THE TSAR'S LAST
ARMADA

PREVIOUS BOOKS BY
CONSTANTINE PLESHAKOV

The Flight of the Romanovs
Inside the Kremlin's Cold War

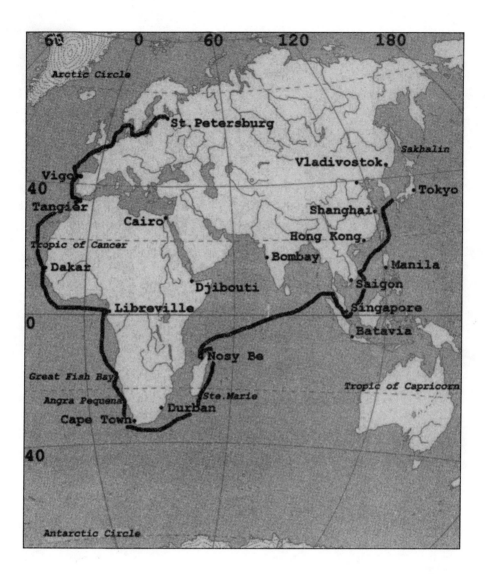

60   0   60   120   180

Arctic Circle

St. Petersburg

Sakhalin

Vladivostok.

Vigo

40

Tokyo

Tangier

Shanghai

Cairo

Hong Kong.

Tropic of Cancer

Bombay

Manila

Dakar

Saigon

Djibouti

Libreville

Singapore

0

Batavia

Nosy Be

Great Fish Bay

Tropic of Capricorn

Angra Pequena

Ste.Marie

Durban

Cape Town.

40

Antarctic Circle

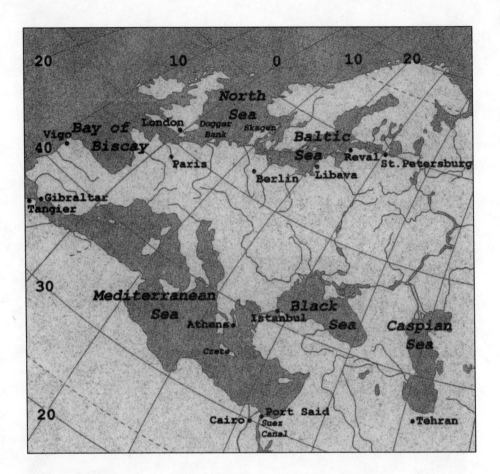

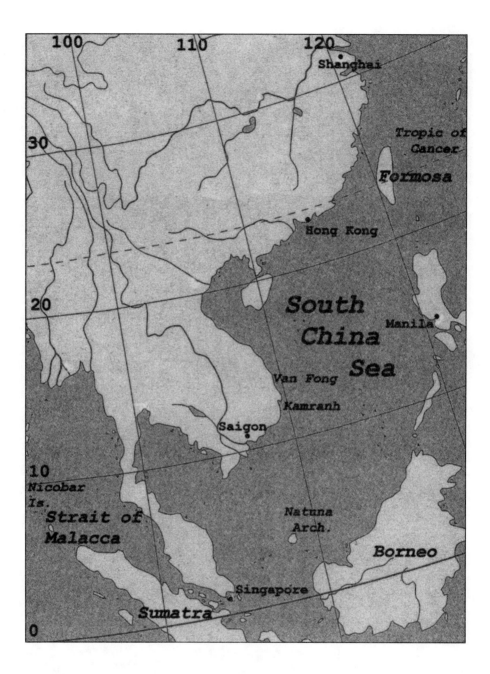

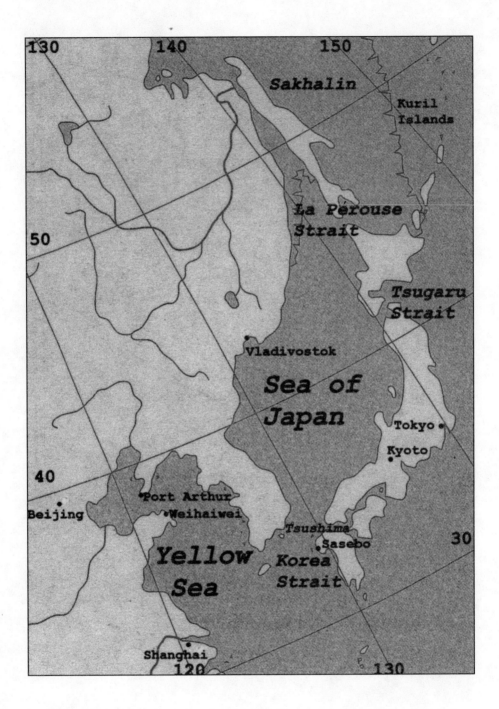

THE TSAR'S LAST
ARMADA

The Epic Journey to the
BATTLE OF TSUSHIMA

CONSTANTINE PLESHAKOV

BASIC
BOOKS
A Member of the Perseus Books Group

Published by Basic Books,
A Member of The Perseus Books Group

Designed by Trish Wilkinson
Set in 12-point AGaramond by The Perseus Books Group

Library of Congress Cataloging-in-Publication Data
Pleshakov, Konstantin
    The Tsar's last armada : the epic journey to the Battle of Tsushima / Constantine Pleshakov. — 1st ed.
        p.   cm.
    Includes bibliographical references and index.
    ISBN 0-465-05791-8
    1. Tsushima, Battle of, 1905. I. Title.
DS517.5 .P58 2002
952.03'1—DC21   2001052532

First Edition

02 03 04 / 10 9 8 7 6 5 4 3 2 1

For
Elza—books you did not read, Anton—fish we
did not catch, and Anya—flowers we did not plant
because of the story I had to tell, in appreciation,
from Son/Dad

It is my profound conviction that apart from the literature of the last two centuries and, perhaps, the architecture of the former capital, the only other thing Russia can be proud of is its Navy's history. Not because of its spectacular victories, of which there have been rather few, but because of the nobility of spirit that has informed its enterprise.

—JOSEPH BRODSKY, IN A ROOM AND A HALF

Contents

Foreword   XV

Acknowledgments   XIX

PART ONE   RACE

  1   "The First Ball of the Tsar," 1890–1904   3

  2   "Master the Sea!" January–August 1904   25

  3   "Rumors from the Bazaar," August–October 1904   69

  4   "This Is a Miserable Fleet," October 4–23, 1904,
      Western Europe   91

  5   "We Have No Coast Batteries in Dakar!"
      October 23–December 16, 1904, African Coast   115

PART TWO   LINGERING

  6   "The Yacht Squadron," October 1904–January 1905,
      Red Sea   151

  7   "Nossibeisk," December 16, 1904–March 3, 1905,
      Madagascar   169

  8   "Ten Guns Done Up in India Rubber," March 1905,
      Indian Ocean   203

9   "A Hole Coated in Iron," March 26–May 1, 1905,
     Indochina   217

10   "Be Prepared for Full Steam Ahead," May 1–13, 1905,
     Pacific Ocean   247

PART THREE   **BATTLE**

11   "They Are All There!" 6:30 A.M.–5:30 P.M.,
     May 14, 1905   261

12   "Follow the Admiral," 5:30 P.M., May 14–1 P.M.,
     May 15, 1905   277

13   "Slutty Old Geezer," May 14–21, 1905   287

14   "Throw Me Overboard," 5:30 P.M., May 14–6 A.M.,
     May 16, 1905   299

15   "Return Soon," May–November 1905   309

16   "The Insulted Russian People," November 3,
     1905–January 1, 1909   321

Notes   339
Select Bibliography   371
Index   377

Foreword

THE MODERN WORLD WAS BORN AT THE TURN OF THE LAST CEN-
tury. Correspondence gave way to telephone conversation. Electric
lights added spirit to the most despondent dumps. Steel and steam
ousted wood and sail. The globe became united not by roads but by
cable—international telegraph, the initial prototype of the World
Wide Web. No element remained unconquered; planes conquered
space, submarines the deep sea.

There were also more sinister accessories of modernity. In South
Africa, the British built the first concentration camps. Physicists in
Paris were exploring radioactivity. Narcotics, until then available only
in the Orient and to the unhappy few in the West, began spreading
worldwide. Means of manslaughter—gun shells, bombs, mines, and
torpedoes—multiplied in a fierce arms race. Theoreticians of totalitar-
ian terror, like Lenin, developed strategies of political cannibalism.

It was at the turn of the last century when the Russo-Japanese War
occurred. It went on for twenty months in 1904–1905 and resulted in
unprecedented human losses and material destruction. Hundreds of
thousands were killed, dozens of ships were sunk, hundreds of settlements were raided, looted, and devastated. It was the first war of the
modern age.

It is largely forgotten in the West, ousted by memories of another
military holocaust—World War Two. When in 2000 a British poet

published a long poem about the battle of Tsushima, a reviewer in the *Times Literary Supplement* wondered why the poet had chosen such a subject. At most, the newspapers might report on an exhibition in Washington, D.C., of the Japanese propaganda woodblock prints related to that war or on the treasure hunt involving one of the sunken Russian ships in the Sea of Japan. Shares of a bankrupt South Korean construction company surged 41 percent in one week after the company spread a rumor about its intent to salvage the *Dmitri Donskoi* cruiser, having generously ascribed her with the most impossible hoard of gold, 14,000 metric tons. The latter story is quite exemplary. Boldly exploiting the shroud of oblivion surrounding not only the humble cruiser but also the whole war in question, the company hadn't bothered to check the *Dmitri Donskoi*'s specifications. In fact, she was a very old and slow ship, one of the notorious clunkers with which the Russian sailors were so frustrated—a very unlikely candidate to be entrusted with transporting a tenth of all the gold ever mined in the world, not to mention that even though Tsar Nicholas II was rather thickheaded, he would never have ordered the transport of such a large amount of gold by ship from St. Petersburg to Vladivostok when he had the Trans-Siberian Railroad at his disposal.

But if the rest of the world forgot about the 1904–1905 war, Japan and Russia did not. The victory of the former and the defeat of the latter shaped the two countries' histories. To Japan, the war of 1904–1905 delivered hegemony in continental East Asia, which lasted until 1945. This victory also boosted the Japanese national ego enormously; it was the first time an Asian nation had defeated a European power. To Russia, the defeat brought revolution, which eventually developed into the dark tsardom of Bolshevism; peasants and workers rebelled against the government, which kept sending them into the hellish furnace of war without the slightest prospect of winning it, while defiantly exhibiting the two worst features of autocracy—ineffectiveness and corruptness.

The naval battle at the Tsushima Islands in the Korea Strait, separating Japan from mainland Asia, was the pinnacle of that war. It stands among the top five naval battles of human history, equal to those of Lepanto, Trafalgar, Jutland, and Midway. The admiral who led the Japanese fleet at Tsushima, Togo Heihachiro, is still unanimously praised as an unsurpassed military genius—not only in history books but also on the Internet, where numerous sites reverently describe him and his battleship, the *Mikasa*. As for Russians, ships traveling through the Sea of Japan still put wreaths on the waves when passing through the Korea Strait. The remains of thousands of Russian sailors are lying on the sea bottom there, within and around the battered hulls of battleships, cruisers, and torpedo boats.

At some point, an author is invariably asked how and why he became interested in the subject. The origins of my interest are pretty conventional. Thirty years ago, as a boy growing up in the coastal town of Yalta on the Black Sea, I discovered an old book in my grandmother's closet. Like everything else in that murky comfortable space, it smelled of cherry preserves and dust. It was a book about Tsushima. It had been published in the 1930s and contained wonderful pictures of ships, layered with sheets of thin, sheer paper. I read and re-read it. Even then it struck me as incomplete. It was a Soviet account of the event with obvious political biases, which are too boring to be discussed here. Much later, after having moved to America, I started checking other volumes; even those that had been conscientiously done were still weak, relying exclusively on printed sources. Gradually, my research commenced.

The Russian and British archives that I have used allow one to tell the story of Tsushima with some hope of being objective and complete, yet, I know that my research is deficient. I do not read Japanese, and without Japanese archival evidence it is not possible to write anything truly comprehensive about the war. So this is the story of Tsushima told from a Western perspective, as it was seen through Russian, British, French, and German eyes—nothing more, but also, hopefully, nothing less.

Two more disclaimers are due. By definition, historical sources contradict each other. However, in modern naval battles, destruction is so overwhelming and instantaneous that witnesses are particularly un-reliable. At the time of Tsushima, no black boxes existed; navies of to-day do not carry them either. Therefore, for practically any evidence, there is counterevidence. In the process of selecting the probable from the improbable, a writer can be guided chiefly by common sense—and also, perhaps, by what he has learned about his characters. It should be emphasized that no matter how rich the archives may be, the story of Tsushima will always remain subject to interpretation.

Readers familiar with the military history of the twentieth century may be confused about certain dates in this narrative. Until the Bolshe-vik Revolution of 1917, Russia had used an old calendar; in the twenti-eth century it lagged thirteen days behind its more advanced Western counterparts, hence the disparity in dates. However, I thought it would be extremely awkward to switch to the Western style; this would have resulted in phrases like, "on Christmas Day, January 7." The Russia de-scribed in this book was a very peculiar country, but not to that extent.

Acknowledgments

FOR THE SOURCES FOR THIS BOOK, MY THANKS GO PRIMARILY to two very different archives: the Russian State Naval Archives in St. Petersburg, a hassle-free vault bravely struggling with poor financing and outmoded equipment and run by very understanding and caring people, and the Public Record Office in London, which is so modern and efficient that it surpasses any imaginable peer. My acknowledgments also go to the Bakhmetieff Archives (Columbia University, New York), the State Archives of the Russian Federation (Moscow), and the Russian State Military History Archives (Moscow).

The person who is to be credited for having encouraged me to launch this project is John Curtis Perry, a delightful writer, a splendid speaker, a seasoned North Pacific hand, and a soul mate. Another dear friend, Edwina Cruise, provided invaluable linguistic support; among other things, she edited the model chapter of the manuscript so that publishers wouldn't stumble on my very imperfect English. Stephen Jones, not only an accomplished historian but also an expert yachtsman, advised me on the arcane rituals of the British Navy. Katia Egorova supplied me with an invincible logistical lance, striking through the armor of the most obnoxious bureaucrats in Russia. Lev Bronislavovich Doubnitsky, a.k.a. Colonel, Valera Petrov, Marty and Susan Sherwin, Katia Ozhegova, Mikhail Moliukov, Sasha Sumerkin, Slava Mogutin, Lenya Kolpakov, Sasha Zotikov, Valera and Galia

Maximenkov, Lenya Serebriakov, Joyce Seltzer, Bill Taubman, Elfed Roberts, Marina Solovieva, Volodya Larin, and Volodya Solomentzev helped cushion the emotional strain of writing by giving me their unreserved friendship. Jerry Bauer enhanced my self-esteem by supplying me with a dashing photographic image of myself.

My agent, Gerry McCauley, made sure the manuscript would not end up in a dustbin. At Basic Books, Don Fehr demonstrated strong faith in the project, thus carrying me through the stressful months of research and writing. My editor, Sarah McNally, saved me from the limbo of uncertainty with her intense interest in the manuscript; her editorial assistance was extraordinarily helpful. Equally important to me was her genuine (I hope) enthusiasm for the story. When I walked into her New York office to show her some pictures for the book, she looked at the photograph of Mad Dog, the ferociously handsome Admiral Zinovy Petrovich Rozhestvensky, and exclaimed, "So this is the man!"

I think a non-native English speaker owes the audience a refreshing ethnic touch, so I want to end my acknowledgments with a very Russian twist. I am extremely grateful to those people who persistently discouraged me from writing this book. They did not like me, or the project, or in most cases, both. Thank you—your hostility fortified my will and made me work harder.

PART ONE

RACE

1

"The First Ball of the Tsar,"
1890–1904

1

A TELEGRAPH'S INCESSANT CLICKING INTRUDED INTO THE FROZEN stillness of the northern gloom. The thin, tattered tape started uncoiling ominously on the operator's table. The man must have read it in panic and disbelief. In all likelihood, he was the first person in the vast empire of the tsar to learn the dreadful, top secret news. Dispatched by the Viceroy of the Far East, Admiral Alexeev, from Manchuria several hours earlier, the telegram brought word of a great disaster:

> Petersburg. TO HIS IMPERIAL MAJESTY
> Humbly reporting to YOUR IMPERIAL MAJESTY. Around midnight January 26–27th, Japanese torpedo boats undertook a sudden attack on our squadron stationed at the outer roadstead of the Port Arthur base. The battleships *Retvizan* and *Tsesarevich* and the cruiser *Pallada* have been ruptured; the degree of damage is being determined. Will report details to YOUR IMPERIAL MAJESTY later.
> General-Adjutant Alexeev

That night, January 26, 1904, the sovereign was not at home. The long-anticipated New Year season of balls and entertainments had recently begun, and Tsar Nicholas II was presiding over an elite audience, listening to an opera at the Imperial Mariinsky Theater.

The Mariinsky looked like an oversized gilded cake. Designed to impress, it symbolized the empire's wealth, might, and grandeur. Like a nesting doll or a Fabergé egg, the big cake contained a smaller one—the royal box. Elaborately ornate and conspicuously large, it served as an august podium for the Romanov dynasty. Like precious jewels, the tsar and his family sat there for everybody to see—to adore, or to hate. The sovereign was not popular in the capital, and the looks he received at Mariinsky were mostly cold, hostile, or condescending. But that night the tsar was enjoying himself thoroughly.

The shining lake of diamond-encrusted evening dresses and gold-embroidered military uniforms bobbing beneath the royal box was unsettled this night. Admirals, generals, ministers, industrialists, bankers, foreign ambassadors, spies, and their wives and children kept turning to the royal box, scrutinizing the impervious handsome face of the tsar. Everybody was agitated and anxious. Three days earlier the Japanese mission had left the Russian capital, having made a point of burning their archives. The tsar was known to have said, "War—so be it, peace—so be it, but the current uncertainty is really bothersome."

The Mariinsky company was having a hard time. Completely ignoring the performance, hundreds of eyes scanned the gilded box where the autocrat of the one-sixth of the earth, Tsar and Emperor Nicholas II, sat. That night the tsar was like the sun, commanding the attention of sunflowers on an immense field. He was finally savoring the taste of power, opiate and sweet.

After the opera, not in a hurry to get home, he accompanied his mother to her palace, the Anichkov, and had late tea there. The Dowager Empress was anxious and once again warned her son about the perils of his reckless Far East venture. Polite and noncommittal, the tsar listened to everything she had to say and then left quickly. Throughout the whole day he had been in an excellent mood.

It took him just a few minutes to reach his main residence, the opulent Winter Palace on the Neva River. The magnificent Nevsky

Prospect, straight as an arrow and barren on a cold winter night, provided a convenient shortcut between the two royal homes. In the Winter Palace the tsar was handed the viceroy's telegram.

He was relieved. The uncertainty of the past few weeks had come to an end. Also, he could now feel good and self-righteous; the Japanese had attacked without warning, proving that his utter contempt toward the "macaques" was well deserved. "God will help us!" the tsar said hopefully.

Before going to bed, he sent copies of the telegram to the foreign and war ministers. The courier had orders to wake up the dignitaries if necessary. The minister of foreign affairs, Count Lamsdorf, was indeed fast asleep, but the minister of war, General Kuropatkin, was nervously shuttling between various parlors; two hours earlier, at 10:30 P.M., he had received unconfirmed news about the attack from a private source in Port Arthur and was now desperate to verify it.

The next morning brought more news from Manchuria. The Japanese had bombarded Port Arthur. The Russian and Japanese fleets had engaged in their first battle, and four Russian ships were damaged.

It was the beginning of the Russo-Japanese War. The tsar issued a war manifesto, blaming Japan for having "challenged" Russia. "Pursuing peace, so dear to Our heart," the tsar solemnly declared, in the best tradition of autocrats speaking in august plural, "we have done everything to maintain tranquillity in the Far East." Necessary to satisfy the public taste for justice, this statement made insiders smile sarcastically. The sovereign's policy in Manchuria had been anything but pacifist.

At 3:30 P.M. all the Romanovs present in St. Petersburg assembled in the Golden Hall of the Winter Palace. Led by the head of the family, the tsar, they gravely made their way through the dense, cheering crowd to the palace chapel where a special mass, a prayer for victory, was sung. Younger people had never heard this beautiful but belligerent tune before. Nicholas's father, Tsar Alexander III, had secured an unprecedented twenty-five-year peace for Russia. The chapel was packed like the rest of the palace, mostly with army and navy officers. Thrilled and moved, they cried a deafening "Hurrah!" to the dynasty and its imperial cause. The Romanovs, appropriately enthusiastic and pleased, returned to the Golden Hall, where Grand Duke Alexei, one of the patriarchs of the clan, commander of the Imperial Navy, and now even more full of self-importance than ever, pompously read to awed relatives the recent cable reporting more casualties in Port Arthur.

In the next few days, St. Petersburg saw multiple patriotic demonstrations. For a while, people rallied around their monarch—something not seen during the nine years of Nicholas's reign. Even students, notorious pro-revolutionary troublemakers, marched to the Winter Palace to sing "God Save the Tsar." Nicholas and his wife, Alexandra, watched them from the window and, deeply touched, bowed. In the last days of January 1904, it looked like the sore gap between the rulers and the ruled was being filled with patriotic sentiment. Things finally began looking brighter for the Romanov monarchy.

Nicholas felt that the wave of patriotism was his personal success. At last, people were with him. And the ill-wishers, all those haughty know-it-all advisers skeptical of his Far Eastern policy who had been humiliating him for years with their seemingly overwhelming expertise, had been proven wrong. The tsar had always felt his glory would be earned in the Pacific. Now the moment had come.

Passing in a carriage by the house of Sergei Witte, the former minister of finance, fired for his antiwar warnings several months earlier, the tsar looked up at his window. To his delight, Witte was there, sulkily watching the triumphant sovereign, the true heir of Peter the Great. The tsar put on his best new nonchalant victorious look, as the face of his enemy disappeared from sight.

2

Nicholas had first heard about the wonders of Asia twenty-three years earlier, in 1881. He had been thirteen and doing studies with tutors at home, as heirs to the throne were disqualified from attending any—even military—school.

The year 1881 had been a terrible one for the family. On March 1, Tsar Alexander II was killed by a terrorist's bomb. The adolescent Nicholas was present at the terrifying death of his grandfather and had seen the convulsing body lying in a puddle of blood. The ensuing long state funeral was accompanied by the stench of quickly decomposing torn flesh. Though the boy was not particularly sensitive or fragile, he was nonetheless shaken by the violent, cruel, and undeserved death of Tsar the Reformer. Further aggravating his depression, his father, the new Tsar Alexander III, moved the family, for security reasons, away from the capital to the remote, gray, and gloomy Gatchina Palace in the suburbs. The new tsarina, Maria Fedorovna, watched her children with anxiety. She vowed to use every possible chance to brighten up their lives. Always abreast of the latest trends, be it fashion, jewels, or geography, she invited Nikolai Przhevalsky to Gatchina in May 1881.

In 1881 Przhevalsky was the rage of the day. Explorer of Central Asia, Tibet, and Western China—and employed by the Russian government as a spy—Przhevalsky would disappear for months at a time into the mountains and deserts to collect specimens of previously unknown flowers and animals—and pieces of invaluable strategic intelligence. He became one of the senior players in the Great Game—the fierce struggle between Britain and Russia over Central Asia, full of covert operations, secret expeditions, treacheries, bribery, and murder.

A man like Przhevalsky was exactly the kind of person who could impress an adolescent screened by privilege and a loving family from the real world. Adventurous, chivalrous, and reckless, Przhevalsky was the perfect model of the great explorers and manipulators of the imperial age—men like Cecil Rhodes and Lawrence of Arabia. The area that Przhevalsky had chosen for his exploits was even more appealing to the general public than South Africa or the Middle East; Tibet and Mongolia were wilder than Arabia and richer culturally than Rhodesia. His journeys were spectacular, and so was his presentation of himself and his numerous accomplishments. In 1881 he was at the peak of manhood and behaved like a self-assured conquistador, a modern nomad, the demon of the steppes.

Of course, Przhevalsky *was* unique. Boastful (he had named at least twelve new specimens of plants and animals after himself), daring, and industrious, he had acquired a unique knowledge of continental Asia, home to ancient kingdoms and improbable beasts. He also was quite familiar with teenagers; preparations for months in the wilderness normally started with a discreet search for a young male, preferably a sixteen-year-old, to lure into adventure and to teach to skin animals and dry plants—and to share his tent at night.

Przhevalsky's charms worked on the young and shy heir to the throne. Nicholas immediately fell for this powerful character and, more importantly, for the lands described in his thrilling tales. However, his fascination with Asia would probably have remained unfulfilled if it hadn't coincided with a nationwide drive toward the Pacific.

Russia was born in the western corner of the great Eurasian forest. As late as the seventeenth century, a squirrel could easily have traveled from the Baltic Sea to the Pacific Ocean without ever having touched the ground. Though perfect for beasts, the forest rejected humans. Transportation there was virtually impossible. The forest was too dense and full of treacherous swamps. Here and there inaccessible mountains fortified it. The famed Silk Road—the only land artery connecting East and West—never dared go north; a desert is a much better avenue than a forest.

In the absence of roads, Russians used rivers. Exceptionally bad navigators, they sailed primitive boats, often carved from a single trunk of a gigantic tree, normally oak. In winter they fared much better. Thick ice turned rivers into smooth highways for sleds pulled by horses. However, with very few exceptions all rivers flowed north to the lifeless Arctic Ocean, and the further they went and the wider they became, the less inhabitable their shores were.

To aggravate matters, 90 percent of the forest grew on permafrost—an uninterrupted shield of ancient ice coated by a thin layer of weak soil. Permafrost kept bodies of dead mammoths intact for millennia exactly because it was hostile to life. No agriculture was possible there. Hence, there was one more challenge to a traveler: ongoing hunger.

Other unavoidable hazards like snowstorms, floods, and predators also prevented the penetration of the immense wilderness. As a result, between 900 and 1600, the Riurikovichi, the first Russian dynasty, had only barely glimpsed Siberia. For all people knew, dragons might have inhabited the lands to the east of the Ural Mountains.

The Romanovs broke the spell of the forest. However, it was not that the new tsars were particularly ingenious or insightful—they were just lucky. The ascendance of the first Romanov to the throne in 1613 coincided with a new technological age. Firearms solved the problem of bears, tigers, and wolves. They also provided great tools for hunting, and starvation became just a faint ghost. The science of cartography, developed in Portugal and Spain two centuries earlier, finally reached Moscow. Meanwhile, merchants from London and Hamburg were bringing fine gems, luxurious silks, and precious porcelain from India and China. Suddenly Russians realized that only a vast expanse of no-man's-land separated them from the treasure trove of Asia. Not a single state had to be conquered in the east—only barren space, sparsely populated by generally peaceful tribes. The great Eurasian forest was no longer just a place where people killed squirrel and mink for their furs; it became the barrier that had to be crossed to reach the riches of the East.

The tsars started sending people over the Urals. Eventually they reached the uninhabited Pacific coast, the immense foggy wasteland stretching between China and the Arctic.

The Chinese were unwilling to populate these areas, full of natural riches, but cold, barbaric, and distant. The Russians decided otherwise. Accustomed to severe climate and being children of the forests themselves, they began settling down in Siberia and the Far East at the southern border of the permafrost. Their settlements were few and small, sometimes populated by religious dissenters, the sullen Old Believers, and kept secret from authorities. However, in the absence of competition, the empire was slowly but surely absorbing Siberia and the northwestern coast of the Pacific, building military settlements, churches, and roads. The tsars also ordered the construction of prisons. Few could escape from Siberia, and the land received a new, sinister fame.

By the mid-nineteenth century, Russia had become deeply enough involved in the Pacific to provoke the British-French fleet to attack a fort in the Kamchatka Peninsula during the Crimean War. The attack symbolized a greater trend. Western powers had made up their minds to check Russian expansion in the area.

The tsars were becoming greedy. They dreamed of taking over the Ottoman Empire and reaching the Mediterranean Sea. Ten centuries earlier, Russia had received its religion, culture, and even its alphabet from Byzantium, and it regarded all former Byzantine lands as its true heritage, stolen by the vile Turks. However, the Crimean War of 1853–1856 had resulted in Russia's complete defeat, and now expansion to the Mediterranean Sea looked problematic. The idea was not completely abandoned (Russia fought a victorious war against Turkey in 1877–1878), but it was looking too risky—and too costly—to undertake.

The Great Game in Central Asia had also come to an impasse. The two spheres of influence, British and Russian, were sealed for the indefinite future in an acceptable stalemate. British and Russian officers were willing to watch each other through binoculars, but not through a rifle's target-finder. Given these circumstances, there was only one outlet left for Russia's expansion—the Pacific. If Russia was not allowed to conquer Constantinople on the Bosporus, it was going to create a new Bosporus in the Far East.

One of the best harbors in the northwestern corner of the Sea of Japan was renamed the Golden Horn by Russian settlers. The original Golden Horn, the gorgeous harbor of glamorous Constantinople, was securely fenced from them by the concerted efforts of Turkey, England, and France.

In 1860, a military outpost was founded there. It was named Vladivostok, which means "Rule the East." Soon it became the main Russian naval base in the Pacific. On May 19, 1891, the heir to the throne, Nicholas, visited the town and inaugurated the construction of the Great Trans-Siberian Railroad, which would connect Vladivostok to the imperial capital.

It was a Romanov tradition to send an heir to the throne abroad on his coming of age so that he could see the world and the world could see him. All of Nicholas's ancestors had gone to Europe. However, his father, Tsar Alexander III, decided that Asia had become important enough to be the stage of the future tsar's debut.

Nicholas traveled from the Mediterranean Sea to the Pacific Ocean on a Russian naval ship. Dignitaries in each country on his route went out of their way to pay courtesy to the Russian prince, but the more they tried, the more confined and bored the twenty-two-year-old felt. Official dinners and formal talk did not interest him in the least. He longed for real adventures, ones like those described by Przhevalsky ten years earlier, but the best Nicholas could find were imaginative prostitutes—a spicy treat, no doubt, but hardly an adventure.

In his letters home, the heir tried to demonstrate an interest in state matters, naturally expected from him. He shared the Romanov distrust of Britain, and letters to his father, the emperor, from India looked almost like spy reports, monitoring the movements and morale of the enemy's troops. Then adventure arrived.

Nicholas had reached Japan and was visiting the town of Otsu. Suddenly, in the street, a disturbed samurai threw himself on the Russian heir. The madman ferociously hit Nicholas on the head with a sword. To the consternation of those in his entourage, Nicholas's blood "shot out like a fountain." The heir panicked and thought he was going to perish under the attack of the lunatic. Help came not from the Russian officers, but from a Greek Romanov. His young cousin and friend, Prince George of Greece, sent the madman to the ground with a single powerful stroke.

The wounded head soon healed, but the world press, to the utter embarrassment of the Japanese hosts, immediately publicized the incident. The Russian heir now felt hatred and vengeance toward the land of the rising sun. Unable to regard the Otsu incident as just an unfortunate episode, he jumped to conclusions about the nature of the Japanese people and their intentions toward their northern neighbors that he held for the rest of his life.

Angry Nicholas arrived in Vladivostok directly from Japan. His head was still bandaged "like that of an old general's," in his own words. In spite of his wound, he was more determined than ever to launch the Trans-Siberian Railroad immediately. In a letter to his father, he called the public mood in Vladivostok on May 19 "feverish." All the people seemed to realize they were present at a historic event; the Trans-Siberian Railroad was to be the longest in the world. Nicholas himself inaugurated the steel artery with malicious joy; he knew it could be used as a weapon against the Japanese whom he now profoundly hated.

Although the railway construction was underway, Nicholas had to cross Siberia like everybody else did in those days—by horse, a tiring experience for even a young and sturdy officer. Yet, notwithstanding the natural hardships of the journey, and perhaps even due to them, the heir couldn't help being impressed by the gigantic Asiatic sector of his empire. Pathetically underdeveloped and undisturbed by urbanization, Asiatic Russia treasured its riches in silence. It was like a sleeping princess, waiting to be awakened by a kiss. Nicholas decided he was the prince to do so.

Another young man was taking almost the same journey at about the same time. Whereas the heir circled Eurasia counterclockwise, Anton Chekhov circled it clockwise. Both were driven by the same impulse—to discover new frontiers.

A journey to the Far East was very untypical for a Russian prince, but it was even more so for a Russian writer. Before Chekhov, Russian literature, though rich and diverse, had never crossed the Urals. Ironically enough, none other than the same engaging Przhevalsky had awakened Chekhov's interest in Asia. Not privileged enough to meet the hero in real life, Chekhov had been a "passionate reader" of the famous adventurer's books as a boy. Belonging to the same generation as the future tsar (Chekhov was born in 1860, Nicholas in 1868), Chekhov was also seeking challenge and adventure in the East. In April 1890, he set off on a four-thousand-mile land journey toward the Pacific. It lasted three months and left him coughing blood. In July he reached Sakhalin Island, the Russian Far Eastern outpost, used by the tsars as a natural jail for felons—a Russian Australia or Devil's Island. He stayed there until October, collecting material for his barely readable, but extremely consequential book *The Island of Sakhalin,* in which he wrote about prisons and the treatment of convicts.

Chekhov returned to Russia via Vladivostok, Hong Kong, Singapore, Ceylon, and Suez and in the Red Sea crossed the path of the heir, heading east. It is quite possible that within the interval of just a few days the two young men encountered the same prostitutes; sharing with Nicholas more than just fascination with the Orient, Chekhov was also an enthusiastic habitué of brothels.

He summed up his impressions in a very revealing way: "I can say I have lived! I've had everything I wanted. I have been in Hell, which is Sakhalin, and in Paradise, which is Ceylon."

While Chekhov's trip to the East was the fulfillment of all his dreams, Sergei Witte described Nicholas's journey through Asia as his "first ball."

3

Arguably, Sergei Witte was even more important in discovering Asia for Russians than Przhevalsky. An energetic and ruthless self-made man, he had realized early on that the path to Europe or to the Middle East was blocked by Western powers. Instead of threatening London, Paris, or Berlin with pan-European war, which was the inclination of many of his colleagues, he suggested an alternative option: Shift the imperial spearhead to the Pacific.

Liked and trusted by Alexander III, Witte easily persuaded the monarch that the Far East had a great future. The first step in that direction was obvious: Build railroads. Witte had started his career by managing railroads in European Russia and fully appreciated the potential of steam power.

At the turn of the last century, the steam engine was what the jet is today. Monarchs boasted about their railroads more than their armies.

Railway stations, be they in Leipzig or New York, St. Petersburg or London, resembled palaces. Fortunes were spent to construct opulent depots with cathedral ceilings and ornate façades. A midsize European city could easily commission a railway station rivaling St. Peter's Cathedral in Rome.

The Great Trans-Siberian Railroad, which inspired so many writers and spies, was Witte's brainchild. When the heir was present at the inaugurating ceremony in Vladivostok, he was on Witte's mission. When his father, the reigning tsar, appointed him Chairman of the Trans-Siberian Construction Committee, Nicholas, again, had to bow to Witte's iron will and exceptional qualities of persuasion.

Witte always seemed larger than life. His physique alone invariably inspired awe; he was tall and heavy, and his prominent nose was fractured, which made people say he "looked like a crocodile." Sergei Witte deserved the metaphor; he was cunning, tireless, and fierce. The future tsar, extremely insecure, shy, and secretive, felt enormous resentment toward this dominating figure of Russian politics. For his father, Tsar Alexander III, the self-confident, peace-loving giant towering over continental Europe in a way no other Russian monarch did, Witte was merely a clever and efficient associate. For Nicholas, Witte became a problem. Witte, in his turn, did not make a secret of the contempt he felt toward the heir.

Tsar Alexander III died prematurely in October 1894, at merely forty-eight. His son, though twenty-six at that point, was totally unprepared to assume the crown. He explicitly said so to his closest friends. Of course, he could have rejected it, but he did not. Instead, he started looking for something capable of turning him into a respected ruler. War looked like the easiest option. Having briefly considered the Middle East, Nicholas moved to the Pacific. Here his plans interfered with Witte's.

In order to reach its eastern terminus, Vladivostok, the Trans-Siberian Railroad had to cross the whole of continental Eurasia. Because the Russo-Chinese frontier in the Far East curved northward, further costs were added to the already enormous expense of completing the railway. Witte decided a shortcut was possible—through Chinese territory in Manchuria.

In 1896 Witte persuaded China's strongman Li Hongchang to sign a treaty. China acquired an ally against Japan (there had already been a war between the two countries in 1894–1895), and Russia got a free hand in Manchuria.

By that time, several other foreign powers had already become involved in colonial annexations in the Far East. Russia was late to the feast and therefore had to be very careful. War with England over China was unlikely. With Japan—absolutely possible. It had almost occurred in 1894–1895, during Japan's first powerful thrust into China's flesh.

In such a situation, the tsar's personal insecurities and idiosyncrasies were of paramount importance. He did not have to secure the nation's support for launching a war. He was an autocrat and could order any war he wanted.

In November 1897, the worst happened. The tsar's cousin, Kaiser Wilhelm II of Germany, ordered his troops to land on Shandong Peninsula in the Yellow Sea.

The two monarchs were competing in politics like boys comparing who can do more push-ups or whose genitals are bigger. Now Nicholas felt he had to demonstrate equal strength. He sent Russian ships to the tip of Liaodong, a peninsula barely one hundred miles away from Wilhelm's new colony. Witte's plans of peaceful penetration of China collapsed.

More ships were sent to the Yellow Sea, and a naval base was founded there—Port Arthur. It had a spacious deepwater harbor, ice-free throughout the whole year. Known to the Chinese as Lushun, it had been used as a staging post since the second century B.C. No ship going from Bo Hai Gulf to the Yellow Sea can avoid the area, and Bo Hai Gulf is the gateway to the Chinese capital, Beijing.

Liaodong and Shandong are like two hands guarding—or for that matter, squeezing—Bo Hai. Port Arthur lay on the very tip of the northern peninsula, Liaodong. It quickly became the most noticeable stronghold on the Manchurian coast. The capital of Manchuria, Harbin, was merely 500 miles to the northeast; Vladivostok was 600 miles away; the Korean border just 200.

Japan was enraged. It regarded China as its natural prey. Now two outsiders, Russia and Germany, were controlling the naval path to Beijing, and Russia was speedily turning Manchuria into its protectorate. In 1894, Japan had captured Port Arthur. Then, under pressure from Russia, France, and Germany, it had abandoned its claim. Now the Russians were stealing the area for themselves.

To Russia, Japan's involvement in continental Asia was the typical overstretch of a parvenu. Until the end of the nineteenth century, the Japanese had never expressed any interest in reaching the world outside their beautiful archipelago. The nation had remained largely self-absorbed, preoccupied by domestic feuds, maintaining its low-cost, closed-circuit economy and lingering in its amazingly rich cultural cocoon. However, in the mid-nineteenth century, this calm came to an abrupt end. Western guns awakened Japan.

When Western ships reached Japan, the nation was left with two alternatives: modernize or continue to hibernate. Their biggest neighbor, China, had chosen the latter and turned into a semi-colony. The Japanese decided to act.

An ambitious program of sweeping reforms was launched. This period is now known as the Meiji era—after Emperor Meiji who ascended the throne in 1867. In an amazingly short period of time, Japan developed its own version of a modern state, based on the supremacy of money and technology. The pursuit of profits led its industrialists to continental Asia. Battleships provided an impressive convoy.

Unlike Russia, Japan reined in its absolutist monarchy. Officially, the semi-divine sovereign was still in full control. He declared wars, made peace, and concluded treaties, and Parliament had no say in these matters. However, in reality Emperor Meiji had surrendered his authority to a group of oligarchs.

Tsar Nicholas II kept his power intact.

4

By 1904, Nicholas had been on the throne for nine years, presiding over the largest country on earth. The tsar disliked grandeur, however, and he spent his time in bourgeois pursuits. He read books to his wife and daughters—mostly Russian humor, sometimes Chekhov—exercised, took long relaxed walks, wrote letters to relatives, and took photographs—a fashionable novelty in those days. He was rightfully described as "a most polite young man," "with the education of a colonel of the Guards from a middle-class family."

State affairs were not of great interest to him. The first place in his heart was firmly occupied by his wife and children. God came second. The pursuit of glory came third. He managed the huge empire very poorly. In order to secure his attention during an audience, a minister had to incorporate as many anecdotes as possible into a report. Hiding insecurity and incompetence, the tsar would often take the advice of the last person he had spoken with and then curtly inform his ministers, "This is my will."

The tsar also presided over the Romanov family—several dozen haughty individuals, each extremely wealthy and full of self-importance. Some he could command, some he could ignore, and some he still obeyed. All of the Romanovs were part of a greater European royal family.

The most notorious relative was Kaiser Wilhelm. Wilhelm was a grandchild of Queen Victoria, as was the tsar's wife. Of course, that alone did not make "Willy" and "Nicky" (as they addressed each other) close. Their Uncle Bertie, or King Edward VII of England, was closer to republican France than to any of his royal relatives in Russia or Germany. The kaiser had a specific reason for cultivating the bond with the tsar: He wanted the two nations to become allies. This is why Willy kept insisting on being intimate with Nicky. He posed as a soul mate, an elder brother, a mentor in the arcane art of politics and war. The sentiment was not returned. Willy's was a difficult mission.

Eccentric, despotic, and rude, the kaiser was the *enfant terrible* of European royals. Fond of masquerades, jewelry, exclusively male society, and loud military camaraderie, the kaiser was, perhaps, repressing a same-sex desire. Many people suspected that Wilhelm envied open homosexuals among his relatives and friends like King Ferdinand of Bulgaria, the Duke of Saxe-Coburg-Gotha, and Count Philipp Eulenburg. No matter what was gnawing the German emperor, it was becoming worse over time. Erratic behavior developed into recurrent fits of rage and offensive escapades. With Wilhelm, people always felt they were "sitting on a powder keg." Any remark, even a harmless one, could cause his "violent objection." Once he playfully slapped the King of Bulgaria on the behind in public; the tsar's uncle, Grand Duke Vladimir, suffered from his field-marshal's baton; to the King of Italy, Wilhelm always sent aides "whose tallness accentuated the diminutiveness" of the Italian monarch.

The Romanovs disliked him and his nation profoundly, calling Germans "filthy." But above all else, they must have loathed the day in July 1869 when the future kaiser had first set his eyes on the sea.

Wilhelm was fascinated with the ocean despite being prone to seasickness. He was an avid sailor and a patron of the navy, and he even painted marine pictures (like Nero, he aspired to master all arts). His infatuation with warships had a strong impact on his cousin Nicholas who felt obliged to compete with the kaiser in everything.

Wilhelm suspected that the tsar did not like him, but he also knew he could manipulate Nicky, like a capable boy scout leader manipulates shy teenagers in search of a role model. Willy hoped Nicky would eventually forsake his alliance with France and join Germany's camp. He was unable to persuade the tsar to do this—though he came pretty close—to the consternation of his own diplomats and the rest of Europe. But he succeeded in something else: pushing Nicky toward war in the East.

Wilhelm repeated that the tsar should become "Admiral of the Pacific," leaving him, the kaiser, "Admiral of the Atlantic." These exhortations were extremely self-serving; the kaiser wanted Europe for himself, magnanimously letting his cousin expand in Asia. However, Wilhelm was sincere about his hatred of the Japanese. He detested the "pagan" East and maintained that it was the duty of every Christian monarch to oppose the "yellow peril."

Nicky was sympathetic to this. First, he was a very fundamentalist Christian himself. Second, he still carried a scar left by the Japanese madman's sword back in 1891. Each year he quietly celebrated his miraculous survival in Otsu.

Nicky never liked Wilhelm. He suspected that his cousin was insane. However, Wilhelm hypnotized him with so much assertiveness and regal stature, which the tsar totally lacked, that Nicky yielded: All right, he would leave Europe alone and try to conquer the East instead.

However, he ran into a problem. Seeking personal glory and viewing Asia as the ideal place for his military debut, Nicholas nonetheless felt intimidated by people like Witte. He decided that he needed his own, secret policies, bypassing his ministers. For that, he had to select a private cabinet, almost a shadow government.

There were plenty of people to choose from. The Far East excited hotheads all over Russia. Nicholas could not seek advice from the person who had ignited his passion for Asia. Przhevalsky, the great spy and adventurist, had died in 1888, just forty-nine years old. But there were others.

A Tibetan healer, Peter Badmaev, had created a sensation in St. Petersburg society by distributing exotic drugs among the aristocracy. However, Badmaev believed that his true mission lay not in treating insomnia and impotence but in guiding Russian policy in Asia. Using his court connections, he had bombarded Tsar Alexander III with long, bizarre memorandums, claiming that the heartland of Asia—Tibet, Mongolia, and perhaps even China—longed for Russian rule. He asserted that the Orient still cherished an ancient legend of a "White Tsar" from the North who was destined to rule over the whole of Asia.

Alexander III did not believe him. He disliked exotic drugs, exalted immigrants, and esoteric concepts. But his son did not inherit this healthy skepticism. Nicholas listened intently to Badmaev. Later in life he would even start taking medicine from the healer. But that was yet to come.

Another person he listened to was a relative. Grand Duke Alexander was a cousin and the most trusted friend of his youth. Together they had cruised St. Petersburg, out for every kind of mischief, sharing amorous adventures and binge-drinking parties. Infinitely more self-confident and intelligent than the heir, Grand Duke Alexander was a lasting influence on Nicholas. He loved the good life, beautiful women, sea voyages, remote places, and crazy adventures. He also sought glory—which was hardly available to him, only a minor member of the Romanov dynasty. Probably it would be unfair to say that he had married Nicholas's sister, Xenia, for the sake of his career. In any case, he mercilessly exploited the affection of his brother-in-law, manipulating him for his own ends.

Grand Duke Alexander was a born troublemaker. He became an enthusiast of the Far East. But unlike Witte, he supported a militant stand in the area. A naval officer and later an admiral, the grand duke advocated challenging Japan for naval supremacy in the Pacific. He wrote a memorandum to that effect and sent it out to all of the top officials. In this piece, he pointed out that Russia was only "two days sea voyage" from the coast of Japan. He maintained that the chief target of Russian foreign policy should be Korea, as a Russian presence in Manchuria was already secured. Conflict with Japan, insisted the grand duke, was inevitable.

Surrendering to the pressure of his energetic brother-in-law, the tsar added Korea to his wish list. He also created a Merchant Marine Department and put the royal adventurer in charge.

Another troublemaker was Captain Alexander Bezobrazov. Low-born and undistinguished, he was the type of "favorite" who had plagued European courts in the Middle Ages. Talkative, fearless, and imaginative, striking people as extremely vulgar and surprisingly unrestrained, he was refreshingly different from polished courtiers. Completely charmed, Nicholas entrusted Bezobrazov with independent policies in the Pacific.

Korea particularly attracted the entrepreneurial man. Bezobrazov came out with a fantastic plan of creating a quasi-private company, involved in forestry and mining, which would acquire Korea for Russia in a peaceful manner. The tsar nodded. His brother-in-law had already persuaded him that Manchuria was not enough. Expansion on the Korean Peninsula began.

This was more than Japan could take. In 1903 the country started preparing for war. The tsar was aware of this. Now all he had to do was to find an officer in the military to conduct the war for him. In August 1903, he appointed Admiral Evgeny Alexeev viceroy of the Far East.

Alexeev was named commander-in-chief in the Pacific, with both ground troops and the navy under his helm. This meant that the Foreign Ministry, the Admiralty, and the Ministry of War were now powerless in the strategically important area.

Nicholas had every reason to trust Alexeev. The admiral was his bastard uncle, sired by his grandfather, Tsar Alexander II. Alexeev was also very close to his half-brother, Grand Duke Alexei, who commanded the navy; as young officers, they had raided the better part of European brothels together.

Grand Duke Alexei was inclined to audacious statements and heroic poses. The kaiser, a known connoisseur of male beauty, thought "his handsome face and figure resembled that of some Germanic chieftain from the Sagas." A tall, imposing man, a bachelor by choice, an insatiable chaser of women, and a darling of Parisian salons, cabarets, and restaurants, he sighed each time he had to return to St. Petersburg and his boring duties. He was a courageous man but preferred to demonstrate his courage not at sea, but on private ground, standing up to an angry husband or arguing his right to carouse in front of the tsar.

Grand Duke Alexei had had his share of marine adventures; back in September 1868, thirty-six years earlier, he had nearly drowned with the sinking of the frigate *Alexander Nevsky* on the western coast of Yutland—and had been telling the story ever since. If Europe knew him as a lover of "fast women and slow ships," Russian sailors had an even less flattering nickname for him—"seven *puds* [250 pounds] of august flesh." Uninterested in either strategy or diplomacy, the grand duke wasn't averse to war against Japan; he wanted to claim victory for the navy he commanded.

A number of dignitaries, although having little interest in foreign affairs or the Far East, supported the war party in St. Petersburg for other reasons. Domestic unrest was growing, and a shadow of revolution was starting to materialize in urban centers and in the countryside. Minister of Interior Pleve coined a phrase: "In order to prevent revolution, we need a *little victorious war*."

Inspired by his new independence from meddlesome ministers, the tsar created and chaired the Far Eastern Committee. With sadistic pleasure, he fired Witte. Now the only peace-loving dove left was the foreign minister, Count Lamsdorf, but he was unable to fight the war party alone.

Quiet and withdrawn, a deeply closeted homosexual, and unlike many peers in St. Petersburg, too afraid to defy the mores of the time, Lamsdorf lived a frustrated and sheltered life. Refined and aristocratic, he shied away from society and hated to speak in public, even at cabinet meetings. Caustic and sarcastic with subordinates, he expressed himself best in correspondence. A workaholic, a "walking archive" of the Foreign Ministry, he had spent forty years in diplomacy. He never opposed the tsar openly but rather skillfully persuaded him that peace in Europe was to be maintained at all costs. The tsar, however, had recently started turning a deaf ear to his warnings.

Japan could not be held responsible for the forthcoming war. Oligarchs in Tokyo were prepared to compromise. As late as October 1904, Foreign Minister Komura voiced this position. He suggested recognizing Manchuria as a Russian sphere of influence; Russia, in its turn, had to renounce claims on Korea. The tsar would not agree to the latter. As a result, negotiations with Tokyo ended in a stalemate.

Meanwhile, Nicholas got absolutely carried away by his grand design for Asia. He sent a Cossack officer and a Russian Buddhist monk to Tibet "to raise Tibetans against the English." Characteristically, he kept this secret from his foreign minister. Tibetan healer Badmaev wrote Nicholas, calling Tibet "the key to Asia" and insisting that "a real

Russian" would never "allow the English to enter Tibet." The healer concluded his memo to the tsar by stating resolutely that "the Japanese problem is nil when compared with the Tibetan one." The tsar probably felt reassured.

In any case, it was high time to send reinforcements to Port Arthur. A detachment of ships—the battleship *Oslyabya* and the cruisers *Aurora* and *Dmitri Donskoi*—led by Admiral Virenius was hastily dispatched to the Far East. By January 1904 they were in the Red Sea. There they met two brand-new Japanese cruisers—the *Nishin* and the *Kasuga*.

The *Nishin* and the *Kasuga* had a story behind them. They had been bought by Japan from Argentina. Argentina had been preparing for war with its neighbor Chile, and both countries had embarked on an ambitious naval arms race. But by 1902 the conflict had been resolved through diplomatic means. The two nations were stunned at the money wasted; Argentina had ordered two ships from Italy, and Chile, two ships from Britain. Russia and Japan both rushed to buy them. Russia failed. Japan succeeded. Now the two cruisers were being taken to the Far East, their crews commanded by officers of the British naval reserve. Agents reported that they were proceeding east with sinister speed.

Meanwhile, a special cabinet council in Japan started finalizing the war plans. It was decided that it was necessary to strike first.

On January 6, Willy cabled Nicky from Berlin: "Signal from Admiral of Atlantic to Admiral of Pacific. News from trustworthy Chinese source has arrived; governors of Yangtze valley have been apprised by Japan that, war with Russia being unavoidable, they were to lend their protection to foreign commercial interests."

On January 22, an imperial conference of Japanese oligarchs decided to start immediately. On January 24, Japan informed Russia that it was severing diplomatic relations with St. Petersburg. At that time, Admiral Togo Heihachiro, leading the main force of the Japanese fleet, was already steaming for Port Arthur. Two days later the war began.

"Master the Sea!"

JANUARY—AUGUST 1904

1

ON JANUARY 29, TWO DAYS AFTER THE PORT ARTHUR SQUADRON was attacked, another piece of bad news arrived from the Far East: The transport *Yenisei* had hit a Japanese mine and sunk, taking the captain, three officers, and ninety-two men with her. "A terrible event," the tsar wrote gloomily in his diary.

Yet, more horrors were to come. On January 31, the tsar learned that the cruiser *Boyarin* had also hit a mine—this time a Russian one—and sunk. The navy appeared terribly unprepared for war. This was exceptionally disheartening. If Russia had a national pet, it was its navy.

By 1904, the Russian navy was two centuries old. It had been built by Nicholas II's ancestor, Tsar Peter the Great, virtually from scratch. In his efforts to catch up with the rest of Europe in the 1690s, he understood that he did not have a chance unless he supplied his country with a modern fleet. Tsar Peter employed skilled experts from Holland to build the new Russian ships. Earlier, the tsar had spent some time in the Low Countries himself, working on the wharf as an ordinary carpenter.

Peter's devotion to shipbuilding is often described as one of the essential elements in the modernization of Russia. But one cannot help wondering if he wasn't actually modernizing Russia for the sake of his own marine dreams. Nothing pleased Peter more than spending a day at the wheel of a naval ship. He had won several major land battles that changed the face of Eastern Europe, but his insignificant skirmishes at sea brought him much more satisfaction.

The marine child of Peter the Great became the darling of his descendants. They showered sailors with honors, though in strictly military terms the navy had never been instrumental for Russia's security. Random sea engagements were always secondary to land battles. The Russian empire was built not by sail but by hoof, and was held together not by anchors but by bayonets. Yet, Russians held their navy in highest esteem, still thrilled by the very fact that they had one. The profession of sailor was seen as heroic, and naval officers were the stars of the nation. In the land of woods and steppes, boys dreamed about masts and hulls.

To people like Grand Duke Alexander, the navy looked like the decisive weapon. Cooler heads like Witte insisted, to no avail, that Russia should use the natural benefits of its continental nature. The nation demanded a grand future for its grand navy.

Tsar Nicholas II was among the strongest proponents of a naval buildup. This was partially due to the *Zeitgeist* at the time; at the turn of the last century, the navy was firmly and universally associated with national might. That had not been the case a century earlier. Tall ships had been very important, such as in the Battle of Trafalgar, but one simply could not compare the age of sail to the age of steam.

It had been a revolutionary change. Finally, people did not have to ask the gods for the right type of wind. With sails, a carefully planned attack on an enemy's squadron or port could have easily failed just because of calm weather or a storm. The fate of the Spanish Armada was the perfect example of this. Now, at last, people were in control. Poseidon was downgraded to a minor deity, and Vulcan, the divine blacksmith, took his place.

The revolution involved more than steam, however. Industry was producing bigger shells for more accurate guns and thicker armor for faster ships. Skillfully placed mines could bar an enemy from any area and required no maintenance. Torpedoes compressed distances, destroying old notions of naval might. Now a tiny boat carrying torpedoes could easily defeat a huge, heavily armed hull. With some luck, several torpedo boats could sink a squadron.

Battleships became floating fortresses. Their gunnery intimidated both enemy ships and enemy ground fortifications. Coastal cities like Copenhagen, St. Petersburg, and New York started looking terrifyingly vulnerable. A squadron of battleships could easily devastate any of them in a matter of minutes.

In 1895, Britain launched the *Majestic*—the battleship of a new generation. Securely armored and heavily armed, she was also very fast—with a top speed of 17.5 knots. Her shells could penetrate 18 inches of armor at 15,000 yards. A leviathan like that could easily change the outcome of an entire battle.

Cruisers were also putting on armor. Traditionally, the major asset of cruisers was speed and speed only. Now the British started building "protected," or armored, cruisers. If battleships were fortresses, the new generation of cruisers could be likened to speedy artillery batteries, capable of speeds between 20 and 24 knots. Those cruisers that bore heavy gunnery were close to battleships in their destructive potential.

The invention of the self-propelled torpedo revolutionized naval tactics. Now a powerful torpedo could maintain a speed of 30 knots as it also became more accurate. In 1897 the British launched the *Viper* torpedo boat, which became the model for French, Russian, German, and Japanese torpedo boats. They were invaluable escorts for battleships and transports; they also were like hounds chasing game—used not only for attack, but also for reconnaissance purposes. Most of them were incredibly small (350 tons), but fast (26 knots).

A totally new class of ships also emerged: submarines. Though they were clumsy and unreliable, they were hailed by the public. A warship could now become invisible, capable of bringing instant death.

Everybody was experimenting with radio. The ocean ceased being a desert. It was clear that in the near future, communications between base and ship would be able to be maintained anywhere in the world.

All major nations were launching large-scale shipbuilding programs. Alfred Thayer Mahan in the United States declared sea power the power of the future. European royals spent weeks showing off aboard their yachts. Kings paraded fleets in front of foreign relatives. Only half a century before, they had been parading hussars.

New naval strategy looked exciting and promising, but it was as yet only theoretical. Since the coming of armor and steam, no major naval battle had been fought. Theory had yet to be tested in practice. In 1904, the new technological era was still largely terra incognita.

The British were the strongest naval nation by far. Others were trying to catch up. Russia was trying especially hard. However, its enterprise was severely handicapped.

The country was run not by an elected government or by elites, but by the tsar and his relatives. Almost all Romanov males had important military duties. Ambition, competition, and vanity blurred their vision and interfered with their judgment. Moreover, Romanov naval leaders, such as grand dukes Alexander and Alexei, were only amateur sailors, but their authority was absolute.

Bureaucracy and corruption, the two traditional Russian maladies, affected the fleet strongly. Even the most minor decisions had to be approved by Admiralty in St. Petersburg. The naval bureaucracy repressed initiative. It stole. It lied. It cheated.

People could be promoted to high rank just because they looked imposing or cultivated the right grand duchess. In 1904, Russia had 100 admirals. England, with the biggest fleet in the world, had 69, France had 53, Germany had 9. Many Russian admirals had never been to sea as captains. More than one-third had not been to sea for more than ten years.

Happily embezzling state funds, the bureaucracy tried to economize on essentials. Too many ships remained in port to save money. Expensive gun shells were not to be "wasted" on practice. Maneuvers were rare, and maneuvers of bigger, squadron-size units, almost unheard of. Nepotism thrived. Angry officers labeled sons and nephews of important people "auntie's children." Of course, nobody paid any attention to their grievances. If anything was changing at all, it was only for the worse. Admiralty prevailed over fleet, desk administrators over sailors.

In addition to the problems of bureaucracy and corruption, the Russian navy fell victim to the country's geography. Russia's European oceanic outlets—the Baltic Sea and the Black Sea—were disabled by the bottlenecks of narrow straits. Ports in the north, on the doorstep of the Arctic Ocean, were of little use during most of the year. Vladivostok, on the Pacific, was also locked by ice in winter. It was the search for a warmer place that drew the Russians to Port Arthur and the Yellow Sea—where the Japanese were waiting for them.

2

Originally, Russians did not think highly of the Japanese navy. It had had an even later start than the Russian navy, having been established during the Meiji reforms. When the Russian fleet was dying in Sevastopol during the Crimean War, Japan had no fleet at all; but only fifty years later, Tokyo was commanding one of the mightiest armadas in the world. On the verge of war with Russia, Japan had six battleships, eight armored cruisers, sixteen lighter cruisers, twenty destroyers, and fifty-eight torpedo boats.

Seventy percent of the Japanese ships were foreign built, largely in the docks of their European ally, Britain, but national shipyards were growing quickly. So was their major naval base—Sasebo. An obscure fishing village before 1886, it was now famous.

Japanese scientists had made an important unexpected breakthrough. They had invented a thin-skinned shell that allowed more weight to be allotted to the charge—10 percent instead of the normal 2 to 3 percent typical of European shells. This provided for a much greater explosive effect. Also, a new explosive—*shimosa*—set fire to almost anything. Shells stuffed with it turned enemy ships into floating grills.

On the eve of the war, the Japanese combined fleet consisted of two units with two battle divisions each. The overall command was given to Admiral Togo Heihachiro. This proved to be an excellent choice. Throughout the winter of 1904, Togo kept the Russian fleet blockaded at Port Arthur. His ships enjoyed full control over East Asia's waters. The Russian tsar received invariably bad news from the area. Yet, Togo's success was only partially explained by his military genius. He did not have to make Port Arthur into a trap; it had been one from the start.

Port Arthur was located on the very tip of the Liaodong Peninsula. An enemy had only to occupy the adjoining area to cut off the fortress from the army completely. Also, its harbor was confined within a ring of hills. Enemy artillery placed on any of them meant the end of the fortress and of the fleet. The entry to the harbor was shallow. Battleships could use it only at high tide. Otherwise, they were locked within. A squadron fleeing to Port Arthur could not enter the haven until the tide changed. The harbor itself was not spacious enough, prohibiting ships from maneuvering freely. Every departure was an ordeal. The Japanese commander-in-chief watched the Russians agonizing from a distance.

Togo Heihachiro came from an ancient family of warriors that traced it roots to the thirteenth century. Thus, at least in length, his ancestry was equal to that of Nicholas II. He was born in 1848 in the little town of Kajiya and received an education proper for his rank, mastering calligraphy and the works of Confucius. At the age of eight, he surprised people with his fencing prowess; in a matter of a few minutes, with his sword, he cut and caught about fifty carp in a stream flowing through a rice field. He was sharp-witted and stubborn and from time to time displayed shocking disobedience to his elders. In 1860 he reached the age of majority—twelve. According to custom, he shaved off his front hair and received an adult name—Heihachiro.

He became a copyist at his clan's office with the salary of half a bushel of unhulled rice a month. But the boy was not going to remain a clerk for the rest of his life. He started learning gunnery. This proved helpful. In August 1863, his lord, the great Daimo of Satsuma, went to war with the British Empire.

The Daimo's father had had an infuriating encounter with foreign devils. On his way from Yokohama to Yedo, he met four Englishmen on horseback trotting across the path of his procession. A young samurai of his entourage exploded with rage at this unheard of breach of etiquette and rushed upon the intruders. A fight started. One Englishman was killed, two others wounded.

When the news reached London, Her Majesty's government, very much displeased, instructed the British chargé d'affaires in Japan to demand indemnity. The chargé d'affaires thought he needed a stronger contingent and summoned a fleet of seven men-of-war to the Kagoshima Bay.

The Satsuma clan had expected precisely that. All ten forts around the bay had been hastily fortified, twelve light boats were prepared for sea action, and three mines were laid in the water near one of the forts.

The British, sneering at this naive war effort, immediately seized the clan's steamships. The Satsuma forts opened fire. Surprised, the British responded.

The streets of the town caught fire immediately. A local ammunition factory burned to the ground. Guns in the forts were disabled. Many samurai threw off their clothes and went to the shore with their swords unsheathed, prepared to fight at close quarters and die.

But the British never came ashore. In the dusk the squadron anchored. They had done a good job; the shore across the bay was ablaze with flame. To celebrate the event and teach the Asian barbarians a lesson, captains ordered musicians on decks. Merry tunes started drifting over the fires. The bands played late into the night.

That was the end of the battle, and the clan paid indemnity. One of the youngest samurai fighters to mourn the defeat was Togo Heihachiro. Perhaps it was the day he decided to become a sailor. No matter how much he must have hated the British, the only place to get superb naval training was England. He dutifully went there and was assigned to the training ship *Worcester* at Plymouth.

Togo was twenty-four years old. His English was very bad, and he made very slow progress. However, he was good at mathematics, and he surprised local hosts with his keen interest in the Christian church. His acquaintances reported that he attended services regularly, even singing hymns with the use of a hymnal. It might have been merely a desire to master the language—many a foreigner learned English with the help of the King James Bible—yet an unlikely rumor had Togo baptized as a Roman Catholic. His training over, he was ordered to stay in England to watch the construction of a new Japanese ship. Then he returned home.

The Japanese navy had its debut in the war against China in 1894–1895. Togo participated in the campaign with distinction. Among his exploits was the occupation of the Pescadore Islands in the middle of the Formosa Channel and of Formosa itself. He was noticed and promoted.

By the time he became rear admiral, he had acquired the awe of subordinates, rheumatism, an amazing ability to endure physical pain, and a good reputation with his superiors, but not fame. This was to come later, with the war against Russia.

Togo had set off for Port Arthur several days before the war. On the way, his fleet captured a Russian merchantman, named the *Russia.* Taking this as a good omen, sailors started saying to each other, "Russia is taken."

Togo dispatched Rear Admiral Uryu to cover the Japanese landing in Korea, and Togo himself led the main force to Port Arthur. On the night of January 27, his torpedo boats attacked the harbor and disabled several ships there. The first blow against Russia in the war had been orchestrated by Togo.

The next day, seeking revenge, the Russian squadron left the base to face Togo's fleet. A long-range artillery duel ensued. The Japanese losses were minor; several Russian ships were hit badly. In anguish and anger, the Russians headed back for their base. The temptation for Togo to finish the enemy then and there must have been very strong, but this would have meant fighting at close quarters, and the admiral was still apprehensive about his adversary's guns. Demonstrating wisdom and a cool head, Togo turned back.

Togo then decided to put Port Arthur under siege. Keeping his flag on the brand-new *Mikasa* battleship, he started cruising the Yellow Sea, keeping the Russian squadron locked in its base and waiting for the right moment to destroy it completely. He spent much time away from Port Arthur. He was not in a hurry to attack the doomed fortress. He knew patience was his best ally.

This paid off on the stormy night of March 30–31, when a Japanese ship laid mines in Port Arthur waters.

3

Russian losses in the Far East caused anger throughout the nation. Even Anton Chekhov, now a famous author, was so disturbed by the war that he now planned to go to the front as a doctor and war correspondent.

The commander of the Port Arthur squadron, Admiral Stark, was apparently incapable of providing leadership in time of war. The Viceroy of the Far East, Admiral Alexeev, played with the idea of commanding the fleet himself. Typical of his imaginative but vain mind, he considered the possibility of making Tsushima Island in the Korea Strait his base. The island was so close to Japan that Togo would have annihilated the Russian garrison there in a matter of hours. When asked about Alexeev (or, for that matter, Stark), sailors in St. Petersburg and elsewhere responded with obscenities. Having to consider public opinion for the first time in his life, the tsar decided to send another commander to Port Arthur. The candidate was obvious: Admiral Makarov.

Stepan Osipovich Makarov was the most charismatic admiral in Russia. Independent, impervious to court politics, courageous, demanding, and stern, he was also an acknowledged expert in oceanography. Leo Tolstoy, the first Russian pacifist, called Makarov an "excellent machine of slaughter." Hardly intended as a compliment, this definition must have frightened Makarov's adversaries, the Japanese.

On a cold, sunny day, February 4, the tsar received Makarov. Having received the blessing of the sovereign, the admiral left for the Far East the same day by the recently completed Trans-Siberian Railroad. The cousin of the tsar, Grand Duke Kyril, a naval officer longing for glory, departed with him, as did the leading Russian battle painter, Vasily Vereshchagin, Makarov's classmate and an artistic witness to all the wars of his lifetime.

The sovereign soon started receiving the first good news of the war. Makarov was in firm control, ships were quickly repaired, and land fortifications were strengthened. "Thank God," Nicholas wrote in his diary on March 23, "everything goes smoother and faster than planned!"

A week earlier, on March 17, Port Arthur had celebrated an anniversary. Six years earlier, Grand Duke Kyril, representing the monarch, had raised the Russian flag at Golden Hill. The grand duke's great-grandfather, Tsar Nicholas I, used to say, "Wherever the Russian flag has been raised it never comes down again."

On March 31, Makarov, Vereshchagin, and Grand Duke Kyril were standing on the bridge of Makarov's flagship, the battleship *Petropavlovsk*. The squadron had left the harbor and was looking for Togo. Suddenly quiet talk on the bridge was interrupted by the report of an excited officer: The Japanese squadron had been spotted on the horizon! Vereshchagin went below to fetch his sketchbook; at this moment a terrible explosion shook the *Petropavlovsk*. The grand duke turned to Makarov; the admiral's body, still vertical, was decapitated.

The first thought everybody had was of a Japanese submarine. But it had been a mine laid by the Japanese the night before. The *Petropavlovsk* was cloaked in a dark cloud, her bow diving into the sea, her stern high in the air and propellers still whirling. Under the rays of bright springtime sun, in mocking proximity to the friendly shore, the battleship sank in a matter of minutes. Among the numerous bodies never recovered was that of Admiral Makarov.

4

Masses were celebrated for Makarov nationwide. Many sailors wept openly. In St. Petersburg, the tsar also went to mass. He felt "sad" and was glad that the service had been appropriately "solemn." His European cousins sent letters of condolence. The kaiser cabled from Syracuse:

> Rumor has just reached me that Makarow [sic] fell in battle and went down with his ship off Port Arthur. Is this true? If so allow me to express sincerest and heartfelt sympathy to you at the loss of so brave an admiral, who was personally well known to me. And so many brave sailors.

The loss of the *Petropavlovsk* was hard to live with. The sinking of a battleship was not the end of the world, but the loss of Makarov left a hole in the Russian universe. There was no other admiral equal to Makarov in stature.

The position of Port Arthur did not look hopeless yet, but it was likely to deteriorate. Even if the fortress stood firm for many months, the fleet had no chance of getting control over East Asian waters. Without this, no victory over Japan was possible. For Russia to win in Manchuria, the Japanese army there had to be cut off from the homeland. This challenge was a tough one.

The *Petropavlovsk* catastrophe affected the tsar and other Romanovs deeply and personally. Too independent-minded, Makarov had never been popular with the royal family, but one of the kin—Grand Duke Kyril—had almost perished in the maelstrom. The tsar disliked his ambitious cousin, but the shock was nevertheless great.

In mid-April, two weeks after the *Petropavlovsk* sank, Nicholas decided to send more ships to the Far East to rescue Port Arthur and eventually master the sea. Ships had to be borrowed from the Baltic Fleet. They were to become the 2nd Pacific Squadron. The Port Arthur ships from now on were referred to as the 1st Pacific Squadron.

It was a most audacious plan. No other fleet in history had ever attempted anything like it. Squadrons traveling from European metropolises to colonies in Asia, Africa, and America had always been conveniently tight, manageable, homogeneous, but the 2nd Pacific Squadron had to be big and diverse. Practically all Russian ships suitable for action were to be dispatched with it. The squadron the Russians had in mind could be compared only with the infamous Spanish Armada of the sixteenth century—but its route was infinitely longer. The squadron had to start in the Baltic Sea and reach the Far East. Furthermore, new technology, ironically enough, involved new challenges.

In the days of sail, ships were propelled by nature, and all that captains had to worry about was food, fresh water, and ammunition. But modern ships had to be fed liberally. From where was one to get all this coal? Who would provide transports for this? Would any foreign nation violate its neutrality and allow Russia to use its ports in Africa and Asia?

Even food and fresh water were more of a challenge now than several decades earlier; the crew of a single battleship could easily consist of nine hundred men. To find supplies for this multi-thousand-person fleet more transports and more friendly bases would be necessary.

However, what would prevent the Japanese from intercepting the fleet in an ambush made possible by modern means of communication—telegraph and radio? Would they lay mines on the squadron's route? The whole armada could easily perish like the unfortunate *Petropavlovsk*. Which route would be the safest? How could they monitor the enemy's activities? Which nations would assist the Russians in the areas where they had no presence of their own—say, in tropical Africa?

But the most important question was, who could lead this un-precedented fleet on its unheard-of mission? Though the Russian navy had one hundred admirals, only a few looked fit for such a role.

Many favored Grigory Chukhnin, director of the Naval Academy. Other candidates were Fedor Dubasov, and to a lesser extent, Nikolai Skrydlov and Alexei Birilev. These four names had come up in January when the tsar was looking for a commander for the Port Arthur squadron, but he had rejected them all in favor of Makarov.

All of the short lists, both in January and now in April, included one more name: Rear Admiral Zinovy Petrovich Rozhestvensky.

Uncharacteristically, Nicholas this time decided quickly. On April 19 he signed the much anticipated decree. Rear Admiral Rozhestvensky was ordered to raise his flag over the 2nd Pacific Squadron.

Some said Makarov's ghost would be angry; Rozhestvensky had never been respectful of the now deceased admiral. But it is difficult to respect a man if you are involved with his wife, even one so renowned as Makarov.

5

Zinovy Petrovich Rozhestvensky was reported to have an iron will and an iron hand. Everybody who saw him on the bridge agreed that the man inspired immediate awe. Tall, powerfully built, his balding head a proud well-proportioned dome hinting at determination and obstinacy, Rozhestvensky, at the age of fifty-five, was one of the handsomest admirals in the Russian navy. He was frightfully imposing, almost the embodiment of a savage Russian admiral, which he was in the eyes of many. Bushy eyebrows did not hide his bright eyes, which were lit sometimes with passion, sometimes with uncontrollable rage, and occasionally accompanied by a sarcastic smile. A short, graying beard partly concealed sensual lips more accustomed to foul obscenities, by virtue of his métier, than to words of tender passion, which they were nonetheless fluent in.

When he so desired, Rozhestvensky's self-control was complete. He could be irresistibly charming and pleasant—when chatting with a woman he liked or with an enemy he hated. However, his subordinates and colleagues knew a very different man: stern, demanding, as often as not rude, and sometimes violent.

Rozhestvensky's explosions of rage caused total horror in his victims. Many a sailor lost a tooth on encountering Rozhestvensky's boxer's fists, and people suspected he wished he could beat his officers. He believed in discipline, was punctual and precise himself and was determined to make others respect orderliness at any cost.

Men were terrified by him. His stern glance alone was enough to make them turn pale. They hid from him in the dark corners of the ship, which was best if they happened to be wearing a soiled shirt or were guilty of leaving some dirt on the rails. When he was furious but unable to instantly reach the object of his wrath—such as the captain of another ship—he would growl with anger and throw his binoculars overboard.

At the same time, he generously gave poorer colleagues money from his modest salary and paid the tuition of several students. He was one of the few people in the Admiralty who had not been tainted by corruption. No matter how much people hated Rozhestvensky, nobody could say he was an embezzler—a rare distinction for a person of his rank in Russia.

He was a splendid speaker. His vocabulary was rich, his voice extremely persuasive. The presence of dignitaries, including the tsar himself, never made him shy. Witnesses insisted it even added force to his presentation.

He despised doctors and ignored sickness. People thought his iron will healed him, but it hardly helped his kidney problem or his rheumatism, which caused him a lot of pain though almost no one knew.

People who liked the admiral were doggedly devoted to him. For them he was a difficult, thunderous, but fair and wise head of family. But regardless of whether they liked him, everybody agreed that Rozhestvensky was one of the most capable admirals in Russia.

Zinovy Petrovich Rozhestvensky was born on October 30, 1848. He was nine months Togo's junior, but unlike his Japanese counterpart, he was lowborn. That was obvious from his first name. No person of any prominence would have given his son the name Zinovy. Zinovy was a name favored by petty shopkeepers and village priests. His father was neither, but his social status was not much higher; he was a military doctor. Fortunately, that was good enough to enable his son to become a cadet at the Naval Academy (no child of a peasant or petty merchant could gain entry to this prestigious institution). The boy entered the academy in September 1864 when he was almost sixteen years old.

The mid-1860s were difficult years for Russia and even worse for its navy. Only a decade earlier, the nation had been defeated in the Crimean War. As a result, Russia was prohibited from having any navy in the Black Sea. The former Black Sea fleet had met a most tragic fate, sunk by its captains in a desperate attempt to block the channel to prevent the French and the British from entering Sevastopol harbor.

Russia had not suffered such a blow to its national pride since Moscow had been occupied by Napoleon back in 1812. The tsar, Nicholas I, died before the peace was signed—allegedly having taken poison. His son, Alexander II, realized he had to do something if he wanted Russia to remain a great power. He decided on a new course: reform.

Tsar Alexander II emancipated peasants, introduced juries to Russian courts, and softened censorship, bringing to life the first Russian *glasnost*. He also started reforming the military, bringing it from the Dark Ages to modernity. Soldiers now did not have to spend twenty years in the army, and officers could no longer flog them to death at their whim. The person to reform the navy was his brother, Grand Duke Constantine.

Atypical for a grand duke, Constantine was a liberal. He was pressing his hesitant elder brother, the tsar, for more reform, perhaps even for constitutional monarchy. As for the navy, he wanted to raise it from the dead.

The Naval Academy found itself under his special patronage. He aspired to raise a generation of sailors who would never taste defeat. The school was small—just fifty cadets were accepted each year—and very elite. Any boy who received entry would be noticed by the court, more attention than those who entered the army received.

The navy was more egalitarian financially, too. A person of modest means (like Rozhestvensky) was unable to join the elite regiments of the army. The expense of a thoroughbred horse alone amounted to a fortune, to say nothing of the almost obligatory spending at the most expensive clubs in St. Petersburg. On a ship, class difference was less noticeable. Also, very few members of aristocracy would fancy a career demanding constant travel in moveable barracks in largely bad weather away from society. All in all, the navy embraced meritocracy.

Rozhestvensky became one of the best students in the academy. He mastered English, which was mandatory, and also French. By the time he graduated, he had spent 227 days at sea. The Russian Baltic coast became familiar to him and so did naval science. He graduated with honors—fifth in the class of 1868—and joined the Baltic Fleet. His ship was the first big Russian ironclad, appropriately named *Pervenetz* (Firstborn). Two years later, having spent twenty-one remarkably long months at sea, he received the first officer's rank of midshipman. He chose naval artillery as his specialization. This was a very unorthodox choice, generally ignored by professional sailors. To pursue his studies, he joined the Mikhailovskaya Artillery Academy and graduated in 1873, again with honors and by that time with a rank of lieutenant.

For the next four years he went to sea on several ships, both under sail and under steam, and then got involved in testing guns, shells, and armor as a member of the Artillery Committee. This was a distinction for a person his age. To his superiors, Rozhestvensky embodied the new spirit of the time: He sought challenge and courted science. While on the Artillery Committee, he audited courses at the St. Petersburg College of Transportation, translated articles on new naval technology from the foreign press, and even participated in a contest involving the installation of electricity in St. Petersburg's theaters.

In the midst of these pursuits, Rozhestvensky somehow found time to become a family man; he married Olga Antipova, a young woman of similarly modest background. She did not bring him any dowry, and presumably it was a love match. On December 22, 1877, they had their first and only child, a daughter, Elena. By the time the baby was born, her father had already learned what war was about.

Seeking revenge in the Black Sea, the empire was preparing an assault on Turkey. Rozhestvensky was dispatched to the south to collect guns from local fortresses for use on merchant vessels; the navy in the Black Sea was still handicapped. In several weeks he had six floating batteries ready, protecting the harbors of Odessa, Ochakov, and Kerch. In April 1877, soon after the war started, Rozhestvensky's efforts were recognized, and he was appointed supervisor of the Black Sea Fleet artillery.

Rozhestvensky went to sea several times—usually on merchant boats armed according to his instructions. In July 1877, his hour struck. He boarded the armed steamer *Vesta*, commanded by Nikolai Baranov. The *Vesta* was old and small, but she carried new artillery Rozhestvensky wanted to test. On July 10, the *Vesta* left Odessa with the mission to attack all small Turkish ships she found. But on the dawn of the next day, she met not a schooner but a Turkish battleship.

Having answered the battleship's first salvo, Baranov ordered the crew to flee. There was no chance that the *Vesta* could win the artillery duel. The battleship, hungry for a victory, pursued. Baranov maneuvered cleverly, preventing the enemy from approaching the *Vesta* from any side; from the stern, any ship, particularly a small one, is a difficult target.

After three hours of successfully averting the battleship, Turkish gun shells started hitting the Russian steamer. After several officers were disabled by enemy fire, Rozhestvensky assumed command of the *Vesta's* guns. He performed well. One of the *Vesta's* shells hit the battleship's bridge. The Turkish commander, cursing his bad luck, retreated.

Rozhestvensky was credited with "having saved the steamer." He was promoted to lieutenant captain and received two honors, the

Order of St. Vladimir and the Order of St. George, the latter a very prestigious distinction. He was also sent to St. Petersburg to report to Grand Duke Constantine in person. Then he returned to the war zone and spent the rest of the campaign at the Danube. Rozhestvensky did not get another chance to participate in battle. Instead, he unexpectedly became a political combatant. He did not seek fame; he was guided by a guilty conscience.

The war was won by Russia, but on land. The efforts of the navy had been totally irrelevant. The august naval commander, Grand Duke Constantine, was painfully envious; his brothers, grand dukes Nikolai and Mikhail, had been commanding Russian land armies and were now praised for having wrestled victory from the Ottomans while he and the navy remained in shadow. Grand Duke Constantine thought that a bit of self-promotion was in order. The *Vesta*'s modest accomplishment started to be trumpeted as a great feat.

Rozhestvensky did not want to be the fake hero of a fake battle. But what was he to do? He sought the advice of a renowned commander, Vice Admiral Butakov. He told the admiral that the St. George Cross was "burning" his chest. All the *Vesta* had been involved in, he said, was mere fleeing. Was he to renounce the award he did not deserve?

Admiral Butakov listened to the confession patiently, then calmly told the young man that *his* St. George Cross had also been undeserved. However, he had received no reward for three subsequent—and quite extraordinary—battles, and thus now claimed the cross as his just distinction. He advised Rozhestvensky to use his future career to justify the "burning" item in question.

Dissatisfied with his interview with the cynical old man, Rozhestvensky talked to several other people and finally decided to rebel. He published an article called "Battleships and Merchant Cruisers" in a popular newspaper. It was camouflaged as a piece on naval strategy. His major thesis was that hastily armed merchant vessels could not fight battleships. He casually mentioned the *Vesta*'s battle, saying that all the heroic ship had been doing was fleeing for five and a half hours from a much stronger adversary.

The article met a stormy response. Not only Captain Baranov, but also another war hero, Stepan Makarov, publicly accused Rozhestvensky of slander. Baranov even suggested that Rozhestvensky should be prosecuted for libel.

The scandal had no immediate impact on Rozhestvensky's career—either good or bad. He returned to his duties on the Artillery Committee, lingered ashore, pursued his fascination with electricity, traveled to Germany to monitor the processing of Russian military orders, and visited familiar Black Sea fortresses. Suddenly, in July 1883 he was given a new role that he could never have expected.

Five years earlier, having defeated Turkey, Russia managed to carve out an independent Bulgaria from the Ottoman lands. Prince Alexander Battenberg of Germany became the compromise candidate for the Bulgarian throne and eventually took it. Battenberg was German and disliked Slavs, but his only chance at governance was as Russia's vassal. St. Petersburg approved Bulgaria's constitution and sent Russian officers to create a Bulgarian army and navy.

Rozhestvensky was appointed commander of the Bulgarian fleet. It was not much of a fleet; Russia had given Bulgaria several steamers and cutters and that was about it. But still, Rozhestvensky was the naval commander-in-chief of an independent nation, while his classmates were still commanding canon boats. This unexpected promotion had been well deserved. He was daring, creative, self-reliant, abreast of the latest technological innovations, familiar with the Black Sea strategic terrain, a hero of the recent military campaign, and already a capable administrator, known to many in the corridors of power in St. Petersburg.

Immediately after he arrived in Bulgaria, he made it clear that he did not want to be a figurehead. After his persistent requests, Russia gave Bulgaria two torpedo boats. Not everybody in Sofia rejoiced. Bulgarian politicians were skeptical about the necessity of having a navy.

In a memo to the Bulgarian minister of war (another Russian), Rozh-estvensky expressed his concerns. The vessels given to Bulgaria were not being utilized properly, he said. The war ministry was using them as cargo ships. That was unacceptable. Normally, he continued, a na-tion would spend not less than one-third of its ground troops budget on its navy. Bulgaria was spending only one-twenty-fifth. Rozhestven-sky pushed and pushed, and in only a few months his navy was granted its fair share. He achieved another difficult goal—to raise the first generation of Bulgarian seamen. He began a technological society (remembering his own enthusiasm during the first decade of electric-ity) and a naval museum (he was a firm believer in uplifting symbols and rituals).

As the creator of a new navy, Rozhestvensky felt obliged to come out with something of a general manifesto. He prepared a special re-port in which he summarized his views. He thought a navy was a vital attribute of any developed state. Bulgarian politicians were hinting that a strong navy belonged only in an autocracy like Russia. He ar-gued that democracy and a strong navy were totally compatible. "The English people," Rozhestvensky wrote, "for three hundred years enjoy-ing the most free institutions in the world, have a national anthem that starts and ends with the words

> *Rule Britannia, rule the waves*
> *Brittons never shall be slaves.*

Of course, he did not become Bulgarian in spirit—but he was not expected to. He was merely a mercenary. Like all other Russians serv-ing in Bulgaria, he had had to nominally quit the Russian service, and the Bulgarian ruler, Prince Alexander, issued a special decree saying Russian servicemen would not be held responsible in Russia for what they did in Bulgaria. However, Prince Alexander could not speak for the Russian tsar.

Though merely a guest on Bulgarian soil, Rozhestvensky took his duties extremely seriously. In 1885, he spent 195 days with his navy—

maneuvering or conducting artillery practice. He would often visit Budapest, Vienna, and Bucharest. His title and mission must have raised many eyebrows, for in the eyes of many, "Bulgarian navy" was an oxymoron, but he had become an insider of intricate Balkan politics.

Unexpectedly, his tenure came to an abrupt end. The industrious Battenberg decided to annex a neighbor, Eastern Rumelia, in spite of St. Petersburg's objections. The Russian tsar, Alexander III, did not want to risk another major war in the Balkans, and to punish the arrogant upstart, the tsar ordered all Russian officers in Bulgaria to go back home immediately.

Having spent two years in Bulgaria, Rozhestvensky returned to the ranks of the Imperial Navy. During 1886–1889, he sailed in the Baltic Sea as a senior officer, which was a painful backtrack. He had become accustomed to having a position of authority, but now he was a mere administrator again. However, he performed his duties with precision and excellence, and in 1890 an award arrived. He was appointed to the Far East as captain of a ship. That was a breakthrough. If he was successful in the role, he could aspire to further promotion.

The ship Rozhestvensky was assigned to command was the *Kreiser* clipper, a fine tall ship equipped with an engine. For several months, he and his crew patrolled the North Pacific. In America Bay, the clipper hit a rock not marked on the map. Rozhestvensky ordered the unloading of some coal and succeeded in rescuing the ship and bringing her back to Vladivostok. On another occasion, during a ferocious storm, the crew was too frightened by gales to climb the mast and lower the sails. They probably expected their captain to use his fists, but instead Rozhestvensky calmly ordered officers to perform the dangerous operation. Men, ashamed, instantly climbed the mast.

He stayed in the area for only a few months. In the fall, he took the clipper to Kronshtadt, via Hong Kong, Singapore, Colombo, Suez, Port Said, Cadiz, Cherbourg, and Copenhagen. He knew that he had been a tremendous success as a captain. Very few naval commanders could boast the unwavering loyalty of subordinates, a successful salvage, and a trans-Eurasian journey—all in less than a year. Now his credentials were fully established: an administrator, a war veteran, a diplomat, a captain. What next?

As in 1883, a surprise was awaiting him in the capital. Having spent barely a month commanding a ship in the Baltic Sea, he was appointed naval attaché to England. He attained the rank of captain soon after his arrival in London.

In 1892, the position of naval attaché, or naval agent as it was called in Russia, was somewhat different than what it had become by the late twentieth century. Rozhestvensky had virtually no diplomatic functions and few contacts with his embassy. His chief errand was to gather intelligence, and in this he was a lone hunter. Unlike his peers in today's world, he had no staff or network of agents. He was also responsible for monitoring Russian government orders placed with foreign producers and searching for cheap deals and new inventions. If he was lucky, he could purchase a winning weapon from an inventor desperate for cash.

In 1892, London was a thrilling place to be. It was the capital of the world. Pleasure-seekers were going to Paris, and art-lovers to Rome, but money, science, and power dwelled in London. Rare orchids and diplomatic secrets, blueprints of the most recent torpedoes and stock exchange news could all be found there. As for naval affairs, if something sought could not be obtained in London, it could not be found anywhere.

Three years earlier, the First Lord of Admiralty, George Hamilton, had persuaded the parliament to adopt a new and most ambitious shipbuilding program. Now Britain was following a "two-powers standard"; her navy's strength was to surpass that of the next two most powerful naval fleets combined. The arrogance of this strategy had no equal in history, but few doubted Britain would succeed. Indeed, in 1894 Great Britain already had forty-six battleships; Russia and France had just thirty-five, seven of them wooden.

London astounded visitors with its fast pace and noise. Five and a half million people lived there. Thousands of cabs rattled at street corners, and enormous railway stations spat fast trains in all directions twenty-four hours a day. The underground train, built twenty-nine years earlier amid the foundations of the Plantagenets and the Tudors, tied the city in a single steel web. It had been the first subway in the world, and in 1892 only one other city had one—not Paris or New York but British Glasgow. Whistles of factories mingled with whistles of boats from the River Thames. London streets were filling up with the first automobiles. A totally new sound could be heard behind the closed doors of Mayfair mansions and Whitehall offices: telephones. The squeaking of pens had gone and so had the scribes; thousands of female typists filled the air with the racket of typewriter keys.

In such a city, a Russian felt like a poor relative visiting obscenely wealthy cousins. Hardly inhibited by London's might and splendor, Rozhestvensky must have nonetheless felt resentful and frustrated. London's conspicuous glamour alerted him to the dangers of Russia's appalling backwardness. However, he had a mission: to represent the interests of the Russian fleet in the naval center of the world. He pursued it stubbornly.

His primary task was to assess the chance of war. Political declarations of statesmen, parlor gossip, publications in professional journals, and comments of the free press all had to be analyzed, compared, and verified. Almost every week he sent a parcel to St. Petersburg that contained the First Lord of Admiralty's recent statements, a technological advertisement from the *Times,* blueprints of the most recent boiler, or samples of new armor stolen from a shipyard. He was also supervising Russian orders at local plants (British private companies did not care about strategic rivalry as long as they got paid in full). For this, he traveled all over Britain. A relatively minor, but still essential responsibility was to look out for new books that might be of interest to Russian naval experts.

The British secret service kept a close eye on Rozhestvensky. From time to time, he had to deal with remarkably friendly Englishmen requesting his services for delicate missions. As often as not, these men represented the British intelligence community. However, if Rozhestvensky lacked anything, it was not distrustfulness.

He wrote all reports himself in longhand; there was no secretary or typewriter. When he asked the Admiralty to hire a retired naval officer as his assistant, St. Petersburg, economizing on essential expenditures as usual, refused. More importantly, the Admiralty frowned when he tried to bring its attention to the corruption flowering among Russian bureaucrats placing orders with British industrialists. In a terse letter, the naval minister recommended that he minded his own business.

Rozhestvensky spent two and a half years in Britain. He had already spent considerable time abroad, in Bulgaria, but as an ally. In Britain he was an alien, if not a foe. Although he admired British naval skills, he developed a patriotic distaste for everything else coming from the British Isles. Also, he became quite ill there. During his years of sailing he, like Togo, had acquired rheumatism, and his ailment worsened in the damp and chilly English climate. He was glad when his ordeal in London ended. In July 1894, he was appointed commander of the *Vladimir Monomakh* cruiser and left for Russia.

Although the *Vladimir Monomakh* was the first big ship he commanded, this appointment was hardly a promotion. The Russian Admiralty had not forgiven him for his anticorruption zeal, potentially dangerous for its embezzlers, and put him in charge of an old-timer; the *Vladimir Monomakh* had once been a frigate. On October 2, 1894, Rozhestvensky took her from Kronshtadt for the Mediterranean Sea.

Just like in the Pacific several years earlier, he inspired awe in the sailors. He could be brutal to his men, but he hired German dockers to load coal in Kiel, because his crew felt too tired. Very few captains would have done that.

The *Vladimir Monomakh* visited Lisbon, Algiers, and Piraeus. In Piraeus, Rozhestvensky was introduced to the Queen of Greece, Olga, a Romanov grand duchess by birth. She was the daughter of none other than Grand Duke Constantine who had commanded the navy. Nostalgic, she made herself into the patron saint for Russian crews in the Mediterranean.

It is unknown what passed between Rozhestvensky and Olga, but ten years later she still expressed profound distaste for the man. Of course, there was plenty of space for conflict; both were stubborn and opinionated. Queen Olga thought the best way to deal with sailors was to give them icons, blessings, and religious instruction. She must have been appalled by Rozhestvensky's coarse ways, just as he must have sneered at her belief in miracles.

Also, in the last months of 1894, every Romanov was overwrought; the patriarch of the family, Tsar Alexander III, the Peacemaker, died in the Crimea on October 26, at only forty-eight. Queen Olga had been at his deathbed and was heartbroken. The new tsar, young Nicholas, was an unknown to most people, but the family knew how insecure he was.

Rozhestvensky was developing another important relationship at about the same time in the same waters: Admiral Makarov had been appointed commander of the Mediterranean squadron. Makarov had not forgotten the *Vesta* case and his accusation of slander against Rozhestvensky. But in his reports to the Admiralty, Makarov had to acknowledge Rozhestvensky's energy and initiative and also the perfect order he maintained on his ship. He soon got a chance to test his subordinate's abilities.

On the evening of January 24, 1895, Makarov received an urgent cable from St. Petersburg. He was to take his ships to the Far East as soon as possible. Japan was crushing China, and Russian interests in Manchuria had to be protected. The Japanese captain who had shot the first salvos in that war was Togo Heihachiro.

The *Vladimir Monomakh* was the first ship to leave Piraeus. It took Rozhestvensky just two days to prepare her for a transoceanic voyage. She was the only one in the whole squadron that could act on such short notice.

In less than two months, the cruiser entered the harbor of Nagasaki. Soon Makarov brought other vessels to the Far East, and the unit started cruising the coastal waters of China.

In spite of mutual deep resentment going back to the *Vesta* episode, Makarov's respect for Rozhestvensky grew. In that campaign, he regarded Rozhestvensky as his closest collaborator. The issues they had to discuss were extremely grave; war with Japan could start at any moment.

There was another admiral in the squadron, and his relations with Rozhestvensky were also strained. Evgeny Alexeev, a Romanov bastard, patronized by his august relatives, had grown up to be haughty, careless, and megalomaniac. Now he kept his flag on Rozhestvensky's ship. Rozhestvensky did not like Makarov but acknowledged his talent. For Alexeev he did not have a single good word.

Conflicts among top commanders could have influenced the unit's performance in battle, but, fortunately, Japan yielded to Western pressure and the battle never came. However, for Rozhestvensky the campaign brought a personal disappointment; after it, his career stalled. Admiral Alexeev had not forgiven the outspoken captain and decided to make life difficult for him.

After Rozhestvensky brought the *Vladimir Monomakh* to Kronshtadt, he was showered with very demanding but definitely obscure commands: the battleship *Pervenetz* (which was now a thirty-year-old relic); the artillery school for noncommissioned officers, and a special unit for crews practicing onshore. This would have been a stretch for any other man but not for Zinovy Petrovich. If his ill-wishers hoped to exhaust him, they failed. Rozhestvensky was a tireless workaholic. His superiors could not deny him that. Within three years, he was elevated to the command of the Artillery Practice Unit, the floating artillery academy of the Russian navy. On December 6, 1898, he was promoted to rear admiral.

He was fifty. He had had a good career, exceptional in many respects, but now had every chance of getting stuck at his present rank. Russia had too many admirals already and too few good jobs for them. His command was an inconspicuous and unappealing one, a backwater for failures and obstinate perfectionists. But it was difficult to overlook Rozhestvensky.

In 1900, an important errand came out of the blue. He was entrusted with a most difficult rescue mission. The battleship *General Admiral Apraxin* had shipwrecked at Gogland Island in the Baltic Sea. Several attempts to take her off the rocks had failed. Rozhestvensky was asked to give it another try. There was no reason to believe he would succeed, and his enemies gleefully anticipated a spectacular failure.

He started working on Gogland in the middle of winter when the sea was still coated with ice. Again, he proved to be a tough disciplinarian, but unlike other disciplinarians in the navy, his discipline was not affected by class concerns. Officers suffered from his wrath as often as subordinate crew members. Of course, the major difference was that he could not beat his officers even when he badly wanted to, for instance when he discovered, to his immense rage, that the crew was being fed what he called "greasy garbage." Having dealt with the personnel problems, the admiral addressed the technical matters.

Instead of attempting to pull the *Apraxin* off the rocks, which might have led to her total loss, he decided to extract the rocks themselves. For that, he identified a civilian mining company, which destroyed them in a series of micro-explosions. His ingenuity paid off. In early May, the salvaged *Apraxin* was brought to Kronshtadt.

The ill-wishers had miscalculated. Instead of being added to a list of early retirees, Rozhestvensky's name became famous. He was showered with flattering cables from Makarov and other admirals. The tsar's influential cousin, Grand Duke Alexander, also joined the congratulatory choir.

In his turn, Rozhestvensky complimented Makarov on the brilliant performance of his brainchild—the unique icebreaker *Ermak*. Rozhestvensky doubted the *Ermak*'s potential, but after using it, he was ready to credit Makarov. He also made sure the *Ermak*'s officers were properly awarded.

There was a special reason for Rozhestvensky to be particularly generous to his rival, and St. Petersburg society was quite aware of this. He had developed a close relationship with Makarov's wife, beautiful and intelligent Capitolina.

Capitolina Makarova was a lioness and a *femme fatale* looking for a sympathetic shoulder and handsome face. Makarov could be very difficult, and he was obsessed with ships and oceanography. He also cultivated a *muzhik* beard, and although he was the same age as Rozhestvensky, he looked much older and rather unkempt. He was more distinguished than his wife's new friend (among other things, Makarov had been the youngest admiral in the Russian navy), but what Rozhestvensky lacked in stature, he made up for in courtship. If Makarov devoted his whole self to his profession, Rozhestvensky, who was working just as hard, always reserved some secret garden for himself. And with his dazzling looks and poise, he was infinitely more attractive than the bearded oceanographer. Rozhestvensky and Makarova's affair became the talk of the day, and Rozhestvensky acquired a reputation for being not only a good admiral but also a lady-killer.

At the same time he managed to placate his wife. He shared with her everything he thought about his fellow admirals—and in no uncertain terms. Hardly seeking advice, he nevertheless sought understanding. But when he felt misunderstood or mistreated, he never hesitated to explode. His wife, though intimidated by his temper, remained an opinionated woman, which did not promote marital peace. She was intensely jealous of all his affairs (Makarova was not his only infatuation) and closely interrogated his orderlies. But they knew better than to betray their stormy master.

Although the triumphant rescue operation of the *Apraxin* brought praise, no immediate career breakthrough resulted. Rozhestvensky resumed command of the Artillery Practice Unit. The armistice with Makarov also came to an end; Makarov had been appointed commander of the port of Kronshtadt, and Rozhestvensky immediately started nagging him about long overdue repairs. By irritating Makarov, he was making Capitolina's life more difficult, but Rozhestvensky never cared about women as much as he did about ships.

Finally, his devotion to the navy was rewarded when he attracted the attention of the tsar. Nicholas visited Rozhestvensky's unit and was impressed by the fine gunnery and general orderliness of the ships. In July 1902, the tsar's cousin, Kaiser Wilhelm II of Germany, a notorious naval enthusiast, visited Russia, and Nicholas chose Rozhestvensky's unit to perform for the critical guest.

The monarchs watched an artillery exercise from the bridge of Rozhestvensky's flagship. They were accompanied by Russian and German naval elites, who were sure to be an unforgiving audience. The day was a real test for Rozhestvensky.

Remarkably, he seemed not to be disturbed by the presence of the august visitors and the unfriendly eyes of fellow admirals. Absorbed by what his ships were doing, he completely forgot about them. When one of the ships faulted, Rozhestvensky cursed and threw his binoculars overboard. The tsar noticed and smiled.

Artillery practice went very well that day, and Kaiser Wilhelm praised Rozhestvensky to the heavens. Makarov and the other ill-wishers had to swallow their envy. Nicholas immediately promoted Rozhestvensky to general adjutant—the highest court rank for the military.

After that practice, the tsar took a strong liking to the admiral. He was glad he had been able to impress Cousin Willy, but there was more to it than that. Rozhestvensky was distinctly different from other courtiers. It was hardly possible to impress the tsar with the right French accent or flowery flattery. Nicholas was fluent in four languages and had mastered the art of hypocrisy in adolescence. Quiet, withdrawn, and slightly effeminate, the tsar was invariably attracted to earthier males. An admiral who cursed and threw binoculars overboard appealed to him more than one who gave compliments to his wife and danced well. Also, Rozhestvensky must have reminded the sovereign of his late father, Tsar Alexander III, who, when once enraged by an Austrian ambassador, tied a silver fork in a knot and threw it all the way across the table toward the culprit's plate.

In the fall, Nicholas took Rozhestvensky on a trip to Sevastopol. During the trip, his admiration grew even larger. The following March, 1903, he appointed Rozhestvensky Head of Naval General Staff.

6

Now Rozhestvensky was one of the top dignitaries of the empire. He had a totally new lifestyle—pompous and lavish, requiring constant lies and maneuvering. He did not enjoy it.

It became customary for him to host as many as forty guests for dinner. This was stressful for the admiral and for his household. Servants started preparing for such occasions three days in advance.

Everything had to be immaculate, from the silverware to the menu. The Head of Naval General Staff could only have the best—and St. Petersburg's standards for fine dining were among the highest in the world. By the time the first guests arrived, the crisp white tablecloth was already laden with dishes. Russians traditionally started with abundant appetizers: smoked salmon, rich ham, several kinds of caviar, pickled cucumbers, each smaller than a "lady's little finger," various salads, oysters on ice, lobster, herring, jellied pork, game, and fowl elaborately decorated with their original feathers as if still flying. Guests were offered several brands of vodka flavored with herbs and berries. In an hour or two, dinner itself would start.

As in all countries fond of food, there was a ritual to dining. Broth with pastries was accompanied by sweet madeira. This was followed by trout with white wine, then by beef with red wine. Then artichokes and asparagus arrived that were supposed to be too delicate to be accompanied by any wine at all. The ensuing turkey with salad and quail demanded champagne. Dessert, fruit, cheese, and coffee were served with liqueurs or cognac.

Many people who came to these dinners belonged to St. Petersburg's elite. Rozhestvensky was at the pinnacle of Russian society. There were only two posts higher than his in the navy: naval minister (officially called Manager of the Naval Department) and general admiral, a position occupied exclusively by Romanovs, in 1903 by Grand Duke Alexei.

The Head of Naval General Staff was the true day-to-day commander of the fleet. He was held responsible for everything. Rozhestvensky's promotion to this post of top authority was exceptional. The navy had twenty-three vice admirals who were senior to him, still merely a rear admiral, and he was surrounded by envious looks and malicious whispers.

His superiors liked him, though. They were glad they could rely on somebody. The naval minister, Vice Admiral Fedor Avelan, though an experienced sailor, was no match for Rozhestvensky in terms of personality; he was glad to have someone with a strong will who could take command. General Admiral, Grand Duke Alexei, the tsar's uncle, though a bully himself, rarely interfered in Rozhestvensky's domain. He was not particularly interested in the sea, ships, or battles and rarely had any opinion on naval matters. His interests were limited to fine dining and quick courtship. With Avelan too weak and the grand duke too disinterested, Rozhestvensky had only one real superior—the tsar.

He spent ten months and ten days at his new post before the war with Japan started. His short tenure did not bring any dramatic change to the slow and inefficient naval bureaucracy. As for strategic matters, the tsar had his own inner circle of advisors. He liked Rozhestvensky but never invited him to join that group.

Rozhestvensky's bluntness prevented him from becoming a good courtier. He could lie to superiors, but he would periodically feel an insurmountable desire to be honest, like he had in the *Vesta* case. Now, like any other top official of the empire, he had to maneuver through the perilous Byzantine reefs of the Russian court. He had to be sure he never praised Grand Duke Alexei in front of Grand Duke Alexander and vice versa. He probably could bad-mouth Admiral Alexeev in front of Grand Duke Alexander, but never in front of Grand Duke Alexei, who was his half-brother and buddy. He had to be careful about what he said about both grand dukes in front of the tsar; Nicholas revered his uncle, closing his eyes to all his shortcomings, and admired his cousin's ingenuity but envied him for having several sons while the tsarina kept giving birth to only girls. Each pregnancy of the tsarina was more important than a shipbuilding program. Her strained relations with her mother-in-law, the Dowager Empress, had to be watched more closely than Japan's military deployments.

Of course, the forthcoming war in the Far East had been Rozhestvensky's major preoccupation for several months. He was very critical of using Port Arthur as a base and suggested moving the fleet to another location. But, of course, it was already too late. He had a low opinion of the Viceroy Alexeev, who managed Far Eastern affairs practically single-handedly, but the tsar could not care less.

Rozhestvensky was angry at the way that Far Eastern issues were dealt with. On January 14, he was asked by a subordinate whether war with Japan was inevitable. He curtly replied: "Hostilities do not always start with artillery fire. I think the war has already started. Only the blind would not see this."

The uncommunicative tsar, moody grand dukes, corrupt subordinates, bad leadership in the Far East, and mainly, his virtual inability to change things for the better in spite of his high position did not improve his temper. His orderlies reported thunderous fits. They recounted that the admiral was crushing furniture in his apartment in anger.

Rozhestvensky felt out of place in the Admiralty, better suited for the bridge of a ship than for a bureaucrat's desk. But when he was offered command over the Port Arthur squadron, he refused to go, briskly saying to Naval Minister Avelan that Viceroy Alexeev was impossible to work with.

However, as soon as Japan attacked, Rozhestvensky volunteered to go to Port Arthur with reinforcements, replacing Admiral Virenius who at the end of January was lingering in Djibouti. But it was agreed that Virenius would return to Kronshtadt; his unit was not strong enough to be of any real service to Port Arthur. Although there was some confusion in the first days following the attack, it was believed that Port Arthur had a charismatic and capable commander in Makarov. Then, on March 31, Makarov went down with the *Petropavlovsk,* and the tsar decided Rozhestvensky would take the 2nd Pacific Squadron to the Far East.

7

Rozhestvensky did not want the job. He was skeptical about the success of the enterprise. He hoped that some other admiral would assume the command, Birilev or Skrydlov. When he was informed that the tsar would see him in the next few days, he grimly announced to his associates that superiors "had decided to get rid" of him.

In a sign of appreciation, the tsar ordered him to keep his post at the Naval General Staff, but it was now a mere symbol. From now on

Rozhestvensky had to concentrate on the squadron. Virenius, recently returned from the Middle East, replaced him at the General Staff.

Courtiers close to the tsar disliked Rozhestvensky intensely and accused him of quiet sabotage. The admiral kept openly saying that he was not sure the expedition was necessary. Nicholas remained true to himself. He turned a deaf ear to the criticisms of his favorite—but he also turned a deaf ear to Rozhestvensky's anxieties.

Rozhestvensky was busier than ever. Each morning the admiral got up at seven o'clock. At eight, he was in his study going through numerous letters, memos, and reports. His comments in the margins were lengthy and decisive, often unprintable; like many Russians, Rozhestvensky had an inclination for emphatic obscenities. His handwriting was terrible, especially when he was angry.

Until ten o'clock, people consulted with Rozhestvensky about their personal affairs, like pensions, promotions, and leaves. From 10 A.M. until 1 P.M., Naval General Staff officers reported to him. The phone on his desk rang incessantly. Cables arrived in overwhelming numbers. Rozhestvensky answered each one immediately. At one o'clock he had his lunch, and at two he departed for various visits and conferences. At four o'clock, he returned home where industrialists and officers, both Russian and foreign, awaited him. Between seven and eight, he had dinner. At eight, he was back at his desk. At eleven, his associates were allowed to leave, but he called them to give instructions for the next day at as late as two o'clock in the morning.

Preparing the squadron was a long and excruciating mission. It was June 16 before Rozhestvensky's deputy, Rear Admiral Dmitry Gustavovich Felkersam, raised his flag on the cruiser *Admiral Nakhimov*. Another junior flag officer, Rear Admiral Oskar Enkvist, moved to the *Almaz* on July 1. Rozhestvensky did not go to his flagship, the mighty new battleship *Prince Suvorov*, until August 1. He did not intend to depart for another four weeks. He was still in the process of polite bargaining with the tsar, hoping that the sovereign would change his mind and cancel the reckless expedition.

For Tsar Nicholas II, 1904 was a year of mixed blessings. In spite of numerous defeats in the East, the tsar was happy; on July 30, his wife finally gave birth to a son. Although fond of his four daughters, Nicholas had been deeply depressed by the absence of a male heir. Like all royals, he wanted *his* line of the dynasty to supply further rulers for the empire. Happy and relaxed in spite of the disastrous news from Manchuria, the tsar met Rozhestvensky several times. He liked the admiral very much.

Soon Rozhestvensky realized that nothing would make the sovereign cancel the expedition, and he proceeded to do everything he could to ensure its success. He knew that if he wanted to get things done, he had better not delegate power to anybody. He stopped informing the naval minister and Naval General Staff about his decisions. He had formed his new staff and now dealt with all governmental departments and ministries directly. But the system he tried to circumvent eventually had its revenge.

The most debated question concerned which ships were to be sent to the Far East. Naval bureaucracy was thinking numbers. Rozhestvensky was thinking quality. Older and slower ships were a burden rather than an asset, but Naval Minister Avelan and the commander of the port of Kronshtadt, Birilev, were insisting on sending all available ships, including the clunkers—obsolete battleships of coastal defense. Grand Duke Alexei and the tsar agreed: the more ships, the better.

Rozhestvensky rebelled. The clunkers were much too slow and unreliable, and he would not take them. The tsar grudgingly yielded. Nevertheless, a number of other antiquated ships, such as the cruiser *Dmitri Donskoi*, were imposed upon the admiral. He was very upset about this but never opposed the imposition categorically. That was an issue of ego. He realized that he would have been accused of sabotaging the whole mission—which in turn would have been attributed to cowardice. He preferred stature to reason.

Another issue on which he eventually surrendered was repairs. Repairs required time, but the tsar demanded speedy work. Again, the admiral gave up. He capitulated one more time—and in the sphere that he knew best: artillery. The ships were given too few gun shells—enough for a battle but not enough for regular artillery practice on the long way to the East. Again, he was too proud to say that it was making his mission virtually impossible.

A number of problems were unavoidable. First of all, the crews lacked battle experience. The peaceful reign of the tsar's late father, Alexander III, had secured peace for two generations. Only senior people in their fifties, like Rozhestvensky, had had some wartime experience. Junior officers and men had never been to war. And the Russo-Turkish War had hardly supplied Rozhestvensky with real battle experience. The *Vesta*'s five-and-a-half-hour flight had been the war's climax for him. He remembered how it felt to be under enemy fire and to see death around him, but only vaguely, for it had happened twenty-six years earlier.

Many in the squadron lacked *any* experience. War with Japan was a great grinder for the empire: It needed more cannon meat than it had trained. Hastily assembled crews were rushed into service. Some men were drafted from prisons in Kronshtadt and St. Petersburg where they had been kept for minor felonies.

A fleet of ships do not make a squadron. A squadron, particularly on a voyage such as this, should be a living body—trained, fit, balanced, coordinated. Of course, Rozhestvensky had had no chance to organize his flock, and no grace period would be granted him. As soon as his ships left Kronshtadt, the lack of coordination would become conspicuous, and they would have no other way but to learn from their own mistakes, some of which could be perilous.

Another huge problem was coal. Rozhestvensky knew that no neutral power would allow him to buy coal in its ports, so he needed foreign steamers to supply the squadron with coal throughout its long voyage. A deal was struck with a German company, the Hamburg-American Line, which promised to deliver the necessary amounts of coal to the armada's ports of call outside Russia. And the squadron also needed other supplies delivered to it. Rozhestvensky started looking for a merchant who could be entirely trusted. Eventually, such a person was found. His name was Ginsburg.

Moisei Ginsburg was born in 1851 in Russia to a destitute Jewish family. At fifteen, he left the confining world of the Pale and hitch-hiked his way to Europe. He pumped water from the holds of a schooner for forty-six days, while the ship slowly made her way from Liverpool to New York; he built railroads in the American West; in Yokohama he sold goods to Western sailors. At the age of twenty-six, he opened his own business and started catering to ships in eastern waters—for nostalgic reasons, preferably, the Russian navy.

Ginsburg's was a floating supermarket. He could deliver food or boots, books or soap, depending on what the client ordered. He became the chief supplier for Port Arthur and stayed there during the first weeks of the war. Four days before the sinking of the *Petropavlovsk,* Admiral Makarov sent Ginsburg to St. Petersburg and gave him a flattering letter of recommendation. But it appeared that Makarov had underestimated the merchant's fame. When Naval Minister Avelan complained to the tsar that Rozhestvensky's squadron would face supply problems, Nicholas quickly retorted, "But you have Ginsburg!"

That response was the equivalent of a contract. Ginsburg was issued credit for ten million rubles. He promised to supply the squadron with all the essentials. Even official—and highly sensitive—correspondence between Rozhestvensky and St. Petersburg would often go through his couriers.

These and many other problems had to be sorted out by Rozhestvensky. Overwhelmed by stress, he would lose his temper when faced by inefficiency or outright stupidity. On June 15, Grand Duke Alexander presided over a meeting appraising ships built on public donations. Rozhestvensky angrily declared that torpedo boats built by the Nevsky shipyard were appallingly bad and not properly constructed. A heated argument followed. The next day, in Kronshtadt, Rozhestvensky assembled his captains to talk about Port Arthur. But no debate was possible, for the admiral started shouting that the commander of the Port Arthur squadron, his classmate Admiral Witgeft, "deserved to be hanged." He would not take his ships into the harbor but instead kept them at the roadstead, thus repeating the "madness" of January 26, when the same mistake had cost Russia its first casualties of the war.

No matter what Rozhestvensky was saying, Witgeft was having a hard time in Port Arthur. But for a while, so was Togo.

After Makarov's death, Togo seemed to be running out of luck. In May, under protection of fog, the Russians laid mines in the waters off Liaodong. The next day, the cruiser *Yoshino* hit one of the mines and capsized. The same day, the battleships *Hatsuse* and *Yashima* also struck mines and sank. The loss of these battleships was particularly painful; now Togo's fleet had lost one-third of its armored strength.

Japanese ground troops were more fortunate; Port Arthur was besieged. If the Japanese captured any of the strategic heights surrounding the fortress, which they were very likely to do, both the fortress and the fleet would be annihilated by their artillery in a matter of hours. The tsar ordered Witgeft to flee.

Witgeft was instructed to leave Port Arthur with six battleships, four armored cruisers, and eight torpedo boats. His destination was Vladivostok, a remote base rarely approached by Japanese ships.

Witgeft abandoned Port Arthur on July 28. The Russians found Togo's forces scattered. However, warned about Witgeft's departure by spies, Togo immediately started pulling his ships together. He made good use of radio communication, and when his ships faced Witgeft's soon after noon that day, the two squadrons, matched in heavy guns, encountered each other.

Both admirals were unwilling to get engaged in a close artillery duel, and a cat and mouse game started. Witgeft outmaneuvered Togo and headed full speed away for the Korea Strait—a gateway to Vladivostok. Using his superior speed, Togo successfully pursued. In late afternoon, he opened fire at 7,000 yards. But it looked like the gods were making fun of him. The Japanese ships were heavily impaired. Their flagship *Mikasa*, an obvious target for the Russians, suffered damage. Then suddenly the gods smiled.

Two Japanese shots struck the bridge and conning tower of Witgeft's flagship. Witgeft was instantly killed. His ship, disabled, continued in a circle. The Russian battle line collapsed. Togo closed to 5,000 yards and started massacring the adversary. Witgeft's second in command signaled the ships to follow him back to Port Arthur.

The Russian retreat was disastrous. Two of the ships sank; three went to neutral ports and disarmed there; the rest returned to the slaughterhouse, the cursed Port Arthur.

After dusk, the fortress plunged into complete darkness, with screened windows and deserted streets. All women and children had been evacuated long ago. The only people who visited Port Arthur now were Chinese laundrymen and coolies. The Russians rightly suspected that many of them were Japanese spies.

From the walls of the besieged city, the Russians could watch the ships of Togo's fleet on the horizon. As was customary for sailors in those days, they recognized each ship by her dim silhouette. As far as they could see, all of Togo's ships were fine.

The Japanese kept shelling the harbor and the city, often hitting Russian ships, now almost useless. The Russians responded, but they could not really retaliate. Their only hope was Rozhestvensky.

8

The plight of Port Arthur demanded immediate action. On August 11, the tsar held a conference in his summer residence, Peterhof, the Russian Versailles, an opulent gilded palace on the seashore. He invited Grand Duke Alexei, Grand Duke Alexander, Naval Minister Avelan, Minister of War Sakharov, Minister of Foreign Affairs Lamsdorf, and Rozhestvensky. That day the admiral was facing the wise men of the empire.

Rozhestvensky was almost sure that the Port Arthur squadron would be annihilated before he reached the Far East, and he energetically insisted that his squadron receive reinforcements. He had a concrete proposal. He wanted the tsar to buy seven cruisers from

Argentina and Chile (the follow-up of the deal that had collapsed several months earlier). He longed for these ships and even kept photographs of some of them in his desk.

The dignitaries agreed. But Rozhestvensky should not wait for these cruisers to arrive in Kronshtadt, they said. The new cruisers would join him later, after he circled Africa and made a stop at Madagascar.

Rozhestvensky wasn't satisfied. He demanded that the squadron's departure be postponed for several weeks. First, he needed that time for training. Second, in this case the squadron would reach the Far East next March—when the Vladivostok harbor would be free from ice. This implied that he had no hope for Port Arthur whatsoever.

Unexpectedly, War Minister Sakharov supported the admiral. He announced that after the terrible defeats of the previous few months, the army would not be able to attack sooner than the following spring. By that time, Port Arthur would, of course, have fallen, he predicted. Therefore, it was essential that the arrival of Rozhestvensky's squadron in Far Eastern waters coincide with the realities of land warfare.

The conference was taking a new turn. Both the commander of the squadron and the war minister were actually saying Port Arthur would perish pretty soon. Everybody knew Vladivostok did not provide a safe haven either. The Japanese could besiege it just as they had besieged Port Arthur. Thus, it might make sense to keep the squadron in the Baltic Sea until the following spring, train it, arm it, buy Argentine and Chilean cruisers, and only then send it to the Far East. That was what Grand Duke Alexander suggested.

Rozhestvensky objected. No, he said. The squadron should leave in the fall. If its departure was delayed, it would be impossible to go through the immense preparations again—for instance, to freight colliers. It would be better to leave now and wait for reinforcements at Madagascar. Naval Minister Avelan supported him. Everybody agreed.

Encouraged, Rozhestvensky demanded more. Port Arthur was likely to fall before he reached the Yellow Sea. Therefore, he needed permission to put up in some Chinese port. Using it as a base, he could disrupt Japanese communications—exactly what was expected from him.

Foreign Minister Lamsdorf exploded in indignation. Impossible, he said. Putting up in any Chinese port would mean violating China's neutrality. Of course, China was too weak to protest, but Britain and America certainly would.

What about the Pescadore Islands then, Rozhestvensky asked. No, others objected. To defeat the Japanese there would be too difficult. The squadron would need all its might in Port Arthur or Vladivostok. If he needed a base before he reached Russian shores, he could use only the Korean or Japanese coast, perhaps, or some minor archipelago there.

That was the end of it. The fate of the squadron was sealed. It would leave Russia in a few weeks, head for Madagascar, and wait for reinforcements there. Then it would proceed east, in all likelihood to Vladivostok, to reach it by March of the following year. However, to inspire hope in the crew members, the task of the squadron was officially formulated as "to reach Port Arthur and together with the 1st Squadron master the Sea of Japan."

After the conference, Nicholas took the admiral to the tsarina. Alexandra introduced Rozhestvensky to the little prince, Alexei, a weak infant twelve days old. Rozhestvensky got a small icon as a token of the heir's blessing. This was the ultimate farewell of the tsar.

9

The 2nd Pacific Squadron was a weird collection of ships. Its major assets were five modern battleships—the *Prince Suvorov*, *Alexander III*, *Borodino*, *Orel*, and *Oslyabya*. The former four were brand-new, and all five could do up to 18 knots. Two older battleships—the *Sisoi Veliky* and *Navarin* could do 15 knots if they were lucky. Four cruisers out of the seven—the *Oleg*, *Aurora*, *Zhemchug*, and *Izumrud*—were fast, well armed, and new. The *Dmitri Donskoi* was twenty-one years old. The *Svetlana* and *Almaz* were fairly new and fast (20 knots), but both had been yachts; the former belonged to Grand Duke Alexei, the latter to his half-brother, Viceroy Alexeev. Designed as royal toys, they were poorly protected from enemy shells and even more scantily armed. Five light, poorly armed auxiliary cruisers were added to that force: the *Ural, Kuban, Terek, Rion,* and *Dnieper.* They were hardly anything more than just fast steamers with several random guns. Nine torpedo boats were to escort the bigger ships.

Naval tradition explains the names. Battleships had to be associated with something grand. The *Prince Suvorov* was named after a famous Russian generalissimo, the *Borodino* after the battle with Napoleon in 1812, *Oslyabya* had been the name of a monk warrior of 1380, the *Alexander III* was named after the tsar's father, *Orel* meant "eagle" and eagle was the symbol of imperial Russia, and *Navarin* was a reminder of a victorious naval battle with the Turks.

Cruisers also represented glory. *Oleg* had been one of the early Viking princes, rulers of Russia, *Aurora*—the Greek goddess of dawn, the *Zhemchug* stood for "pearl," the *Izumrud*—for "emerald," the *Almaz*—for "diamond," and Prince Dmitri Donskoi had defeated the Tartars in 1380. Names of torpedo boats were adjectives praising fierce warlike features; the *Buiny* meant "wild," the *Bystry*—"fast," the *Bedovy*—"reckless," and so on.

Rozhestvensky was making final preparations for the journey. If there was one thing he could be satisfied with it was that he knew what to expect from each ship and each captain. The squadron was not an abstract agglomeration of hulls and men for him. He knew many of them personally, like a gardener knows his soil and his plants.

His deputies, the two junior flag officers, had been his acquaintances for forty years; he graduated from the Naval Academy in 1868, Rear Admiral Dmitri Felkersam in 1867, and Rear Admiral Oskar Enkvist in 1869. Bruno Fitingof, commander of the *Navarin,* belonged to the class of 1870. Felkersam had been in the same squadron with Rozhestvensky in the Far East in fateful 1895. The commander of the *Dmitri Donskoi,* Ivan Lebedev, had been invited by Rozhestvensky to Bulgaria back in the 1880s. The *Orel's* senior officer, Shvede, had served under Rozhestvensky on the *Vladimir Monomakh.* Rozhestvensky's staff engineer, Evgeny Politovsky, had participated in rescuing the

Apraxin in 1900. He was also taking to sea children of his classmates and colleagues; his deputy at the Naval General Staff, Nidermiller, for example, was sending to war his twenty-three-year-old son.

Rozhestvensky also knew the naval commanders. His deputies at the Naval General Staff, Virenius and Nidermiller, had graduated from the Naval Academy at about the same time as he did—in 1869 and 1870. Admiral Witgeft, recently killed in the Yellow Sea, had been his classmate. So was the commander of the port of Libava, Iretzkoi, and the current director of the Naval Academy, Kriger, who had trained the younger officers of his squadron. The Viceroy of the Far East, Alexeev, had been his fellow officer in the Far East in 1890 and then his admiral in 1895; they even shared a ship—the *Vladimir Monomakh*. Naval Minister Avelan had been his flagman in the Mediterranean Sea in 1894.

The squadron also had one very special ship—the hospital vessel *Orel*. It carried the only women in the squadron—nurses who had volunteered to go to war. To distinguish her from another *Orel*, a battleship, the hospital ship was nicknamed White Eagle. Rozhestvensky had vested interests in that ship: the head nurse there, Natalia Sivers, was his current passion. True to himself, this man with an insatiable taste for action was now combining war, politics, and love. Two women who loved him—his wife and Makarov's widow—were to wait in St. Petersburg; the third was to share the perils of the voyage with him.

All of the ships were assembling in Kronshtadt—the major naval base of the empire. Founded by the tireless Peter the Great in 1703, Kronshtadt lies on Kotlin Island. It is the guardian of St. Petersburg, barring the way of any intruder. The first red brick forts there were built by Tsar Peter himself. His successors added more. Several artificial islands were created, each bearing a Romanov name—Peter, Paul, Constantine—and each boasting a small fortress. No enemy could reach St. Petersburg without having first conquered this marine redoubt. The British and French during the Crimean War had tried and failed; the grandfather of Nicholas II, Emperor Alexander II, could calmly watch from nearby hills the adversary's fleet bobbing on anchors in front of Kronshtadt.

Now Kronshtadt was not as much a fortress as a naval base. Ships docked there, sailors lived and studied there. Its numerous parks and canals provided calm and privacy, though its streets boiled with life. In summer, Kronshtadt was a pleasant place to be. But Rozhestvensky's doomed squadron veiled the island in gloom.

Many officers and men were sure that their expedition was charged with disaster. Their superiors did little to dissuade them. When the captain of the *Donskoi* told the commander of the port of Kronshtadt, "We are going into the tropics and we need a refrigerator," the admiral cheerfully replied, "Refrigerator! You will find yourself on the bottom of the sea anyway and you will not need it there!"

As a result, many were wildly celebrating their last days in Russia. The captain of the *Donskoi,* Ivan Lebedev, set a bad example for his officers. An adventurous man who had served in Bulgaria under Rozhestvensky, then retired and moved to Paris, earning his bread by translating French novels into Russian before joining the navy again, he was now drinking from the cup of life greedily. Every day Lebedev would go ashore for carousing and return late at night by a small steamer, the *Dachnik,* which left St. Petersburg at three o'clock in the morning. Sailors called her the Drunken Boat, for most of her passengers were intoxicated officers heading for their ships. Lebedev used the boat so often that he even kept his pillow there. When at the end of August, on the very eve of departure, Rozhestvensky forbade officers from going ashore, Lebedev started quietly going to the nearby *Oranienbaum.* Fortunately for him, the *Donskoi* was anchored at the edge of the squadron. The captain would return at three o'clock in the morning, cleverly steering his small boat to avoid the *Prince Suvorov*'s searchlight. Rozhestvensky had his flag on the *Suvorov.*

At the end of August, the tsar started visiting the ships. He would take his mother, the Dowager Empress, and other relatives on these trips. Nicholas was in an excellent mood. The ships looked great to him, the days were sunny and warm. He remarked that the sea was still "like a mirror."

When on August 29 Rozhestvensky took his ships from Kronshtadt to Reval for the first leg of their journey, the tsar saw his sailors off on his mother's yacht, the *Tsarevna*. All the ships of the squadron fired a deafening salvo to their sovereign. "A very solemn and beautiful picture," the tsar wrote in his diary that night.

Unlike the tsar, some other Romanovs felt the presence of doom. His sister, Xenia, was shaken after visiting the ships and wrote in her diary that it was "horrifying to think what awaits them!"

The sailors suspected what awaited them. The captain of the battleship *Alexander III*, Bukhvostov, shocked a party that had arrived to bid farewell to him and his officers: "You wish us victory. It goes without saying we wish it too. But there will be no victory! I am afraid, we will lose half the squadron on our way to the Far East. If this does not happen, the Japanese will annihilate us. Their ships are better and they are real sailors. I can promise you one single thing: we will all die but never surrender."

3

"Rumors from the Bazaar,"
AUGUST—OCTOBER 1904

1

ON AUGUST 29, ROZHESTVENSKY TOOK HIS SHIPS FROM Kronshtadt to Reval. This was not the formal departure. The squadron had to wait for several ships to finish repairs. Some practice in domestic waters was also essential. An experienced shepherd, Rozhestvensky wanted to try his flock where nobody could disturb or watch them. Another stop in a Russian port, Libava, was planned before the squadron would go into the alien world.

The route of the squadron had been discussed and approved. The shortest route from the Baltic Sea to the Yellow Sea was through the Suez Canal, but only a few ships were to take this path. The others would have to circle Africa—an extremely long and tiresome journey. The official explanation was that the canal was not deep enough for the gigantic hulls of the newest battleships, but this was a lie. There was another reason to bypass the Red Sea: In the Suez, Rozhestvensky's squadron could become hostage to the British.

Animosity between London and St. Petersburg had started sixty years earlier when the two empires collided in the Middle East. The bear and the whale had confronted each other in the Great Game, in which the ancient lands of Turkey, Bukhara, Afghanistan, and Iran were contested. With the Russian occupation of Manchuria, they clashed in the Far East as well. Now the belt of Anglo-Russian rivalry stretched from the Mediterranean Sea all the way to the Yellow Sea. The British kept talking about the menacing, violent, and barbaric Russians. The Russians snorted at the British jingoism and warned that the current generation of politicians was taking militant nationalism to extremes. Grand Duke Alexander, one of the creators of Russia's Far Eastern policy, was convinced that Britain tried to "hurt" Russia whenever it could.

In 1902, Britain sided with Japan. The two countries concluded a formal alliance to contain the empire of the tsar within continental Eurasia. Let Russians rule their immense, barren, and cold wasteland. They should never be allowed to settle on the warmer seas of the Orient. Japan and Britain would drive the bear back into Siberian snows.

When the war struck, London became a zealous defender of Japanese interests, although the British Empire was technically neutral. King Edward VII published a manifesto starting with the words, "We are happily at Peace with all Sovereigns, Powers, and States." He instructed his "loving Subjects to govern themselves accordingly, and to observe a strict Neutrality." Russian and Japanese ships were banned from all ports and roadsteads of the British Empire—in Europe and elsewhere. But in reality theirs was a very biased neutrality.

The Russians suspected that Britain would eventually openly join Japan and attack. At the beginning of the war, Russian ships in the Red Sea were warned by the Admiralty of the possibility of attack by "Anglo-Japanese torpedo boats." This was far-fetched, yet in the same Red Sea, Britain was preventing Russian cruisers from checking the flow of war contraband smoothly streaming to Japan via the Suez Canal on board ships belonging to neutral nations. Soon, more serious favors to Japan followed. When Togo closed Port Arthur, the British decided to give him a hand.

Togo worried that upon the fall of Port Arthur, the Russian fleet would try to take refuge at the British colony of Weihaiwei, a hundred miles across the sea. For him, that would be a horrible sight; he had spent half a year waiting for a chance to finish these Russians off. Tokyo informed London of its concerns.

London took the matter seriously. The British Cabinet was inclined to avoid "any inconvenience" to His Majesty's Government. It couldn't fail its ally, but it also did not want to enrage Russia. The decision taken by the British Foreign Secretary, Lord Henry Lansdowne, was wise. It was decided "to close the port to both belligerents." But at the same time, the British commander-in-chief of the China Station was instructed to withdraw the fleet from Weihaiwei, "as its presence there would, under the circumstances, be undesirable." In other words, the British chose to wash their hands of the problem. If the fleet were in Weihaiwei, it would have to do something about Russian ships seeking refuge there. With the harbor empty, they would not be forced into the conflict.

The Japanese were "greatly disappointed." They were certain that in the absence of His Majesty's fleet, the Russians would go to Weihaiwei "if hard pressed." They wanted more commitment from the British. The ambassador to Japan, Sir Claude MacDonald, seconded the grievance of his hosts. In his cable to Lansdowne, he emphatically stressed that "a ship running before a hostile fleet is not likely to consider declarations, but to enter the nearest empty port." The Japanese ambassador to London visited Lansdowne and explicitly said that the Russians would be less likely to take refuge in Weihaiwei "if British ships were in occupation of the harbour."

Lansdowne yielded to pressure. The British fleet was ordered back. Lansdowne also promised Tokyo that any Russian ship that entered Weihaiwei would be interned without the usual option of leaving within twenty-four hours and detained in British custody throughout the remainder of the war. In other words, as good as sunk. Thirteen days later, Admiral Witgeft tried to break from Port Arthur to Vladivostok, and his ships were soon unable to go anywhere.

War between Russia and Japan accentuated all the tensions between London and St. Petersburg. St. Petersburg protested against Colonel Younghusband's recent expedition in Tibet. Russia unequivocally accused London of intending to turn Tibet into a British protectorate. London denied that it had any aggressive plans for the "Roof of the World."

The British harbored their own suspicions—quite absurd at that point; Russia was too busy fighting Japan in Manchuria to encroach on British interests elsewhere. Nevertheless, in the beginning of 1904, word spread within the military in Asia that the tsar was planning to invade India and Afghanistan. The Cabinet hardly believed this but suspected that Russia was preparing a strike in the Persian Gulf. In June 1904, the Foreign Office representatives in the Gulf reported that two Russian men-of-war "would come shortly" to the Gulf to annex several islands there. The Admiralty advised the Cabinet to send troops to occupy a strategic "position at the entrance to the Gulf." The commander of the Aden Division of the British navy, in a fit of imperial paranoia, reported that a "few years ago a Russian gunboat had annexed a portion of land and hoisted the Russian flag" at Bab El Mandeb and had surveyed other areas of the Red Sea coast.

It was silly to suspect that Russia, weak as it was and stuck in war with Japan, would attack an empire over which the sun never set. With colonies all over the globe, Britain could assist Japan and harm Russia in practically every region, be it the Middle East or Africa, or the Pacific. The most urgent problem Russian strategists had to solve was how to minimize this harm, not how to attack Britain.

On the surface, relations between St. Petersburg and London were friendly; a blood bond united the two countries. The Russian Dowager Empress was the sister of the British Queen Alexandra. The two sisters, former Danish princesses, were extraordinarily close. King Edward VII referred to the Russian tsar as Nicky, and the Romanovs called him Uncle Bertie. Nicholas II's first cousin, Georgie, the Prince of Wales, sent him a warm cable with condolences on Makarov's death, saying that every sailor would mourn the sinking of the *Petropavlovsk*. "Thank God Cyril was saved," the Prince of Wales remarked, referring to the miraculous survival of their relative, Grand Duke Kyril, who had been aboard the ill-fated battleship.

However, royal blood did not dictate foreign policy at the turn of the last century. Interests of nation-states came first. In addition, the late Queen Victoria had disliked Russia and its dynasty profoundly, believing them to be uncivilized and rude. Her son, King Edward VII, was more tolerant of other people's deficiencies, but he himself had too many for a Romanov's taste.

Edward had become king at the age of fifty-nine, having spent almost six decades as the Prince of Wales, kept by his jealous, dominating, and disagreeable mother uninformed and unemployed. Throughout these empty years of anticipation, Bertie had developed a taste for debauchery and carousing. His circle of friends included actresses and industrialists, and his promiscuity was legendary. His wife, the tsar's aunt, Queen Alexandra, had to tolerate her husband's escapades, even mistresses, whom he openly paraded in continental Europe. To Nicholas, the son of a model family man and a model family man himself, the behavior of Uncle Bertie must have been repulsive. Reportedly, his aunt, Queen Alexandra, wore a wide pearl and diamond choker at all times because she had made an unsuccessful attempt to cut her throat. This was probably untrue, but in any case, Uncle Bertie was, undoubtedly, a black sheep.

Another relative, Kaiser Wilhelm, had set his heart on disrupting the remains of cordiality between London and St. Petersburg. He wanted to establish a military alliance with Russia against France and Britain.

Kind Edward VII hated Wilhelm wholeheartedly. His German nephew's taste for insincerity and intrigue had always disgusted him. When Edward's mother, Queen Victoria, was dying, Wilhelm had made a total nuisance of himself, grieving loudly and possessively.

Wilhelm despised the British king and feared the British army and navy. He never hesitated to bad-mouth England in front of the Russian tsar, especially after Nicholas had started war with Japan. In April 1904, the kaiser reported to the tsar from his Mediterranean cruise:

Malta very interesting. Mediterranean fleet in splendid condition. Interest in war most keen, and quite pro-Japanese. To my utter amazement prevail body firm conviction that ultimately Japan will total beat Russia and impose peace on her! *This is strictly confidential!* Willy. "Admiral of Atlantic."

Nicholas did not trust Wilhelm, but the kaiser's Anglophobic remarks were falling on fertile ground. Each time the tsar saw his minister of foreign affairs they talked about Britain's role in the current war. One constant subject was London's determination to overlook war contraband going to Japan from Europe.

Terminating war contraband is essential in every war. No nation is self-sufficient in strategic supplies. Thus, intercepting goods destined for the enemy is absolutely crucial. It was particularly important in the Russo-Japanese war because Japan's domestic resources were extremely limited.

Therefore the Russians began an intensive search for "war contraband"—a very loose term. For instance, how did one categorize wheat? Or cotton? Or rice? In 1904, many British ships shuttled between Europe and the Far East. Very few were transporting ammunition or guns. The Russians applied the term "war contraband" very broadly. As a result, almost every time Russians intercepted a British ship, London became thunderous.

Russia sent two cruisers—the *Petersburg* and the *Smolensk*—to the Red Sea. It is not easy to ship contraband quietly; the Russians would act on intelligence collected by agents in foreign ports worldwide. Intelligence provided the name of a ship and her route. When the suspect was located, Russian cruisers signaled, "Stop immediately." If the merchant did not stop, the cruiser fired a couple of blank charges across her bows. Then another command followed: "Reverse engines." The merchant would have no choice but to obey.

Several Russians would board the suspect ship. They would demand her papers and examine her hold. If they found anything suspicious, they would transfer all of the crew to the Russian ship. There the crew would be interrogated. Sometimes sailors would betray their mission out of fear or in revenge against their captain. A Russian crew would board the captured ship—or if the Russians were in a hurry or did not have enough men, they would sink the merchant vessel. Crews were detained for several days and then released in the nearest port. Russian officers made a point of being meticulously polite to them.

War contraband was just one of the subjects constantly discussed in London and St. Petersburg. The British ambassador to Russia, Charles Hardinge, argued incessantly with the Russians, and St. Petersburg often retorted with bravado and haughtiness. But Russia was powerless. If London wanted, it could send Rozhestvensky's squadron to the bottom of the sea in a matter of minutes.

2

The worst fear of the Russians in the summer and autumn of 1904 was that Rozhestvensky would not be able even to reach the Far East. Agents reported that the Japanese, backed by the British, were preparing an ambush on Russia's doorstep—in the Baltic Sea.

In 1904, there were no professional spies. The days of cloak-and-dagger training centers hidden in the woods and conspiratorial secret service bureaucracies wouldn't arrive until well into World War I. Governments were hiring agents at random. It could be a well-known writer, like Somerset Maugham, a cabaret dancer, an aristocrat, or a cabbie. One or two officials in the war ministry or foreign office would organize a network of agents, and several institutions would compete, parading their agents' reports and eventually neutralizing each other's efforts. As often as not, those who ran spy rings had other responsibilities. They could be ambassadors or military attachés, or even private merchants. Intelligence service at the turn of the last century did not differ much from spying in Renaissance Italy or the Byzantine Empire. The only major exception was the British. Their secret service had been founded three centuries earlier, under Queen Elizabeth, and now thrived.

As soon as war in the Far East broke out, the Russians realized that they lacked an intelligence network that could be used against the

Japanese. A rush for agents started. In 1904 Russia had five independent spy rings, each operated by a separate institution: the War Ministry, Military High Command in Manchuria, Naval General Staff, Police Department, and Foreign Ministry. Personal rivalries prevented coordination. Interference of a competing department was rarely tolerated, and if it had to be, then the data its agents produced was treated with suspicion or ignored.

The Military High Command in Manchuria was fully autonomous. Viceroy Alexeev did not want anybody interfering in affairs of his jurisdiction. He believed it was *his* war. Officers and civilians approved by the viceroy operated in three countries—China, Korea, and Japan. In Japan and Korea only a handful of people, normally Europeans, were willing to risk their lives for a steady flow of cash. The information they provided was of little value, normally based on hearsay and trivial observations, their pay largely unearned. Also, in spite of new technology, communication remained the greatest obstacle. Reports from Korea and Japan were reaching Russian headquarters in Manchuria by telegraph via private addresses in Paris and then St. Petersburg, which guaranteed at least a twenty-four-hour delay.

In Manchuria, Russian ground troops commanders had numerous agents among the Chinese. They spied on Japanese movements and were sometimes involved in sabotage, such as setting a military depot on fire. A normal reconnaissance trip would take from fourteen to twenty days. Each agent had a special numbered pass, allowing him to go through the Russian front line. These passes were small so that they could be hidden in shoes or clothes. Of course, the very fact that they existed but carried no photographs gave the Japanese enormous opportunities for abuse. After a Russian spy was arrested, a Japanese scout could use his pass to infiltrate the Russian rear. Also, most of the Russian agents were Chinese peasants absolutely unsuitable for the job; their experience was nil, their knowledge of military matters very superficial, their loyalty problematic. To verify reports, Russian officers demanded that each spy bring something from the final leg of his expedition to prove that he had been there, but, of course, no material object could be definitive proof.

The army also did routine reconnaissance, sending out small units to determinate the enemy's location and collecting papers from Japanese officers killed in action. But no grand strategy could be betrayed by a letter from home found on a dead boy from Nagasaki. Gossip collected by Russian diplomats worldwide was a better source.

It was virtually impossible to distinguish the job of a diplomat from that of a spy. Every Russian legation—be it in the Mediterranean, the Pacific, or North America—was instructed to monitor Japanese activities closely. Foreign Minister Lamsdorf received piles of telegrams from Brussels, Trieste, Hamburg, Athens, Algeria, Malta, Cairo, Beijing, Shanghai, Bangkok, Singapore, Colombo, Melbourne, and New York and forwarded the most important ones to the tsar.

The life of a diplomat abroad was boring. Unless stationed in a major capital like Berlin or London, the routine consisted of trivial matters. Intelligence missions gave diplomats a feeling of self-importance. In search of new contacts, a diplomat started frequenting port taverns buying drinks for every seedy character prophesying familiarity with the world of bootleggers, unlicensed pilots, and secret inlets. He visited lighthouses and secluded fishing communities. He bribed customs officials and skippers. In order to justify their pay, the recruited agents had to fish for gossip or just to make things up. One did not get a bonus for monotonous, though truthful reports of "All is quiet on the Baltic coast." But a report on a suspicious schooner or sinister blinking lights on the horizon at night earned extra cash. A tourist from the Far East was branded a spy or saboteur; a village idiot pacing the beach at dawn could be sending signals to the Japanese seafaring hounds. Processing the reports in his shabby office, a diplomat was dreaming about promotion; people knew that the tsar took keen interest in the spy reports, partially due to his hunger for adventure, unquenched in youth, and partially because of his anti-Japanese paranoia.

Some amateur spies were serious people with consequential duties. The most noticeable among these was Alexander Pavlov, the former envoy to Korea. He lived in Shanghai as a private person with considerable power, his mission personally approved by the tsar. He could even send minor military ships, like gunboats, as couriers. Sometimes he would go on reconnaissance cruises himself and supply Russian command with firsthand information about Japanese ships, military and merchant, and goods carried by the latter.

The War Ministry in St. Petersburg ran its own spy web, managed by military attachés. These General Staff officers were believed to be the stars of the army. However, their knowledge of the East was appallingly inadequate. One of these self-proclaimed Japan experts had maintained before the war that one Russian soldier was worth three Japanese. They did not speak the language, which inevitably handicapped their expertise. In 1904 the whole Russian army had just eleven Japanese interpreters; out of these eleven, only two could read Japanese. Military attachés were lucky if they could hire foreign journalists or businessmen who would be willing to supply them with important data. However, most intelligence was gleaned from a quick visit to the docks or a pub frequented by sailors.

The Naval General Staff had a parallel network of naval attachés stationed abroad. For Rozhestvensky's purposes, this was more helpful, for these people were at least professional sailors and had a clearer idea of what information was needed. However, there were few agents, and among these, many were inclined to use their imaginations liberally.

As head of the Naval General Staff, Rozhestvensky had been supervising the attachés himself. Going through their cables, he groaned. He was enraged that spies were paid lavish sums of money for doing absolutely nothing. There were too many Westerners who maintained that they had state secrets to sell and too many Russian attachés who wanted to report suspect information that was easily come by. Rozhestvensky felt obliged to review voluntary submissions from a former British naval officer, Mr. Edward Lowdill, who had given the address of his club as prestigious 99 Piccadilly; from, as the Russian attaché in the United States put it, a "seasoned" citizen of Bridgeport, Mr. Vinecken—and so on. His boss, Naval Minister Avelan, was very generous in giving awards to spies. Rozhestvensky was frugal. His typical response was "Give So-and-So two months to prove his services are worth his allowance."

Logically enough, in a country as heavily policed as Russia, the Police Department possessed the best secret service. Its agents had been trained to pursue Russian revolutionaries within the empire and in all major European cities. Now the department was determined to use this network fully—in spite of the fact that its provocateurs were well connected only within the conspiratorial circles of left-wing exiles.

Certain relatives of the tsar did not hesitate to add to the mess. The entrepreneurial Grand Duke Alexander was constantly involved in cryptic correspondence and private secret missions. If Nicholas II was sending undercover agents of his own to Lhasa, his cousin aspired to penetrate the Middle East.

Inevitably, the Japanese were only too glad to use the rivalry and chaos to their advantage. Sometimes their clever play would lead to a real interdepartmental scandal in Russia. In August 1904, Lamsdorf's spymaster in the Far East, Pavlov, sent an alarming cable to the minister. A person called Bekker, "a decent-looking German," had visited one of Pavlov's agents. He insisted that Admiral Skrydlov in Vladivostok employed him as a spy. Now he was asking to forward a cable to the Russian military attaché in Berlin. He dutifully provided the text and asked the Russians to send it using "their code."

The Japanese trap was boldly primitive. Comparing the text prepared by themselves with the coded message sent from Shanghai, they would learn how to break the Russian code. Pavlov smelled a rat. He asked Lamsdorf to check out whether the "decent-looking German" was really employed by Admiral Skrydlov.

Apparently very gleeful, Lamsdorf contacted Naval Minister Avelan. Avelan, in his turn, cabled Skrydlov at Vladivostok. Skrydlov responded that he had never met Mr. Bekker and that he "had no agents at all." The issue was clarified in just eight days, but the disconcerting

news was that the naval minister had no idea whether one of his commanders had his own network of spies.

In 1904, the ill-equipped Russians had to compete with two hostile
spy rings: the Japanese and the English. The Japanese had hundreds of
agents in China and Korea and some in Europe and the Middle East.
Britain's secret service was by far the best in the world.

Russia could hope for cooperation with France and Germany—
France a diplomatic ally, Germany a dynastic one. However, these alliances did not amount to much, though Pavlov, for example, was able
to travel on the French cruiser *Pascal* from Chemulpo to Shanghai. By
and large, both the French and the Germans did little to assist Russians in the regions where they lacked agents completely—namely, in
Africa and Southeast Asia.

3

The admiral was receiving reports from all five Russian spy rings. The
numerous agents, amateur and professional, were almost unanimous:
The Japanese were preparing an ambush. Rozhestvensky's fleet would
not be allowed to reach the Yellow Sea.

According to the reports, many Japanese officers had been dispatched to the Baltic Sea coast. They carried torpedoes, which could
be launched from smaller ships or from shore. Some reports insisted
that Britain had built six torpedo boats for Japan, which had disappeared since the beginning of the war. Hidden in secret inlets, these
torpedo boats were still around and ready to attack Rozhestvensky as
soon as he left Russia.

Reports confirming this terrifying conspiracy were reaching St.
Petersburg daily. The British vice consul in the coastal town of Nyborg, Denmark, had been instructed to inform the British Admiralty
of the passage of any military ship through the Great Belt Straits. The
Russian Police Department had intercepted two communications
from Japanese embassies in London and Paris: "Discuss seriously the

possibility of using electric torpedoes," and "It is necessary to do research on all aspects of the attack." An agent of the Russian naval attaché in France had delivered several briquettes of coal with a camouflaged hole in each—presumably for installing explosives. If put into a furnace, such a device could immediately sink any of Rozhestvensky's ironclads.

The last menace—charged briquettes of coal—looked very real. Naval Minister Avelan immediately ordered vigilance on ships and in ports. But what about the ambush? Who could prevent it? Rozhestvensky and Avelan decided to cooperate with the Police Department.

The Russian police had a permanent representative in Europe. His name was Arkady Mikhailovich Garting. Stationed in Berlin, he was fluent in surveillance, provocation, investigation, deceit, and probably murder.

Garting's real name was Abram Gekkelman. Twenty years earlier he had made the choice, very untypical for a Jew in Russia, to become a police agent, and he had penetrated revolutionary circles. Soon his exploits became legendary. He hunted down underground printers, lured people into making bombs only to betray them subsequently to the police, and spied on major revolutionaries in exile. He also provided security cover for Romanovs traveling abroad. When needed, on the tsar's orders, his people would even follow a grand duke suspected of an inappropriate love match that threatened the dynasty's prestige. In short, he was a Russian James Bond.

In June 1904, Garting was hastily summoned from Berlin to St. Petersburg and entrusted with a grandiose task: to protect Rozhestvensky's armada from a likely Japanese attack. The rough estimate of costs was 150,000 rubles. The Naval Ministry transferred the funds to Garting personally.

He returned to Europe and immediately started sending alarming reports. Fishermen at Skagen, Denmark, had noticed a torpedo boat carrying no flag. Two more unidentifiable torpedo boats had been spotted in the same area by a ship he had hired. A suspected agent of the Japanese was seen onshore the night of September 1, signaling somebody in the sea with a red lantern. The Japanese mission in Stockholm was hosting five mysterious males.

Garting divided the coast of Denmark, Sweden, and Norway into districts. In each he selected "locally respected" agents. The Danish coast alone consisted of thirty-nine districts, the Swedish and Norwegian, twenty-one. The German coast was also watched. Garting's agents were people experienced with the sea and ships—port managers, lighthouse keepers, pilots, border guards, merchants, skippers, and fishermen. He also freighted steamers to watch out for alien ships. By September 1, nine steamers were cruising the Baltic.

Denmark was very friendly to Russia; the Danish king was the grandfather of Nicholas II. Danes were proud that their princess was held in high esteem in Russia as Dowager Empress and were sympathetic to her son's plight in the Far East. The Danish Naval Ministry ordered lighthouse keepers to take note of all suspicious ships and forwarded all relevant reports to Garting. The Danish Ministry of Finance instructed port authorities to report all suspicious cargo.

Pressed by Garting, the Danes forced Japan's consul general to leave Copenhagen (a measure demanded by Rozhestvensky personally). Danish police arrested two other alleged Japanese spies and deported both. The Danish minister of foreign affairs confirmed that police had been instructed to watch out for Japanese agents in coastal areas, and the Danish government sent a squadron to guard the straits connecting the Baltic Sea with the North Sea.

Garting visited Russian consulates in the area and instructed the diplomats to closely monitor the nearby coast. He made a list of the most dangerous places. The diplomats were obliged to follow all "suspicious Asians," "suspicious cargoes," and privately freighted ships. The consuls took their mission very seriously and in their turn started employing lighthouse keepers and fishermen.

Garting chose Copenhagen as his base. He lived in the Phoenix Hotel under the name of Mr. Arnold. His activities were reported to the tsar directly. The sovereign enthusiastically approved of them all.

Assisting Garting in his mission, Russian diplomats approached Scandinavian governments with stern warnings and highly demanding requests. The Russian envoy in Sweden visited the Swedish minister of foreign affairs to deliver a harsh statement: "It would be hardly pleasing for your Royal Government if the Japanese chose Sweden as the base for their sorties." The terrified Swedes, who had lost the southern coast of the Baltic to Russia only two centuries earlier, dispatched a battleship to hunt for Japanese torpedo boats.

In the fall of 1904, the Baltic coast was in arms. Similar measures were taken by Russians in the Red Sea; several ships of Rozhestvensky's squadron were to go via the Suez Canal.

Meanwhile, still in friendly waters, Rozhestvensky took his flock from Kronshtadt to Reval, which they safely reached on August 30. Three weeks later, new and alarming reports reached him there.

4

On September 19, the director of the Police Department forwarded the translation of a Japanese cable to the Naval General Staff. Allegedly, it had been sent from the Japanese embassy in The Hague to Foreign Minister Komura.

> We have stationed our people in various places, and they have to report to us all the enemy's moves and, if they can, to impede them. . . . The squadron, which is to go on a rescue mission, will depart this month; this is why we have taken measures to prevent this. . . . Everything that can be done will be tried.

The intercepted telegram looked scary. It quoted the time frame for the actual departure of the squadron correctly. Rozhestvensky planned to leave Reval quite soon and then briefly visit another Russian port, Libava.

Reval was one of the oldest cities in the empire, a place that had seen many masters. Reval was its German and alien name. The native Estonians referred to it as Tallinn. Its cozy walled lower town, gloomy hilltop citadel, and magnificent Gothic churches looked like a setting for a Scandinavian fairy tale. Russian naval officers liked being stationed there. Though somewhat slow and sleepy, Reval gave them the advantage of living in Europe without leaving Russia.

Every hotel in town was full. Relatives, reporters, officials, and spies streamed to Reval that week. Ashore, crowds shaking hands, extending blessings, and giving occasional kisses to future heroes mobbed Rozhestvensky's officers. Receptions and banquets abounded, and many windows sported Russian flags.

The squadron could not boast a unified mood. Some officers and men were hopeful and ready for the journey; others expected nothing but disgrace and perhaps disaster. The pessimists would get drunk every evening to drown their sorrows, but they had to do so quietly, for the admiral was vigilant.

Rozhestvensky spent his time in Reval tutoring the armada. Maneuvers and torpedo, mine, and artillery practice took most of his time. He made sure everybody worked hard; exercises started at 6 A.M. and did not finish until 10:30 at night. Still angry at his officers' debauchery in Kronshtadt, the admiral banned any communication with shore and with other ships after 7 P.M. Any boat not responding to signals was to be fired upon by sentries after the second warning. Officers complained, but order was maintained.

There was another problem very much on the admiral's mind: Several ships were still not ready to depart. The Kronshtadt shipyard was infuriatingly slow. He even considered moving his flag back to Kronshtadt to one of the handicapped ships, sure his presence would make the workers hurry. But, of course, it was unimaginable that he would leave the squadron. His junior flag officers, Enkvist and Felkersam, would inevitably loosen their grip, and the debauchery of the despairing would restart. It would be better to leave without a few ships than to lead a drunken fleet.

At nine o'clock in the morning of September 26, the tsar arrived at Reval. As always, he admired the sharp skyline of the fairy tale city. He was anticipating a busy but highly pleasant schedule.

The sovereign arrived by train. His yacht, the *Shtandart,* was waiting for him in the harbor. He placed a lot of significance on this trip and even brought his son, his "little treasure," and wife with him.

He started with a tour of the five newest battleships. The day was sunny and the sea rough. In the evening, when Nicholas was hosting a dinner for the admirals and captains onboard the *Shtandart,* the sea calmed down, and the emperor enjoyed talking to the warriors on deck, in the cool but clear night.

During the sunny day of September 27, the tsar continued visiting the ships. He brought along four relatives: the Dowager Empress, Queen Olga of Greece, Grand Duke Alexander and his wife, the tsar's sister, Xenia. The tsar presented ships with icons, while Olga, the Queen of Greece, weeping, kissed captains three times as the Orthodox custom demanded and left mother-of-pearl crosses for those sailors who would be on the upper deck during the battle. The crosses came from the main church of Jerusalem, Golgotha.

Nicholas took his duty conscientiously. All in all, he visited twenty-two ships, from battleships to torpedo boats. However, Rozhestvensky was something of a disappointment to him during this time. Bidding farewell to the sovereign, he repeated that in all likelihood by the time he reached the Far East, the Port Arthur squadron would no longer exist. But even this did not spoil the emperor's good mood. On the night of September 27, he left in good spirits. He never saw the squadron again.

On the day of the squadron's departure from Reval, September 28, thousands of people came to the embankment. Relatives and friends of the officers assembled from all over the empire to say good-bye. The crewmen did not have relatives there. At best, some of them, blissfully drunk, were embracing girlfriends from the docks.

According to a witness, "weeping and tears, embraces and kisses" lasted until a whistle signaled all cutters and boats to leave the shore.

"The crowd started moving, bobbing" and stayed long after the boats had left.

The admiral was not at all happy that day. He had to leave behind a number of ships that were not ready for the journey. Hopefully, they would catch up with the squadron later. On September 28, he took the armada to the last Russian port, Libava.

5

Quite a few unfriendly eyes watched his ships leaving Reval. If at sea Russians had to deal with Japanese men-of-war, on land they had to resist British espionage.

The British secret service was the oldest in the world and by far the best. It monitored all fleets, making good use of the new technology—photography—and circulated lists of "foreign war vessels of which photographs are required," as the document was officially called. On the eve of the war between Russia and Japan, many vessels were still to be photographed—Togo's flagship, the *Mikasa,* and Rozhestvensky's *Suvorov* among them. But by the end of September 1904, the British secret service had filled in many gaps.

Captains of British warships were instantly reporting all encounters with Russian vessels, be it a battleship or a collier. Sometimes the Russians had no choice but to hire a British steamer to transport cargo to Port Arthur or elsewhere. In that case, their war plans could easily be exposed; masters of merchant ships were willing to share instructions given by Russian admirals with inquisitive British officers.

The British monitored Russian ships talking to each other by radio, or as it was known in 1904, wireless telegraphy. In many cases, the British were able to take in Russian communications, naively made in the open. When the British could not intercept radio communications, they would not hesitate to investigate "rumors from the bazaar," in, say, Port Said.

Radio in general provided a new tool for spying. Russians were aware of that. Viceroy Alexeev was alarmed by the way radio was used in the Yellow Sea. He insisted that some Western correspondents on board neutral vessels were transmitting news to the Japanese by radio. If arrested off the coast of Manchuria, he warned, such people would be treated as spies and vessels seized as prizes.

Viceroy Alexeev had a point. The London *Times* had indeed chartered a vessel, the *Haimun,* and *Times* correspondents were using her radio to communicate with the British colony Weihaiwei. A special radio mast had been erected on shore. It was 170 feet high. The *Times* reporters expected to be able to send messages at 140–200 miles. The senior officer of the navy at Weihaiwei had rendered the *Times* "considerable assistance," and so the *Times* magnanimously agreed that His Majesty's Navy would be allowed to send their communications through that installation too, "provided they do not interfere with the *Times* messages."

This time the British Admiralty, seeing this as a dangerous precedent, unexpectedly sided with the Russian viceroy. Lords of the Admiralty announced that "if Great Britain were at war, the presence of press steamers fitted with wireless telegraphic apparatus would . . . be so prejudicial to naval operations that it could not be tolerated."

Ironically enough, they were thinking about war with Russia. At about the same time, the British Admiralty kept insisting that the Danish straits, leading to the Baltic Sea, should remain a free passage for everybody, otherwise the European part of Russia "would become inviolable and unapproachable"—and His Majesty's Navy always had to "get into touch with hostile fleets with the least possible delay," as the Admiralty wrote to the Foreign Office.

The new power of the independent press was too alarming to pass unnoticed. Even before Lords of the Admiralty snarled at the *Times,* the commander-in-chief of the navy's China Station had already warned his senior officer in Weihaiwei:

You are to have nothing to do with wireless telegraphy arrangements. . . . Cancel any arrangements you may have made as to their receiving signals from men of war. Inform commissioner that I consider that the transmission of messages for public use by wireless telegraphy from the sphere of operations, unrestrained by censorship, does not conform with the obligations of neutrality and should not be officially sanctioned.

The Japanese became alarmed, too. The *Times* radio transmitter was a double-edged sword: Russians could intercept it as well. But for the Japanese, the solution was easy. By May, they had a Japanese officer always stationed on board the *Times'* vessel, censoring all communications.

Rozhestvensky's squadron became the number one target for British intelligence—not only the squadron itself, but everything related to its journey. In the Baltic Sea, London had agents reporting activities at Russian naval bases. British ambassadors sent urgent cables to the foreign secretary, informing him about all movements of Russian ships. Consular officers investigated all purchases of vessels that could be armed and consequently used as light cruisers. Some of the information collected was passed on to the Japanese.

But the Japanese allies were not in a hurry to reciprocate. London had to rely upon reports of official British representatives. Captain Hutchison was sent to Japan with the "purpose of obtaining naval information connected with the war," as the ambassador to Japan, Claude MacDonald, put it. The ambassador also selected two other officers, Captain Pakenham and Commander Jackson, for the same mission. From time to time, the Japanese allowed them onboard warships on military expeditions.

On October 1, Foreign Secretary Lansdowne was informed that Danish pilots had left for Reval to board Russian ships and pilot them through Danish waters. As the pilots and their families had been instructed to keep their destination secret, the British ambassador in Denmark concluded, "I have been unable as yet to get absolute confirmation of the fact that they have gone to Reval, but I believe that there is no doubt about it."

6

It took the squadron just two days to get from Reval to Libava. It was going to be a very short stay. In Libava the squadron had to take on coal, water, and food. It was the last chance to get supplies on friendly terrain.

The day scheduled for departure, October 1, dawned gray and overcast. Low clouds covered the sky, and fog mixed with drizzle. Faces looked gloomier than ever. "Perfect weather for a funeral," somebody on the *Suvorov* said. Officers were nervous and angry; at low tide bigger ships had become stuck in silt. Rozhestvensky was furious. "Some port!" he noted caustically.

Rozhestvensky passionately wanted to finally start his expedition. Several days earlier, he had sent a letter to his intimate friend Capitolina: "I cannot think about anything else now and am living solely by the desire to overcome."

But that day they did not make it to sea. The *Sisoi* lost her anchor, and the squadron had to linger in the harbor like a pack of impatient hounds waiting for an old and sick peer.

The next day, October 2, they left Libava. The day was quiet and dark. It drizzled again.

The armada departed in four units. Admiral Enkvist led the cruisers; Admiral Felkersam, the older battleships; Captain Yegoriev, the transports. Rozhestvensky left last with the newest battleships.

At 1:01 P.M., Libava's telegraph dispatched Rozhestvensky's laconic cable to the tsar: "With ships arrived from Reval, departed from Emperor Alexander III Port."

That night Nicholas wrote about the squadron in his journal: "Bless its path, Lord, let it reach its destination whole to fulfill its hard mission for the good and benefit of Russia!" Deeply moved, the emperor even added an unusually emotional supplement to his plea: He drew a cross.

4

"This Is a Miserable Fleet,"
OCTOBER 4–23, 1904,
WESTERN EUROPE

1

ON OCTOBER 7, RUSSIAN DOWAGER EMPRESS MARIA FEDOROVNA, now vacationing in her native Denmark, reported to her son, the tsar: "This morning our squadron has safely passed Skagen. May God grant them a good voyage." Zealously loyal to Russia, Maria Fedorovna felt it was her duty to add to the pile of cables her son was receiving that day from all over Europe.

The reassuring telegram of the Dowager Empress was sent from Copenhagen at 3:07 P.M. It arrived three hours after an ominous cable from Garting. On highest alert now, he reported: "29 ships of the squadron taking on coal at Skagen. Two Japanese suspected to be secret agents had tried to hire a boat, but were detained by authorities."

Three days earlier, on October 4, the squadron had anchored in Danish waters at the entrance to the Great Belt Straits. The journey from Libava to Denmark had taken two troubling days. Rozhestvensky's worst fears were proving justified. The ships were unreliable, the crews undisciplined, and many captains careless.

The *Sisoi*, the one that had lost her anchor at Libava, now said she needed repairs. On the *Zhemchug,* a pair of davits broke, and a cutter fell overboard and sank. A rudder on the newly built battleship *Orel* had to be fixed. The torpedo boat *Prozorlivy* had a permanent leak in her condensers that could not be fixed at sea. Another torpedo boat, the *Bystry,* had rammed the *Oslyabya*—fortunately, lightly. While taking on coal, the Russians had damaged three Danish colliers, and indemnity had to be paid. The favorite child of Makarov, the icebreaker *Yermak,* commanded by an incompetent merchant marine officer, was jeopardizing other ships by her dazzling maneuvering. When the *Yermak* did not answer the admiral's signal, Rozhestvensky ordered the *Suvorov* to fire several shells across her bow. That helped, but he did not want such a ship around. He commanded the *Yermak* to return to Libava immediately, along with the *Prozorlivy.* The rest of the squadron was ordered to take on coal.

Rozhestvensky's arrival in Danish waters did not pass unnoticed. Hours after the Russian ships had anchored, Lord Lansdowne received an urgent cable from Copenhagen: "Russian fleet of twenty-four vessels at anchor at Langeland Belt." Presumably, Japanese agents were watching Rozhestvensky's ships from the shore, too.

At noon on the following day, Rozhestvensky sent a celebratory telegram to the tsar from the small town of Rudkobing. October 5 was the name day of the little prince, Alexei. The tsar was moved. The court was full of spongers and silver tongues, but Nicholas sensed that Rozhestvensky was truly loyal. He decided to encourage his protégé. At Skagen, Rozhestvensky learned that he had been promoted to vice admiral. He replied, "My life and energy belong exclusively to Your Imperial Majesty."

While in Skagen, the admiral had to make an absolutely crucial decision: to finalize the route for the squadron and then, as soon as possible, notify Russian representatives, allies, and spies all over the world of his choice of passage.

The allies to be informed about his intentions were the French. To Rozhestvensky, they sounded wishy-washy. They clearly did not intend to damage their relationship with London for the sake of St. Petersburg. Now Paris was nervously demanding to know what Rozhestvensky's exact plans were. Did he plan to put up in any French colonial ports? Had he chosen the passage around the Cape of Good Hope or around Cape Horn? If he chose the route around the Cape of Good Hope, he would have to visit quite a few French colonies. Didn't he think he should go via Cape Horn after all, thus saving the French allies the immense embarrassment?

Rozhestvensky ignored the pleas of Paris. He kept silent and took his time. As for their embarrassment, he couldn't care less. He expected to make his decision before he left Skagen, but an urgent piece of news ruined his plans.

While the admiral was exchanging wires with the Continent, his squadron was frantically taking on coal, hoping to grab as much of it as possible, because beyond Cape Skagen lay the North Sea, the domain of the hostile and powerful British. The squadron's captains were extremely surprised when before the end of the day of October 7, Rozhestvensky halted coaling abruptly and gave orders for immediate departure. The captains did not know that their admiral had just learned that Japanese torpedo boats had been spotted in the North Sea.

The first warnings arrived from Garting's agents in Norway. People believed to be Japanese saboteurs were hastily departing the fjords. Some spies even insisted that they'd seen Japanese torpedo boats. The admiral got another piece of evidence, from a fellow seaman. The Russian freighter *Bakan* reported that on the previous night, her crew had seen four torpedo boats, cruising the sea with top lights only, barely distinguishable in the dark from fishermen's ships.

Until Skagen, the squadron had felt reasonably safe. The enemy was unlikely to attack Rozhestvensky in Denmark's narrow coastal waters. King Christian IX of Denmark had also dispatched several gunboats to protect the fleet of his grandson, Tsar Nicholas II of Russia. But prolonging the armada's stay at Skagen was asking for trouble.

Skagen lay on the northern tip of Denmark, at the entrance to Skagerrak, a wide strait leading to the North Sea. Skagerrak's ninety-mile width allows a generous margin for any ship wanting to slip unnoticed from the North Sea into the Baltic Sea. The Japanese could sneak into the area at night and attack the squadron at Skagen, coming on it like sharks from the high sea. That was the way they had attacked the Russian fleet at Port Arthur eight and a half months before, on the first night of the war. The only prudent choice, Rozhestvensky concluded, was to remove the squadron immediately, set it in motion, and put it on high alert.

Again, as in Libava, he divided his fleet into four detachments, each under separate command. He himself kept the newest and most precious battleships—his own *Suvorov,* the *Alexander III,* the *Borodino,* and the *Orel.* Detachments were to travel fifty miles apart from each other. If the worst came, at least some ships would survive the torpedo attack. Captains were informed that such an attack might occur any time after dusk.

2

Rozhestvensky spent the night of October 7 on the bridge, his binoculars glued to the dark waters of Skagerrak. His fleet was entering a major avenue of world history. On the seabed beneath them lay Roman triremes with Italian wines and Aristotle's manuscripts, Viking ships with their precious loot, negligently plied by drunken crews, Hansean vessels with mead and furs. The North Sea, famous for its fog, rough waters, and treacherous coast, had claimed a dreadful toll from European history.

However, the sea itself gave the admiral no cause for worry. The night was cloudless, and Skagerrak shone in the moonlight like Nordic silver. By dawn the ships reached the North Sea proper, and the Japanese demons—if they were there—were less likely to detect the squadron.

At Skagen, Rozhestvensky had chosen Tangier as the rendezvous for all detachments. Now many in the squadron wondered which route Rozhestvensky would take to reach Morocco—a shortcut along the coastline of Europe or a longer route around the British Isles. The longer route was safer, with fewer ships and wider spaces, but perhaps the Japanese were hoping he would take exactly this bait. Rozhestvensky ordered navigators to steer right through the English Channel. He would risk a shortcut.

The morning breeze from the southwest brought thick fog that rendered binoculars and searchlights useless. Men on board looked like phantoms in the smoky veil. The sirens of Rozhestvensky's ships wailed continuously, their giant voices quickly rising to a climax and then slowly dying away. The flagship, the *Suvorov*, began, and as soon as she ceased, the *Alexander III* followed, next the *Borodino,* then the *Orel.* The transport *Anadyr*, the smallest by far in the detachment, shrieked in the rear, "as if to announce some terrible misfortune." If Rozhestvensky wanted to announce his arrival to the Japanese, he could find no better way.

Eventually the mist cleared, but the calm did not last long. In the dusk, the sea became choppy, and it started raining. At 8:45 P.M. on October 8, the repair ship *Kamchatka* reported an attack.

The first radio cable that Rozhestvensky received said, "Chased by torpedo boats." The admiral frowned in disbelief. The *Kamchatka* was the most worthless of all the worthless ships—old, slow, and with a tendency to break down at the most unsuitable moment. Why would the Japanese single out this pathetic wreck? He himself could see no sign of a torpedo boat whatsoever. Still, he signaled the detachment, "Be ready for torpedo boat attack from stern." Meanwhile, radio cables from the panic-stricken *Kamchatka* continued:

"All lights shut down."
"Attacked from all directions."
"Torpedo boat closer than a cable length."
"Steering in different directions to escape torpedo boats."
"Heading east at 12 knots."

East? Was the wretched *Kamchatka* going back to Skagen?

Rozhestvensky ordered her to turn west immediately. He kept scrutinizing the darkness surrounding him. He could see nothing. When at 11:20 P.M. he called the *Kamchatka* and asked, "Do you see any torpedo boats?" the answer was the infuriating, "We cannot see any."

Fog returned shortly after midnight. The detachment was passing the Dogger Bank, a large shoal sixty miles east off the coast of England. The armada was frighteningly close to hostile shores. If secret agents had been telling the truth and the Japanese torpedo boats were using England as their base, this was the best place and the best time for them to strike.

At 12:55 A.M. Rozhestvensky saw dark silhouettes. Several small ships were quickly approaching the *Suvorov*. They carried no lights.

The admiral's first thought was of torpedoes. Following his abrupt command, the *Suvorov* changed course. He ordered all searchlights on and the sea, dark just a moment before, became ablaze with light.

All hell broke loose on the *Suvorov*'s bridge. Captain Ignatsius groaned, "We should open fire!" The flag navigator Filippovsky excitedly counted suspicious vessels. The flag captain de Kolong pleaded with the admiral to not hesitate and shoot.

Rozhestvensky remained absolutely silent, scanning the sea through his binoculars. Suddenly, to the right of the *Suvorov*, in the bright beam of a searchlight, the admiral saw a torpedo boat. To the end of his life he was sure that it had been a torpedo boat and never regretted the order he gave. "Open fire!" The night filled with roaring. The *Suvorov*'s heavy frame shook.

Rozhestvensky could not see the torpedo boat any longer, but in a moment, the *Suvorov*'s bow searchlight flashed on a steam trawler ahead of the ship. The gunner next to the admiral, drunk on fear, showered it with shells. Rozhestvensky's gigantic hand grabbed the man by the shoulder and threw him away from the barrel like a kitten. In total fury, the admiral thundered, "Have I ordered this? Can't you see a fisherman!"

He commanded the starboard searchlight of the *Suvorov* to be raised forty-five degrees up, which meant, "Do not fire at this target."

Then he signaled to all the ships, "Do not fire at steam trawlers." Now the guns of the ironclads were sending shells only at darker and swifter silhouettes.

A witness wrote, "Bugles blared; drums rumbled; rails rattled under the weight of handtrucks laden with shells; heavy guns were fired from the starboard and port turrets, lighting the darkness with flashes as they discharged and stirring the night with echoing thunder."

Suddenly, the admiral saw flashes of searchlights to the left. Before he could say anything, the *Suvorov*'s guns fired a salvo in that direction. A moment later, he realized that the ships under fire were desperately flashing the familiar signals of the Russian navy. The flagship was gunning the *Donskoi* and the *Aurora*.

Rozhestvensky loathed his crew. "Cease fire!" he yelled. "Searchlights up!" he cried at the top of his voice. Remarkably, even in the noise of the battle, his voice was heard. In a moment, all the searchlights of the *Suvorov* were extinguished. Only the port one hit the sky, the signal for all ships to stop shooting.

The shooting lasted for few more moments. "The officers, cursing the men and belaboring them, dragged them from the guns, but the gunners broke away and continued shooting." For a while they felt possessed. Finally, it became deafeningly quiet. The clocks showed 1:05 A.M. The shooting had lasted for less than ten minutes.

Rozhestvensky knew some of the fishermen's boats must have been hit, but he did not give much thought to them. His utmost concern was the ghostly attackers. He was sure that the torpedo boat to the right of the *Suvorov* had been hit several times, but the second one, which he at some point had seen to the left, "was lucky to have disappeared."

In the silence and cold of night, the detachment kept moving southwest. It did not stop to pick up the fishermen it had sent into the drink. In his report to the tsar, Rozhestvensky wrote, "Since the fishing trawlers' behavior looked suspicious and since I was not sure that all the torpedo boats participating in the assault had been disabled, I left the injured to the cares of their comrades."

3

In four days, on October 13, the squadron anchored at the Spanish naval station Vigo, having safely and uneventfully passed through the English Channel and the rough seas of the Bay of Biscay. Throughout all four nights, Rozhestvensky had been on the bridge, affording himself only quick naps in a chair and glasses of tea to stay awake.

Several men on the cruisers *Donskoi* and *Aurora,* which had been shelled by the *Suvorov,* were wounded. The condition of Chaplain Anastasy of the *Aurora* was critical, and the captain of the ship sought Rozhestvensky's permission to take the wounded to an English port. Rozhestvensky snarled: "Permission not granted. If he dies, this will be God's will." The chaplain developed gangrene. A monk from a poor and tiny monastery, thirty people in all, in rural Russia, he became the first person in the squadron to die.

Near the rocky shores of Spain the admiral learned that his squadron had gunned English fishing boats, that Europe was on the verge of war, and that he was held responsible.

Unwilling to entrust his feelings to telegraph, in his first cable to the tsar from Vigo he was laconic: "Arrived with the first detachment of battleships."

The cable reached the tsar in the country. October was the peak of hunting season, and he was out shooting game. He had scored twenty-seven that day and was very pleased. Rozhestvensky's cable was delivered to him in the forest, during the third round of shots. By that time, the tsar already knew that European newspapers were flashing alarmist headlines—"English Fishing Fleet Sunk by Russian Guns"—and that London was demanding vengeance.

The next day the tsar held a short meeting with Grand Duke Alexei, Lamsdorf, and Avelan. Although nobody in St. Petersburg wanted another war, the prevailing mood was that London's behavior was much too "audacious." Nicholas now referred to the British as "our filthy enemies." Presumably, he included his uncle, King Edward VII, in this insult.

The Dogger Bank was one of the most well-known fishing grounds in Europe. Famous for cod, turbot, and herring, it attracted fishermen from several countries. Sinking any fishing boat there would have created trouble, but sinking English vessels was disastrous.

The fishermen had come from the city of Hull in Yorkshire. One of their trawlers had sunk "like a stone," and several others had been damaged. The British public was enraged that the squadron had continued on its way without attempting to rescue its victims.

When the news reached London, Britain began rattling its sword. Popular resentment toward Russians reached a critical point. The Russian ambassador, Count Benkendorf, was barraged by protest at Charing Cross Station, and the police had difficulty protecting him from the mob. The British press was unanimous in demanding reparation and apology and insisted that the officers responsible for the massacre be punished. Newspapers urged the British fleet to chase the Russian armada and detain it until that was done. Many even hinted at the desirability of war.

King Edward VII was boiling with indignation. The stylish and pleasure-seeking monarch, who preferred a carnation in his buttonhole to military medals and cabarets to paperwork, for once took matters seriously. He called the Dogger Bank affair "a most dastardly outrage." His subjects couldn't agree more. In Britain, Rozhestvensky's armada was nicknamed the "squadron of mad dogs."

His Majesty's Navy started preparing for battle.

4

The Home Fleet, which had been on maneuvers in the north of Scotland, was gathering in the English Channel. The Mediterranean Fleet, which had been scattered all over the Levant, was recalled to Malta. The Channel Fleet assembled at Gibraltar and began preparing for action. The situation that most of Europe had dreaded for four decades seemed to be coming true: Russia and England were heading for war.

The Channel Fleet was awesome. Consisting of nineteen superb men-of-war, it alone might have been worth the whole Russian navy. But the British were taking no chances. Six battleships, all armored cruisers, and all available torpedo boats from the Mediterranean Fleet were also ordered to Gibraltar.

On October 14, the British Admiralty was informed that Rozhestvensky had arrived at Vigo. The rest of his squadron was believed to be off the Spanish coast, heading for Tangier; for safety reasons, the admiral kept his armada split. Captains at Gibraltar were ordered "to make all preparations for action and be ready at a moment's notice."

Amazingly enough, the concentration of naval might in Gibraltar was not motivated only by vengeance. The Admiralty suspected that Rozhestvensky was capable of attacking the British stronghold. Ships there were instructed "to sink any vessel" attempting to force the Gibraltar harbor. Torpedo boats patrolled the Gibraltar Strait from sunset until dawn. The commander of the Channel Fleet, Charles Beresford, sent a confidential memorandum to his captains, starting with an ominous phrase: "Bear in mind what occurred at Port Arthur before war was declared."

All ships in Gibraltar idled with steam up, ordered to be ready to steam at 12 knots with one hour's notice. Powerful searchlights were hitting the sea from the moles. Patrolling ships were told to watch out for Russian mines and inspect all people trying to get into the harbor. Beresford cabled the Admiralty requesting that "all filled shell and other ammunition due to Gibraltar, also 25 percent of ordnance stores beyond ordinary reserve, be sent to Gibraltar at once."

On Friday, October 15, five cruisers proceeded to Vigo "at full speed to watch the Russian fleet." They arrived the next day. The *Lancaster* entered the harbor, and her captain saluted the Spanish flag and then the flag of the Russian vice admiral. Salutes were returned. Rozhestvensky sent an officer to the *Lancaster* with his compliments, and the *Lancaster* captain hurried to call upon the Mad Dog.

Rozhestvensky received the British officer with marked cordiality. After conversing in French on general topics, he asked the captain "to let him speak in English, and at once began to express his great concern for the terrible tragedy which occurred off Hull." Rozhestvensky assured the British officer that "firing on the fishing boats was a horrible mistake, but with his searchlights he had seen on either bow a low craft with three funnels steaming at high speed toward him. He felt there was nothing to do but open fire."

The *Lancaster* captain, in his own words, listened "sympathetically as he related the sad occurrence, with evident emotion. His whole manner and tenor of speaking conveyed to me how deeply he felt his position. On rising to go he grasped me warmly by the hand. I could do no less than return a grasp, which expressed such deep feeling."

The next day, Rozhestvensky visited the British cruiser. By now, the *Lancaster* captain was totally charmed. The captain did not know that when he cared to, the Mad Dog could soften a heart of stone. But that week the *Lancaster*'s captain was probably the only British officer who empathized with Rozhestvensky. His commander, Lord Beresford, was preparing for war. It looked like he would engage Rozhestvensky in battle before Togo would.

Beresford was ready to fight both Russian units—Rozhestvensky's in Vigo and the rest in Tangier. "Being quite satisfied with the excellence of the gunnery of the Channel Fleet," he wrote to the Admiralty, "I should only have engaged the Russians at Tangier . . . with four of my battleships, at a distance of from 5,000 to 6,000 yards. It appeared to me that this would only be chivalrous, under the circumstances. If the Russian ships had commenced to knock my ships about I would have engaged them with the whole eight Channel Fleet battleships."

Beresford had planned to order Russian ships in Tangier to enter the moles of Gibraltar, to land all officers and half the ship's companies, and to disable the ships' engines. "Having accounted for the Russians in Tangier, I intended to proceed to the northward and meet the Vigo squadron."

But Rozhestvensky saved Beresford the trouble of traveling northward. At noon on October 19, Beresford learned that the Russian admiral had unexpectedly left the Spanish port four hours earlier, steering south to join the rest of the squadron at Tangier.

Beresford decided that the worst had come. He cabled the Admiralty: "I have steam for full speed ready and am prepared to proceed immediately on receipt of telegram from Admiralty. . . . When ordered to act I shall order all Russian Fleet at Tangier into Gibraltar and if disobey they will be sunk and I shall then proceed to meet Vigo Fleet, my cruisers already having orders never to leave them." Eleven battleships, three cruisers, seven torpedo boats, and three destroyers prepared to depart for combat mission. The British ships fired their guns and hoisted Blue Peter, the flag of imminent departure.

5

If in October 1904 there was a European monarch angrier than King Edward VII, it was his nephew Tsar Nicholas II. "I have no words to express my indignation with England's conduct," Nicholas confided to another relative, the German kaiser. The entire Romanov family shared his feelings. The Dowager Empress wired her son from Copenhagen: "How very unpleasant. With God's will everything will be fine. I do not doubt that those rascals the Japanese were there." When her sister, Queen Alexandra, had left Denmark on October 8, the Dowager Empress had decided to stay in Copenhagen just in case. Now the extension proved to be extraordinarily helpful; from Copenhagen it was infinitely easier for her to apply her charms on European courts.

If there was a happy monarch in Europe at that time, it was Kaiser Wilhelm. He had been trying to ally with Russia for several years, and the Dogger Bank incident was a perfect occasion to demonstrate his loyalty to Nicky.

On October 14, Kaiser Wilhelm sent the tsar a sweet-and-sour telegram. "I am sorry for the mishap in the North Sea," he wrote, continuing with the advice that "the use of guns, especially in European waters, should be restricted as much as possible." If Rozhestvensky was afraid of night attacks, the kaiser expertly elaborated, "the use of searchlights alone would suffice to guard the ships from being surprised."

Willy also assured Nicky that the situation in Britain was not that alarming: "The press and mob make noise, the Admiralty some fuss," but "government, court, and society look with greatest calm at the event as an unhappiness arising from the great nervousness."

Yet, he told the tsar that the British danger

> would have to be faced in community by Russia and Germany together, who would both have to remind your ally, France, of obligations she has taken over in the treaty of dual alliance with you, the *caesus foederis*. It is out of the question that France, on such an invitation, would try to shirk her implicit duty toward her ally. Though Delcasse [the French foreign minister] is an anglophile *enragé*, he will be wise enough to understand that the British fleet is utterly unable to save Paris.

In 1904, Europe was decadent, corrupt, and full of gossip, and few secrets were safe. The French learned about Wilhelm's bad-mouthing through their spies and panicked: The kaiser was trying "to get the Tsar to destroy the Franco-Russian alliance!"

Even without Wilhelm's interference, the situation looked quite precarious to Paris. France badly needed alliances with both Russia and Britain, as they felt seriously threatened by Germany, their bitter enemy. They had made an alliance with Russia ten years before but had signed the Entente Cordiale with Britain barely half a year earlier, in April 1904. The French were outraged by Russia's arrogance and Wilhelm's scheming, but perhaps they were most angered by Britain's sword rattling. Foreign Minister Theophile Delcasse complained, "I can see that there's more to fear from the English side than from the Russian at the moment."

Delcasse was worried that war might start because of an accidental technicality, say, a mere delay of an important telegram. What if the British said something irrevocable, having failed to receive a Russian response in time, "and a few hours later, a conciliatory reply shows how disastrously hasty they have been! Would anyone in his senses agree that peace between two great empires depends on a matter of hours?"

Delcasse decided to speak "very strongly and plainly" to the Russian ambassador in Paris, Alexander Nelidov: "It is absolutely vital for your government to immediately send a chivalrous and apologetic message which alone can avert a crisis. There isn't a moment to lose. . . . Just think for a minute; tomorrow morning an English Squadron may very well receive instructions to open fire on your ships."

Nelidov trusted neither the French nor the British, nor, for that matter, the Germans. His personal conviction, expressed to friends, was that "Russia has been pushed into war in the Far East, so that she might get distracted from the Near East." Moreover, his son was a lieutenant on one of Rozhestvensky's battleships. The ambassador grimly responded that public opinion in Russia was as roused as public opinion in England, "because it regards England as the traditional enemy, an enemy hated far more than the Japanese." Delcasse exclaimed, "But that is all the more reason for your government not losing a moment in saying the word that can still settle the whole trouble!"

Russian diplomats knew that they had a weak case but tried to defend Russia: "The Russian government had received numerous reports to the effect that Japanese agents were visiting" Britain for the purpose of organizing attacks on the Baltic Fleet, "and in these circumstances it was perhaps not unnatural that the captains of the Russian ships should have been alarmed at finding" the Hull trawlers in close proximity to their men-of-war.

St. Petersburg was willing to pay reparations and perhaps apologize. But London insisted that Rozhestvensky and his captains be punished. It also demanded "that security be given to us against a repetition of such incidents." Foreign Secretary Lansdowne provocatively asked, "What was to prevent the Russian Fleet, during its long journey to the Far East, from carrying death and destruction with it throughout its course?"

The Russian naval attaché to Britain, Captain Bostrom, sent a private cable to Rozhestvensky at Vigo describing this pan-European turmoil. Rozhestvensky responded with information so important that Bostrom and Ambassador Benkendorf decided to send it to the British Cabinet immediately.

Knowing that the tsar always liked to have scapegoats, Rozhestvensky was more than willing to fill the role. The language of his telegram would have made the most tolerant man in the world lose patience. It read:

> The North Sea incident was occasioned by the action of two torpedo boats which steamed at full speed under cover of the night, and showing no lights, toward the ship that was leading our detachment. It was only after our search lights had been turned on that it was remarked that a few small steam craft bearing resemblance to trawlers were present. The detachment made every effort to spare these craft and ceased firing as soon as the torpedo boats had disappeared from sight.

And Rozhestvensky made another statement. The British press were accusing the Russians of ignoring the fishermen's plight, based on reports by the Hull fishermen that one of the Russian vessels, a torpedo boat, had remained at Dogger Bank until dawn, never attempting to save the Englishmen from the sea. Rozhestvensky triumphantly wrote:

> The Russian detachment did not include any torpedo destroyers, and no Russian vessel of any kind was left behind upon the scene of the incident. It follows that the vessel which is declared to have remained in the neighbourhood of the small fishing boats until daylight must have been one of the two enemy's torpedo boats, which had only sustained some injuries, the other one having been sunk.

But London was not swayed by the telegram. The ship, which had stayed at Dogger Bank until dawn, they said, must have been the Russian *Kamchatka*. The British government again demanded that Rozhestvensky and his captains should be "recalled and placed on trial."

Privately, however, the Cabinet agreed that Rozhestvensky's testimony demanded more investigation and began an unsuccessful search for the mysterious torpedo boat. They made inquiries with neighboring countries like Denmark, asking whether their torpedo boats had been in the vicinity of Dogger Bank that night, but no one ever learned the identity of the mysterious ship. It was quite possible that the fishermen were mistaken and that no ship had been there at all.

Negotiations between St. Petersburg and London proceeded with great difficulty. London insisted that until the crisis was resolved, Rozhestvensky with his battleships should remain in Vigo. The flamboyant Spanish port was becoming a jail.

From their ships, the Russians could see the lofty crests of the Pyrenees and the azure of the southern sea. Many sailors had never been to such a spacious harbor before; Vigo's bay provided ample room for a hundred ocean-going vessels.

The port was a historic site. Twice, in 1585 and 1589, Sir Francis Drake had attacked it. Now it looked like the Russian battleships might join old wrecks on the sea bottom; the British ships were cruising the adjoining waters menacingly.

Spain was neutral, but its authorities, wary of London's wrath, forbade the Russians to take on coal. There was a reason for their zeal.

King Alfonso XIII was eighteen. Charming and quick-witted, born a king (his father had died six months before his birth), Alfonso was now one of the most sought after bachelors in Europe. Both Kaiser Wilhelm II, who had a remarkable stock of strong-willed German princesses, and King Edward VII, who had several nieces, were interested. In this situation, the last thing King Alfonso wanted to do was offend any monarch in Europe, but when he had to choose between offending Nicholas II and offending Edward VII, he logically opted to offend the Russian tsar.

Yet, Rozhestvensky never surrendered easily. He kept nagging, and finally, the governor of Vigo yielded. Rozhestvensky's ships were allowed to take a token amount of coal—four hundred tons per ironclad and lesser amounts for the smaller vessels.

The coaling started. "Everyone lent a hand: bluejackets, stokers, artificers, petty officers, clerks, officers, and all. The men were told that two extra tots of vodka would be served if the work was well and quickly done." The crews worked through the night until ten o'clock the next morning. By that time they had taken aboard twice the allowance specified by the Spaniards.

Technically, the squadron could now move on, having enough coal to reach Tangier, but London kept the jail door shut. The European press reported that if Rozhestvensky broke the blockade, he would have to fight twenty-four battleships and eighteen cruisers. When the awed staff read him the warning, the admiral just snorted: "We will be able to fight only the first four battleships, and it does not matter how many others will finish us off then—twenty-four or one hundred and twenty-four."

The Vigo public was sympathetic to the squadron and its admiral and cheered Rozhestvensky on the streets of town. The Spanish could not forget the loss of Gibraltar to the British. A local newspaper wrote, "The enemy of our enemy's ally is our friend."

Meanwhile, Rozhestvensky was waiting for instructions from the tsar. Unable to make any decision before the conflict with Britain was over, on October 14 the tsar wired a meaningless but encouraging telegram: "All my thoughts are with you and my dear squadron. The difficulty will soon be settled. Russia places all her faith and has implicit confidence in you."

The admiral had the telegram read to all of the crews and dutifully replied: "The entire squadron bows as one man before the throne of Your Majesty."

On October 16, Nicholas ordered his foreign minister to send to London a proposition "to subject the whole question to an international commission of inquiry as laid down in The Hague Conference protocol."

That day, Kaiser Wilhelm was pheasant hunting along the Russian frontier—a special courtesy of the tsar. Willy did not like Nicky's new appeasing mood at all and, having hastily collected his trophies, composed a war-mongering telegram. He reminded his cousin that the fishermen "have already acknowledged that they have seen foreign steam craft among their boats, not belonging to their fishing fleet, which they knew not. So," summed up Willy significantly, "there has been foul play."

But this time Wilhelm achieved nothing. The tsar himself was already quite sure that there had been foul play. But in regard to the conflict with London, he had made his choice: peace.

London accepted. It was agreed that an international commission, composed of admirals, would investigate the Dogger Bank incident. Rozhestvensky had to leave four officers in Vigo as witnesses. The case was also submitted to The Hague Tribunal. Rozhestvensky himself was free to proceed to his fateful rendezvous with Togo. However, everybody knew that from now on, the shadow of the Dogger Bank would follow the armada. A top Russian diplomat sighed, "You can imagine what the environment will be for the future voyage of the squadron."

Yet, the flagship officers were sure that the admiral was full of vigor. They did not know that on the night before the departure, Rozhestvensky had sent a bitter letter to his wife: "We have become miserably weak, and with this general sick weakness, the crazy enterprise of our notorious squadron can hardly count on anything, even on sheer luck."

At seven o'clock in the morning of October 19, the squadron steamed out of Vigo. The British cruisers followed at a distance. Rozhestvensky recognized three of them: the *Lancaster,* the *Hermes,* and the *Drake.* He was very glad they were there. "We could not get better guardians," he remarked. The Japanese saboteurs would never dare to attack while the British were around. Now Rozhestvensky could allow himself a night of sound sleep in his cabin.

During the day, he remained on deck though, unable to turn his eyes away from the perfect maneuvering of the unfriendly British detachment. "What a squadron!" he finally said. "What seamen! Ah, if only we were this way. . . . "

The Admiralty informed Beresford, the British naval commander in Gibraltar, that battle with Rozhestvensky was to be postponed. Beresford was ordered to "avoid wounding susceptibilities of Russian admiral by overt shadowing of his fleet. Sufficient if cruisers do not lose them." In another cable, the Admiralty explicitly said, "It is our imperative duty not to take any step that will make war inevitable until we are quite certain that we cannot obtain complete satisfaction without war."

Beresford responded: "Understand your wish. . . . Cruisers and destroyers have imperative orders to do nothing to wound susceptibilities." Ships in Gibraltar were instructed to let the fires die out in boilers that were not necessary for 10 knots at four hours notice—not high alert by any means.

Yet, the crisis lasted for ten more days. Only on October 29 was the British navy informed that "Government considers crisis past."

The conflict was settled. Russia apologized, promised to pay reparations, and agreed to submit the case to an international commission. England dropped its demand to put Rozhestvensky and his captains on trial and stopped insisting on guarantees against a repetition of such incidents in the future. The Dowager Empress left Copenhagen, the tsar went back to hunting, King Edward VII returned to womanizing. However, well-informed people like the German Admiral Von Tirpitz were sure that Rozhestvensky's squadron would create yet graver problems for European diplomacy. As Von Tirpitz caustically remarked, "Only a few more episodes of a like nature are required during the voyage of the Russian argonauts."

6

While the squadron was waiting at Vigo, the admiral had made a critically important choice. The Russian Admiralty officially informed Paris that Rozhestvensky had rejected the Cape Horn–Polynesian Archipelago route, which the French, intimidated by London, wanted him to take. Rozhestvensky's explanation was that the marine perils of this route were too great, and his men and officers were not fit for such a challenging voyage. He would proceed instead to the French colony of Madagascar and be joined there by the ships of his squadron that would go by way of the Suez Canal.

The infuriated French, now fully exposed to British criticism, were on the verge of refusing to host the squadron in their waters. But, quite predictably, fear of the kaiser made them more cooperative. The French Foreign Ministry did not want to see what "the capital Germany would make out of it" and preferred "the lesser evil." Rozhestvensky could count on their limited hospitality.

He was obliged to send them his itinerary: Tangier in Morocco, Dakar and Libreville in French Africa, Portuguese Mossamedes, German Angra Pequena, and finally, Sainte-Marie in French Madagascar. There was little doubt that the French would notify London about the admiral's plans. Then it would be just a matter of hours before Togo would learn of them, too.

The French Foreign Ministry started "making all the arrangements for coaling, the transmission of news from spies and certain secret missions." Rozhestvensky could only hope that they would not share the sensitive information with the British. Beyond this, the French involvement in the intelligence network made Rozhestvensky's squadron extremely vulnerable. Spies had led him to disaster at Dogger Bank. Most probably, the provocative rumor of "an ambush in the North Sea" had been told to Russian spies by their Japanese colleagues. The shower of alarming reports defeated the admiral's natural skepticism and made him overreact on the ill-fated night of October 8. One could only wonder what other mishaps might occur when the Japanese would have a chance to play with the French secret agents, too. Yet, cooperation with the French was crucial; the Russians did not have any spy network in Africa beyond the Suez Canal.

Rozhestvensky's detachment reached Tangier at 3 P.M., October 21. The British cruisers had disappeared shortly before his arrival, having made sure he was indeed heading for Tangier. In Tangier, other ships of the squadron were waiting for the admiral impatiently. They had reached Morocco safely and without any trouble.

Rozhestvensky immediately ordered his fleet to split into two groups before dusk fell. He himself would lead his detachment of newer battleships and a number of other better ships around the Cape of Good Hope, and Admiral Felkersam would take five older warships and several transports through the Suez. The two detachments would meet at Madagascar. Felkersam left at nine o'clock that night. Anticipating another ambush or even a military conflict with Britain, the admirals wanted to save at least some of their ships.

The separation had been planned long before the Dogger Bank incident, back in St. Petersburg. Originally, it was intended that Admiral Enkvist would lead the Suez unit. He was related to Naval Minister Avelan and therefore was expected to receive an independent command. But Rozhestvensky knew Enkvist was good for nothing and changed the arrangement at his own risk.

After Felkersam departed, Rozhestvensky rushed his captains to coal as fast as possible. He still had good reason to expect the worse. The British fleet was only fifty miles to the northeast, across the narrow Gibraltar Strait.

Worried about Rozhestvensky's possible intentions, the British were monitoring all his moves closely. The warship *Diana* was placed in Tangier with precisely this mission. The captain of the *Diana,* Phippo-Horaby, visited the *Aurora,* which struck him as "a very nice ship with clear decks and is said to steam well and be handy." But by and large, the Russian ships seemed lousy to the British. They tended to roll considerably. "The men looked well fed and healthy," but "the general appearance of the ships did not give one an idea of being well disciplined and organized for war." The snobbish captain of the *Diana,* coming from a country with notorious class distinctions, noted in his report, "Though some of the officers looked to be of a good class, the majority of those I saw, especially of the lower ranks, seemed of a decidedly common type."

Interestingly enough, the British captain, generally very critical of the squadron, made an exception for Rozhestvensky's detachment of battleships: "Very powerful fighting vessels and carry large crews who look healthy. This division looks better prepared for war and better found in every way than the other divisions."

Receiving visitors on their ships, as naval etiquette dictated, Russian officers told their inquisitive British counterparts stories about the Dogger Bank incident, insisting that several enemy torpedo boats had been seen there. The British could see for themselves that the *Aurora* had been damaged during the skirmish; her chaplain had died of gangrene in a French hospital ashore.

The Russian ships burned searchlights at night and sent boats on patrol. Their British watchdog, the *Diana's* captain, in his own words, "also continued to prepare for war as far as could be done without being visible from outside the ship."

Tangier was the last Western port the squadron visited, the final farewell to a familiar world. Built on chalky limestone hills, in 1904 Tangier was one of the busiest and loveliest ports of the Mediterranean. Its old town, enclosed by ancient ramparts, struck the eye with dazzling whiteness; The sultan's palace and the Great Mosque created a spectacular sight, but the Russian sailors spent little time on the narrow curved streets of the city, famous for its prostitutes, hashish, and good food. The armada left Tangier in sixty-four hours.

Apprehensive of Rozhestvensky's possible reaction, the British Admiralty canceled its previous order to follow the Russian ships closely. The only information required now was whether they were proceeding via the Mediterranean or the Atlantic.

On the morning of October 23, Rozhestvensky's squadron departed from Tangier. It steered west. The British destroyer *Ariel* followed for a few hours, reporting that the Russians had turned west-southwest. The Mad Dog's squadron was going around Africa.

When they were leaving Tangier, the transport *Anadyr* discovered she could not lift her anchor; the wretched ship had got caught by an underwater telegraph cable.

Rozhestvensky became furious and spewed all the obscenities he knew, then signaled the *Anadyr*: "Cut the cable and go to your place in the column immediately." With this order, he essentially terminated telegraph communication between North Africa and Europe.

On the eve of the departure, he sent two messages to Russia. One was a telegram to the tsar; it was the tenth anniversary of Nicholas II's ascension to the throne. "May God send joy to Your Majesty's heart," the admiral said politely. The second message was to his wife, again full of complaints: "One has to order five times to do some most trivial thing and then to check five times more whether they have forgotten the order or not. . . . This is a miserable fleet."

5

"We Have No Coast Batteries in Dakar!"

OCTOBER 23–DECEMBER 16, 1904, AFRICAN COAST

1

ON LEAVING TANGIER, "MAD DOG" ROZHESTVENSKY'S MEN were told their next destination, the city of Dakar, in French Senegal. To reach it, the squadron had to travel two thousand miles southwest from Gibraltar, skirting the Sahara and then tropical rain forest. Seasoned sailors warned not to expect anything good down there; they prophesied unbearable heat and itching rash.

With Admiral Felkersam's ships now crossing the Mediterranean, Rozhestvensky's squadron was smaller. He organized it into three columns. He himself led the right one on the *Suvorov*, followed by the other four huge battleships—the *Alexander III*, the *Borodino*, the *Orel*, and the *Oslyabya*. Six transports, the *Kamchatka*, the *Anadyr*, the *Meteor*, the *Korea*, the *Malaya*, and the *Rus* proceeded in a parallel column to the left. The poor *Kamchatka* was leading not due to her superb naval qualities but precisely because of her total lack of such. After her erratic performance at Dogger Bank, Rozhestvensky wanted to watch her as closely as possible. Admiral Enkvist on the *Nakhimov* followed in the rear, leading two other cruisers, the *Aurora* and the *Donskoi*. The hospital ship *Orel* and the French refrigerator ship *Esperance,* carrying 1,000 tons of frozen meat, did not join any column. This was essential for keeping their "neutral" status. Hopefully, it would make them immune to any potential Japanese attack.

Even now, with Admiral Felkersam's ships traveling separately, this was an enormous fleet, with around 7,500 people. Every human eccentricity and frailty must have been represented in it. According to statistics, 1,500 of Rozhestvensky's men must have had allergies, 800 could suffer from depression, 700 from anxiety disorder, and at least 20 were likely to become suicidal before they reached the Far East.

Rozhestvensky was responsible for them all. No matter how despotic Russia was and how powerless people were, military orderliness demanded that attention be paid to individuals. All casualties had to be reported to St. Petersburg. The death of an officer was an emergency, demanding an immediate cable to the tsar. Naval officers were the elite of the nation, quite a few of them personally known to foreign royalty and benevolently mentioned in august correspondence. Their men were not that privileged, but even though they were frequently abused physically, they still had to stay healthy, well fed, and stable, much more so than their peers in the army. The worst thing a depressed soldier could do was to shoot his commander. An unhappy sailor could destroy his whole ship.

Rozhestvensky's crews had every reason to become depressed. Modern warships looked mysterious and unfriendly to many of the men. Most of them had come from villages only a few years or months earlier and could barely read. Until they were drafted, they had never seen an electric bulb or heard the sound of an engine. The most sophisticated weaponry they had ever come across would have been their landlord's hunting gun. They did not understand the reason for the countless cables, meters, and pipes inside a ship. Huge hulls stuffed with machinery looked sinister to them. In letters back home, men described their ships as "iron monsters."

Officers were not depressed by steam and steel, but they had their own concerns. They were still called "stars of the nation"—but "cannon meat" seemed more appropriate. Their journey was charged with disaster. Togo appeared almost omnipotent. To this was added the claustrophobia inherent to naval life. True, some hulls, like the *Suvorov*, were as huge as floating cathedrals, but they were overcrowded—eight hundred men manned them. A warship provided no privacy, no extra space, and no real comfort. Of course, in terms of private space, officers were far better off than the crew, but they were also more spoiled and therefore more vulnerable to hardship. In working-class slums or peasant huts, nobody had an individual bedroom anyway.

Another concern was the strict hierarchy—confining, conservative, and often repressive. Crewmen could find consolation in the anonymity of a mob, but an officer was always in the unwelcome limelight. Almost all aspects of an officer's life were strictly regulated and watched by his men and his superiors.

Wardrooms were presided over by senior officers, never by captains. The latter had meals in their cabins. The idea was to create a distance, providing captains with special stature, but as often as not this resulted in a split between the captain and his subordinates.

Daily routine was harsh. Watches were serious business—especially when ships were traveling in columns at uncomfortably close distances. An officer keeping watch was in total charge of his ship, his authority delegated by the captain. The most hated watch, from 2 to 4 A.M., was called "dog." In the darkness, time crawled excruciatingly slowly; it was easy not to notice the threatening hull of the next ship; it was tempting to close one's eyes and drift into a nap. Meanwhile, the squadron was led by the thunderous admiral, who seemed to be all-seeing and ever vigilant and never hesitated to severely punish a negligent officer.

Each warship was a miniature replica of Russian society. The divide between officers and crew was sharp. It was the division between stern and bow. In the stern, officers had their own tiny cabins. Battleships like the *Orel* even had reserve space, in case the admiral and his whole staff decided for some reason to move from the *Suvorov*. The crew lived in the bow. Their joint quarters were so cramped that the upper row of hammocks there had to be taken away for the day to allow at least some space.

Torpedo boats had even less space. This could result in a special feeling of naval camaraderie between all people on board. Officers from bigger and more snobbish ships, like the *Suvorov,* cultivating aristocratic detachment, were shocked when they learned that torpedo boat officers gave each other birthday presents. Occasionally, an officer on a torpedo boat would be spotted ironing his uniform—an appalling sight even for liberal-minded peers on bigger ships.

The small world of a torpedo boat allowed a captain to cultivate his idiosyncrasies to extremes. Lieutenant Otto Richter, the captain of the *Bystry*, for example, liked to dress as a private, did his washing together with his men, and spent a lot of time in their company telling bawdy stories they much appreciated. Sometimes he even wore a private's uniform onshore and was seen walking around in the company of his orderly, saluting bypassing officers. This flamboyant cross-dressing, when the captain was openly enjoying the eroticism of submissive role-playing, would be unimaginable on bigger ships.

Every officer had an orderly, normally a young peasant lad. A good orderly was not only a valet who washed the deck, did the laundry, and ran various errands but also a nurse, a cook, a tailor, and sometimes a friend (in the case of Lieutenant Richter, a lover). However, the Russian language, with its two forms of "you," one familiar and one respectful, accentuated the inequality of these friendships. Officers invariably addressed men with the familiar *"ty."* Men had to address them not just with the respectful *"vy"* but with a very formal *"vashe blagorodie,"* Your Honor.

The Russian Navy was based on strict, almost obsessive discipline. Officers aspired to control every aspect of sailors' lives, including the spiritual. Russia's state religion was Eastern Orthodoxy. A good Russian was Orthodox. Although some officers and bureaucrats of German or Baltic descent remained Protestant or in some cases even Catholic, no diversity was possible on a warship. Each of the large vessels, like the battleships and cruisers, had an Orthodox priest or monk for her chaplain. Aside from professional chores, such a figure was also encouraged to spy and report on the crew. In some cases, a sincere confession could cost a sailor dearly.

One way to discipline crews was to make church attendance mandatory. Many men hated going to chapel and would hide in the bowels of the ship, as they put it themselves, "like cockroaches." Non-commissioned officers searched for them, cursing and sweating. When found, the culprits would be rewarded with liberal punches. Few of the officers enjoyed the masses either, but they felt obliged to set a good example.

Class tensions were much worse in the navy than in the army. A soldier would meet his officers exclusively during service hours. He had no idea how they ate or drank or spent their free time. Ships were another story. Sailors watched their superiors constantly. There was not much that an officer could conceal from their prying eyes.

In theory, men ate well. Meals were to be cooked with fresh meat, but it was impossible to stock enough cows or pigs to feed eight hundred men for several weeks. When the livestock supply onboard was exhausted, meat had to be taken from the refrigerator of the *Esperance*. After the *Esperance*'s stock was emptied, crews were fed *solonina*—meat preserve of a yellowish color, often stinking and generally nauseating. On such days some sailors refused to take meals at all.

Officers had their own supply of everything. Each meal consisted of several dishes. Good cooks prepared them. Probably no officer in the Imperial Navy had ever eaten *solonina*—except when obliged to check the crew's menu. Fine wine and elaborate spirits were served in the officers' wardroom. It was both a restaurant and a club. Sounds of opera arias and Chopin mazurkas mixed with smells of exquisite sauces, coffee, liqueurs, and cigars. These sounds and smells told men of an infinitely better life. If this ignited anything in their hearts it was bitterness, if not outright hatred. No sailor could hope to become a commissioned officer. For that, he had to be born into a privileged class.

Some officers still beat their men. Many captains discouraged or prohibited this, but everybody knew that Rozhestvensky himself rarely felt guilty about giving a man a thrashing. When an officer was impressed with a sailor's performance, he would buy him an extra shot of vodka or two. It was commonly believed this was the only kind of encouragement the brutes would appreciate.

For men on a warship, the day started at five o'clock in the morning, announced with a shriek of a flute on the upper deck. Immediately after that, noncommissioned officers started rousting the men. They never hesitated to use obscenities or fists; bullies by design, they usually made the point of being deliberately cruel. For this they were rewarded; some of them even shared a cabin for just two. Hundreds of sailors hastily jumped from their berths and hammocks. They had only a few minutes to dress and turn hammocks into neat, numbered cocoons. Then the cocoons had to be taken to the upper deck and put into special niches. The crew was ordered to wash. Elbowing each other, they hastily rinsed their faces with harsh seawater. The next order was "To prayer!" A priest arrived to sing the day's hymns. Hundreds of voices on deck accompanied him.

Breakfast of bread, butter, and tea took half an hour. At seven o'clock the cleaning-up started. Decks had to be washed, brass polished, walls brushed. Shortly before eight, everybody had to be on deck in a solemn formation. The captain received reports from his senior officer, the doctor, and others. At eight o'clock sharp, simultaneously with Rozhestvensky's *Suvorov*, all ships raised the St. Andrew's Flag, a blue cross on white that was the trademark of the Russian navy. Officers and crewmen took their caps off. Horns and drums played. The day was launched.

For two and a half hours, training proceeded. Then the cook brought a portion of the crew's lunch to the captain: a bowl of meat soup, slices of bread, and salt. The captain had to taste the soup, and if he approved, the senior officer and head of watch had to taste it, too. All used the same spoon.

At eleven o'clock, flutes announced lunch. Men rushed to the deck where vessels with vodka already stood. Each was poured half a glass. If the meat was fresh, the soup was good: meat, cabbage, potato, beet, carrot, onion, pepper, and some wheat flour. After lunch, the crew rested for two hours, took tea for thirty minutes, and then returned to work. At half past five, all labors were finished. At six o'clock, dinner arrived, and vessels with vodka were brought to the deck again. After that the crew was free to relax. The only ceremonies remaining were the lowering of the flag and evening prayer.

Normally, crews were well fed and worked only eight hours a day, with a three-hour break in the middle. However, if something went wrong—be it the interruption of food supplies or some other emergency—the crew was the first to suffer.

Apart from these ugly discrepancies brought to the squadron by a semi-feudal society, Rozhestvensky's ships also encountered a number of ad hoc difficulties.

They were quickly running short of supplies. Some essential items were becoming scarce, for instance, soap designed to be used in seawater (ordinary soap would not lather). Officers, almost all of them smokers, suffered from a shortage of cigarettes, and crewmen were running out of tobacco for rolling. They were not sure when and where they would be able to restock. Other supplies brought from home, like sweets, also started looking precious.

They were experiencing a feeling of total abandonment. The Russian navy was accustomed to long voyages, but had never taken such a desolate route. Usually the Russians kept to the busy traffic lanes like the Mediterranean, Red Sea, or North Pacific. Officers complained that they were to visit places they had never heard of before, or if they had, then only long ago in school.

The heat became unbearable. Sailors sweat profusely and slept naked, "wearing only crosses," as they joked to each other. Officers, exploiting the privacy of their cabins, stayed naked in daytime, too. After dark, although the heat was especially oppressive, no one was allowed to open portholes: Rozhestvensky did not want any unnecessary lights.

Drawers would not close; humidity had made the wood damp and swollen. Towels and underwear would not dry. Ventilators were working all day long but did not help. Everybody looked "sluggish and sleepy."

They were thirsty all the time. Officers greedily consumed soda water with ice, and crews made *kvas*, a village bread cider.

Several ships had proven totally unreliable and basically unsuitable for such a journey. Their engines would break down frequently, making the whole squadron stop and wait until the unfortunate ship coped with the problem. This was especially infuriating, because it usually happened to transports. Although it had been impossible to acquire better battleships or cruisers, the Admiralty definitely could have found better cargo ships. On October 26, for example, the transport *Malaya* kept the whole squadron waiting for six long hours.

The fact that steam was still relatively novel aggravated tensions. Many of the captains had been trained in the days of sail and regarded mechanical problems with irritation. They were unable to apprehend the built-in frailty of machinery and thought that a turbine must be as easy to fix as a rope.

Rozhestvensky himself was somewhat guilty of that misperception. Relative technical conservatism, amplified by bad temper, was leading him to horrendous explosions of wrath aimed at those ships that broke down regularly.

But everything seemed to be provoking his wrath that fall. In a letter to his wife, he called the *Suvorov* a den, a word Russians used to describe a messy and totally mismanaged place. "I never thought a warship could be like that." And some other ships were even worse.

Rozhestvensky was extremely displeased with his captains and staff: "Tons of papers, various instructions—but all wrong. . . . When they face a grandiose task they faint. . . . If the army has the same kind of people too, then there is no hope left." Why did he have so many inept people? Because other admirals, like Makarov and Alexeev, had already taken all the best men. "The people who were left had been rejected by them."

Tolerance was definitely not one of his virtues. When angry at the *Suvorov* captain and in need of sending orders to the front bridge where the culprit was, Rozhestvensky would roar, "Tell the den to do this and that." The kindest words he would use on these occasions were "this bunch of fools."

Soon everybody on the *Suvorov* knew that when the admiral was cursing the Slutty Old Geezer, he was referring to his junior flag officer, Rear Admiral Enkvist, a man of imposing looks but no substance. The captain of the battleship *Orel*, vain and nervous Jung, he called the Polished Fidget; the captain of the *Borodino*, Serebrennikov, who had flirted with revolution in his youth, the Brainless Nihilist; the captain of the *Alexander*, Bukhvostov, a proud member of the Imperial Guards, the Guards' Uniform Hanger. Of the ships, the too quick *Aurora* was the Whore, the too slow *Donskoi* was the Cabbie, and the hateful, unreliable *Kamchatka* was the Lecherous Slut. When a ship misbehaved, Rozhestvensky yelled at her, as if she, five miles away, could hear. When exasperated, the admiral howled in impotent rage, "Whores, all whores!" and pitched his binoculars overboard. His staff, quite aware of this habit, had ordered fifty pairs when they were leaving Kronshtadt. But the Dogger Bank incident definitely hadn't improved Rozhestvensky's disposition, and the optical stock was being exhausted even more quickly than the staff had expected.

The admiral regularly issued orders to the squadron, delivered to every ship by messenger. He used these for severe scolding. They exhibited sarcasm, bitterness, and passion for discipline. Some of the orders were long remembered for their blunt language. One of them dealt with signals.

The *Suvorov* was, naturally, setting the pace for the whole squadron. To this end, special black balls were raised on her mast to indicate ordered speed. However, with enormous indignation, the admiral noticed that most of the mast was normally occupied by the crew's underwear so that, Rozhestvensky wrote sardonically, those following the flagship "could see a lot of waving pants, but no signals at all."

In 1904, radio was still temperamental and unreliable, so the main way to communicate with other ships was to raise a combination of special flags on the mast and to monitor the flags on their masts carefully. Obviously, in this case, no communication remained private. A way to bypass it was to use hand semaphore—a signal discernible only from close range.

On one occasion the admiral ordered a signal sent to the battleship *Orel* via hand semaphore. It took the *Orel* captain an hour and a half to respond. In a special order, Rozhestvensky warned that during the forthcoming battle, all masts could be destroyed, and the semaphore might prove to be the only means of communication. If the captains did not learn to use the hand semaphore properly before that, he continued, during the battle the squadron would become "a flock of sheep," "losing their unwashed hair" to the Japanese.

Communication was one of the major problems that kept sending Rozhestvensky's binoculars overboard. The year 1904 was an interesting time in this respect. Radio was still very new and somewhat untested. Transmitters were extremely volatile, and their range excruciatingly short. Marconi, a leading maker of radios, was vague about the potential of its own products, quoting a range of ten to three hundred miles. It was rarely longer than fifty. Even the British, as always the most technologically advanced, constantly expressed their frustration. They experimented with radio a lot and scrupulously recorded grievances: "atmospherics very bad"; "no definite signals received"; signals "mostly unintelligible." As often as not, all a radio operator could hear would be "a few ticks." He would not be even able to distinguish which language was being transmitted.

Telegraph could also be problematic. First, it was slow. Very few direct links were available, and it took an eternity to get a message transmitted through several terminals. All messages, even top secret ones upon which the fate of the world depended, were transmitted through the general telegraph network. To transmit an extremely sensitive message from an embassy to the home capital, one had to use alien telegraph lines. With codes being rather basic, spying was easy and no information was secure as soon as it plunged into the cable web. For Russians, the situation was particularly bad. Their enemy, Britain, controlled a lot of telegraph terminals, especially outside Europe. In 1904, the safest way to conduct business was by letter.

Communications were playing a sinister role in the fate of the besieged Russian fortress in Manchuria, Port Arthur. Very soon it found itself isolated from the rest of world; the Japanese had cut the underwater telegraph cable that led across the sea to Chefoo. The Russian consulate in Chefoo had a radio station, and foreign correspondents assembled in the dark around the building to watch the antenna's mysterious blue gleam. Although the Japanese consulate asserted that the use of radio by the Russians was a violation of Chinese neutrality—and the Chinese asked the Russians to stop—the sad reality was that the Russian consulate could not talk to Port Arthur at all. Its transmitter used the same wavelength as the Japanese fleet, and the Japanese were jamming the Russian signals.

The Russian consul in Chefoo was forced to start buying the services of Chinese smugglers to deliver messages to Port Arthur and back. Finding the new business very profitable, junks of outlaws began shuttling between Shandong and Liaodong. Every ninth junk perished on its way. Some were intercepted by the Japanese, who occasionally shared their catch—for instance, a Russian officer's letter—with the British.

The Russians were quite aware of this and took precautions. Messages were written in code on tiny pieces of thin paper, and two or three smugglers carried the same message. Occasionally a junk also took a Russian officer-courier to Port Arthur and back. The consul experimented with dove mail, too, but not a single bird succeeded in covering the eighty miles separating Chefoo from the fortress.

Of course, Rozhestvensky's situation was infinitely better. He and his crews could expect to get mail in almost every port on his route. Officers had left thorough instructions for their families on how they could be reached. All personal mail had to go through intermediaries—

either through the St. Petersburg post office, or Ginsburg's Odessa headquarters, addressed to "The Second Pacific Squadron." For security reasons, it was prohibited to use international mail.

Officers' letters home were not censored; nevertheless, the ban on independent communication was broken in every port. In Tangier many had sent cables back home, and the lucky ones even got a response. But now, barely a month after they had left Russia, officers complained that they felt totally isolated. They were bored, and books and magazines were in great demand.

For the admiral the isolation was much worse. It was an issue not of emotional comfort but of survival. He had no idea how the Russian army was faring in Manchuria. Was Port Arthur still in Russian hands? Was Vladivostok threatened? What was going on in Russia proper? When the squadron left Kronshtadt, many had been talking about the approaching revolution. Had it arrived? What did Tsar Nicholas II think about the revolution, war, and peace? What were his plans for Rozhestvensky?

2

At eight o'clock on the morning of October 30, the squadron reached Dakar in French Senegal. October 30 was Rozhestvensky's birthday, and the *Suvorov* officers expected a party.

He gave a festive lunch that day indeed. A surprise awaited the guests: nurse Natalia Sivers from the hospital ship *Orel*. The admiral's affair with this thirty-year-old blue-eyed, emotional blonde was becoming public knowledge.

Rozhestvensky's angel must have been smiling down on him. He was partying with the woman he was infatuated with, and ten German steamers with thirty thousand tons of coal were waiting for him in the harbor. He hoped to start loading soon and announced that no one was to see the shore until all the coal was taken onboard. But suddenly problems arose.

In the morning, the French governor was very friendly, but by afternoon he had received new instructions from Paris: The Russians were forbidden to take on coal. That new technology, the telegraph, had unexpectedly interfered with the admiral's plans.

A number of Western reporters in Dakar had been impatiently awaiting Rozhestvensky's arrival. At the turn of the last century, the public was developing a taste for quickly delivered news. A century earlier, in 1815, by the time the European periphery got the news about Napoleon's landing in France, he had already been defeated. Now news traveled fast, sometimes too fast, influencing and shaping politics.

When the German colliers arrived at Dakar, the press reported the news immediately. Even before Rozhestvensky himself showed up, European diplomacy had been set into motion. London energetically protested to Paris that allowing Russians to take on coal in French waters was breaching France's neutrality.

Paris was unpleasantly surprised, to say the least. It had hoped Rozhestvensky would be able to take on coal quietly before the world knew anything about it. In that case, Paris would have held the local governor responsible, and that would have been the end of it. Now things were becoming more complicated.

The governor went to the *Suvorov* and solemnly informed the admiral that he was withdrawing his permission to take on coal. Rozhestvensky emphatically objected. Wasn't France Russia's ally? he asked angrily. The Frenchman smiled and responded that, yes, it was indeed. He personally had nothing against Rozhestvensky. He was just following instructions from Paris. Rozhestvensky brightened up. "Then we understand each other. You obey your orders from Paris, and I shall carry out my instructions from St. Petersburg. I shall continue coaling until your coast batteries stop me." The governor replied mischievously, "Your Excellency surely knows that we have no coast batteries in Dakar!" Immediately after the guest left, Rozhestvensky ordered coaling to begin.

The work was frantic. Discrimination was put on hold; all had to participate. Officers worked shoulder to shoulder with crewmen. On the

Suvorov, even the priest joined in. To motivate his crews, Rozhestvensky promised prizes for the fastest ships. His battleship won all three. In one hour, she took 120 tons of coal, breaking all known records.

The work lasted for twenty-nine hours in suffocating heat. Those men unfortunate enough to be sent into the holds were working stark naked. Many fainted and had to be taken up to the deck and showered with water. In the scarce hours of rest, people slept "in the mixed juice of sweat and coal dust." All drinks became unpleasantly warm, thirst was terrible and impossible to quench. Ice cream served at the officers' mess was steaming. Lemonade bottles were consumed by the dozens. All that people could talk about was coal and coal alone. Faces were black with coal dust, and the air over the decks was hazy with it. Dust was everywhere—in beds, drawers, and wardrobes.

Several sailors died from heatstroke. One of them was Lieutenant Ivan Nelidov. Rozhestvensky had to personally report this death to the tsar by special cable; Nelidov was the son of the Russian ambassador to France. His mother had patronized the hospital ship *Orel* where he died. She had collected 120,000 rubles to equip the hospital ship for her son's journey. After the funeral mass, Nelidov's body was brought ashore, and a French steamer took it to Europe for his parents to bury.

Though built picturesquely on the oceanic shore and several small islands, Dakar did not strike the exhausted Russian sailors as a particularly beautiful place. Yet, the mixture of African and European cultures was fascinating. The European compound of Dakar, with its straight narrow streets and simple two-story houses with shadowy verandas, was pierced here and there by native huts. Most Russians had never seen Africans before and watched them with great curiosity.

The blacks went to the squadron in tiny narrow boats. There they performed a trick, familiar in the days of high colonialism. Sailors threw coins into the water, and blacks dived in to catch them. But the next day they tried to sell back the coins: *Kopeika* was useless in Dakar.

The Russians were impressed by the culture: people in white and colored tunics, naked children, everybody wearing amulets instead of crosses. Of course, the Russians mixed only with the local French, preferably officers. They noticed that there were no elderly Europeans in Dakar. They would spend just few years there and leave; Dakar was known for its yellow fever.

The Russians complained there was nothing to do in town. Out of boredom and curiosity, the *Suvorov*'s doctor picked up an unknown fruit and ate it. He was sick for the next several hours.

Two Japanese were spotted in town. Everybody believed they were spies. St. Petersburg informed the admiral that the Japanese were planning an ambush. Three Japanese cruisers were reported to be near Ceylon, allegedly carrying formidable torpedoes. The message concluded sinisterly, "It is believed that the Japanese know the place of our squadrons' rendezvous in the Indian Ocean."

Also of crucial importance was where they could next take on coal. The French government knew that Rozhestvensky intended to make a stopover in Libreville, the capital of another French colony, Gabon. Paris thought this embarrassing and proposed that Rozhestvensky go to Cape Lopez, a deserted roadstead a hundred miles south. Admiral Virenius, managing the Naval General Staff in Rozhestvensky's absence, questioned the French naval attaché, Captain de Saint-Pair:

"Is there a good anchorage at Cape Lopez?"

"First class. I'll show it to you. Give me a chart."

After twenty minutes' search, an officer reported to Virenius, "The Admiralty doesn't possess any charts of the African coast."

While the Russian Admiralty was combing its files for maps of Africa, King Edward VII still perceived a ghost of war between Britain and Russia. In a talk with the French ambassador to the Court of Saint James, the king blamed the Romanovs for the forthcoming disaster:

> There is a war-party there which is longing to pick a quarrel with us, by way of diversion after all the disasters in the Far East. The Grand Duke Alexis hates us; the Grand Duke Alexander is pressing for war. The Emperor is a man of peace, inspired by the best intentions, but he always takes the advice of the last person he's been speaking to.

The king kept repeating that a war between Britain and Russia "would be a cataclysm, a cataclysm." As he justly suspected, his other nephew, Kaiser Wilhelm, was stirring up trouble, sending incendiary letters to the tsar. Neither the tsar nor the kaiser knew that the Russian Minister of War, General Sakharov, terrified by the possible fruits of the kaiser's private diplomacy, was reporting the kaiser's messages to the French military attaché in St. Petersburg. As a result, being now fully aware of the kaiser's efforts, Paris was getting more and more anxious about the possibility of a Russo-German alliance and less and less inclined to sacrifice its friendship with London for the sake of St. Petersburg.

Amazingly enough, London still suspected that Russia was capable of launching a war against the British Empire. The Viceroy of India reported, "Influx of troops from European Russia has recommenced, 2,000 men having recently arrived at Krasnovodsk [a Russian port in the middle of nowhere on the Caspian Sea]." Any minor pro-Russian activity in Asia was now watched with caution. A British representative in Teheran warned, "Persian ambassador at Constantinople will shortly proceed to St. Petersburg to congratulate Emperor on birth of Tsesarevich."

Prime Minister Balfour succumbed to the paranoia, too. He wrote to the king that "in the event of Port Arthur falling" Rozhestvensky might "adopt some course hostile to British interests—for example, the occupation of a port in the Persian Gulf." The cabinet had decided, Balfour continued, that it was not desirable to send British troops to land in the Persian Gulf yet. Instead, it had decided "to have a superior force of battleships ready at Bombay, and to request the Russian Government to abstain from anything in the nature of a landing." The Cabinet was prepared "to withdraw our Ambassador from St. Petersburg," if necessary.

In the Orient, His Majesty's Navy was preparing to meet Rozhestvensky's squadron. Three top naval commanders of the Asian Pacific—the commanders-in-chief of the China, Australia, and East Indies stations—met in Singapore on the HMS *Glory*. "Under the present condition of affairs," the participating admirals gravely stated, "it is especially necessary to consider our being involved in a war with Russia and France, with Japan as our ally." Such a scenario was not news to them. As early as December 1903, almost a year earlier, a special letter from Admiralty had notified the commanders that war with Russia could become a reality. Now the admirals were preparing for action against France as well, planning "a successful attack" against their current ally. Even before hostilities started, they planned to watch French naval bases in Indochina and shadow their armored cruisers in the area.

London had other anxieties. Prime Minister Arthur Balfour informed the king that "a most embarrassing question of international law" had arisen: "British colliers are supplying the Russian fleet with the coal necessary to take them to the Far East." "Under the Law of Nations," Balfour wrote, "it is perfectly legitimate for the citizen of a neutral to supply, at his own risk, coal and munitions of war to a belligerent. It is *not* legitimate, however, under our own Foreign Enlistment Act." Balfour informed the king that "it was decided to write a letter for publication, explaining, as far as possible, how the matter stands."

The letter was not too persuasive. It warned British merchants that their profiteering may have possible negative consequences, but stated that "neutral traders may carry on trade even in contraband with belligerents subject to the risk of capture of their goods."

The government kept lists of all ships—British and foreign—supplying Rozhestvensky with coal. These lists provided information on owners, ships, cargo, and destinations. Destinations of colliers revealed the route of Rozhestvensky's squadron. British consuls around Africa were requested to report any information relevant to Russian coaling. When a British collier failed to report to a local British consul, the latter would take "measures to ensure that she should not be allowed to leave this port." After that, skippers usually agreed to collaborate. Meanwhile, consuls briefed not only the Foreign Office but the nearest naval command on the colliers' destinations.

The Japanese also had the names of vessels and companies supplying Rozhestvensky with coal and pressed London to prohibit British subjects from getting involved. Japanese knowledge was substantial: They knew each ship's location and the amount of coal she carried.

The Japanese were prodding their British allies for more significant help. They indicated they were "very greatly disappointed" that London had not insisted on Rozhestvensky's prolonged detention at Vigo. At the same time, official Tokyo never tired of thanking London for its "many courteous and friendly acts."

Marquess Ito Hirobumi, a former prime minister who had secured victory over China ten years earlier, came to dinner at the British legation, "speaking English better and better as the evening wore on." He said Japan neither wanted Manchuria nor was strong enough "to maintain large garrisons indefinitely on the remote borders of that province." Japan would respect the integrity of China, he said. "Manchuria would thus be restored to China." The railway built there by the Russians would be maintained internationally. It was unprofitable for any country, Ito continued, "to endeavour to go beyond those limits which appear to have been set by nature to its powers."

While Japanese diplomats kept trying to persuade Europe that it did not have to fear Japanese hegemony in continental Asia, Admiral Togo was preparing to meet Rozhestvensky's squadron. On November 8, Minister of Foreign Affairs Baron Komura Jutaro met with the British ambassador. "It had been found imperatively necessary," he said, "to dock and effect repairs to the vessels of the Japanese fleet, so that they might be in a fit state to cope with the numerically superior force" being brought against them. It had been decided, the foreign minister continued, "to make another general assault on Port Arthur," this time "quite regardless of loss of life, and to endeavour to capture a fort, or forts, which commanded the entire harbour, and from there either to destroy, or to drive out in a damaged condition, the Port Arthur squadron to be dealt with by Admiral Togo's ships outside." The emperor "had ordered that the fortress must be taken at any cost." The attack was scheduled for November 12.

By that time, Rozhestvensky was heading further south. He had departed from Dakar on November 3, having sent a coded cable to the tsar: "Left for Gabon." As if to emphasize the confusion of this ill-fated war, and to the extreme annoyance of the august addressee, the telegraph distorted "Gabon" into "Gabulen."

3

As the squadron was leaving the inhospitable Senegalese shore, a detailed report about its stay in Dakar was heading for London to be read by Lansdowne personally. The author of the report had done thorough spying. He had registered not only the death of Lieutenant "Jean de Nelidoff" (the French spelling of the Russian name indicated that the British scout had been using documents of the local colonial administration) but also a number of more political matters. He reported that the French governor had taken "no efficient measures" to prevent Rozhestvensky from coaling. As a result of this, the Russians had been able to take on tremendous amounts of coal. The scout enclosed figures for each warship—very important information, allowing the Admiralty to calculate how far Rozhestvensky would be able to travel. However, the British agents had been unable to get verifiable information about Rozhestvensky's next destination, for "great secrecy has been maintained on the subject." Basing his judgment on an overheard conversation between two supercargoes from German colliers, the author of the report suggested that Rozhestvensky had departed for Cameroon or some other German colony to the south of Dakar. He was wrong. Rozhestvensky was taking his fleet to yet another French settlement.

The rains started after they left Dakar. Beginning in the early hours of the morning, and lasting for three to five minutes, they were so ferocious that they broke tents on decks and soaked sailors sleeping underneath.

Morning brought heat, and heat brought itching rash. Fresh water was the only known cure, but it was available only from rain. Seawater made itching worse, yet many could not resist the temptation to get temporary relief from its coolness.

The heat lasted all day long. At lunch and dinner, thirsty officers drank everything they could: water, mineral water, white and red wine, beer, lemonade. Rozhestvensky suffered from heat more than others. After all, two weeks earlier he had turned fifty-six. The air temperature in his cabin was reaching 45 degrees Centigrade; 27 degrees was the best he could hope for, with the ventilator on and all portholes opened.

Around six o'clock, night came. The tropics do not have twilight. The sky blushes purple and scarlet for a few moments and then darkness falls. Each evening brought relief to the squadron.

Men, former peasants from the northern plains, had never seen so many stars. The nights were ablaze with them, and they were much brighter and bigger than in the north. Officers searched the sky for the magnificent constellation of the Southern Cross. Few had seen it except in astronomy textbooks.

At night the ocean was calm and motionless, almost mirror-like. "The monster slept and guarded its repose." Absolute silence was interrupted only by the sound of propellers. Each ship left a glowing wake; the ocean, still unpolluted, became phosphorescent with the passing ships.

Men and officers all slept on deck now. Their sleep was not peaceful. A new annoyance had manifested itself on the ships: rats. One of the beasts attacked the *Suvorov*'s senior officer every night, piercing its sharp teeth into his leg.

The weather suggested leisure, but the admiral was permitted none. The *Suvorov* nearly rammed the *Orel*, throwing the squadron's formation into disarray. The *Borodino* became handicapped and for thirty-six hours was unable to proceed faster than 7.5 knots. Eleven hours later, something went wrong with the *Malaya* transport, and the whole squadron had to stop and wait. Then the *Donskoi* reported sand in her Kingstone valves. This incidence presaged potential disaster; the ocean was much shallower than the map suggested. Ships immediately turned seaward.

The expected time of their arrival at Gabon had come and gone, but they were still on the high seas. Rozhestvensky demanded explanations. His navigators had to admit that they had failed to calculate their position correctly and now did not know where the mouth of the Gabon River was. Rozhestvensky showered them with well-deserved reproaches. Fuming with rage, he sent the steamer *Rus* to search for the Gabon.

The *Rus* did a good job. On November 13, the squadron reached its destination and anchored at the mouth of the Gabon River, three miles from shore, outside French territorial waters.

German steamers were there, and the admiral ordered coaling immediately. It was their first coaling in the open sea. He promised his crews a reward: visits to shore after the coaling was completed. The coal rush started once again.

The local French governor sent Rozhestvensky some fruits and vegetables and a request not to enter the mouth of the river. The capital, Libreville, was twenty miles upstream.

There were no cables waiting for Rozhestvensky in Gabon to inform him of developments at the front. Also, Gabon did not receive news service from telegraph agencies, and the French officers themselves knew nothing about what was going on in the world. When cables from St. Petersburg finally arrived, they did not improve Rozhestvensky's mood: the Admiralty recommended moving the squadron even further away from Libreville, for its present anchoring was too embarrassing for French allies. Rozhestvensky ignored the order.

News from the front was mixed. The Russian army in the Far East had been assigned a new commander, Alexei Kuropatkin, who was believed to be a good general, but no offensive had resulted, and a lingering lull fell over the whole of Manchuria. Port Arthur, to the contrary, was in the middle of a storm. So far, all Japanese attacks had been rebuffed, but the future looked gloomy.

Admiral Felkersam was heading for Djibouti in the Red Sea, and Captain Dobrotvorsky, bringing more cruisers and torpedo boats from the Baltic, was making for Tangier. But the news most shocking to Rozhestvensky was that the tsar was considering sending another force to the Far East—the 3rd Pacific Squadron.

The 3rd Pacific Squadron was the brainchild of Commander Nikolai Klado. Klado had been Rozhestvensky's chief of naval intelligence on the *Suvorov.* After the Dogger Bank incident, Rozhestvensky had sent him to St. Petersburg, together with three other officers, to testify before the international tribunal for Russia. However, the ambitious officer was not content to be a mere witness to history; he wanted to shape it. Using his strong court connection—he had been a tutor to two Romanovs, the tsar's brother Michael and his cousin Kyril (the lucky survivor of the *Petropavlovsk*)—Klado started advocating reinforcements for Rozhestvensky. He published impassioned articles, he cruised high society parlors, and he talked to the tsar.

Of course, Rozhestvensky did not mind reinforcements. If Russia had bought ships from Argentina and Chile, as the tsar had promised it would, Rozhestvensky would have willingly taken them. But what Klado was suggesting now looked incredibly silly: assembling all the leftovers of the Baltic Fleet, most of them old, poorly armed, and slow. These ships would be a burden rather than an asset. To wait for them at Madagascar meant wasting time. Rozhestvensky also understood that the tsar had broken his word, and he would never see the Argentine and Chilean cruisers promised earlier.

While the admiral was still digesting this unsettling information, he got another cable from St. Petersburg that made him absolutely furious. The British government was caustically warning him that there was a flotilla of British fishing boats in the Indian Ocean near Durban.

Rozhestvensky exploded with rage. "I beg you to ask the English government," he cabled the Admiralty, "to warn their African fishermen not to intrude into the squadron's route at night with their lights off, otherwise they will be sunk without any mercy." To make sure his message was heard by the British immediately, Rozhestvensky sent it uncoded.

St. Petersburg winked. Foreign Minister Lamsdorf, quietly cursing Rozhestvensky, did transfer the warning to the British but also asked the Admiralty to do something about the belligerent admiral. Lamsdorf's patience was exhausted, and from then on he was Rozhestvensky's bitter enemy.

Libreville, the capital of Gabon, which crews were finally allowed to visit, did little to improve the sailors' spirits. Fifty-five years after it was founded in 1849 by freed slaves, Libreville was still not much of a sight. Only a few hundred Europeans lived there. In the last two months, cannibals had eaten four.

Russian officers visited the local king. He was taking a nap, but the bored visitors insisted on an immediate audience. Still sleepy, the king proudly sported several wives and an old uniform of a British admiral. The dowager queen, pathetically drunk, begged for money. The senior and elderly lady-in-waiting, Margarita, did not wear any clothes at all.

This mock court became the favorite attraction of the Russians. The king shook hands and readily posed for pictures. Another entertainment for officers was visiting shops to buy rusty weapons and teeth of wild beasts.

The only thing Russians liked about Gabon was its lush vegetation. They called it a "botanic garden." Located on the edge of an immense tropical rain forest, it breathed with exuberant life. Huge majestic trees trimmed the shore. Each visit to the nearby plantations provided a tour of tropical miracles: pineapples, bananas, lemons, baobabs, mangoes, mimosas, and a myriad of other trees, flowers, and fruits unknown to Russians.

The wildlife also amazed them. One of the butterflies that reached the *Suvorov* was a foot wide. Sharks, tortoises, and pythons were abundant. Officers started buying pets. A local Jesuit priest sent Rozhestvensky a parrot. One can imagine the flood of unprintable remarks this gift caused; the commander-in-chief did not like pets or, for that matter, Jesuits.

The relaxed anchoring at Gabon brought a collapse in discipline. Younger officers were acquiring dangerous devil-may-care attitudes. The most outrageous case involved the cruiser *Donskoi* and the hospital ship *Orel*.

The *Orel* nurses were the greatest temptation for Rozhestvensky's men. He himself was infatuated with Natalia Sivers and courted her faithfully and not too discreetly. The *Donskoi* officers invited another nurse from the *Orel,* Miss Klemm, whom they had known in St. Petersburg. She was an amateur singer and promised to perform in the *Donskoi* wardroom. The *Donskoi* captain, Ivan Lebedev, readily granted permission; he was a great fun-lover himself. The officers enthusiastically headed for the *Orel* to fetch their silver-tongued prize. However, the party was destined for calamity.

Rozhestvensky had banned all communication between ships after five o'clock. Dinner with Miss Klemm was scheduled for six. But a solution was available that particular day: The *Donskoi* crew was loading coal on the *Orel,* so a boat traveling from the hospital ship to the cruiser after the curfew would not look suspicious to the vigilant admiral.

The dinner went very well. Miss Klemm was a huge success. Yet, in 1904 a woman could not possibly spend the night on a ship in the company of strangers. The *Donskoi* signaled to the *Suvorov,* asking for a permission to send a boat to the *Orel.* The *Suvorov* signaled back, "Not allowed." Then the *Donskoi* officers made a fatal mistake: They signaled again, asserting, falsely, that it was necessary to bring back some crew members still loading coal on the hospital ship.

Rozhestvensky immediately became suspicious and answered, "Do not send a boat under any circumstances." The *Donskoi* captain, a perfect gentleman, kept Rozhestvensky's response from the merry young woman. He sent a boat to the *Orel* at his own risk. Three intoxicated officers accompanied Miss Klemm.

The admiral gasped. His order had been disobeyed! After the boat safely delivered its precious cargo, Rozhestvensky ordered it to the *Suvorov.* Beside himself with rage, he kept the boat at the *Suvorov* stern for more than an hour. This was a traditional and very humiliating punishment in the Russian navy. But the three officers would not quiet down. Totally drunk, they kept making incoherent and noisy protests. Rozhestvensky summoned them to the bridge. The flow of obscenities he poured on them was extraordinary even for him. Next morning he sent them over to Libreville, to proceed to Russia on the first steamer—to be shamefully discharged from service for "disobedience." The debonair nurse, who had indeed behaved as if she had been on a country picnic, was punished, too. If she had forgotten, Rozhestvensky was commanding the squadron, he reminded her. The admiral banned her from visiting shore for three months.

The gallant captain of the *Donskoi* reported that it had been entirely his fault, but Rozhestvensky ignored his plea. When Lebedev came to the *Suvorov,* the admiral refused to see him.

4

From Libreville they headed farther south. The equator was barely forty miles away. The day of its crossing was always a holiday in the navy; since Peter the Great, Russians had held the tsar of the sea, Neptune, in high regard.

The *Suvorov* scheduled a feast for 9 A.M., November 19. Rozhestvensky, the captain, and all the officers stood on the bridges, men on the decks. Performers were half-naked and painted all imaginable colors: black, green, red, yellow, blue. The bearded Neptune carried a trident. His suite included devils, tritons, and Venus. As they marched toward a basin made of canvas, a hellish orchestra stepped in. When the introductory march was over, the devils pointed fire hoses at the crowd. Rozhestvensky was the first one to take the shower.

Those who were crossing the equator for the first time were thrown into the basin. Then even the veterans joined in—among them the captain and almost all the officers. They were shaved with a mock two-and-a-half-foot razor made of wood. The priest fell victim to this liberating pagan carnival, too.

The next day, November 20, Christianity took its revenge. The Christmas fast began. All ships had a mass, and the men and officers were dressed in white. Hymns sounded appropriately solemn. Rozhestvensky ordered the whole squadron to observe the fast. However, it was too much to force people to abstain from meat, as the strict rules of the church demanded, so the primary requirement was to attend mass.

The admiral hoped that this would discipline the crews. He expected to reach the shores of Japan in two months, by the end of January.

After the ships crossed the equator, the temperature started dropping to the comfortable mid-twenties. They were approaching the Great Fish Bay.

The spacious harbor they reached on November 23 looked good to the admiral. It was superb for anchoring, and hence for coaling. The German colliers were already there, and so was a single gunboat, the *Limpopo,* sent there by the Portuguese to assert their control over the otherwise unclaimed wild coast of Angola.

The *Limpopo* was under the command of 1st Lieutenant Silva Nogueira. Facing the awesome Russian armada, the lieutenant was unable to ask his superiors for instructions, as Great Fish Bay had no telegraph. The brave officer decided to protect Portugal's neutrality by his own means.

He reached the *Suvorov* and in a brisk manner, befitting his reckless conquistador ancestors, informed Rozhestvensky that there would be no loading of coal, food, or water and that the squadron would have to leave within twenty-four hours.

Rozhestvensky knew Portugal was leaning toward siding with Britain. He was also aware of one particular danger: The Portuguese could invite British warships from the adjoining Mossamedes in southern Angola. To the best of his knowledge, the *Barrosa* cruiser was lying there right now. As a result, his reply to the Portuguese captain was sardonic but calm: "We can only thank the Lord that He has made the entrance of the bay wider than six miles, and that between the two strips of Portuguese territorial waters, the neutrality of which is, of course, sacred to me, He has placed a narrow strip of sea, open and accessible to all."

The lieutenant, carried away with the feeling of self-importance, was silly enough to say that in that case he would be compelled to drive the Russian squadron from the Portuguese territorial waters by force, if necessary. With obvious pleasure, Rozhestvensky responded that "he would look forward to an attack from the river gunboat on the Russian fleet." The infuriated officer threatened to call for help from Mossamedes. Rozhestvensky shrugged his shoulders. As the gunboat was angrily steaming away, he ordered coaling to begin.

Great Fish Bay did not impress the sailors with its beauty. The settlement was tiny, some houses difficult to see even through binoculars. Sand spread in all directions. But captains of steamers were allowed ashore and reported that the beach was covered by beautiful shells and was full of pink flamingos.

Their stay was short. The next day, November 24, at 4 o'clock in the afternoon, the squadron departed.

Meanwhile, the British were shadowing their enemy cautiously but persistently. The HMS *Barrosa* was cruising West Africa's coast, dispatched there by the commander-in-chief of the Cape Station. It had visited Great Fish Bay two weeks earlier. On November 23, the day Rozhestvensky arrived, the *Barrosa* was further north, in Elephant Bay. Alerted there that Rozhestvensky had left Gabon heading south, the *Barrosa* captain steamed for Great Fish Bay again.

He reached it on November 25 and found only shells and flamingoes. He was informed that Rozhestvensky had left the previous day, after coaling. The British captain ordered immediate departure. He went to Mossamedes where he found the very angry *Limpopo* captain. The Portuguese officer gave his British colleague a rather heroic version of his encounter with the ferocious Mad Dog. The Portuguese believed Rozhestvensky was heading for a German port, Angra Pequena.

The captain of the *Barrosa,* apparently very excited, immediately shared this news with his commander-in-chief at the Cape. The calm telegraphic response sent him to the peaceful Walvis Bay instead. There was no need to pursue Rozhestvensky. He had no other option but to round the Cape. His Majesty's Navy could save on cables and coal.

5

The armada's journey was becoming monotonous: whales and waves. The *Malaya* had more mechanical problems, and the crews were getting accustomed to the absence of news from home and to the admiral's angry snarling.

A storm began, but bigger battleships like the *Suvorov* were hardly disturbed by it. The ships had crossed Tropic of Capricorn; it was becoming much cooler, and many developed colds. Albatrosses were fearlessly cruising the sky right over the ships' bridges. The Russians had never seen bigger birds.

Each ship had her own set of pets, usually dogs and parrots. The *Suvorov* dog was appropriately called Flagman. He had sneaked on the battleship in Kronshtadt on the same day as Rozhestvensky's staff. Loved by the crew, a regular guest at the officers' mess, Flagman also made himself useful as a rat-hunter. He hated rats passionately and could sit for several hours sniffing at a suspicious-looking hole.

The Southern Hemisphere was lavishly demonstrating its wonders. The sun moved in the wrong direction, the new moon looked like the old moon. On November 28, in a storm, the Russians saw Angra Pequena.

It was an old place with little history and no apparent future. Discovered and named by a famous Portuguese navigator, Bartholomeu Dias, back in 1487, it remained neglected until a Hamburg merchant, Franz Adolf Luderitz, persuaded Berlin to annex it. It became the first German settlement in Southwest Africa.

The Namib Desert diamonds would not be discovered for four more years, and in 1904 Angra Pequena struck the Russians as a "disgusting dump." For the sake of justice, it must be said that it was hardly a lovable place.

Its harbor was poorly protected from oceanic winds and waves, and the wind was terrifyingly strong that day. For several hours, Rozhestvensky could not dispatch a boat ashore. Not that the shore itself looked hospitable. Barren rocks and sand covered it. The settlement could not be seen from the roadstead, but it reportedly did not amount to much. Only ten Germans lived there.

Still, Angra Pequena happened to be the first friendly port since Tangier. Local Germans gladly assisted the Russians. There was no love lost between Germany and Britain.

The commander of the port, a German major, announced that he was not a diplomat, that nobody had officially informed him that the Russians were coming, that he could not see their ships from the windows of his house, and that he had no cruiser at his disposal and could not be expected to "patrol the coastline in a native dugout." Therefore, Rozhestvensky was free to do as he pleased.

Glad of this opportunity, Rozhestvensky ordered coaling, but on this occasion the weather was against him. The wind was so strong that it was virtually impossible to take coal directly from steamers; the *Suvorov* damaged her side attempting to approach one of them. As a result, the Russians used smaller boats as intermediaries—a slow, dangerous, and very work-intensive procedure.

On December 1, the commander of the port visited the *Suvorov*. Rozhestvensky gave him a royal reception. A lot of champagne was consumed during lunch. When the major was departing, the *Suvorov* band played the German national anthem and guns saluted him. The German was delighted and drunk. Probably, that day was the most memorable of his entire tenure at Angra Pequena.

The friendly German major reported a suspicious steamer in the local waters, cruising the sea at night and piercing the darkness with searchlights. The *Suvorov* officers suspected a Japanese scout or even worse, a saboteur.

He also informed Rozhestvensky that a flotilla of schooners had put in at Durban, a seaport located on the other side of the continent, on the Indian Ocean coast. German spies were saying that the British had built these schooners for the Japanese in Bombay. Allegedly, the schooners were equipped with torpedoes.

Rozhestvensky ordered utmost vigilance. At night searchlights scanned the horizon. The ocean was roaring and the wind howling. The port commander said such weather was typical for Angra Pequena.

A British newspaper brought by a steamer from Kaapstad (Cape Town) reported gross misfortune in Manchuria: Port Arthur had been bombarded by the Japanese from Vysokaya Hill. Another newspaper said Admiral Felkersam's ships had been attacked and damaged by the Japanese in the Red Sea.

The admiral was alarmed by the news—especially about Port Arthur. He summoned Commander Semenov, a veteran of the Port Arthur campaign.

"Vysokaya Hill?" the admiral asked in a strange voice, staring right into the officer's eyes. "What does this mean?"

"This means the end of the fortress or at least of the squadron. The roadstead and harbor are clearly visible from it."

The Japanese kept the promise they had made to the British three weeks earlier. They had captured a hill commanding the area and were now decimating the Russians. It became clear that Port Arthur would fall in a matter of weeks, if not days.

Rozhestvensky dispatched the hospital ship *Orel* to Kaapstad. For several weeks he had had no confidential reports from Manchuria, only newspaper reports and hearsay. Although private correspondence could wait until Madagascar, war plans could not. He suspected St. Petersburg was desperately trying to get in touch with him. He was right, but for a while he was unable to learn the most urgent message. It was stuck somewhere between the Admiralty and Southwest Africa.

6

After Angra Pequena, the squadron headed for Sainte-Marie, a small island off the northeastern coast of Madagascar, designated by Rozhestvensky as the meeting place for all his ships. A huge distance of about 2,500 miles separated it from Angra Pequena. Rozhestvensky suspected an uneasy journey, and he was right.

Ominous signs were plentiful. When the squadron was leaving Angra Pequena on December 4, a schooner was anchored suspiciously close to the Russian warships. The officers dispatched to inspect her were told she was carrying the British flag and had arrived to pick up guano. The next day, December 5, a steamer was spotted at the horizon. She did not come closer, but by the end of the day sped up and headed for Kaapstad.

December 6 was a special occasion: St. Nicholas' Day. St. Nicholas was the patron saint of the Russian navy. Not particularly religious but superstitious like most sailors, Rozhestvensky ordered a mass and a salvo, which sounded like the thunder of a naval battle.

Soon a real tempest came. It was an unusual storm for the sailors—huge swells, the ocean turbulent but with no wind. However, it was typical for the high seas between Antarctica and Africa. Its waves looked like mountain ranges. Some were forty feet high.

From their rolling ships, the Russians could see the shores of South Africa in the distance. They looked gloomy and unforested. Now the squadron was at the southernmost point of Africa, at the longest distance from St. Petersburg as a crow flies. They were also on St. Petersburg time again. Until then, they had been going further and further away from Japan, but now they started their approach toward the Pacific.

They were passing Kaapstad or Cape Town, the capital of South Africa and the base of their British foes. War had ended here only two years earlier, when the British finally defeated the Boers in 1902. Russia had been sympathetic to the Boers. Many still vividly remembered the British policies of scorched earth, barbed wire, concentration camps, and blockhouses. More than 20,000 Boer women and children had died in epidemic-ridden locked and fenced camps. Although bullets had silenced Boer commandos, South Africa still looked like an ominous place.

Rozhestvensky was waiting for an encounter with suspicious schooners. However, he was somewhat reassured because the storm was definitely hazardous for smaller vessels. When waves hit the *Suvorov*, they sounded like artillery guns. No schooner could attack in such weather.

On December 9 the worst of the tempest struck. It was so ferocious that the captains completely forgot about the Japanese. Bartholomeu Dias, the first European to round the cape in 1488, had appropriately named it the Cape of Storms. The misleading name of Cape of Good Hope was later assigned by King John II of Portugal, obsessed with the mind-boggling prospects of Asian commerce.

The *Suvorov* rolled from one side to the other, and her hull squealed as if begging for mercy. All portholes and doors were locked, but water kept pouring in. Inner decks were flooded, and water found its way into the engine. It was impossible to stay on deck especially at the stern. The waves were running at the *Suvorov* vertically, in terrifying walls. The battleship *Alexander III,* following the flagship, was an awful sight. The sea played with the huge ship like a toy. When she was diving, her deck looked almost vertical to the people on the *Suvorov.* At such moments, they could see her from bow to stern, as if they were flying in the air high above her. If the engine of the *Alexander* or any other ship collapsed, it would be a death warrant. It was unthinkable that another ship would be able to help. The steamer *Rus* sped up to escape the worst and disappeared from sight. Then the wretched *Malaya* stopped.

The squadron did not slow down but passed her by, leaving the ship to her fate. The last that the *Suvorov* saw, the *Malaya* was bravely putting up sails. Believing her to be lost, the warships proceeded east.

Storm or not, Rozhestvensky was not inclined to deviate from his routine. He invited officers to lunch in his quarters. While they were sitting down to a very formal meal, a huge wave covered the ship and flooded the deck, turning it into a pool. Crewmen had to be summoned, and the officers sat with their feet up in the air waiting for the mess to be cleaned up.

The storm stopped on December 10. The good news was that the tempest had carried the unit to Madagascar much faster than the ocean would have normally. The admiral started sending signals to the lost *Malaya,* but he received no response. Suddenly, the other regular troublemaker, the *Kamchatka,* started to lag behind. Her captain raised a signal: "Bad coal. Cannot keep up steam. Seek permission to throw 150 tons of coal overboard. Would be able to proceed then." Rozhestvensky answered: "Tell them that I allow only saboteurs to be thrown overboard."

Remarkably, the *Kamchatka* continued quite nicely. But that was not the end of her plight. On the night of December 12, she sent a report on her engine. The *Suvorov* signalman read it as, "Do you see the torpedo boat?" The officer on duty commanded an alarm before the misunderstanding was clarified.

Amid these troubles, large and small, Rozhestvensky had to think about the future. The admiral was anticipating problems in Madagascar. He was not sure Felkersam and Dobrotvorsky would make it. But even if they arrived safely, how was he expected to turn these three diverse units into a single military force? On December 12, still on the ocean, he wrote to his wife: "Where will I assemble this stupid pack? Untrained, how it can be useful, I have no idea."

After the storm, the *Suvorov* officers noticed that the admiral had suddenly aged. That was not remarkable, for he had spent the previous ten days on the bridge, taking only an occasional nap in a chair. But he recuperated quickly. He needed not rest, but stress.

On December 14, the *Suvorov's* boilers started leaking. The crew acted heroically, risking death in hot steam. Rozhestvensky ordered all the men on deck, praised them to heaven, and distributed awards from his own wallet. He looked younger again. The *Suvorov* doctor grinned. "This kind of person can get tired or sick only when he is off duty."

On December 16, Rozhestvensky's ships reached Sainte-Marie Island off the Madagascar coast. But the admiral was scanning the horizon in vain; Admiral Felkersam's ships were not there. The Japanese might have sunk them after all.

PART TWO

LINGERING

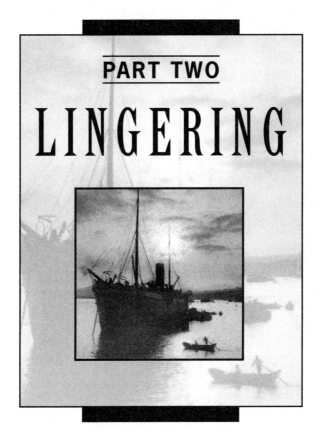

6

"The Yacht Squadron,"

OCTOBER 1904–JANUARY 1905, RED SEA

1

On November 1, the hostess of a fashionable St. Petersburg salon, Mrs. Bogdanovich, always abreast of the latest gossip, discussed the war with her guests. They agreed that Rozhestvensky would be unable to reach the Pacific before the beginning of March. They suspected that the strain of the journey would be too much for him and that he would become crippled by some illness—"How very terrible!"—and in that case the squadron would be led by "the impossible Felkersam who would ruin it."

On November 1, the "impossible" Admiral Felkersam was on Crete. Ten days earlier, in Tangier, Rozhestvensky had entrusted him with independent command and ordered him to bring five Russian warships to the rendezvous in Madagascar.

Dmitry Gustavovich Felkersam was far from being "impossible," but he was not an outstanding character either. He came from a more privileged background than most of his peers; the Felkersams were Baltic barons and were therefore entitled to an impressive "Von" preceding their family name. He had graduated from the Naval Academy in 1867 as the top student in his class. His path had crossed with Rozhestvensky's, first in school (Rozhestvensky was a year younger), then in 1895 in the Far East where they both commanded ships, and then in the Artillery Practice Unit. Felkersam had a good reputation among officers, but privates were not impressed with him. In their eyes, his appearance did not fit his rank. Felkersam was fat and walked in little quick steps, his face was puffy, his voice thin, almost "womanish," and when he got angry, stern words of command sounded rather comic when pronounced by his round mouth, "small like a thimble."

No matter what privates thought, Rozhestvensky liked and trusted Felkersam. To give him independent command in Tangier, he had bypassed Oskar Adolfovich Enkvist, a relative of the naval minister, thus asking for trouble. Yet he had done it.

Felkersam's ships left Tangier on October 21. His detachment consisted of two older battleships, the *Sisoi* and the *Navarin*, three cruisers, the *Svetlana*, the *Zhemchug*, and the *Almaz*, and several torpedo boats. His were the least reliable ships in the squadron. The *Navarin* belonged to an older generation of armored vessels. Built in 1895, it left the shipyard already outdated. The *Sisoi* was another aged veteran. The *Zhemchug* cruiser was fast and well armored, but the *Almaz* and the *Svetlana* were just armed yachts. Grand Duke Alexei had turned the *Svetlana* into a floating villa. After he gave her back to the navy, Rozhestvensky vindictively ordered the dismantling of her luxurious salons, but by and large she remained a grand ducal toy.

There was one serious problem with Felkersam. He was seriously ill, apparently with cancer, and suspected his condition was hopeless. He considered retiring, but instead decided to stick to his post; he did not want to seem cowardly. But now most of his energy was consumed by his struggle with illness. Felkersam was a very tolerant and kindhearted man by nature, and the combination of kindheartedness and sickness proved disastrous. Now he was tolerating almost everything—including excessive drinking by officers and crewmen alike.

His unit had to cross the whole of the Mediterranean Sea before it would reach the Suez Canal. Having passed by Gibraltar, controlled by British foes, the unit reached friendlier waters. Soon it was in the Greek archipelago, where Russian sailors always felt welcome. The Queen of Greece, Olga, passionately patronized the Russian navy. Another—though opportunistic—well-wisher, Kaiser Wilhelm, resided in his favorite haunt, the Achilleion castle, on nearby Corfu. There, on its spectacular marble terraces, amid blooming roses, antique statuary, and soothing springs, the kaiser sported suits of raw silk and dreamed of glory.

On October 28, Felkersam's detachment reached Soudha on Crete. Greek Soudha was a port hospitable to Russians. The Russian gunboat *Khrabry* was permanently stationed there. The town had a sad reminder of Russian involvement: The local cemetery contained the graves of two officers and twenty-six men who died after an artillery shell had exploded aboard the battleship *Sisoi* in the so-called "Cretan catastrophe" of 1897. The since-repaired *Sisoi* was now visiting again. This time she did not bring disaster—but she definitely brought trouble.

Felkersam's men, allowed ashore for the first time since Reval, were unleashed by the warm weather, the soft-spoken admiral, and the general sense of impending doom. They used their license in an unimaginative but nevertheless effective way. They got drunk and got into a horrendous fight with the locals.

The Reuters news agency reported the episode widely, insisting that intoxicated Russian hooligans had killed several locals. This resulted in another scandal; the Mad Dog's squadron was as dangerous on land as it was at sea!

Felkersam pleaded not guilty. In his report, hastily sent to St. Petersburg, he mentioned just "several fights in the vicinity of liquor stores and in certain special blocks of the town" (the euphemism for brothels). Also, there were some skirmishes with Italian soldiers. "One should be tolerant of the somewhat violent behavior of 600 sailors . . .

who haven't been ashore for more than two months," the Russian consul in Soudha wrote. In any case, this was not another Dogger Bank. Nobody attempted to detain the Russians in Crete.

From Soudha, Felkersam proceeded to the Suez Canal. This striking artificial waterway, providing a dramatic shortcut between the Atlantic and Indian oceans, was at that point barely thirty-five years old. It extended for one hundred miles; the Nile River delta lay to the west of it, with the arid Sinai Peninsula to the east.

Felkersam's primary concern was a possible Japanese attack in this tight bottleneck. Russian spies had been informing the Admiralty for several months that the Suez Canal and the Red Sea, in general, was a likely place for a Japanese ambush.

As early as April 1904, the Russian Police Department informed Rozhestvensky that an alarming spy report had arrived: The Japanese were aware of his intention to send at least some of his ships through the Red Sea with a stopover in French Djibouti. Russian naval leaders immediately included the area in their security planning.

After preliminary evaluation, it was acknowledged that Russia did not have a reliable spy network in the area. It had to be started from scratch.

Foreign Minister Lamsdorf discussed the situation with the tsar. Nicholas ordered the creation of a substantial secret network "quickly and energetically." Acting on the tsar's mandate, the Foreign Ministry sent several people to Egypt, some diplomats, some using false names and papers.

A retired French navy captain, Maurice Loir, was hired to do all the dirty work. He was to command agents in Alexandria, Port Said, Suez, Cairo, Ismailia, Djibouti, and Aden. He chartered several yachts for sea watch. Agents were dispatched to spy on Japanese visitors in various ports of the Middle East. Suspicious people were identified in advance, and at least on one occasion an agent was sent from as far as Cairo to Aden to board a ship carrying Japanese suspects. A Russian diplomat, Maximov, stationed in Cairo, was coordinating the whole operation, which was estimated to cost 500,000 francs. All details were reported to Rozhestvensky directly.

However, after the Dogger Bank incident, the foreign minister, caustic and cautious Lamsdorf, had lost faith in spies. He had been appalled by that disaster, which, at least partially, had been the result of spies' imaginations and alarmism. Instead of applying cloak and dagger methods, he decided to talk openly to the British ambassador in St. Petersburg. On October 28, two weeks before Felkersam's expected arrival at Port Said, Ambassador Hardinge promised Lamsdorf that the British would guard Felkersam's detachment themselves to prevent another Dogger Bank–type debacle. Egyptian police, the ambassador said, would be cruising the harbor around the clock, preventing any vessel from approaching Felkersam's ships. Both sides of the Suez Canal itself would be heavily patrolled as well.

Meanwhile, Japanese spies were monitoring the Russian ships' movements. They knew that Rozhestvensky and Felkersam were to meet at Madagascar. They were relieved to know that the squadron carried no submarines but were concerned that it was equipped with wireless telegraph and anti-mine sweeping nets. Whether to ambush or spy on Felkersam, Japanese agents would be waiting for him in the Red Sea.

And, of course, British eyes and ears were surveying the field. British agents had no doubt about what kind of operation the Russians were staging in the Red Sea. One of the people they shadowed most closely was Maurice Loir. They followed the movements of the yachts chartered by the French mercenary, including the one reserved for himself, the *Fiorentina II*. Loir was an easy target. Each time the *Fiorentina II* unexpectedly returned to port and Loir informed the port authorities that "the sea was too rough for the ladies" on board, the British scouts, chuckling, checked with the post office to find out the length of the cable he had sent to St. Petersburg that day. They disdainfully called Loir's fleet the "Yacht Squadron."

Felkersam's ships reached Port Said early in the morning of November 11. The admiral had every reason to be grateful to the British. The day before, the harbor had been cleaned of fishermen's boats and other small vessels. All merchant and postal steamers had been ordered to leave Port Said "by a somewhat harsh letter of the Canal's administration."

By the early hours of November 11, "normally so animated and full of various voices and sounds, Port Said's harbor became empty and quiet."

In the first rays of the rising sun, Felkersam's ships started entering the harbor. They moved in smoothly and steadily, as if "at well-rehearsed maneuvers."

Felkersam had his flag on the *Sisoi*. Maximov, the chief of the Russian security net, immediately went aboard the battleship. It was decided that the detachment would get 1.5 million rubles in golden coin then and there and 5,700 tons of fresh water.

There were several cables from the Admiralty waiting for Felkersam in Port Said. They sounded most disturbing. One warned that thirty-seven Japanese privates and three officers had passed through Singapore heading west. Another informed that three hundred Japanese were already living in the suburbs of Colombo on Ceylon, using the island as a base for spying and sabotage. More had been dispatched from Japan to Shanghai and Hong Kong and possibly further on. Many Japanese were disguised as Chinese. Could they be planning to man ships in the Indian Ocean to attack Russians there or even in the Red Sea? Felkersam was instructed to brief Rozhestvensky on all this. But no matter what the Admiralty was saying, Port Said looked safe to the Russian admiral.

Felkersam felt relieved and grateful to the local hosts. That night he even gave a small dinner aboard the *Sisoi* for Russian ladies living in Cairo. He also sent a request to the Admiralty to watch the port of Trinkomali in Ceylon very closely. He regarded it as a likely Japanese base for attacking his detachment in the Indian Ocean.

The next morning, the ships weighed anchor and, one by one, started entering the Suez Canal. Crowds assembled on the embankment to gawk at the Russian argonauts. Diplomats representing France, Italy, Austria, and other powers attended. The *Navarin* orchestra played the "Marseillaise" to thank the French. The British, although behaving very helpfully, did not hear "Rule Britannia."

The detachment spent the night at the Bitter Lakes in the southern part of the canal and on Saturday reached Suez—an ancient port used for centuries for the spice trade and for pilgrimages to Mecca. There they met their watchdog, the British *Hermione*. Felkersam's *Sisoi* and the *Hermione* exchanged greeting salvos—thirteen guns. At Felkersam's request, official calls were waived; he did not have enough time, intending to spend just fifteen hours in Suez. The next day, he proceeded to Djibouti.

The *Hermione* captain duly reported to the high command all details of the encounter. Now the watch was being transferred to the East Indies Station.

Many perceived the Red Sea to be the most dangerous leg of Felkersam's journey. Commander Klado, making loud predictions in St. Petersburg, insisted that it would be "in the narrow Red Sea, with its desert shores over which no supervision is possible, that our enemies will be able, without hindrance, to carry out their reckless plans."

But Felkersam reached Djibouti safely. Even if Japanese saboteurs were hiding in the deserts of Arabia, they did not attack.

No Japanese attack occurred in Djibouti either. Instead, Felkersam encountered a diplomatic ambush. At about the same time, Rozhestvensky was facing the same problem in Africa: The French were unwilling to host the squadron. But Felkersam had no idea where Rozhestvensky was or what he was up to. He had to make his own decisions. The Admiralty cabled him at Djibouti saying that Japan was "energetically protesting" against France violating its neutrality by allowing Russians to take on coal in its ports. Now Paris was asking Felkersam to leave Djibouti immediately and move to some other place—for instance, "to the very convenient" Merbal Bay in Arabia, between Aden and Masqat.

Felkersam curtly replied: "The administration of Djibouti has not objected to coaling yet. The colliers haven't arrived; hurry them up." But more trouble lay ahead.

On November 21, Admiral Virenius at the Naval General Staff reported that Paris, intimidated by Japan, was refusing to host the Russian squadron at Diégo-Suarez, suggesting instead the small island of Nosy Be or some other inconspicuous place in Madagascar. Virenius stressed that he had sent the same message to Rozhestvensky at Libreville on November 17, but the admiral had failed to respond. Now he was asking Felkersam to decide.

Felkersam protested emphatically:

In order to let the squadron's ships meet, I have to reach the spacious, healthy, quiet, well-described Diégo-Suarez Bay which has been selected for this purpose. Cannot find another bay of the same qualities. Nosy-Be possesses some essential qualities but the way to it is insufficiently described and therefore doubtful. By ruining the existing plan I can put the commander of the squadron in a dangerous position. This is why I am punctually following the instruction to wait for him at Diégo-Suarez. I think, as in Djibouti, it will be rather possible to get the silent consent of the French government and I am asking for your energetic assistance in getting such.

In spite of Felkersam's sound reasoning, St. Petersburg panicked. The admiral was ordered to skip the meeting place at Diégo-Suarez and proceed to Nosy Be directly.

Felkersam exploded with indignation: "I am being ordered to take my detachment by a route which is known to be dangerous and to ignore my nearest commander's order in war time." He repeated his argument that Nosy Be was hardly known to sailors and that bigger ships had never visited it.

Virenius was a seasoned bureaucrat. He understood that Felkersam was on the verge of disobeying and hastily rallied top support for the Nosy Be option. Naval Minister Avelan cabled Felkersam: "Nosy Be's spacious bay is a splendid place for the whole squadron's anchoring; it is sheltered from hurricanes, which last there from January to May."

But Felkersam was still stubbornly protesting, so on November 27, Avelan sent cable number 5305 to Djibouti: "HIS IMPERIAL HIGH-NESS, General-Admiral, ordered you not to call on Diégo-Suarez and proceed to Nosy Be directly."

Felkersam responded: "Orders given by cable number 5305 will be obeyed with a heavy heart. . . . The occurring change of the meeting place makes chances for the expedition's success slimmer."

Meanwhile, spies reported that two Japanese cruisers were positioned at the Mozambique Channel. Madagascar itself was infiltrated by Japanese agents, two of them stationed in Mahajanga.

The island of Nosy Be was located in the Mozambique Channel, and the town of Mahajanga was just 180 miles southwest. That sounded like a warning call to Felkersam.

Yet, all premonitions and fears proved hollow. On December 15, Admiral Felkersam safely brought his ships to Nosy Be in Madagascar.

2

Captain Dobrotvorsky's detachment left Libava on November 3, when Felkersam was plowing the Mediterranean and Rozhestvensky was taking on coal in Tangier. It comprised ten ships: two new armored cruisers, the *Oleg* and the *Izumrud*, two auxiliary cruisers, the *Rion* and the *Dnieper*, five torpedo boats, and the training ship *Ocean*. Like many of the captains, Leonid Dobrotvorsky was an old acquaintance of Rozhestvensky. In 1904 he was forty-eight. Entrepreneurial, stubborn, and opinionated, he had asked for unusual assignments and expected early promotions. Back in 1893 he went to England to prepare ships for a scientific venture in Siberia and then commanded the expedition itself—on the Yenisei River, a northern giant that streams into the Arctic Ocean. He received his first independent command in 1901; the two ships he had commanded were the gunboat *Gilyak* and the old cruiser *Donskoi*, the latter now rounding Africa with Rozhestvensky.

Dobrotvorsky was immensely ambitious. He thought he was better fit for top command than any of the admirals he knew. Now he was heading for a breakthrough in his career. The independent command entrusted to him hinted at the possibility of receiving admiral's epaulettes pretty soon.

However, by the time he departed from Libava, his mission was looking problematic. News from Manchuria was disturbing; Port Arthur was nearing its fall, Rozhestvensky's squadron had become involved in the infamous Dogger Bank incident, and at the time of Dobrotvorsky's departure, it was struggling for coal and shelter at the periphery of Europe.

As a result of all this, the mood of the crew was highly polarized. On the one hand, many of the sailors were roaring patriots. One nearsighted young mechanic, recently drafted into the navy, had bought a revolver and was now carrying it at all times in case he needed it for "active participation in battle." Others, on the other hand, had descended into apathy, fatalism, and indulgence. A medical attendant on the *Izumrud* became a drug addict, pumping himself with stolen morphine. He nearly died from an overdose on a day the unit had anchored on the Danish coast and a Japanese torpedo attack was expected.

Just like Rozhestvensky a month before, Dobrotvorsky was getting alarming reports from Russian spies. A mysterious submarine had been spotted at Skagen. Denmark allegedly still swarmed with Japanese agents. Dobrotvorsky ordered his crews to watch out for torpedoes. Just 300 miles away from Russian shores, men slept at artillery guns with their clothes on, unsure "where they would wake up"—in heaven, in icy water, or still aboard their warship.

The place off which they anchored was called Frederikshavn. A dense fog raised its veil for a while to let the Russians peep at the tiny quiet town and then descended again. The Russian consul informed Dobrotvorsky that the Danes were asking him to leave immediately. Their friendliness toward Russia had evaporated. The small nation was now afraid of getting dragged into a larger European conflict.

But Dobrotvorsky ignored the plea; he had to take on coal first. At the end of the day, a Danish torpedo boat approached the detachment. Her captain used a loudspeaker for a severe warning. He asked the Russians to leave the neutral country's shores immediately.

Dobrotvorsky didn't react. The torpedo boat left and then returned. Her captain announced, "After the third warning, I am ordered to have you arrested."

Grudgingly, Dobrotvorsky stopped coaling. The detachment had to leave without even taking on fresh water. The Danes also attempted to prevent Dobrotvorsky from sending any mail ashore, but the captain of one of the private foreign transports accompanying the detachment, the French *Mimi,* unabashed, quipped, "*Pst, c'est pour les enfants,*" and volunteered to carry the mail to Danish terrain.

The morning of November 11 saw the detachment already in the North Sea. The sea was rough and the ships rocked. Officers were wet, unhappy, and cold; they had spent the night on the bridge watching for a possible Japanese attack. The heat system was turned off; Dobrotvorsky had ordered energy conservation measures.

The next day, the storm calmed down. The detachment was passing Dogger Bank. Quite a few fishermen's boats were around. They did not demonstrate any fear, crossing the path of the Russian men-of-war freely without raising any signals.

Meanwhile, the shortage of fresh water was becoming a big problem. It was risky to try reaching Tangier with their limited resources; the journey would take at least eight days. Dobrotvorsky had to decide which port to call on—French Le Havre or British Dover. His choice was an unexpected one: Dover. Enemies, he thought, might be more understanding than false allies. On the evening of November 13, the detachment anchored two and a half miles away from the English shore.

The night was foggy. Still, sailors could see the dim lights of the Dover promenade and numerous careless boats. One steamer nearly rammed the *Izumrud.* It was a huge oceanic liner, ablaze with lights.

The frightened passengers were gawking at the angry Russians from the peaceful decks. Yet, nobody prevented the detachment from taking on water. As soon as they were done, the ships left the unfriendly coast.

The journey from the English Channel to Tangier was largely uneventful. In Tangier, Dobrotvorsky's officers had a chance to visit the shore. Arabs, Bedouins, and Sudanese filled the maze of medieval alleys. Many of them were barefoot and armed with antique rifles. Tangier was noisy, full of the loud curses of horsemen and the pestering whispers of pimps, inviting officers to visit underground dens. The women of Tangier were reputed to be extremely beautiful and willing to dance naked, but it was believed to be unsafe for Europeans to walk around at night.

A British torpedo boat paid a visit, "sniffed around" like a hound, and departed. The next morning, November 23, Dobrotvorsky left Tangier. Having passed by the Trafalgar battle site, the detachment entered the Strait of Gibraltar.

The Rock of Gibraltar to the north was like a fortress. In the harbor beneath, British naval ships anchored, six gigantic battleships among them. The Russians felt envious and depressed. A bit further on, the detachment came across a British battleship under a vice admiral's flag. She was conducting gun practice but was polite enough to fire a thirteen-salvo salute.

Soon, the *Izumrud* had to stop; there was a leak in the boilers. Her commander asked Dobrotvorsky for permission to go to Malaga for repairs. Dobrotvorsky tiredly signaled back, "Go wherever you want." In several moments he added, "Buy some wine for us."

The last signal was barely visible on the horizon. The *Izumrud*, much relieved, headed for Malaga; the weary but determined *Oleg* went on to Crete.

The two ships finally reunited at Soudha. Unexpectedly, the envy that the *Oleg* officers felt toward their lucky *Izumrud* brethren was somewhat compensated. Having indeed enjoyed Spanish wine, meals, grapes, fireworks, and *señoritas* ("beautiful," but "eat too much garlic"), the *Izumrud* crew had a most unpleasant journey from Malaga to Crete. They encountered a storm so fierce that it was impossible to sleep; the rocking ship pitched sailors from their bunks like kittens. It was also impossible to cook meals. Soup, for example, would flood the stove, so for five sleepless days and nights the crew had to fast, loathing their bad luck and paying no attention to the scenic views of the Messina Strait and charming islands of the Greek archipelago.

In Soudha they could finally rest; its bay was protected from wind by high mountains. However, November was a bad month for a visit. It was too hot during the day, too foggy, damp, and cold at night. Of course, there was a British ship in the harbor, the *Merlin,* who kept cabling news about Dobrotvorsky's ships to the commander-in-chief in the Mediterranean.

There was no mail waiting for the crewmen. Only those officers who had violated the vow of secrecy and told their families the itinerary now boasted letters from home. Dobrotvorsky angrily cabled the Naval General Staff: "Officers who have broken the law got their mail, others did not. Am asking for justice."

Of course, he knew he would not get any from St. Petersburg. His paramount concern was to leave the place as soon as possible and to move on toward Madagascar. The last thing in the world Dobrotvorsky wanted to be reproached for was keeping the rest of the 2nd Pacific Squadron waiting. But his unit was unable to move: The *Izumrud* kept having problems with her engines, and the torpedo boats had reported a number of breakdowns, too. The officers could curse the Nevsky shipyard as much as they wanted (Rozhestvensky had done so publicly in St. Petersburg last summer), but now they had to rely on the skill of their own mechanics.

The European press had made Dobrotvorsky's unit a target of sarcastic comments. St. Petersburg kept bombarding Dobrotvorsky with angry cables, demanding to know when he would finally leave Soudha. To make the situation worse, now the *Oleg* too developed engine problems. In order to have several pipes repaired, they had to be shipped to Athens. In addition, three out of the five torpedo boats had to be sent back to Russia because it was impossible to fix them. One of them, the *Prozorlivy*, had already been discarded previously by Rozhestvensky and had been sent back home from Denmark. Now the wretched ship had to repeat the humiliating journey. The British watched with glee while she crawled through the Danish straits with a damaged propeller.

Discouraged officers openly expressed their doubts about the eventual success of the whole enterprise. Everybody was sullen and gloomy. Quarrels were easily sparked. People had the feeling that they already "had spent three years together."

Instead of the planned fourteen days, the detachment had spent twenty-eight days in Soudha. By Eastern Orthodox Christmas, the repairs were finally finished, and on Christmas Day officers entertained their men. A fir tree was decorated with electric lamps. Cotton from the ship's pharmacy represented the snows of Mother Russia. In a gift drawing, the crewmen received small gifts like socks, wallets, soap, and pencils. Each was presented with some oranges, nuts, tangerines, apples, and Turkish sweets. The best were given money awards. The next day, December 26, the detachment finally left Crete.

In two days, they reached Port Said. The ships spent just eighteen hours there. The Egyptian police in small boats were zealously guarding the Russian ships from potential spies and saboteurs. Dobrotvorsky was informed that a Japanese naval unit had passed the Strait of Malacca long ago and was now hiding somewhere, perhaps preparing to attack his ships.

The police continued to guard the detachment while it was traveling through the canal and anchoring at Suez. Here they took on more coal and got more news about the Japanese: it was reported that they had been spotted in the Chagos Islands in the center of Indian Ocean, halfway between Malacca and Djibouti. Like Felkersam four weeks earlier, Dobrotvorsky suspected an ambush was possible in the Gulf of Aden.

When they reached Djibouti, it struck them as a dump. The tiny town lay on an ugly flat peninsula. Mountains were visible in the distance. Djibouti's harbor was vast and fairly well protected from wind, but the entrance to it was perilous. In the close vicinity lay a huge and shallow coral reef.

The town had just a handful of decent wooden houses belonging to the French. The miserable huts of the locals appalled the Russians. The *Hotel des Arcades* served oysters, but the very first feast, predictably enough, ended in mass food poisoning. The only place of interest was the widely advertised botanical gardens three miles away from the town. All the trees there were young and doing poorly under the tropical sun.

The mountains lay not far from town. Lions and leopards dwelled there. At nighttime lions would come very close to Djibouti, terrifying people with their roaring. The land between the town and the mountains consisted of sand and prickly shrubs; camels fed on scarce plants, and vultures looked for prey. Abyssinian soldiers with luxurious curly hair crossed the wastelands armed with leather shields and lances.

The Russians were stuck in Djibouti. The ships could not proceed any further without repairs. Dobrotvorsky decided to use the occasion to hunt for some war contraband. He dispatched the *Rion* cruiser to sea, but she did not catch anybody. While the *Rion* was hunting, the other ships did some artillery practice, but not much; there were not enough gun shells.

By and large, it was an idle existence. The Russians killed time by observing tropical wildlife. The jellyfish were huge and multicolored. Enormous sharks cruised the waters. Their silvery shadows were always there, watching out for random Russian swimmers. Sharks reacted to the immovable Russian ships with ease and familiarity, like dead tree trunks. The Russians were saying some sharks were "as fat as cows" and kept asking themselves whether one day they might confront them in the water. Sharks were their obsession, but the Red Sea also had other, less conspicuous monsters. People who had had the misfortune of touching the spikes of a colorful but poisonous fish spent the next several hours groaning with pain.

When the wind made ripples in the water and the sailors could not watch the fish any longer, they switched to native children. They would come to the Russian ships in narrow boats and beg for coins, which they would then catch in the water. They were also looking for open portholes from which to snatch something valuable. Each boy had a leather bracelet. It was an amulet against sharks containing a sentence from the Koran. Sailors were fascinated by the fact that the sharks never attacked the native inhabitants.

Russian doctors were busy healing bites, boils, and rashes. But the most common problem was burns—not from the tropical sun, but from repairing the ship's engines. Boredom and the feeling of doom forced many to start looking for artificial stimulants, and the doctors had to lock all narcotics in their cabins. The sailors had begun stealing drugs like ether.

Quarrels flared all over the detachment. Everybody loathed the Nevsky shipyard and complained about the prolonged stay. An epidemic of dysentery could start at any moment, and the doctors began adding red wine into the drinking water. Officers drank wine instead of water. In despair, they longed to leave Djibouti as quickly as possible.

Dobrotvorsky proved to be a bad leader. He was not soft enough to allow his crews to find solace in wine and prostitutes like Felkersam, and he was not strong enough to keep them constantly busy like Rozhestvensky. The morale of his men plummeted. They were eager to "get into the iron hands" of Admiral Rozhestvensky, the sooner the better. But they didn't leave the loathsome place until late January.

The last preparations for the journey were frantic. Crews were pumping fresh water even at night. A full moon lit the decks. Men were quietly stealing water through holes in the hoses. In the sea, they could see sharks' noses, ghastly in the moonlight, looking like they were waiting for them.

Having rounded Cape Guardafui, at the entry to the Indian Ocean, the detachment spotted two steamers. When they realized they had been spotted, they quickly disappeared in the direction of Socotra

Island, barely eighty miles away. Japanese warships could easily be hiding at that desolate piece of rock.

But if they were there, they did not strike. Vigilant but undisturbed, the Russians anchored at the nearby Ras Hafun Bay. It was empty, its hills low, its sands yellow and barren. The local tribe send a delegation in a boat, but the Russians had no way of understanding what these people decorated with birds' feathers wanted to communicate.

When several days later the detachment crossed the equator, morale was so low that they decided to skip the usual ceremony. Dobrotvorsky did not insist. The independent command was too much for him. The commander had sunken into apathy. The superstitious were now saying that angry Neptune would have his revenge.

On the night of January 28, the detachment reached Dar es Salaam. The torpedo boats were flaring the way for the cruisers with their powerful searchlights; the bay was full of reefs. In the morning they saw a most pleasing picture. Instead of barren sands or rocks, the shore was covered with luxurious tropical rain forest. Smaller islands, also covered with forest, were scattered about.

The mouth of the river lay a bit further on. The torpedo boat *Grozny* took a group of officers into a big cove where German ships were anchored. The kaiser's son was a new lieutenant on one of them, the *Gerta*. The Russians arrived in time for participating in festivities; the colony was welcoming the prince. The local police held a parade, the orchestra played merry marches, and the wives of German officers and officials sported their best dresses.

But the Russians did not like the feast. Their faces turned sullen, and they wandered purposelessly about town, entering various shops but never buying anything. Those officers who had decided to spend the night in the hotel were bitterly disappointed; all rooms had been already taken and they had to sleep on the veranda. Actually, they did not sleep at all; the accompaniment of buzzing mosquitoes, the curses of their comrades on the street, and the loud noise made by the Germans singing "Wacht am Rhein" kept them awake.

Soon afterward, the detachment left Dar es Salaam. Early in the morning of February 1, they established wireless contact with Admiral Rozhestvensky into whose "iron hands" they had been so eager to get.

At ten o'clock the same day, they saw smoke on the horizon. It was the 2nd Pacific Squadron practicing at sea.

7

"Nossibeisk,"

DECEMBER 16, 1904—MARCH 3, 1905, MADAGASCAR

1

ON DECEMBER 16, ROZHESTVENSKY'S SQUADRON ANCHORED AT the islet of Sainte-Marie. The roadstead was open to all winds. Madagascar, the fourth largest island in the world, lay only ten miles away. The next day, Rozhestvensky sent the *Rus* to the town of Tamatave, eighty miles south, to dispatch a number of urgent cables. He hadn't been in touch with St. Petersburg for several weeks. One of the cables was addressed to the tsar. As usual in his communications with the sovereign, Rozhestvensky was laconic: "Arrived Sainte-Marie Madagascar."

While the *Rus* was still in Tamatave, another messenger, the hospital ship *Orel*, ordered to Kaapstad from Angra Pequena, brought Rozhestvensky a piece of expected but nevertheless terrible news: The 1st Pacific Squadron had been totally annihilated by the Japanese at Port Arthur, and worse, Port Arthur itself had fallen.

The ship also delivered British newspapers with the unsettling allegation that Russia was on the verge of political revolution. Other reports insisted that a Japanese squadron, consisting of eight armored cruisers and twelve torpedo boats, had already passed Ceylon, heading straight for Madagascar to send the 2nd Pacific Squadron to the bottom of the Indian Ocean. According to rumors, some Japanese cruisers had already reached the island and were now hiding in a secluded bay.

The fall of Port Arthur had been long anticipated. Its garrison had become smaller and smaller, less and less able to keep up the defense. On November 30, the commander of the fortress, General Stessel, reported that the Japanese, having captured Vysokaya Hill, were massacring Russians at Port Arthur with artillery fire. Still unwilling to surrender, the general concluded, "The spirit of my marvelous troops is bold, waiting for help. Have no news from the army."

Having received the cable, the tsar wrote to his uncle, Grand Duke Alexei, "I think we should tell Rozhestvensky that he should not count on the 1st Squadron any longer."

By mid-December communications with the besieged fortress had all but stopped. It was taking Stessel's messages four days to reach the Winter Palace. All cables, even those addressed to the emperor, had to be taken from Port Arthur to Chefoo by smugglers' junks. On December 16, Stessel sent a desperate report to the sovereign: "Will be able to hold just for a few more days. Have almost no artillery shells. Will take measures to prevent slaughter on the streets. Scurvy is ruining the garrison; I have just 10,000 men capable of carrying rifles and all of them are sick."

The tsar did not receive the cable until December 20. On that day, it was already too late to think about artillery shells or scurvy. Another cable, from the Russian consul at Chefoo, Tideman, announced: "The torpedo boats *Vlastny, Serdity,* and *Skory* have arrived and informed that today Arthur is expected to capitulate." Later in the day, at 9:10 P.M., Stessel cabled the tsar in English: "Today forced to sign capitulation about surrender Port Arthur. Officers civil. Officers allowed to wear arms and return Russia under obligation not to take part present war, if not remain war prisoners. I apply to YOUR IMPERIAL MAJESTY for asked obligation."

The cable reached Nicholas aboard a train on the night of the twenty-first. He described the news as "shocking." "It is hard and painful," the tsar commented in his diary. Still, he suppressed his emotions and kept joking with his staff that night. His reserve was misinterpreted by many as outrageous "indifference."

The French Foreign Ministry got the news about the fall of Port Arthur earlier than the tsar did—at 5 P.M. on December 20. Now after the "Gibraltar of the Far East" had fallen, "What about Rozhestvensky's squadron?" Foreign Minister Delcasse asked his collaborators in dismay. "Will it be able to continue its voyage? Wouldn't it be better to turn back and retire to the Baltic again? . . . In any case, we can't let it stay at Madagascar any longer; I can't consent to its doing so; in future we shall be running the risk of an ultimatum from Japan at any moment."

Kaiser Wilhelm, warmongering as usual, telegraphed the tsar: "The defense of Port Arthur will remain forever an example to soldiers of all nations. The hero who commanded your devoted troops [General Stessel] is admired by all mankind, especially by my army and me." Although Paris hoped Rozhestvensky would turn back, the kaiser wanted him to continue.

Of course, Rozhestvensky was not shocked by Port Arthur's fate. He had expected that it would fall and had even said so to the tsar before leaving Russia. In Angra Pequena, he had made inquiries about the significance of Vysokaya Hill and learned that when it had been lost, the fortress was doomed. What made him furious was not the fall of Port Arthur but St. Petersburg's decision to ban him from anchoring at Diégo-Suarez.

Whatever restraints Paris might have had, it was bound to Russia by a formal alliance. And now there he was at Madagascar—controlled by the French since 1895 and settled by them since the time of Cardinal Richelieu—unable to enter a decent port.

He decided to give the Admiralty as good a thrashing as he could: "The order to Felkersam to proceed to the dangerous Nosy Be has ruined the whole plan, which until recently had been meticulously implemented. Am asking you to send Felkersam to Diégo-Suarez immediately."

Of course, it was nobody's fault that he hadn't been informed earlier. The Admiralty had repeatedly tried to reach him, first by cabling

on November 17 to Libreville, then on November 27 and 30 and December 7 to other destinations. Still, he felt betrayed.

To add to his bad mood, the news from Felkersam's detachment,
now anchored at Nosy Be, was disheartening. Practically all of the
ships had had to start repairs of "their old limbs."

But the worst piece of news was that Commander Klado's view
had prevailed. Rozhestvensky was informed that "the 3rd Squadron is
being quickly equipped. The first unit comprises the *Emperor Nicholas
I,* the *Senyavin,* the *Ushakov,* the *Monomakh,* and the cruiser *Rus.* Will
leave between January 15–20 and around February 20–25 should be in
Djibouti bearing the flag of Nebogatov. . . . The second unit . . . is
preparing to depart at the beginning of May." The admiral was to wait
for the reinforcements in Madagascar.

Rozhestvensky was beyond himself with rage. The third squadron?
Consisting of worthless old and slow ships, which he had emphatically
rejected last summer? Under the command of the featureless Nebogatov? Why not some other admiral, whom the navy respected, like
Chukhnin? One more unit departing at the beginning of May, practically in five months?

Rozhestvensky didn't know that the decision to send the 3rd Pacific
Squadron to the Far East had not been an easy one for the tsar. His uncle, Grand Duke Alexei, disliked both the enthusiastic populist Klado,
whom he contemptuously called "a newspaper hero," and the idea of
sending more ships to the Pacific. The Naval Minister, Avelan, shared
both sentiments. But Klado continued campaigning, visiting high society salons one by one and publishing one article after another. For a
while Klado became one of the most popular men in Russia. The
Grand Duke Alexei, to the contrary, was hardly popular at all; in December, unknown avengers smashed several windows in his St. Petersburg palace.

Finally, Klado's argument won the tsar over. On December 4,
when the situation at Port Arthur became desperate, he informed his
uncle that the 3rd Pacific Squadron should be prepared and prepared

quickly. He also hoped it would still be possible to buy cruisers from Argentina and Chile, in spite of the British intrigue.

There was one more problem to solve. Shortly before, Admiral Nikolai Skrydlov had been appointed commander of the Pacific Fleet based in Vladivostok. Theoretically, if Rozhestvensky reached Vladivostok, he would have to surrender command to Skrydlov. Now, said Grand Duke Alexei in his letter to the tsar, this was becoming impossible. To deprive Rozhestvensky of his command would be "extremely harmful for our cause." He had formed the squadron, and he knew all the captains and many officers personally and had guided them through a "most difficult journey."

The tsar, as usual, did not know what to say. Meanwhile, Admiral Skrydlov, seeking fame, was intending to assume command of Rozhestvensky's squadron not in Vladivostok but earlier, if possible, perhaps in Southeast Asia. He asked for a rendezvous—though only God knew how Skrydlov planned to break through the Sea of Japan, now totally controlled by Togo. As always, Naval Minister Avelan found the decision to be too heavy a burden and forwarded the request to Rozhestvensky without comment.

Rozhestvensky loathed Skrydlov for appalling incompetence. Yet, on December 23, he curtly replied from Sainte-Marie, "Sunda Strait January the twentieth." He intended to take the squadron to the Sunda Strait and suspected battle with Togo would occur right there. However, he knew Skrydlov could not make it to the rendezvous, so his response, in all likelihood, was intended as a sarcastic joke.

The only joyful news Rozhestvensky received at Sainte-Marie was personal: Several days earlier his beloved daughter had given birth to a boy. The grandson was named Nikolai; everybody in the family was healthy. Given Rozhestvensky's trust in St. Nicholas, he must have liked the name.

No matter what he thought about Skrydlov, Port Arthur, his grandson, or the Admiralty, he had to attend to two mundane problems: how to take on more coal and where to meet Felkersam.

As for coal, he ordered the loading immediately. While at Sainte-Marie, the *Suvorov* took on 2,500 tons instead of the 1,100 that she was supposed to carry. As for Felkersam, Rozhestvensky had no other choice but to capitulate. He would go to Nosy Be.

Due to rough seas, he took the squadron closer to the coast of Madagascar. He also ordered a full alert. Radio operators had started getting messages that they were unable to read. That might mean Japanese ships were hiding somewhere nearby.

At nighttime one-third of the officers were on deck. Men slept at the guns. Torpedo boats were guarding the bigger ships. For the first time, Rozhestvensky ordered all lights out. People spoke to each other almost in whispers and scanned the dark horizon.

On the morning of December 22, the *Nakhimov* reported she had deciphered a message. It said, "Russian squadron is anchoring with its lights shut down at Sainte-Marie."

Not too many people slept the next night. The *Aurora* reported six lights at her stern. From the *Suvorov* bridge, officers could discern four lights in the sea and one ashore. The lights were flashing as if several groups were talking to each other. The night was murky, the sky overcast.

On the twenty-third at dawn, Rozhestvensky sent the cruisers away. He ordered Admiral Enkvist to take them to Nosy Be. The next day, he himself led the battleships. They had to cover 500 miles, rounding the northern coast of Madagascar. At noon, they met the cruiser *Svetlana* accompanied by two torpedo boats, the *Bedovy* and the *Bodry*—the greeting party sent out by Felkersam. The *Bedovy* carried some letters from home; thoughtful Felkersam had guessed it might be a good idea. The crews were overjoyed.

Rozhestvensky did not join the cheers of the *Suvorov* officers. Observing the three newly arrived ships from the bridge, he snarled: "My own fuckers would have been enough and now I have got three more. I have no idea what I will do with them all."

He had a point. Almost immediately after the joyful reunion, the *Bodry*'s engine died, and the *Rus* had to tow her.

December 25, Christmas Day, was spent moving full steam ahead. After mass, Rozhestvensky addressed the *Suvorov* crew. As custom dictated, he held a glass of vodka in his hand. Thanking every man for his service, he was brief, emotional, and impressive. Officers who stood nearby noticed tears in his eyes. He finished by saying, "I trust in you. Now to her, to Russia!" and drank his vodka in a gulp. The crew spontaneously yelled "Hurrah!" Some wept; many made the sign of the cross.

The way to Nosy Be was precarious; the existing charts of the area were unreliable, the waters abundant with reefs. Instead of figures marking the depth of the sea, the charts carried sinister marks "uncertain," "P.D." for "Position Doubtful" accompanied tentative markings of the reefs.

"It is all right," Rozhestvensky joked. "On our own will we would have never got into this dump. Let's hope Saint Nicholas will take this into account."

He did. On December 27, they safely reached Nosy Be. Mountains towered over the calm bay. Plentiful forests added to the beauty of the place. A boat departed the *Sisoi*. Admiral Felkersam was heading to the *Suvorov* to report to his commander.

2

Rozhestvensky met Felkersam cordially: The admiral had done a neat job. They kissed. That day Felkersam and Enkvist were invited to lunch.

They compared notes. Felkersam briefed Rozhestvensky on his journey, but there was hardly anything in his report that Rozhestvensky had not already experienced himself: Paris unwilling to commit itself, St. Petersburg pushing the squadron into dangerous backwaters to appease Paris, problems with coal and fresh water, spy reports about possible Japanese attacks. However, some of the latter were fairly recent and demanded immediate attention.

A report from the Russian spymaster in China, Pavlov, warned the admirals that on October 25, a special transport had left the major

Japanese naval base, Sasebo. She was carrying three submarines and heading south.

In a more recent cable, Pavlov reported that seven Japanese warships had been spotted at Natuna, north of Borneo. It was alleged that the Japanese had established stations in the Cocos Islands and at Kedah in Malacca and were keeping their auxiliary cruisers, torpedo boats, and perhaps even submarines there.

Both the Sunda Strait and the Strait of Malacca would be full of Japanese mines, agents warned. Several reports mentioned Ceylon as a possible base for Japanese saboteurs. There were pending fears of a clandestine Japanese presence in Durban, across the sea in Africa. Also, the Japanese reportedly planned to hire small boats in Madagascar itself to ram or torpedo Rozhestvensky's ships.

St. Petersburg had absolutely no agents in South or East Africa. Even its consul in Kaapstad (who had had to assist the hospital ship *Orel* on her visit there) was a foreigner who corresponded with St. Petersburg in English. That meant that the reports about Japanese activities in the vicinity of Madagascar were even less reliable than the others.

The Japanese were feeding Russian paranoia. The prime minister, Count Katsura, sinisterly told the British ambassador in Tokyo that "the Baltic Fleet had most certainly not met any Japanese torpedo boats in the North Sea, but there was every likelihood of their so doing in the Indian Ocean." By launching such provocative statements, the Japanese hoped to make Rozhestvensky nervous—and they succeeded.

The Russian naval attaché in London informed Rozhestvensky that a detachment of Japanese cruisers sent to the Indian Ocean was looking for him. Because spies were generally inclined to exaggerate, this was much more alarming than the information that insiders in London actually had: Two auxiliary cruisers, the *Hong Kong* and the *Nippon Maru,* had been sent to cruise around Java and Sumatra to look out for Russian colliers and gain information about Rozhestvensky's itinerary after Madagascar. Another cruiser, the *Niiataka,* had been sighted off Hong Kong. Several detachments were guarding the straits of the Sea of Japan. Almost all battleships were in the dockyards.

Rozhestvensky did not know this. He cabled St. Petersburg: "I ask you not to mention the names of harbors that the squadron will be using in cables addressed to me and in your dealings with foreign governments, for the squadron's arrival should always be a surprise." All in all, the reports about enemy activity he received in Nosy Be promised a gloomy future. However, one cable was laughable: The Portuguese government was informing Rozhestvensky that a Portuguese steamer with troops onboard was heading for Macao. Remembering Dogger Bank, Lisbon begged the Mad Dog to prevent any possible "misunderstanding."

The admiral was determined to leave Nosy Be soon—first for the Sunda Strait and then for Vladivostok. He did not want to wait for Nebogatov or even for Dobrotvorsky. Of course, Togo could intercept him at the Sunda Strait. Well, he thought, the sooner the battle occurred, the better. But first he had to get the approval of the tsar.

While the admiral was corresponding with St. Petersburg, the crews of the two squadrons had a chance to exchange stories. Felkersam's people confirmed that the hurricane that had tortured Rozhestvensky's ships at the Cape of Good Hope had reached them at Madagascar as well. But generally, Rozhestvensky's sailors were envious; Felkersam's journey had been through relatively civilized places with good port facilities, good food, and good brothels. Felkersam had freely allowed his officers and crews to go ashore. He had even tolerated his men's debauchery at Crete.

The tropics continued killing people. On December 30, two men on the *Borodino* died in the bowels of the ship; oppressive heat had activated poisonous gases there. Rozhestvensky issued a harsh order demanding attention to the hazard and attended the funeral mass in person. Yet, there was nothing he could do about the weather, and in the next few days, several people suffered from heatstroke.

The *Suvorov* had its first deserter. In retaliation, Rozhestvensky banned all leave for the *Suvorov* crew. A temptation to disappear forever in the lush tropical landscape, never to see the monstrous steaming ironclads or their awesome commander again, was obviously strong for many.

Bored officers brought wildlife aboard: parrots, monkeys, frogs, chameleons, rabbits. And ships were again inhabited by oxen, pigs, geese, and chickens, but these were for food. On one of the ships, a heap of hay for oxen sheltered a snake. The vermin bit a sailor who barely survived the attack.

Like all the other destinations of the squadron after Tangier, Nosy Be was not much of a place. Life stopped between 10 A.M. and 4 P.M. for a long siesta. The French barred their windows with shades and went to bed.

The town had a decent jetty, a stone church, a convent, a customs house, a governor's villa with a tennis court, a hospital, a post office, a school, and a city hall, plus several shops and three restaurants. That was the colonial town. The rest of Nosy Be consisted of bamboo huts.

The town also had Indians, Jews, Malaysians, Persians, and Greeks—even one gloomy, longhaired, odd Russian who was immediately labeled a Japanese spy. Natives carried Europeans in sedan-chairs.

By the time Rozhestvensky reached Nosy Be, Felkersam had been there for twelve days. The arrival of the Russians had produced a great sensation. Nosy Be had never seen so many naval ships or so many people. Merchants began arriving from Diégo-Suarez—most of them French, some Greek. Temporary shops and restaurants were hastily built from bamboo. Proprietors immediately started importing food in huge quantities to sell to the Russians at ridiculously high prices. Some of them jokingly said that by the time the squadron left, they would have saved enough money to retire to France.

In a matter of days, Nosy Be grew into a smaller and shabbier version of Port Said—a place to satisfy sailors' every wish. Gambling hells appeared from nowhere. Stakes there were remarkably high. Prostitutes from all over Madagascar flooded the place. Overwhelmed by the sudden abundance of options, Felkersam's officers and crewmen felt again unleashed.

Rozhestvensky attempted to bring this orgy to an end. The first thing the iron admiral did was ban gambling and limit the time that officers and crewmen were allowed ashore. But there was not much he could do to fight the spirit of recklessness and debauchery that pervaded Nosy Be.

3

The admiral spent New Year's Eve, 1905, in the *Suvorov's* wardroom. Earlier he had dispatched two cables to St. Petersburg—one to the tsar and another to Grand Duke Alexander. In both, he used exceedingly flowery language, appropriate for official communications. Both Romanovs were touched and kept the telegrams in their desks.

In the *Suvorov's* wardroom, however, the admiral gave a very simple speech: Let everyone present spend the next New Year's Eve in the company of relatives and friends, alive and healthy, and knowing he has fulfilled his duty.

That night Rozhestvensky was very animated; the atmosphere at the table was unexpectedly relaxed, and officers were surprised by his unusual friendliness. He stayed up until two o'clock in the morning and then left the younger men to their feast, which lasted until it was time to raise the flag.

The New Year's festivities again demonstrated Rozhestvensky's amazing powers of self-possession. On January 1, several hours after being so animated and optimistic at the party, he wrote to Capitolina Makarova: "I am not congratulating you with the New Year and do not expect anything good from it. . . . I feel very badly. I am being showered with absolutely useless cables. . . . Bureaucracy in Petersburg does not care a damn about how depressed all people, starting with the most junior sailor, are from this painful lingering."

Yet, it seemed the lingering was coming to an end. Three auxiliary cruisers—the *Terek,* the *Kuban,* and the *Ural*—joined the squadron, having independently reached Madagascar from the Black Sea. They were too lightly armed. The *Ural,* for example, was nothing but a modified German steamer. She still carried paintings and gilded decorations, which irritated sailors immensely. But the main thing was that they had arrived.

On January 4, a French steamer brought a mail shipment. While everybody was busy reading and responding, the departure of the squadron was scheduled for January 6. The post office on the hill was working day and night. Sometimes there were not enough stamps for all those attempting to send letters back home. Officers suspected that battle with Togo would occur in twenty days, at the Sunda archipelago.

Meanwhile, the tsar and his ministers still had no clear idea what to do with Rozhestvensky. They had failed to buy cruisers from Argentine and Chile for him. They had also failed to send him the ships of the Black Sea Fleet as Grand Duke Alexander had suggested. Foreign Minister Lamsdorf insisted that Britain would greatly disapprove of such a move.

On December 26, Naval Minister Avelan sent Rozhestvensky a very respectful cable, seeking his opinion. He mentioned that Nebogatov's squadron was ready to leave Libava in three weeks, in mid-January. The minister wanted to know what Rozhestvensky planned to do now, after the surrender of Port Arthur—wait for Nebogatov at Madagascar, wait for Nebogatov at some other place, or proceed to the Far East on his own. If Rozhestvensky proceeded on his own, the minister asked, where was he to send Nebogatov and also Dobrotvorsky from Djibouti?

Rozhestvensky answered with a short and energetic text: "Being unable to say even approximately" when Dobrotvorsky's detachment would reach Madagascar, "I do not leave any instructions for him. As for Nebogatov's detachment, I am even less sure about what it should do. I myself intend to proceed in seven days."

He was preparing to sail for the Sunda Strait in Dutch Indonesia. Virenius reported from St. Petersburg that the Dutch were scared of Japanese expansion in the area and therefore likely to help the Russians if the latter were discreet. They would prefer Rozhestvensky to call on some quiet place—not the Sunda but, say, the Bali-Lombok, 800 miles further east. Yet, even there, fearful of Japan's vengeance, they would not allow him to take on coal.

Grand Duke Alexei was outraged at the apprehensive Dutch. He thought Japan would never attack Dutch colonies in Asia. He knew it was impossible for Rozhestvensky to continue to Vladivostok without taking on coal in one of the ports of Southeast Asia. The grand duke made his strong views known both to his nephew, the tsar, and the foreign minister, Lamsdorf the peacemaker.

As a result, St. Petersburg exerted pressure on Holland. But the Dutch, caught between the fire and the frying pan, remained noncommittal. They tried to lure Rozhestvensky into some secluded bay outside Dutch territorial waters, where, as the Dutch Naval Minister put it, Rozhestvensky's squadron could stay "as long as it needs."

Rozhestvensky did not like this idea in the least. All of the places suggested to him were in the middle of nowhere: no good anchoring, no chance to buy food, no telegraph. Also, going to any of them meant significantly digressing from his route. Of course, he had another, equally unpleasant option: French Indochina.

He did not inform St. Petersburg of the route he was going to take. He just curtly advised that the colliers were to be sent both to Batavia *and* Saigon. He dryly promised that, in any case, the squadron would anchor "within 1,500 miles" of one of the two ports. In fact, he had already made his choice: destination—the Sunda Strait, departure date—January 6. Rozhestvensky did not know that the tsar had already changed his mind.

On January 3, Naval Minister Avelan sent Rozhestvensky an urgent order: "The Sovereign Emperor has ordered you not to leave Madagascar before getting further instructions." Rozhestvensky did not receive this message in time to cancel his departure. Or he pretended that he hadn't. Nevertheless, he did not sail on January 6. The German colliers rebelled. On the departure day, they notified Rozhestvensky that the enterprise was becoming too risky. They feared that by following the Mad Dog they would run into a Japanese ambush.

The enraged admiral cabled the tsar: "Having prepared to leave today, January the sixth, to proceed further, suddenly was notified by the executive of the German commission that the steamers with coal would not move any further." "Each further day spent at Madagascar is harmful to us," he added emphatically.

In the next cable to the sovereign, the admiral tried meteorological reasoning: "We should not stay at Madagascar. In several days the hurricane season starts. Will lose our ships." In a cable to Avelan, he was asking the minister "not to keep the squadron at Nosy Be" for sanitary reasons: "All living quarters of officers and men are full of food and coal. . . . In this situation many may die of infectious diseases."

He also appealed to the arcane art of diplomacy. Could it be, he asked Avelan, that the colliers had been influenced by Berlin, which wanted to keep the squadron at Madagascar, thus creating problems for France? In that case, he continued, Germany had to be notified that the squadron would go to Dutch East India and get coal there.

The reply from St. Petersburg was slow to arrive. While Rozhestvensky was waiting, the colliers loudly celebrated the kaiser's birthday, as if to mock the Russian admiral. They put up colorful flags and started a drinking orgy, which lasted for three days.

Rozhestvensky was choking with powerless rage. He knew that the intolerable delay was only partially caused by the tsar's insecurities. He was depending on a new technology that was still unreliable: international telegraph.

To send a cable, Rozhestvensky first had to dispatch a fast ship to Diégo-Suarez on the northern tip of Madagascar (seventy-five miles away). From there a cable would be transmitted to Antananarivo in the heartland of the island, then to Mahajanga on the west coast, then by oceanic cable to Mozambique. From Mozambique it would travel to St. Petersburg via Zanzibar and Paris. The Diégo-Suarez–Antananarivo–Mahajanga leg was the most vulnerable one, for there the wire passed through five hundred miles of rain forest and desert. The local custom of closing all offices for a six-hour siesta did not expedite delivery either.

Rozhestvensky complained to Avelan: "Cables sent from St. Petersburg usually reach Nosy Be in four days, sometimes later." "They are long kept on English lines," he concluded sinisterly. Not only was telegraph very slow, it also distorted messages mercilessly.

While the tsar was taking his time, the colliers were still refusing to follow the squadron. Rozhestvensky snarled to Avelan: "I am deprived of a chance to kick out from the roadstead these traitors and watchers, communicating with Japanese spies and agents. Myself, I am not allowed to leave. The squadron will get demoralized in this situation, created by useless negotiations."

Finally, on January 12, Avelan informed Rozhestvensky that the Hamburg-American Line had instructed its colliers to serve the squadron, provided the admiral agree to several conditions. Colliers were to proceed separately. Rozhestvensky was to guarantee their safety. If something did happen to them, Russia was to compensate the Germans. The chief representative of the company had to be given Rozhestvensky's itinerary so that he could be sure all ports and bays of call were neutral.

The admiral had no choice but to agree. At least, he thought, now he was free to go. But the tsar had decided he was to stay.

On a gray, cool day, January 11, after lunch, Tsar Nicholas received Admiral Nebogatov. Satisfied with the interview and reassured of eventual victory, the next day the tsar arrogantly scolded Rozhestvensky:

> Your mission is not to reach Vladivostok with several ships, but to master the Sea of Japan. For this your Madagascar forces are insufficient. . . . It is absolutely necessary for you to wait for Dobrotvorsky's unit at Madagascar, to reinforce your squadron. . . . As for Nebogatov's unit, I do not want to bind you and am waiting for your opinion on whether you find it possible to have him join you in the Indian Ocean, adjusting the squadron's itinerary accordingly.

Nicholas's irritability in mid-January 1905 was understandable: Revolution had started in Russia. The year began with a bad omen; on January 6, during the annual consecration of waters at the Neva River with all the dynasty and imperial dignitaries present, an artillery gun fired cases of shot instead of blanks. Naval Minister Avelan was wounded by a piece of glass from a broken window of the Winter Palace. Everybody thought it was an attempt on the tsar's life. It was not, but it heralded a real disaster. In several days, spontaneous demonstrations and strikes started in St. Petersburg. The government used force to repel these moves, which resulted in the massacre on January 9, Bloody Sunday, of hundreds of people by governmental troops in front of the Winter Palace.

Rozhestvensky was a staunch conservative, but the current unrest in St. Petersburg was not his problem. He had to leave Nosy Be as soon as he possibly could. Dobrotvorsky's unit was still in the Red Sea, and waiting for it at Madagascar meant losing several weeks more. The admiral kept arguing with the monarch: "By staying here, we allow the enemy to repair his main force and to let his smaller vanguard ships become familiar with the southern straits of the Indian Ocean, to study the area and to prepare a concealed trap for us. Out of Dobrotvorsky's squadron, only the *Oleg* will reinforce us and not significantly anyway."

Rozhestvensky's argument about not giving Togo time to have his ships repaired was a strong one. London, for instance, was quite aware of the fact that Togo's ships, having spent twelve months cruising and engaging in battle, were in a pretty bad shape. The Japanese minister of foreign affairs told the British ambassador that the fleet had developed "many defects in machinery and elsewhere." A British observer with Togo's fleet, Captain Pakenham, reported that the ships were "very far from being in an efficient condition." Their bottoms were "very foul, reducing greatly their speed." By and large, Togo's fleet was "very seriously in want of docking and repairing." Of course, in January 1905, Togo was preoccupied with exactly that.

Meanwhile, the tsar had withdrawn the initial compromise. Now Rozhestvensky was to wait not only for Dobrotvorsky but also for Nebogatov. Feeling freer to argue with the naval minister than with the tsar, Rozhestvensky cabled Avelan: "Nebogatov will reach Madagascar in May. Am asking for your order to proceed as soon as Dobrotvorsky's ships will be able to move on."

He also mentioned that salted meat and cabbage brought from Kronshtadt were rotting already and that all other resources were becoming scarce. To wait for Nebogatov at Madagascar would mean once again resupplying the squadron with all essentials. "That would mean the squadron would never move on."

With utmost irritation, Rozhestvensky thought about the role of the British in this war. One of the first cables he sent to St. Petersburg from Sainte-Marie reported his concern: "English cruisers are watching the squadron even in somebody else's waters; as allies of the Japanese, the English are not concealing from them the results of their cruisers' reconnaissance. This means they are reporting our organization, tactical methods, and other things useful to our adversary."

This cable unleashed another diplomatic storm in Europe. The Russian chargé d'affaires in London visited the Foreign Office, demanding explanation. He was informed that "distinct orders had been given to our Naval Commanders to avoid any action which could have the appearance of watching or following the Russian ships." The commander-in-chief of the Cape Station ascertained that "no ships of the Cape squadron had sighted any Russian man-of-war." The Foreign Office insisted that "after the departure of the Russian squadron from Tangier they were not shadowed or even observed by British ships. They might possibly have passed one or two British vessels homeward-bound, but except for this they could not have seen a British vessel after leaving Tangier."

Rozhestvensky's energetic protest had probably been inspired by his paranoid Anglophobia, compounded by his feeling of general frustration. That January, he was taking the blows of fate badly. When his aide, Lieutenant Sventorzhetsky, brought him newly deciphered cables from St. Petersburg, the admiral could barely conceal his anger. He would finger the paper ferociously as if resisting the temptation to shred it into pieces and only then start dictating an answer. He would edit the draft severely, often snapping at Sventorzhetsky. When the cable was particularly displeasing, he would say with forced calm: "Leave it with me. . . . I will write the response myself . . . later." On these occasions when the lieutenant was leaving the cabin, he would often hear the sound of a pencil being broken and the admiral's muffled voice, choking with rage, cursing "traitors."

No matter how frustrated he was, he never shared his thoughts or even the content of the cables with the two junior flag officers—

Felkersam and Enkvist. The only person who was kept informed was his aide, Lieutenant Sventorzhetsky. While preparing cables to the tsar or to the naval minister, the admiral sometimes would burst into a long explanation, voicing the points that he was unable to mention in the correspondence.

First, he had a low opinion of his squadron. Its ships were either brand-new and, therefore, untested, or they were old and proven to be unfit. The crews had been assembled hastily. The squadron had been allowed no time to practice together to develop team spirit or even coordination.

Nebogatov's detachment was a total outrage, "pathetic" and slow—in a word, "archaeological." Rozhestvensky knew what he was talking about; the *Emperor Nicholas I*, the *Admiral Ushakov,* and the *Admiral Seniavin* had practiced under his command in the Artillery Practice Unit. The *Emperor Nicholas I* had also sailed in the same squadron with him in 1894–1895, first in the Mediterranean Sea, then in the Far East. As for their commander, Nikolai Ivanovich Nebogatov, Rozhestvensky knew him, too. Nebogatov had succeeded him as captain of the *Kreiser* and later commanded the *Pervenets,* Rozhestvensky's flagship in the Artillery Practice Unit. Rozhestvensky had not been impressed.

In a letter to his wife he plainly called Nebogatov's squadron "rot." Sardonically, he said that as head of the Naval General Staff he should have probably been nicer to seasoned grasping "pikes" of various salons and chancelleries who were now forcing him to take "bad and out-moded ships" to war on the insistence of Commander Klado, who was, after all, just an ordinary officer.

He was tortured by thoughts about his personal responsibility for the armada. His nightmare was he would become disabled by illness or killed in battle, in which case neither Felkersam nor Enkvist would be able to lead his men. It also was apparent that the tsar did not like him any longer. At least, the sovereign was turning a deaf ear to all his pleas. Overwhelmed with these thoughts, Rozhestvensky came to the conclusion that the armada needed another leader, one who was healthier and more popular with the tsar. He respected the commander-in-chief of the Black Sea Fleet, Admiral Chukhnin, and wanted him to board Nebogatov's squadron in Port Said. When the squadrons eventually met, Chukhnin would become commander-in-chief and he, Rozhestvensky, would step down to junior flag rank. He hoped the tsar would grant him at least that.

4

The rainy season started. To many, it now looked like a gloomy St. Petersburg fall, but it was hot and the Baltic never experienced such violent downpours.

In spite of the admiral's efforts, morale was plummeting and debauchery was escalating. The crewmen indulged in their last gulps of pleasure before they embarked for their final, terrifying destination.

Until their arrival at Nosy Be, Rozhestvensky's crewmen had been confined to their ships since their departure from Kronshtadt, nearly three months and up to four for some. Officers had had just brief glimpses of Dakar and Libreville. The long voyage had been spent on claustrophobic ships allowing little or no privacy and no explicit sexuality. For crews sharing cramped living quarters, even masturbation was problematic. Sexual attraction between men, magnified by solitude, male camaraderie, regular consumption of alcohol, and close exposure of naked bodies, could hardly lead to anything. Lack of privacy, reinforced by social inhibitions, set limits to potential affairs or encounters. Even an officer had to think twice about taking a mate to his cabin.

Now, at Nosy Be, they finally could let out steam. Ladies of the night had rushed to the islet from all over Madagascar like bees attracted to a spectacular bloom. Many native huts welcomed Russian visitors interested in quick copulation, and sailors started cruising dark narrow alleyways. However, class distinctions remained strong. Many officers thought it inappropriate to touch the Malagasy, and crewmen could not afford French harlots.

The crewmen suspected that French courtesans were giving their officers a much better time than local women were giving them. They spied on young midshipmen and lieutenants and then disseminated bawdy stories about "real" debauchery. Once a group of sailors came across an unusual exhibit in the forest. A woman was lying dead drunk on the grass, surrounded by empty wine bottles. Her belly was naked. Two young officers were playing cards on it, and the third one was taking photos of the trio, advising his comrades on how to best pose. Apparently, he thought these pictures would help them to deal with the boredom of seafaring.

Of course, visiting the tropical rain forest was normally an innocent pleasure. Sailors went there to admire hummingbirds, to spot an occasional deadly snake, and to listen to mysterious voices in the woods, making their way through walls of vines and ruining their uniforms.

Officers went out hunting. They would take quinine as a prophylactic against malaria, put on high boots to protect their ankles from snakes, hire a local boy as a guide, and depart for the jungle. There they would head for a big lake lying in a shallow crater. It was surrounded by reeds in which crocodiles were abundant. Its waters were quiet, silent, and enigmatic.

From the lake it was easy to reach their ultimate destination—the river. The path was narrow and full of snakes warming themselves in the sun. The river was shallow but full of rapids. Here and there a hunter would spot a crocodile's head, resembling driftwood. He would fire, but then often be unable to retrieve the trophy amid rapids and brush, and the dead crocodile would be carried by the river down to the ocean where it would float sinisterly on waves, scaring sailors in the squadron.

After the hunt, officers would make a bonfire and have a picnic—a feast frequently interrupted by hordes of mosquitoes. Sometimes, apparently warmed by alcohol, the Russians would venture a very unsafe, though delightful, swim in the cold river, under the blooming trees, with butterflies and white ibises flying over their heads.

But hunting was not for everybody. Most Russian males knew how to hunt, but only enthusiasts ventured to do so amid the heat, snakes, and mosquitoes of Madagascar. Officers normally stayed in town. There, after visiting the brothels, they could go to a restaurant or to a shop. All of the shops displayed signs in Russian, promising "huge discounts." But the post office still never had enough stamps.

Nosy Be soon felt very confining, like a tiny provincial town somewhere in Siberia. The Russians jokingly nicknamed it Nossibeisk, supplying the Malagasy name with a suffix often used in the names of foresaken Russian towns like Irkutsk or Omsk.

Nossibeisk's major attraction was gambling. In spite of Rozhestvensky's orders, underground gambling continued. Stingy French bureaucrats who had come to Madagascar to earn and save money watched reckless Russian officers with shock. The governor was very much displeased; the Russians were setting a bad example. He did not want his colony to continue this way after they left. He visited Rozhestvensky and complained. The admiral knew he could not close all those dens or ban gambling effectively, so instead he banned officers from visiting the shore on weekdays, thus setting limits to the vice.

To control the crewmen, they were generally confined to their ships, and they were beaten if they misbehaved. To fight boredom, the crew turned to fishing; at the turn of the last century angling was a sport for the lower classes.

Nighttime fishing was particularly rewarding. The *Donskoi* crew caught 1,800 pounds of fish in one evening. They used nets and in daylight had to spend considerable time sorting the fish, using the officers' manuals. Normally, the brighter the fish, the less edible it was.

One night, a sailor who was wading the bay suddenly yelled and disappeared under the water. His body was never recovered. Apparently, a shark had snatched him. After that incident, Rozhestvensky scolded the captain and senior officer of the *Donskoi* and banned fishing altogether.

Deprived of this pleasure, the sailors had to seek fun elsewhere. Unexpectedly, they found it in the rain. Many went to the deck naked and soaped and washed thoroughly under the generous tropical torrents.

But everybody was bored and irritated, officers and crewmen alike. Some were unable to spend enough time ashore; others loathed the tropics and foreign lands in general. Some officers had chosen not to leave their ships since Reval. Idleness and the overall feeling of a failed mission magnified all petty problems.

In that climate, even having one's hair cut was an ordeal. Both the customer and the barber (normally a fellow sailor with old battered tools) would sweat profusely, and the client would struggle with the prickling reminders of the operation for hours.

There were other nuisances. The *Suvorov,* like many other ships, was running short of cups. They were not available in Nosy Be in the quantities necessary, and officers were now drinking tea from jam jars. The floor was getting unbearably hot during the day, and officers ordered men to bring chunks of wood to protect feet from burns.

Nights were hot and damp. Virtually everybody went on deck to sleep in relative comfort. Many conventional norms had collapsed. Officers slept on mats stark naked, unabashed by the presence of sailors. When on the eve of a thunderstorm it was too hot to sleep, they would talk about Rozhestvensky, the Admiralty, and the war. A younger officer would make an audacious remark, and an older comrade would cut him sharply in English: "Stop, boy! The sentinel listens . . ." The rain forest would send waves of its sweet narcotic scent, clouds would darken the sky, and finally lightning would cut the dark veil and unleash a flood. The lucky ones reposing under tents could enjoy the relief of the cool air; others had to flee the deck into the sultriness of their cabins.

The *Suvorov* wardroom had a piano, but nobody could play it well, so they were using a pianola instead. When a midshipman from another ship visited and suggested playing the piano, officers were so excited that they started folk dancing in hastily arranged crazy attires, as if at a dress ball.

But one could not dance every day; the pianola was not inspiring enough. Alternatively, they gathered the ships' canines and staged a dogfight, passionately cheering their pets. On another occasion, officers launched a rat hunt, using dogs as mock hounds, but they killed only one rodent.

Seeking variety, officers started collecting tropical wildlife. They were catching chameleons and buying monkeys. Those of the noble class dreamt of bringing them back to Russia to inhabit the gardens of their country estates; expensive heating systems could keep the exotic animals alive all year to the envy of neighbors. Now chameleons were crawling all over the *Suvorov*, absolutely harmless, but detested by many.

The crewmen didn't share the officers' interest in exotic creatures. Most of them were peasant lads, so they were happy taking care of the cows, calves, pigs, and chickens taken aboard as foodstuff. They hated the idea that the animals would have to be slaughtered and were sharing bread with them.

Rozhestvensky seemed not to mind this menagerie too much. He was doing his best to cheer people up. The day started with the solemn raising of the flag and all the orchestras playing the national anthem and then the Marseillaise to honor the French hosts and finally Rozhestvensky's personal march. At the lowering of the flag at sunset, the orchestras played again. Many found these rituals soothing and even poetic.

On Sunday afternoon, the *Suvorov* musicians played outside the governor's villa—a sensation for the local *beau monde;* there was no orchestra in town. French families attended, wearing their best clothes, gawking at young and handsome Russian aristocrats playing lawn tennis. Of course, the aristocrats were showing off—in 1905, no lowborn man could play that game of the privileged. Monkeys were throwing mangoes at the crowd, and the Russians were looking at their watches; the deadline for returning to the boats was 6 P.M. sharp, and many still planned to do some gambling in the afternoon or visit a brothel.

Discipline continued collapsing. A sailor on the *Suvorov* disobeyed the senior officer and threatened the boatswain. A court-martial gave him three and a half years in a disciplinary battalion. The *Malaya* crew rebelled. They did not belong to the navy and assumed that they had no reason to fear Rozhestvensky. They were mistaken. He had the four leaders of the mutiny arrested and put into other ships' coolers. One of them was taken to the *Suvorov*.

The *Suvorov* cooler was horrible. It was excruciatingly hot and had absolutely no ventilation. But there was a worse punishment. Rozhestvensky had promised to leave the four *Malaya* rebels ashore when the squadron departed. One of them burst into tears; such an exile looked worse than jail to him.

On January 10, the *Nakhimov* crew rebelled, too. Her officers had not bothered to import fresh bread from the shore, like the other ships had, and let their men eat dried bread. Finally the crew demanded proper food and refused to disperse after the common prayer.

Under different circumstances, Rozhestvensky would have punished the sailors mercilessly. Now he thought it wise to downplay the whole episode. He arrived at the *Nakhimov* and told the crew: "I knew men on this ship were scum, but not such scum!" Having said just that, he abruptly left the ship. After that, the crew promptly got fresh bread and the officers a ferocious scolding. Rozhestvensky even put four of them under arrest.

Numerous minor episodes occurred, which were symptoms of the same disease: demoralization. A man at the *Oslyabya* stole a church collection cup with money. Four men from the torpedo boat *Grozny* destroyed and sacked a native hut. An officer from the *Suvorov* fell overboard, having drunk too much champagne. The same day, the *Suvorov* crew stole a case of champagne. A sailor from the *Kamchatka* had sneaked into the water and started swimming toward the shore, having first helped himself to two life vests. After he was spotted by a searchlight and brought back to the ship, he explained that he had just "wanted to walk a bit on land." Sailors often returned from the shore dead drunk, carried on stretchers by their comrades. Prohibited from drinking alcohol outside their daily ration of two glasses of vodka, they started buying it from local vendors or from foreign peers.

On torpedo boats, order was becoming especially loose. The *Suvorov* officers were shocked to see a torpedo boat's captain and his mate drinking tea on deck barefooted. On shore, fights between officers and crewmen started. Rozhestvensky reported to the Naval General Staff: "Sub-lieutenant Zaionchakovsky from the *Ural*, debauching ashore and being beastly drunk, was heavily beaten by men. Having court-martialed three participants in the beating . . . degraded Zaionchakovsky to a private." He was warning the naval minister: "If the squadron continues to be prevented from proceeding to the theater of war, discipline will be totally shaken. There is no punishment for most gross offenses, because people die in coolers and sentries there get ill, too. Capital punishment would demoralize crews entirely."

Throughout the whole stay in Nosy Be, Rozhestvensky did not confirm a single death warrant. When an officer dared to hint that he was too soft on men, Rozhestvensky responded: "I am not on the soft side. This just does not make any sense. How can you scare people with capital punishment, if they are following me and I am taking them to death? Before the battle, all arrested men will be set free, and who knows, perhaps they will become heroes."

Even without executions, almost every day somebody would die of heatstroke, heart failure, or drowning. Officers and crew stood at full attention on deck, gravely watching a black, narrow torpedo boat head slowly to sea, churning the water in front of her into white foam. A priest stood at the stern over the dead man sewn into cloth and covered by a St. Andrew's flag. Bands played somber church hymns, and a choir on the torpedo boat sang the funeral mass. After the torpedo boat reached the outer sea, people on other ships heard a single artillery shot. This meant that the body had been dropped into the water. The ceremony over, boatswains whistled, ordering men to discharge. Normal life resumed, but the ominous presence of fate would be felt for several more hours.

Diseases thrived. When the wretched *Malaya* was finally sent back to Russia because Rozhestvensky had lost patience with her defective engine and even less reliable crew, she carried several dozen very sick people with her—including twenty-eight with acute tuberculosis. All through the squadron people complained of tropical rashes and malaria. They were plagued by cockroaches. Legions of these hungry pests wandered around the ships, eating clothes, boots, and books. At night they attacked the sleeping and gnawed at their faces and hands. These savage cockroaches were nicknamed "cannibals."

Many sailors were now wearing bast shoes; their boots had deteriorated and they had no reserves. St. Petersburg had promised to solve the problem, but everybody knew it would take too long. The *Esperance*, which kept the stock of frozen meat, experienced a breakdown of her refrigerator. The rotting carcasses were thrown into the sea, but the current brought them to shore where they continued to rot, contaminating the air with stench.

The ships also suffered in Nosy Be. Their bottoms had accumulated considerable mollusks and seaweed that were bound to slow them down on their way to Japan. It was almost impossible for divers to clean the bottoms. A proper dock was needed. Of course, the Japanese were going to have their ships cleaned before the eventual battle. They were also able to complete all necessary mechanical repairs. The longer the squadron stayed at Madagascar, the better equipped Togo became. The ultimate humiliation would arrive, though, if the Japanese had time to salvage Russian ships sunk at Port Arthur, had them repaired, and then had the *Poltava* fire at the *Suvorov*. Now the Russian officers regretted they had called the Japanese macaques.

On January 20, mail arrived. As usual, it was outrageously muddled. The battleship *Alexander III* kept getting letters addressed to the Alexander III Technological College back in Russia. Some letters were addressed to ships still in Libava and Kronshtadt, and even to the ships already sunk at Port Arthur.

Having greedily read letters from home, people started browsing Russian newspapers. Many were shocked by what they learned: The press was reporting revolution! Much political debate ensued.

Parcels received with the mail were disappointing. For some reason, most families kept sending warm clothes.

Officers were in a hurry to reply and mailed letters or colorful postcards from Nosy Be. The lucky ones were communicating by cable. If a telegraphic response from a Russian addressee arrived in five days, that was considered to be fast.

Rozhestvensky allowed the sending and receiving of private cables through official, supposedly quicker, channels, only in emergencies, such as death or grave illness. In these situations, he never hesitated to monitor the personal affairs of his officers if he thought it would expedite communication. "How is so-and-so's wife's health?" he would ask Naval General Staff. He and other top officers never abused their special access to the telegraph. Naval General Staff would inform them about the well-being of their families only very briefly and infrequently.

The admiral had his share of family problems, too. His wife had decided to go abroad with their daughter and grandson, little Nikolai. Rozhestvensky asked her to postpone travel until the end of the war; he thought it was inappropriate for his family to go pleasure seeking right now. She promised to stay but then changed her mind and informed her husband they were going to the most conspicuous place of all, Nice.

5

In the beginning of February, Rozhestvensky became seriously ill. He developed terrible pain and was moaning through the night, unable even to doze. He spent several days in bed and took all his meals there. Doctors said that it was a bout of his old rheumatism.

Only ice applied to his joints would ease his suffering. When one night the *Suvorov's* refrigerator broke down, an officer was dispatched to search other ships for ice.

Officers who hadn't seen Rozhestvensky since Kronshtadt were saying he looked twenty years older. Some worried a lot, some grinned with glee. There was one particular reason not to like the admiral: His affair with Sivers was becoming an open secret among lonely men.

Almost every day she had lunch with him, accompanied by Rozhestvensky's niece, Miss Pavlovskaya, also a nurse on the *Orel*. Men serving them gossiped that during the meal Rozhestvensky paid no attention to the niece whatsoever, talking exclusively to Sivers. After the meal, the niece would leave to have a chat with her uncle's staff officers, and Rozhestvensky would remain with Sivers alone. Then the door to the admiral's suite would be shut, and his orderly would not let anybody in.

January 19 was Sivers's birthday. Rozhestvensky sent an officer with a huge bunch of flowers to the *Orel* and then hosted a dinner party at the *Suvorov*. The band was playing gay music. They drank champagne.

Every day they exchanged letters and sometimes even parcels—presumably with presents. Rozhestvensky dispatched a special cutter to take his letters to the *Orel*. Once, the French governor sent him an extravagant gift—an enormous plant. He immediately rerouted it to the hospital ship and later scolded the courier for a single broken branch. When the governor threw a dinner for Rozhestvensky, the gallant Frenchman made sure Sivers was invited, too.

The hospital ship, however, didn't enjoy special privileges just because Sivers was on board. On the trip to Kaapstad, Rozhestvensky had ordered her captain to buy fresh supplies for the squadron and to pay for them from the ship's bursary. As a result, the *Orel* had to apply to St. Petersburg for more money.

Seeing apathy all around, the admiral was trying to reintroduce a feeling of purpose to his fleet. Junior officers were obliged to practice daily—astronomic observations, war games, various alarms and drills. Many officers were saying with some satisfaction that when they finished the voyage their naval education would finally be complete.

Another way to practice was to send torpedo boats to attack the squadron at night. Their mission was to crawl as close to bigger ships as they could. At first, each mission was a victory for the torpedo boats and a loss for the squadron, but with each attempt it became more difficult for the hounds of the sea to get to their prey unnoticed.

On January 13, 18, and 19, the squadron went to sea for artillery practice. It was their first joint exercise since Reval. Overall results looked discouraging. In a caustic memorandum, Rozhestvensky said they were "too shameful to be mentioned." In bright daylight, the whole squadron failed to hit any of the targets standing for Japanese torpedo boats, "though the difference between the targets and Japanese torpedo boats was in our favor, for the shields did not move." What was the purpose of keeping gunners on their watch at night, Rozhestvensky sarcastically asked, if they failed to hit targets in daylight?

Maneuvering was also highly unsatisfactory. In his memorandum, Rozhestvensky pronounced that instead of a squadron, he had seen an "ugly mob." On February 8, he took all of the ships to sea to simulate a battle. Felkersam and Enkvist were to play against him. But the result was embarrassing. Instead of attacking their flag, Felkersam and Enkvist got lost.

Rozhestvensky was beyond himself with rage. From the bridge of the *Suvorov,* he violently cursed both, especially Enkvist, the Slutty Old Geezer. He spent the rest of the day assembling the squadron and schooling it in the most basic maneuvers.

The admiral did not have the resources to actually train his men; the stock of artillery shells was limited, and it takes months to turn a number of ships into a squadron. Thus, the maneuvers and practice were not training, but a test—a test that many ships failed to pass.

Many, but not all. One of the ships that Rozhestvensky genuinely liked was the cruiser *Aurora.* Her commander took special care to maintain team spirit on his ship. During traditional Russian pre-Lent carnival, *maslyannaya,* the *Aurora* staged a performance—not just Neptune, clowns, and "natives," but also naked wrestling and shooting and running contests. At five o'clock, the *Aurora*'s numerous boats ran a race in the harbor.

That day, Rozhestvensky was watching the *Aurora* with utmost pleasure. For him, it was one of the few bright episodes in the loathsome stay at Madagascar. A spirit of naval camaraderie, paternalistic treatment of the crewmen, strong and fast masculine bodies, heavy launches lowered into the water or brought back to the deck in a matter of seconds—it was exactly the fleet he would like to have. He had approved the schedule of the festivities the day before. Now he issued a special memo, asking the other captains whether they had bothered to stage any performance at all.

On February 1, Captain Dobrotvorsky's detachment finally joined the squadron. Only the armored cruiser *Oleg* was a valuable asset, but at least now Rozhestvensky could insist again on leaving.

He assembled his captains and junior flag-officers. He finally briefed them on his correspondence with St. Petersburg. The admiral explicitly said that even in the best case scenario they would not be able to master the Sea of Japan, that Nebogatov's ships would be a burden, and that all they could do now was to try to break through to Vladivostok.

In the beginning of February, Rozhestvensky addressed the emperor again. "Your Imperial Majesty," he wrote, "I am doubting the reliability of [the Nebogatov ships'] repairs and if in three months they arrive here with broken boilers, condensers, pipes, my lingering at Madagascar will cause a burst of general indignation." Even without Nebogatov, Rozhestvensky firmly concluded that he could reach Vladivostok only "with losses."

Meanwhile, he was notified that Nebogatov had just started his journey. Naval Minister Avelan cabled, "On February the second, Rear Admiral Nebogatov's unit left Libava for the Far East." The same cable also carried some bad news: "On February 4, in Moscow, Grand Duke Sergei Alexandrovich was killed with a bomb thrown at his carriage. . . . Many plants are on strike again; almost all universities and schools are closed."

Rozhestvensky immediately sent a cable of condolence to the tsar (Grand Duke Sergei was his uncle), condemning in strong terms the new revolutionary turmoil. A principled conservative, he hated those "traitors" sincerely and wholeheartedly.

He did not suspect that revolution in Russia would promote his cause. Tired of arguing and losing interest in the squadron's fate under the pressure of domestic violence and unprecedented threat to the dynasty, the tsar angrily cabled Rozhestvensky on February 8: "I let you decide yourself whether to leave Madagascar without waiting for Nebogatov's detachment or to wait for him there. Your mission is not to reach Vladivostok with some vessels, but to master the Sea of Japan. Repairs of Nebogatov's ships were done with all possible thoroughness. Cable your decision."

In response, Rozhestvensky sent a long telegram:

The 1st Squadron, which before the war had 30 warships and 28 torpedo boats, proved to be insufficient for mastering the sea. The 2nd Squadron, having just 20 warships and 9 torpedo boats, is now incapable of mastering the sea, because there is nothing left of the 1st Squadron but the *Rossiya*. After Nebogatov joins us, our forces still will not be enough for mastering the sea: Nebogatov adds 4 bad warships and 8 transports to defend, which will be a burden for the squadron.

Rozhestvensky thought Admiral Chukhnin with three Black Sea battleships and two cruisers should join Nebogatov in the Mediterranean Sea; the addition of those ships would be useful and such a joint fleet "could master the sea, provided it was constantly supplied." "If the addition of the Black Sea ships is unrealistic, then the 2nd Squadron's nearest task should be reaching Vladivostok and only later, having got rid of transports, would it be possible for the main force to cruise the area of the adversary's communications with metropoly and for the auxiliary cruisers the area through which military contraband proceeds." It was impossible to stay at Madagascar any longer, he argued. The squadron would get totally undermined physically and morally. "Now having the most gracious permission of Your Imperial Majesty, will depart in the last days of February."

Yet, the "most gracious permission" to leave Nosy Be still implied Rozhestvensky would have to set up a rendezvous with Nebogatov—if not at Madagascar, then somewhere else. But the more he heard about Nebogatov's unit, the less he liked it. The Admiralty reported that the cruiser *Rus* had had to be sent back to Libava from Skagen due to a mechanical problem. Rozhestvensky cabled back venomously: "We are very sorry. The *Rus* was the only desirable ship from the whole Nebogatov detachment. Mechanics should be changed. These, it seems, do not want to go to war."

Meanwhile, the international commission on the Dogger Bank incident finished its hearings. Avelan cabled Rozhestvensky on February 17: "In their final statement, the admirals concluded that the actions of Your Excellency and the squadron's officers do not deserve the least criticism and have been absolutely right. . . . The question about the presence of torpedo boats has not been clarified and is not mentioned in the final statement of the admirals." In St. Petersburg, Grand Duke Alexei magnanimously informed Foreign Minister Lamsdorf that "of course" he did not mind paying indemnity to the fishermen of Hull and that he even thought "this had been already done."

Tokyo was disappointed that the international verdict had been so soft on Rozhestvensky. London had a different reason to be upset: The Japanese allies were not keeping the British informed about their war plans. "It is not known where all the units of the Japanese fleet now are, nor what may be their plans for the future," a report from Tokyo stated. Yet, the British were putting on a good face:

This will be known in good time and, meanwhile, there is nothing in the alliance to justify seizing ministers (metaphorically) by the throat, and thus trying to wring their little secrets from them. . . . If allies were engaged in combined war, this strategic secretiveness would be improper, but while the war is confined to the present combatants, the alliance is no ground for claiming from the Japanese any further knowledge of their war schemes than they may find it expedient to offer.

According to British intelligence, Japanese cruisers were patrolling the Sea of Japan straits in February. Repairs were proceeding rapidly in dockyards. However, it was believed that before the end of February repairs would not be finished. Battleships and larger cruisers were still to be "taken in hand for a final refit, docking, and examination of underwater fittings." In other words, every day Rozhestvensky spent waiting for Nebogatov at Madagascar or elsewhere gave Togo more opportunity to prepare for the final encounter. Rozhestvensky realized that. Now he knew that he would be unable to persuade the tsar to let him proceed to Vladivostok without this huge liability, Nebogatov's ships. Leaving Madagascar made no sense if he still had to wait for Nebogatov's clunkers at the Sunda Strait or elsewhere, so he stayed and argued with himself. Gradually, the admiral came to the conclusion that the only real solution was to disobey the tsar. He knew that this could be interpreted as state treason. It took him time to make up his mind.

On the morning of March 2, the admiral received cables from Paris through the Havas telegraph agency. In the solitude of his study he went through them quickly. Today's news was alarming. Nebogatov was hastily taking on coal in Crete and was expected in Port Said shortly. Soon he would be heading for the Indian Ocean.

Enough!

Rozhestvensky banged the door. He summoned his aid. Apparently unsettled, the admiral issued a brisk order to the squadron: Finish all loading in twenty-four hours and be ready for immediate departure.

"Whom shall we cable about the route?" the aid asked.

Rozhestvensky looked at him.

"Nobody, nothing," he said.

He assembled his captains and gave them brief instructions for the voyage to Asia: Be prepared to leave in twenty-two hours, keep up the speed of nine knots, and in case they met Togo, spend ammunition carefully, for St. Petersburg had not bothered to send them any more gun shells.

By the time of the departure, the decks of all the ships were full of sacks of coal. Coal was everywhere, even in wardrooms. The battleships were the most overloaded. If there were a storm or a fire, they would be in real trouble.

During the final loading, all had to join in. Meals were quickly gulped, and all people could talk about was coal. Bands were playing, cheering people up.

Nobody knew the squadron's destination. Rozhestvensky's order was curt and businesslike: Take aboard supplies for forty-five days and be ready to spend the first twenty days on high seas.

Officers wondered whether they were going to the Sunda Strait to fight Togo or to Djibouti to meet Nebogatov. Both guesses were wrong.

On March 4, the French Foreign Ministry sighed with relief; Rozhestvensky had left Nosy Be at two o'clock the day before. The tsar and the Admiralty learned about his departure from the French. Rozhestvensky sent cables to the tsar, Avelan, and Grand Duke Alexei with identical text: "On March third, the squadron departed for its destination." But they did not reach St. Petersburg until March 5. Twenty hours after his actual departure, the Admiralty was still sending cables to him at Nosy Be.

Neither the Admiralty nor the tsar knew Rozhestvensky's destination. "The route of the squadron is unknown to us," the embarrassed naval minister confessed to Nebogatov.

The admiral had eloped. He had disappeared into the immense ocean. With no tools of offshore communications available, for at least three weeks the world would have no way of hearing anything about him—unless cunning Togo intercepted him at sea.

Before disappearing in the Indian Ocean, the admiral sent a final cable to Avelan, asking him to dispatch Chukhnin to Port Said immediately. There Chukhnin could join Nebogatov's detachment. Chukhnin, he continued, should "command the [joint] fleet, and I keep commanding the squadron. Absolutely necessary to prevent anarchy in the case of my death or injury."

8

"Ten Guns Done Up in India Rubber,"

MARCH 1905, INDIAN OCEAN

1

In March 1905, the Russian consul in Singapore, Mr. Rudanovsky, was the busiest man in town. Before the war started, his position had not been an enviable one. Though located at the crossroads of thriving Asian commerce, Singapore was on the periphery of the Russian Empire. Ships commuting between European Russia and Vladivostok passed it by or sometimes made brief stopovers there to replenish food, water, and coal supplies. Occasionally a passenger, overridden by sudden disease, had to be taken care of and sometimes buried in the local cemetery, but that was it. All the Russian consul had to do was to attend to the needs of haughty naval captains and boorish merchants.

Rudanovsky was a conscientious person, energetic and hardworking. Russian naval officers knew and liked him. They thought he was infinitely better than many other consuls, who were notoriously indifferent and lazy. But Rudanovsky's was an unfulfilled life. The consulate work was routine, the British who had founded and now owned the city were snobbish and unfriendly, and the climate was oppressive. In the eyes of the Foreign Ministry personnel, a post in Singapore was almost an exile. Then the war came.

Totally unprepared for the war, lacking any infrastructure in Asia, from navigable ports to coal depositories, Russia also lacked secret agents. In Europe, vital and delicate missions associated with Rozhestvensky's journey could be entrusted to professional spies like Garting. Greedy and self-promoting, those men knew how to run a spy ring, get rid of enemy surveillance, conduct sabotage, and move around unnoticed. Almost no Russian agent in Asia had such skills. They were chosen hastily from those present at the time. Rudanovsky was one of them.

In the fall of 1904, to his surprise, he was given a task of paramount importance: to prepare the scene for Rozhestvensky's safe passage. Nobody knew which route the admiral would take but Singapore looked like a viable option.

Unlike Garting in Denmark or Maximov in Egypt, Rudanovsky was not given much money or many associates. The Admiralty and the Foreign Ministry felt that it would be a waste of time and resources. No matter how much money was spent, the British would not let the Russians run a serious support operation anyway.

Rudanovsky was on his own. He communicated with people in other remote places, also involved in secret missions, but they were all thousands miles away: Commander Polis in Batavia, Ambassador Pavlov in Shanghai, others in Ceylon and Saigon.

Singapore, or the Lion City, was a fairly old settlement by colonial standards. Founded by Sir Stamford Raffles of the British East India Company in 1819, by the twentieth century it was almost a patriarch among imperial outposts. Its roadstead always full of ships, its merchants selling tin and rubber from Malaysia, rubies and sapphires from Thailand, Indian ivory, and Chinese handicrafts, Singapore was the center of commerce and social life for numerous expatriates, bored to death at distant stations lost in the jungle. Spies operated amid the traders, bureaucrats, and officers.

⬙ Kaiser Wilhelm II of Germany had pushed his cousin, Tsar Nicholas II, into annexations and, eventually, war in the Far East. The kaiser was the *enfant terrible* of European royals, aspiring to excel in everything, including seamanship and even painting. Here he holds Divine Service aboard his yacht, the *Hohenzollern*.

⬙ Tsar Nicholas II longed for glory. He thought he could achieve it by occupying Manchuria and Korea.

■ Grand Duke Alexander, a cousin and the most trusted friend of the tsar's youth. A born troublemaker, he supported a militant stand in the Far East.

■ King Edward VII sporting an opalette. Known as uncle Bertie to the tsar, the playboy king was concerned Russia and Britain might go to war in 1904.

■ Admiral Evgeny Alexeev, the Viceroy of the Far East. An illegitimate son of Emperor Alexander II, he was the tsar's uncle. He believed that the war against Japan would be won easily.

The Romanovs were part of a greater European royal family. Emperor Alexander III, Empress Maria Fedorovna, and her sister Alexandra, princess of Wales. [Hoover Institution]

▰ Port Arthur, a Russian naval base in the Far East. It became the apple
of discord between Russia and Japan and also the first Japanese target
during the war. As a base, Port Arthur was very vulnerable; ships could
not leave its harbor during low tide. Also, there was not enough space for
maneuvering in the bay. As for the surrounding hills, they would provide
an excellent site for Japanese artillery in the fall of 1904.

■ The moonlight in Port Arthur. The time is early
1904, and the Russians still do not suspect that Japan
might attack. Meanwhile, Chinese boatmen still freely
visit Russian ships. Later, they will be banned as
potential spies.

◪ Admiral Zinovy Petrovich Rozhestvensky. He fought in the Russo-Turkish War, created Bulgaria's navy, served as Russia's naval attaché in London, headed the Naval General Staff, and finally, led the Russian fleet in the battle of Tsushima. The British press nicknamed him Mad Dog.

◪ The *Kreiser* clipper. Rozhestvensky was her captain in the North Pacific in 1890–1892. She had hit a rock in America Bay, but Rozhestvensky rescued the ship and safely took her back to Vladivostok.

Admiral Stepan Osipovich Makarov, a popular naval leader and Rozhestvensky's rival in everything. He died in the sinking of the *Petropavlovsk* battleship at Port Arthur on March 31, 1904.

April 6, 1904. Admiral Skrydlov, appointed commander-in-chief of the Pacific Fleet after Makarov's death, arrives in St. Petersburg. The Russian public is still enthusiastic about the war, and Skrydlov is warmly welcomed by his fans.

■ Admiral Skrydlov was a popular figure in the navy.
A Russian poster depicts Skrydlov on the bridge of a
ship during a storm. Rozhestvensky thought the admiral
was guilty of self-promotion.

◩ The *Kasuga* armored cruiser. Japan bought her from Argentina. Rozhestvensky had vied for the ship himself and even kept a picture of her in his desk.

◩ September 1904, Reval. The officers of Rozhestvensky's flagship, the *Suvorov*. Almost all will die nine months later, on May 14, 1905, at Tsushima.

The new technology, steam, allowed ships to cross huge distances notwithstanding the weather, but it made them totally dependent on prompt supplies of coal. The ships were also more easily detectable because of the lush plumes of smoke they emitted.

At the turn of the last century, torpedo boats were the hounds of the sea. They were fast and armed with torpedoes. In 1904, the Russians suspected that such a ship could stage an ambush in the Baltic Sea, attacking Rozhestvensky's armada after dark.

☑ A curve of the Suez Canal. The narrow and busy highway looked dangerous to the Russians, who suspected a possible Japanese ambush there. Reportedly, native boats, like the one on the left, could carry torpedoes. The Russians also believed the deserted shores could harbor armed saboteurs.

☑ A British trawler damaged by the armada's gunfire in October 9, 1904. She had been mistaken for a Japanese torpedo boat.

A British ship salutes a foreign flag on high seas.

■ The city of Tangier in Morocco. The armada reached it on October 21, 1904. There the ships split into two units, one going through the Suez, another traveling around Africa. Still anticipating an ambush, Rozhestvensky wanted to save at least some of his ships.

My dear sir,
I shall be pleased to
exchange cards with you.
This is the Admiral
Togo.
My address
is T. Moore
Osaka-
technical-
College Osaka
Japan.

15/VIII – 1906.

▰ Admiral Togo Heihachiro. He masterminded and led all
the major operations of the Japanese navy in 1904–1905. On
May 14–15, 1905, he decimated the Russian fleet at Tsushima.

May 21, 1905. A week after the battle, Admiral Togo visits Rozhestvensky in the naval hospital at Sasebo (a contemporary Russian sketch).

The *Izumrud* cruiser. On May 15, 1905, when
surrounded by Admiral Togo's twenty-seven ships,
she decided to give it a try. The gallant ship made
it through the Japanese blockade but then
shipwrecked on the Russian coast.

The city of Vladivostok. It was the armada's destination, but
only three ships reached it out of the squadron of thirty-eight.

The city, stretching north from the spacious and safe harbor, lay on low hills, covered by spectacular forests. Numerous islets studding the harbor were also covered by tropical groves. The great jungle of the Malaysian Peninsula was very close, across the narrow Johor Strait to the north. Tigers crossed the strait and raided suburbs. Frightened not as much by tigers as by dysentery and malaria, Europeans stuck to their compound. There, in claustrophobic clubs and darkened bars, they exchanged gossip and made deals. In March 1905, the biggest news and the dearest commodity was war.

Consul Rudanovsky was a pessimist by nature. And his country's performance did not encourage optimism. He didn't expect anything good for Rozhestvensky's squadron and hoped only that the squadron would not be attacked in the area of his responsibility.

Rudanovsky reported to St. Petersburg that Togo was inclined to intercept Rozhestvensky's armada before it reached the Far East. According to the consul's informants, Togo planned to attack the squadron in East India. Perhaps there was something to that, for on December 9 Rudanovsky saw two Japanese cruisers in the Singapore harbor.

The consul was sure that the British were quietly assisting Togo. He felt he was living in enemy territory. When St. Petersburg informed him that the Danish consul in the city had been instructed to help him provide Rozhestvensky's squadron with food, Rudanovsky immediately replied, "I have to warn you respectfully that the content of the cable will be reported today to the English government and the Japanese consul."

He kept warning St. Petersburg that Singapore swarmed with Japanese spies—which was certainly true. London was concerned about these allegations. The Japanese were secretive and did not keep London informed about their plans, but these reports gave credence to an earlier statement of the Japanese Foreign Minister. He had told the British ambassador that torpedo boats might attack Rozhestvensky in the Indian Ocean. An attack near Singapore would have been terribly embarrassing for His Majesty's government.

The British Foreign Office contacted the Colonial Office. The latter promised to investigate "the alleged movements of Japanese sailors in the Straits settlements with a view to attacking ships of the Russian Fleet." The governor of Singapore cabled the Colonial Secretary: "A close watch is being kept on suspected agents of both belligerents."

The Singapore police were monitoring the moves of all Japanese subjects in the territory of the colony. They were watching passenger steamers closely, keeping track of all arrivals and departures, and paying special attention to passengers' itineraries. Some of the Japanese were proceeding further west, to Port Said on the Suez Canal, which was a suspicious destination given the current Russian concerns.

As for the alleged Japanese preparations for sinking Rozhestvensky's ships off Singapore, local authorities were skeptical. The chief of police reported to the governor:

> I don't believe a word about the torpedoes and I think I can explain how that story got about. Early in December last, thirty Japanese prostitutes and ten men came here from Japan. The boarding officers were talking about this when young Jennings (who is a reporter for the *Straits Times*) came in. Hearing something about the Japanese, he asked what it was and was told by one of the boarding officers (as a joke) that the Japanese had brought in thirty torpedoes and ten guns done up in India rubber for the Baltic Fleet. He probably told his father, who in turn told the Russian Consul. I may mention that Mr. Jennings, senior, is in the Russian Consul's pay.

Rudanovsky was a simpleton. He believed every rumor he heard. Having swallowed the story of a playful boarding officer, he reported to St. Petersburg that Togo had dispatched torpedo boats and submarines to the vicinity of Singapore.

A grand military strategist like many desk clerks, Rudanovsky thought Rozhestvensky had to attack Togo immediately. He thought the prolonged stay at Madagascar was the admiral's choice and blamed him for that. The squadron finally left Nosy Be on March 3, but after that it disappeared. Nobody knew where it was.

The world was intrigued. Military commanders, kings, presidents, ambassadors, and spies were making bets. Had the Mad Dog received a secret order to turn back to Russia? In that case, would he go along East Africa's coast via the Suez? Or was he heading for East Asia? But which route did he plan to take? The Strait of Malacca, bypassing Singapore, the stronghold of the British whom the Mad Dog hated and who hated him? The Sunda Strait in the south? Or had he chosen neither and was now moving along Australia's northern coast, observed solely by crocodiles but risking losing his ships on one of the treacherous reefs? Or could Togo have already intercepted the Russians somewhere in the Indian Ocean?

The British commander-in-chief of the China Station, Vice-Admiral Gerard Noel, was also at a loss. He believed that war against Russia and France was still likely. At the end of December, the Admiralty had sent him a bellicose cable: "Should Russian reinforcements continue their eastern progress, you will receive orders to take your fleet to Singapore." A month later, another order came: "Be prepared to move your fleet to Singapore on receipt of telegraphic orders to that effect."

Noel felt bound by the warnings. However, now the Admiralty was maintaining an enigmatic silence. And there was no news about Rozhestvensky. Noel's intelligence officers were working hard, but to no avail. After the Russians left Madagascar, four Japanese warships passed by Singapore. Could it mean that Togo had taken his fleet to the Indian Ocean? For all people knew, Rozhestvensky's ships might already be lying on the sea bottom.

On March 20, Rudanovsky received a message from Commander Polis in Batavia. The hastily written letter advised Rudanovsky to be "especially watchful." If everything was fine with Rozhestvensky's ships, he should be approaching Asian shores. Not wasting any time, Rudanovsky started cruising the sea every night on a steam cutter. He did not encounter Japanese ships in the offshore waters. But he did not encounter Rozhestvensky's ships either.

Rudanovsky became hysterical. Admiral Nebogatov's ships, dispatched from Kronshtadt to reinforce Rozhestvensky's armada, were already in Djibouti, preparing to cross the Indian Ocean. Where, in heaven's name, would they meet the resourceful Mad Dog who had disappeared in the sea, having left no instructions or even a hint, as if he were not His Imperial Majesty's general-adjutant but a buccaneer? Where was the Mad Dog's squadron?

2

On March 20, when Rudanovsky, cursing Rozhestvensky, was starting his nightly watch, Admiral Nebogatov's ships were in Djibouti. That same day, as perplexed as Rudanovsky and perhaps just as angry, Nebogatov cabled Naval Minister Avelan: "In three days will be ready to move on. Am asking for instructions on whether I should go to Vladivostok independently or join Rozhestvensky. In the latter case, please inform where the joining can take place, for I have absolutely no information about where he is or which route he is taking."

It had taken Nebogatov's ships less than seven weeks to get to Djibouti from Libava. That was not bad, particularly since the 3rd Pacific Squadron, as it was rather pompously named, was not impressive at all.

The Baltic Fleet did not have many ships remaining. Nebogatov's squadron consisted of older vessels—the battleships *Nicholas I, Seniavin, Ushakov, Apraxin,* and the cruiser *Vladimir Monomakh.* The only ship of any value was the cruiser *Rus.* Last summer, Rozhestvensky had refused to take older ships with him. Now they were forcibly given to him.

In 1905, Nikolai Ivanovich Nebogatov was fifty-six. He was an officer's son born in the vicinity of the capital. He became a naval cadet at the age of sixteen and later served in the Baltic Sea Fleet. At the age of forty, in 1889, he was appointed captain of the gunboat *Grad*—not a desirable post for a man his age. He received the rank of captain when he was forty-five and rear-admiral in 1901, at fifty-two.

In 1904, when the war struck, he was in the Black Sea, commanding its artillery practice unit. Unexpectedly, in September he was transferred to St. Petersburg. In December he was sent to Libava to prepare the 3rd Pacific Squadron for its voyage. It was assumed that some other admiral would eventually lead the squadron to the Far East. Temporarily, Nebogatov raised his flag on the battleship *Nicholas I,* expecting to surrender command to somebody else. Nobody thought that all of the other candidacies would somehow evaporate and that Nebogatov, previously unknown to the public, would receive this high command by default.

On January 11, Nebogatov was received by the tsar. Of course, the sovereign was preoccupied with other matters. Two days earlier the infamous Bloody Sunday had occurred, and now the country was plunging into a revolutionary storm. Probably not giving much thought to it, the tsar confirmed Nebogatov's appointment.

Three weeks later, on February 2, the august chief of the navy, Grand Duke Alexei, laconically blessed Nebogatov's squadron, calling on them to be as heroic as their Port Arthur comrades (most of whom were dead or in captivity). Later that day, the ships weighed anchor.

Like all ships sailing west from Kronshtadt, they were heading for Skagen, the bottleneck of the North Sea. From the start, Nebogatov insisted on constant drills; like Rozhestvensky, he was concerned about a nighttime torpedo attack. Not a disciplinarian at all, cheerful and optimistic, he visited various ships of his detachment regularly and became popular with the crews.

Like Rozhestvensky four months earlier, Nebogatov received alarming news in Skagen: The Japanese ambassador to The Hague was darkly hinting at a clandestine attack in Danish waters. However, this time the Admiralty wisely warned Nebogatov that it might be a provocation, intended to cause another Dogger Bank incident.

From Skagen, Nebogatov sent the cruiser *Rus* back to Libava; her engine was down. Though he was far from the theater of war, he was already losing ships.

Approaching the infamous Dogger Bank, cautious Nebogatov moved closer to the Dutch shore. Radio operators scanned the airwaves that night with extreme care, but heard only reassuring talk in German.

British cruisers were waiting for Nebogatov in the English Channel. Having passed through this sinister screening, the detachment reached the Bay of Biscay, which met them with a ferocious storm. To Nebogatov's delight, the old ships survived the tempest nicely, though three-fourths of the crews got seasick and a lot of furniture and dishes were broken.

After that they proceeded to Tangier and then through the Gibraltar Strait. There Nebogatov, suspicious of British intentions, ordered almost all lights out.

From Gibraltar they headed for Soudha on Crete. Their stay was to be quick and practical: make the most essential repairs and take on coal. Instead, they got into trouble.

With their lights down, Nebogatov's ships could remain inconspicuous at sea, but on Crete they became the talk of the day. It was an exact repetition of Felkersam's debacle three months earlier. Allowed ashore, the men immediately got drunk and started fights with the locals and with sailors of other nationalities. The debauchery continued for several nights.

British newspapers exploded with well-practiced rage. Foreign Minister Lamsdorf, always glad to snap at the arrogant Russian navy, caustically asked Naval Minister Avelan what he knew about "the indecent behavior" of Nebogatov's men. Avelan demanded explanations from Nebogatov.

The commander of the 3rd Pacific Squadron was intimidated. His response sounded silly: "The behavior of the crews ashore is absolutely not something extraordinary." British reports were "overstated," he humbly suggested.

Meanwhile, the behavior of his men was creating problems for one particular Russian: Queen Olga of Greece, the advocate of her homeland's navy. She was heading for Crete to welcome Nebogatov, while his men were punching her subjects. She was sailing on the

Greek warship *Sfakteria,* and the heir to the throne, Prince George, was with her. But Olga pretended that nothing had happened. She received Nebogatov on March 3 and two days later started visiting the Russian ships.

To belittle this endorsement of the Russian war effort in British eyes, her husband, the King of Greece, would have to visit the British squadron at Corfu four weeks later. The plague of the greater European royal family, Kaiser Wilhelm, took advantage of the occasion and sailed to the British flagship on his yacht the *Hohenzollern* to dine with the admiral. He anticipated some gossip, which he could then maliciously report to the tsar.

No matter how flattering the attention of Queen Olga might have been, Nebogatov had another important meeting in Crete: Captain Essen was returning to Russia from Japanese captivity.

Nikolai Essen had been the captain of the *Sevastopol* in Port Arthur. He possessed what Nebogatov and his officers lacked: battle experience. The Admiralty rerouted him from Paris to Piraeus, and the Russian flotilla permanently stationed at Soudha dispatched a torpedo boat to bring Essen to Crete "in strict secrecy."

Essen had many stories to tell. After his battleship had struck a mine in the Yellow Sea and panic broke out, he had to order his men back to their stations with drawn revolver. The *Sevastopol* had survived that calamity only to be sunk six months later off Port Arthur. Among other things, Essen informed Nebogatov that the Japanese were hellishly good at high-speed, long-distance shooting. Alarmed, Nebogatov commanded artillery practice, but that single effort could not help much. Dispirited by the talk with Essen and his crews' lack of discipline, the admiral led the squadron to Port Said.

A month earlier, the Admiralty and the Foreign Ministry had agreed to restore the secret network they had used in the Red Sea for Felkersam and Dobrotvorsky. Now spies were reporting that Japan had several secret deposits of explosives on the Red Sea coast. Maximov reported from Cairo that the number of Japanese visitors to the area had significantly increased again.

Nevertheless, Nebogatov passed through the canal safely and headed for Djibouti. The person to cushion his stay there was the veteran of the previous cloak-and-dagger campaign, Commander Shvank. By that time everybody was tired of spy games, and it was decided that he would not hide and that the French would be notified of his presence and of the purpose of his mission. To Shvank's satisfaction, local French bureaucrats were understanding and accommodating, allowing him to send cables when the telegraph was officially closed at night and during the long afternoon siesta.

Nebogatov spent five days in Djibouti, from March 20 to March 25. He anchored six miles away from shore. It took a steam cutter more than an hour to reach the squadron, and from the port the silhouettes of Nebogatov's ships were barely visible. Nebogatov had done that not because he was afraid of Japanese saboteurs but because he wanted to oblige the French; now nobody could say France was violating its neutrality.

In Soudha, Nebogatov learned that Rozhestvensky had left Madagascar on March 3. In a cable to Nebogatov, the Admiralty evasively wrote that Rozhestvensky was heading for "his destination." The fact was that the Admiralty had no idea what that destination was.

In 1900–1902, Nebogatov had assisted Rozhestvensky in the Artillery Practice Unit and had had a chance to get to know him well. Thus, he was probably not surprised by his commander's unorthodox behavior. Nevertheless, it must have hurt to know that his boss did not want him and intended to skip their rendezvous altogether.

Instructing the embarrassed admiral, Naval Minister Avelan cabled: "Try to find the squadron. We do not know what its route is. . . . Rozhestvensky has set the breakthrough to Vladivostok as his goal. . . . If you cannot join his squadron, go to Vladivostok." That was it.

On March 25, Nebogatov cabled back: "Leaving Djibouti to search for Rozhestvensky; will go through the Strait of Malacca."

Nikolai Ivanovich Nebogatov was not a fighter. He was a soft and polite man. In Tangier, the kind-hearted admiral had discharged a lieutenant suffering from nothing else but seasickness. From Soudha he begged the Admiralty to send to Djibouti "an experienced artillery officer" to finally equip his squadron with a real expert. He continued to tolerate his men's violent debauchery. In the North Sea he had prudently crawled along the Dutch coast to avoid irritating the British. In Djibouti he kept the French happy by staying out of their territorial waters. Probably, he would have been an ideal commander for a fleet pursuing a diplomatic mission. But would he stand up to the challenge of leaving the Middle East and heading for war all by himself? Would he have enough stamina? And where the hell was his irritable but awesome boss?

3

It was seven o'clock in the morning of March 26. A small steam cutter was hastily leaving Singapore harbor. It carried just one passenger— the Russian consul, Rudanovsky. An hour ago, a British mail steamer had arrived, and the skipper had informed the consul that the night before he had seen the Russian squadron between Penang and Malacca. Not losing a second, Rudanovsky ordered his cutter west.

Several hours passed. The cutter bobbed on the waves. There was no squadron. It was quite possible that the skipper had lied or been mistaken. It is not that easy to be sure about what you see in the ocean at night, especially if you notice something too frightening to approach, like the Mad Dog's squadron.

At eleven o'clock, the cutter passed the Raffles lighthouse, thirty miles away from the city. Suddenly, the consul saw numerous plumes of smoke on the horizon. They were from the advance ships of Admiral Zinovy Petrovich Rozhestvensky.

The cutter leaped forward. The enthusiastic consul hoped to board the flagship. The mast of his cutter carried a signal in English: "Want to communicate personally." He wanted to shake hands, congratulate the admiral on his successful voyage, and deliver recent reports about Japanese activities in the area.

But when the cutter approached the *Suvorov*, Rozhestvensky curtly signaled that he was "in haste" and asked the consul to contact one of the torpedo boats instead. Deeply hurt, Rudanovsky took his cutter to the *Bedovy*. He reported to her captain and gave him mail for the squadron.

Not satisfied with this, Rudanovsky then headed for the cruisers *Oleg* and *Donskoi*. Through a megaphone, he told their crews the burning news: In Manchuria, the Russian army had retreated, abandoning huge amounts of foodstuffs; Linevich had become the new commander-in-chief after Kuropatkin had been fired; two weeks earlier four Japanese warships had paid a visit to Singapore; Togo, with the main force, was believed to be at Borneo, probably just 300 miles away; and Nebogatov was in Djibouti. After this public briefing, there was nothing left for poor Rudanovsky, unrewarded by the unsentimental admiral, but to dejectedly follow the squadron in his cutter.

At two o'clock, to the utter amazement of people ashore, the squadron passed by Singapore. The city itself remained seven miles away, but the Russians could see the high spire of St. Andrew's Cathedral.

The fleet passed the hostile stronghold in perfect order and proud silence. Not a single ship, not even the slow and messy transports, misbehaved. Columns were precise, solemn, and dignified.

Rozhestvensky must have been pleased. This time, the hateful British were seeing not a flock of sheep but a disciplined naval formation, speedily and fearlessly proceeding to its destination. Hostile eyes watching the fleet should have been very much displeased with what they saw.

They were. A British report related the scene:

They were steaming N.E. by North at a varying speed of from 5 to 8 knots, the battle squadron in single line ahead at irregular intervals of about three cables, the cruisers ahead and astern at a distance of about one mile, the destroyers on the port quarters of the battle ships. . . . All ships were partially cleared for action, the men-of-war painted black with white funnels with black tops. Some ships were apparently ready for coaling, but whether about to commence or finished was not quite clear.

Having returned to the city, Rudanovsky learned through his informants that the Japanese consul had already sent ciphered telegrams to Padang in Sumatra, Batavia in Java, Makassar in Celebes, Labuan in Borneo, and last but not least, Tokyo.

9

"A Hole Coated in Iron,"
MARCH 26–MAY 1, 1905,
INDOCHINA

1

AT SEVEN O'CLOCK IN THE EVENING, MARCH 26, THE SQUAD-
ron entered the South China Sea. They had reached the third ocean of
their journey, the one in which their final destination lay. The admiral
confirmed the course: NO 21, Cam Ranh Bay in French Indochina.
Keeping the speed of eight knots, the squadron continued in the dark.

Rozhestvensky was satisfied with the last twenty-three days of the
voyage. Having left loathsome Madagascar where the squadron had
stayed for more than two months, ridiculed by the whole world, losing
face and combat spirit, it had safely arrived in East Asia—and in the
most unlikely place of all—the Strait of Malacca. Few had thought
Rozhestvensky would dare do this. His invisible counterpart, Togo,
must have found new appreciation for the Russian leader.

The choice had not been a simple one. The Strait of Malacca,
which separates the Indonesian island of Sumatra from continental
Asia, was one of the busiest commercial venues in the world. The city
of Singapore at its eastern end was the British capital of the area. The

Strait of Malacca was five hundred miles long and often not wider than thirty, shaped like a perfect strategic trap. The Singapore Strait, which continued the Strait of Malacca to the South China Sea, was even narrower—just ten miles—a perfect place for a torpedo attack, particularly with the Japanese naval bases relatively close and the coast abundant with secluded bays of all sorts. Of course, Togo's main force would not be allowed to stage a battle there; that would stain the reputation of the British Empire. But what if Togo waited for Rozhestvensky in the South China Sea right at the mouth of the strait? That would be an unavoidable ambush.

Another option had been the Sunda Strait, eight hundred miles south. The Russian Admiralty had believed that Rozhestvensky would go there. In the beginning of January, he himself had intended just that. It lay between Java and Sumatra and was world famous; the volcano Krakatau in its middle had erupted in 1883, killing 36,000 people. That strait was also kind of a bottleneck, sixteen miles at its narrowest, but it was short—one hundred miles. Even at the creeping pace of eight knots, the squadron could hope to pass it between dawn and dusk.

There were three other gateways: through the Strait of Lombok and the Celebes Sea; by the Timor Sea and the Torres Strait, edging the northern coast of Australia; or by the south of Australia and the Coral Sea. These three routes were extremely long, and the southern seas were full of unmarked reefs, but they would take the squadron through waters were Togo would be unlikely to lie in wait. Western naval experts were publicly advocating them as the wisest options.

When the admiral decided on the Strait of Malacca, it took the world by surprise. When Tsar Nicholas II learned that the squadron had safely passed through that bottleneck, he wrote with admiration in his diary, "Nobody thought it would take this particular route!"

For a battleship like the *Suvorov,* crossing the Indian Ocean was an easy excursion. The ocean covers one-seventh of the Earth's surface, but modern steam and steel could easily deal with such space. For a unit of five new battleships, this would have been a routine voyage.

But for a squadron consisting of forty-five vessels, from the newest ironclads to the oldest transports, the crossing was a challenge.

They had left Nosy Be on March 3. Anticipating a long and boring voyage, officers had acquired numerous companions—exotic beasts. The captain of the cruiser *Aurora*, Yegoriev, brought a python and a young crocodile. His officers brought several crocodiles, two huge tortoises, lemurs, and chameleons. This entire menagerie crept and jumped around cabins and decks. The *Aurora*'s men complained that they were afraid to go to sleep.

The *Suvorov* also carried unusual pets. One of the monkeys there, having stolen an icon and thrown it overboard, earned exile to another ship and the nickname Iconoclast.

The ocean did not tire of exhibiting its own pets. Huge sharks escorted the squadron, nibbling at everything the crews threw or dropped overboard, even wood. The sharks hoped for finer food, of course. An insane sailor from the *Zhemchug* jumped into the water but was rescued before the sharks got him. The day before, another one had dived from the *Kiev* and perished. This terrible suicide had a gloomy impact on the crewmen.

Of course, sailors tried to cheer up. They put lumps of meat on huge hooks and fished for monsters. Sharks were not spoiled by attention in those lonely waters, and in the transparent aquamarine sea, sailors watched them snapping at the bait. It was very difficult to pull a shark from the water, for the wounded creature desperately fought for its life. Once aboard, an officer would shoot it with a revolver, and the shark would die in slow agony. When it was finally dead, sailors would check the contents of its stomach. No human remains were ever found.

At night the squadron proceeded, organized in two columns, each five miles long. The ships were illuminated with multicolored lights, reminding sailors of downtown St. Petersburg with its glorious Nevsky Prospect.

Nostalgic, officers and crewmen thought and talked about home. They started exchanging relatives' addresses; discussing when the battle would come and who would survive it.

Many expected to meet Togo soon. The doctors started giving lectures on first aid. Cruisers, doing reconnaissance at night, reported mysterious lights, suggesting they were Togo's scouts. Others said they were just bright tropical stars crawling over the horizon.

Transports were a disaster. Often, their engines would break down, and the whole armada would have to stop and wait until the transport's crew fixed the problem. The older battleship *Sisoi* became handicapped twelve times. Due to this, sometimes the squadron had to move at the pathetic speed of five knots, while the *Suvorov*, for example, was almost always capable of doing at least fifteen.

To the immense fury of the admiral, no matter how hard they tried, transports could not stay in a disciplined column. When he was not too exhausted by the twenty-four hour watch, Rozhestvensky would summon a guilty ship to the *Suvorov*'s stern and scold her through a megaphone.

Yet, he had no choice but to bring this undisciplined horde with him. Transports were essential; they were carrying coal. By March 8 the squadron needed to coal at sea. From 6 A.M. to 4 P.M., the battleships took two hundred tons each.

The torpedo boats were a headache as well. They could not carry a stock of coal and would therefore run out of fuel before the squadron reached Asia. Often, Rozhestvensky ordered the bigger ships to tow them to save precious coal.

Then there were constant reports about suspicious ships that demanded urgent attention. His paranoia had calmed down, but it seemed the disease was on the rise among his captains. Because of all these concerns, throughout the voyage the admiral rarely left the bridge before nine o'clock at night. That meant dinner at the wardroom had to be postponed, too.

With each day, dinner was becoming less and less satisfying, even for officers. The first ships to run out of good food were, of course, the torpedo boats, and the officers from bigger ships like the *Suvorov* would bring them luxuries: sardines, lobsters, and smoked meat. But by the time the squadron reached the Strait of Malacca, everybody in the *Suvorov*'s wardroom had to eat the detested stinking *solonina*. Even at Rozhestvensky's table, they stopped serving not only vodka and coffee but meat, too. Smokers were running out of cigarettes and matches. Soap became hard to find as well.

The Strait of Malacca was reached at noon, March 23. The squadron was bound to be discovered any minute. Indeed, almost immediately they met a ship heading west. Rozhestvensky ordered exceptional vigilance. Again, at night men slept at the guns; one-third of the officers were ordered on deck. Electric bulbs had been painted dark blue, and human faces acquired an unpleasant deadened shade. Silence fell.

Cruisers probed passersby with powerful searchlights. Alien steamers panicked and steered away. The Mad Dog's squadron, having materialized from nowhere, inspired awe. Rozhestvensky's officers were maliciously saying that steamers had learned their lesson after the Dogger Bank incident.

The admiral wanted to go through the bottleneck as quickly as possible, but this time the gods were against him. The transports were moving excruciatingly slowly. As a result, the squadron was making just eight knots. Meanwhile, everybody knew that Togo's battle speed was fifteen.

Suddenly, Admiral Enkvist reported that he had seen twelve torpedo boats with his own eyes. That was too many even for suspicious Rozhestvensky. No extraordinary measures were ordered, and the squadron continued calmly. The next day, the cruiser *Izumrud* announced that she had noticed a suspicious steamer followed by several "whales." It was clear to everybody that the captain of the *Izumrud*, notoriously overcautious Baron Fersen, thought he had seen Japanese submarines, but did not dare to openly say so.

The British commander-in-chief of the China Station, Vice Admiral Noel, in Hong Kong received "intelligence of the arrival of the Russian Fleet in China Seas" on March 25. At that point Rozhestvensky was already halfway through the strait.

Noel immediately dispatched the warships *Sutlej* and *Iphigenia* to Singapore. They were in a hurry, although the *Thetis* and *Amphitrite* were already there. The two warships headed quickly south "with all boilers alight."

On the night of March 25, the squadron passed the town of Malacca. Russians admired its embankment blazing with lights. But it was also clear that if they could see Malacca's illumination, Japanese spies in town were watching the lights of the squadron, too. Almost all officers stayed awake that night. But nothing happened. It looked like Rozhestvensky had fooled Togo. The Japanese hounds had taken the wrong trail.

The next day at two o'clock in the afternoon, they reached Singapore. The city was clearly visible and so were the two British warships in the harbor. The wind brought scents of flowers in bloom. Tiny coral islets were very close. Looking at them, the crewmen talked about "potatoes, onions, cucumbers, salad, and garlic"—the fresh food they had been denied. Seasoned hands were recounting bawdy stories about Singapore's brothels.

Rozhestvensky was looking at the city, too. He was standing at the left side of the bridge, closest to the shore. "In several minutes the telegraph will report this to the whole world . . . ," he said quietly.

2

With the Strait of Malacca lying behind them, the Russians now expected to meet Togo at the Natuna archipelago in the South China Sea, barely three hundred miles northeast. On the evening of March 26, some officers on the *Suvorov* put on clean clothes and stocked their pockets with cotton to stuff into their ears when the cannonade started.

Rozhestvensky himself thought they might be attacked any moment. If the Russian consul in Singapore was right, Togo was very close. The admiral ordered most lights out. He also commanded the *Aurora* and other ships with too many wooden panels and too much posh furniture to throw it overboard; that would make them less susceptible to fire during the battle.

On March 28, he announced that they might meet Togo's main force any time. The *Oleg* and the *Aurora* had to stay with the battleships, Enkvist, commanding the cruisers *Almaz, Donskoi,* and *Rion, Dnieper,* and the torpedo boats, was ordered to cover the transports. The light cruisers, led by Captain Shein, preceded the squadron in a reconnaissance chain.

But the next day, instead of the Japanese, they met the British. At 5 A.M., the *Sutlej* and the *Iphigenia,* speedily racing to Singapore from Hong Kong, encountered the Russian fleet 150 miles southeast of the Mekong River Delta. The *Sutlej* saluted Rozhestvensky's flag with seventeen guns, "but whether this was returned was uncertain," the *Sutlej*'s captain reported (it was). The *Oleg,* the captain continued, "was sent close under our stern to read the ships' name, and then rejoined her consorts."

At eleven o'clock, the hospital ship *Orel* left the squadron for Saigon. That was a strange move on the eve of a possible battle—to deprive the squadron of its hospital. Some people must have thought Rozhestvensky was evacuating Sivers. However, there was a practical reason for the *Orel*'s departure: She had to carry the admiral's cables to St. Petersburg and, hopefully, bring back the incoming mail. She carried a Red Cross flag and, supposedly, could not be stopped by the Japanese.

The cables sent via the *Orel* were of a critical importance. Rozhestvensky was contacting the three key decision-makers in St. Petersburg—the tsar, his uncle, and the naval minister. He informed them that he was three hundred miles away from Cam Ranh Bay. He planned to go there and wait for orders, unless the Japanese fleet attacked him before that.

In the evening, radios started registering strange messages. Several merchant ships, when met at sea and interrogated, announced that they had seen torpedo boats. These might have been French, but the three fastest cruisers, the *Oleg, Zhemchug,* and *Izumrud* rushed to the horizon to check out all suspicious smoke.

On March 30, sixty miles from Cam Ranh, the squadron suddenly stopped and started taking on coal from the transports. The admiral was behaving oddly that day. Officers on the *Suvorov* looked at him in amazement. Why this urgent coaling at sea when a comfortable bay was only a few hours away?

Rozhestvensky kept his thoughts to himself. He watched the coaling, nervously pacing the bridge, frequently consulting his notebook, and from time to time disappearing into his suite. Sometimes frowning, sometimes smiling to himself, he was apparently involved in some mysterious inner debate. He also demanded a chart of the ocean "between Hong Kong and Vladivostok."

Right before lunch, he suddenly asked all of the ships how much coal they had and whether they were ready for a long voyage. While the captains were calculating, he went to lunch with his officers. Contrary to custom, he kept silent during the meal. Immediately afterward, he retired to his study.

At one o'clock he was on the bridge again. All of the ships had reported sufficient resources of coal; only the *Alexander III* was late in its report. Finally, she sent a signal. It was appalling. Rozhestvensky could not believe his eyes. She was reporting a mistake in previous calculations. Four hundred tons of coal were missing. It was finally clear why the *Alexander* had always been the champion in coaling.

Rozhestvensky looked a broken man. He did not even swear. He stood on the bridge silently, clutching the rail. Then he waved his hand and went below.

His audacious intention to rush to Vladivostok immediately, skipping Cam Ranh, Nebogatov, and the tsar's permission failed. The previous course was reconfirmed: NO 21. In the uncertain light of the new moon, the squadron plowed the South China Sea, approaching Indochina.

3

On March 31, at six o'clock in the morning, the squadron reached the entrance to Cam Ranh Bay. Rozhestvensky ordered torpedo boats to sweep the bay for mines; then he sent the transports in. The other ships, not to remain idle, started coaling. On the morning of April 1, the battleships and cruisers entered Cam Ranh. They had made 4,560 miles from Nosy Be and 16,600 miles from Kronshtadt. All they had to do now was to cover 2,500 miles to Vladivostok.

When Foreign Minister Delcasse of France was informed that Rozhestvensky would doubtlessly stop in Indochina, he "almost jumped out of his skin" and moaned: "What can I do? Refuse Admiral Rozhestvensky an anchorage and thus rob him of any chance of taking in supplies, waiting for his reinforcements and fitting his squadron out for the critical encounter?"

He said his hope was that it would take at least a week to get the official information from Saigon and then send Rozhestvensky a formal order to sail away. "So the Russian squadron will have plenty of time to take in fresh supplies before we compel it to leave our waters."

Cam Ranh was a two-part deepwater bay, twenty miles long from north to south and ten miles wide. It was considered to be the best deepwater harbor of Southeast Asia, perfectly fit to accommodate any armada. The shores were steep and rocky; patches of forest could be seen here and there. Sandy beaches were of two kinds—white and yellow. The bay reminded some of Port Arthur. The comparison was a sinister one.

Rozhestvensky sent torpedo boats and two cruisers to sea to protect the roadstead. To him, Cam Ranh did not look good at all. If the Japanese succeeded in catching the Russians unaware, they could easily blockade the bay and slowly and meticulously annihilate the squadron there. Under these circumstances, vigilance was a necessity. He even dispatched *Suvorov* officers to the torpedo boats, apparently distrusting their captains.

It appeared that the cruisers assigned for the reconnaissance mission could not be trusted either. On the *Aurora,* one of the searchlights' mirrors, essential for surveillance, became dim, and an imaginative officer used chocolate wrappings, rubbed with mercury, to mend its surface. Despite the unusual repair, Rozhestvensky's favorite missed two ships approaching the harbor on April 2—fortunately only a French cruiser and the *Orel,* back from her mission to Saigon. With fear and remorse, they read Rozhestvensky's signal, "Shame on you, *Aurora!*"

At least now the admiral did not have to use messengers to dispatch cables. Cam Ranh had a telegraph and a post office. On March 31, Rozhestvensky received a telegram informing him that seven days earlier, Nebogatov's detachment had left Djibouti. Some of the news was confused and distorted. The Havas agency, for example, was reporting that Rozhestvensky's squadron was involved in battle with Togo off Borneo. What was certain was that five weeks earlier, two Japanese cruisers had visited Cam Ranh.

On April 1, the admiral summoned a conference of captains and flag officers. They discussed how to protect the squadron in Cam Ranh from a possible Japanese attack. They decided that each night four torpedo boats would be dispatched to sea, two cruisers would guard the entrance to the bay, and six torpedo cutters would form a protective chain. All other ships should be prepared for action. Nets were to be put out nightly to guard the squadron from submarines.

Several days after the conference, the only associate Rozhestvensky trusted, Admiral Felkersam, had a stroke. Doctors were fairly optimistic, saying it was a minor one. But days passed by, and Felkersam stayed in bed.

Cam Ranh lay two hundred miles northeast from the colonial capital of Indochina, beautiful Saigon. Indochina had been colonized fairly recently—in the mid-nineteenth century. In the eyes of the French, it was both vulnerable and precious. The natural riches of the Mekong River valley and its excellent strategic location attracted other colonialist vultures. Paris was very nervous when confronted by the two stronger empires in the area—the British and the Japanese. The last thing Paris wanted was a conflict with London or Tokyo aroused by Rozhestvensky's presence in Cam Ranh.

At first, Cam Ranh looked like paradise after the tiring journey. Everybody tried to get ashore. The *Bezuprechny* torpedo boat crew even took their pet goat for a walk there. In terms of indulgent treatment of pets, the *Bezuprechny* crewmen were not an exception. The captain of the *Aurora*, Yegoriev, was passionately fond of his python; the snake coiled next to him while the captain read in his lounge chair. Every other day, the cruiser's doctor would feed the python with meat through a special glass tube inserted into the snake's mouth, sometimes adding cognac to enhance the beast's spirits.

On their excursions to the mainland, officers encountered dense forest, ravines, fat lizards, vicious ants, bright birds, and exotic flowers unknown even to the doctors who represented the knowledge of science in the group. Wild pigeons were easy prey for hunters, bathing was wonderful, the beach full of magnificent coral formations.

At night, the shore was full of dancing flames; a forest fire was taking a nibble at the jungle. The Russians found it "spectacular." French settlers said that after dusk, tigers and panthers came to the beach looking for prey. Watchmen on the Russian ships complained that at four o'clock each morning, some beast roared on the shore, sounding like an apocalyptic messenger, and received an equally awesome response from its mate in the distance. The French said it was a tiger, the sacred animal of the Vietnamese. Engineers constructing the railroad to Saigon complained that elephants had taken a particular dislike to telegraph posts and were persistently destroying all vertical intrusions.

The heat was as bad as in Madagascar. Crew and officers slept on decks in relative comfort. However, their sleep was troubled; they expected a Japanese submarine attack. The nets did not look like a reliable shield against these monstrous challengers.

On April 2, the commander of the French Indochina Squadron, Rear Admiral de Jonquieres arrived at Cam Ranh on a cruiser. He and Rozhestvensky exchanged visits. The French admiral liked the Russians a lot. It was not his fault that Paris had made him a watchdog. Animated and full of life, de Jonquieres openly supported the Russian cause. He thought that Japan intended to conquer the whole of Asia. He said he had honestly believed they would attack French Indochina first. "Let them attack!" de Jonquieres kept saying theatrically. "Let them even target my cruiser! I will take the colors of France to the

border of our territorial waters!" Later, de Jonquieres sent Rozhestvensky a poem he wrote praising the heroic defense of Port Arthur.

Quite predictably, Paris eventually commanded the romantic de
Jonquieres to drive the Russians out. On April 8, he visited the
squadron again. He was heartbroken; the order stated that the Russians had to leave in twenty-four hours.

Nobody in Cam Ranh, de Jonquieres included, knew what was going on in Paris. When Foreign Minister Delcasse was informed that
Rozhestvensky had anchored at Cam Ranh, he frowned: "If there aren't
any French officials at Cam Ranh, there are French cruisers at Saigon;
we can't pretend we are unable to police our coasts. Tomorrow, if not
today" he expected to be handed "an insolent summons" by the Japanese Minister, Motono, and then to be promptly interpolated by the
socialists, which might lead to a full-blown political crisis. He ordered:

> Wire to Saigon for one of our cruisers to find Admiral Rozhestven-
> sky immediately and request him to put to sea again within twenty-
> four hours. . . . Of course, we needn't be inquisitive about where the
> Russian squadron is going next. If it anchors in another bay on
> the coast of Annam after leaving Cam Ranh, we will again dispatch a
> cruiser to ask it to leave. In that way we shall be respecting the letter,
> if not the spirit, of international law and giving Admiral Rozhestven-
> sky time to join up with the battleships that Admiral Nebogatov is
> bringing him.

Delcasse hoped that de Jonquieres would be able to cope with the
problem; the admiral had the reputation of a man "of great ingenuity
and tact." The Japanese ambassador in Paris was told that the Foreign
Ministry did not know exactly where Rozhestvensky's squadron was.
He was also reminded that it was extremely difficult "to police the long,
rocky, and almost uninhabited coast between Touran and Saigon."

These half-truths didn't help much. The "insolent summons" of the
Japanese anticipated by Delcasse began. Tokyo was angry with Paris:
France was "allowing the Russian admiral breathing time to get his

ships into something like order." As a British naval observer in Tokyo remarked, the Japanese were realizing that Rozhestvensky's squadron "was a reality and not a bogey." They trusted Togo, he continued, but could not "get over the fear of what a few lucky shots may do." He was referring to the lucky shot last year that had killed Russian Admiral Witgeft and "virtually settled the fate of the Port Arthur Fleet."

The Japanese press "protested in the strongest language against the action of the French Government." A British report from Japan said that Tokyo was considering ceasing diplomatic relations with France and was appealing to Britain: "Our ally has never been in doubt but that she can rely on the entire support of the British nation."

France had no other option but to give assurances "that she had adopted the necessary measures to ensure strict respect" was paid to its neutrality. That meant, in plain language, that Rozhestvensky's squadron was a homeless wanderer.

Loathing Paris and St. Petersburg, Rozhestvensky decided to move to the outer roadstead of Cam Ranh, outside the territorial waters of France. He promised de Jonquieres that his cruisers would not attempt to intercept any Japanese vessel. The transports were to stay in the bay. This seemed a sensible compromise.

The day his warships left the bay, April 9, Rozhestvensky hosted the second conference of captains. He summarized his earlier orders. During the forthcoming battle, gunners were to target carefully, even if slowly, and not waste precious shells. Sailors were to be instructed daily how to handle their guns efficiently. If torpedo boats attacked, the ships were not to panic, or they would hit their peers. Only a badly damaged ship, unable to sustain the squadron's pace, could leave the column. A special plan was made in case Togo attacked at Cam Ranh.

Rozhestvensky told his captains that St. Petersburg had ordered him to wait in Cam Ranh for Nebogatov. "I will wait," he grimly said. "I will wait at sea until we use up all the coal except the amount necessary to reach Vladivostok. If by this time, Nebogatov does not arrive— this is not our fault—we will move on. . . . Forward! Always forward! Remember this . . . "

Normally a very good speaker, Rozhestvensky was unusually formal and even bleak. After the meeting, many officers cursed Nebogatov and, even more so, St. Petersburg. Nebogatov had been sent just for numerical satisfaction, they said. One officer said, it is always good to have an extra gun, but not "a hole coated in iron."

In three days, another order from Paris arrived: The transports had to leave Cam Ranh, too. Admiral de Jonquieres on the cruiser *Descartes* watched them weighing anchor, then tactfully steered toward Saigon.

Rozhestvensky waited for him to go. Then he ordered all ships north. In the evening, the Russians entered another bay on the same coast, Van Fong.

That was plain cheating. But how could he possibly keep his ships in the ocean for several more weeks while he waited for Nebogatov?

4

By nightfall on April 13, the squadron found itself at a new anchorage. It had taken them only four and a half hours to reach it. Van Fong Bay was badly protected from wind, but it had one great asset: no colonial settlement, no French, no telegraph—nothing. However, even there they were unlucky; a fishing boat was visiting, and from Van Fong she was sailing straight to Saigon.

Within three days, the whole world learned that the cheating Mad Dog was on French territory again. Another order came from Paris to depart, and the squadron steamed away from the shore. Admiral de Jonquieres watched it from the bridge of his cruiser. The next day, however, Rozhestvensky returned. This time he was allowed four days of relative peace before he had to pretend that he was leaving French territory one more time, on April 26. De Jonquieres, the reluctant watchdog, was back on the cruiser *Guichen*.

For two weeks, the squadron yoyoed in and out of Van Fong. Rocky mountain slopes surrounded the beach. The space not covered with stone was covered with forest. The Vietnamese visited the ships in their tiny boats made of bamboo, the universal building material of the Asian tropics. They brought pigs, chicken, tea, tobacco, garlic, oranges, bananas, papaya, mangoes, tangerines—all overpriced. Often they would give change with forged Russian money—indisputably a Japanese invention. Rozhestvensky advised prudence.

In any case, this food was extremely useful, for the squadron was preparing for Easter—always a feast in Russian homes, even if this home was rocking on waves in front of a hostile shore. Officers went into the forest and brought heaps of flowers to decorate the ships' chapels and wardrooms. However, many of the masses had to be canceled: Rozhestvensky commanded urgent coaling.

That year the joyous spirit of the Easter holiday was very subdued. The Russians felt like refugees, betrayed by allies and forgotten by their own government. The Easter mass was depressing. Even on the *Suvorov* many men stood in the chapel barefooted; their boots had rotted, and St. Petersburg hadn't yet bothered to send replacements.

But Rozhestvensky kept most rituals. After mass, he gave his officers "Christ's kiss." He did not share their feast, though; the *Suvorov* wardroom now housed plenty of coal, and there was no space for him or his staff.

Instead, he boarded a steam cutter and cruised the bay, congratulating all of the ships. Bands were playing; people whispered to each other that the strain had become too much for the admiral; he had lost weight and looked unwell.

Officers exchanged visits. In St. Petersburg on Easter Day they would have visited other people's homes; now they visited other ships' wardrooms, all full of coal, their pianos shielded from dust with rough canvas.

Easter was also spoiled by unrest on the battleship *Orel*. The *Orel* crew was not known for its discipline. The crewmen drank and tended to be unruly; recently one had attacked one of the doctors.

On Easter the crew rebelled. A cow onboard the *Orel* had become sick, or perhaps she was just very old. The senior officer had ordered her slaughtered and cooked for the crew. The crew consumed their ration of rum but refused to touch their meat. They demanded a better lunch. Officers panicked and immediately suggested that the sailors pick any two cows.

The next day, Rozhestvensky visited the disorderly ship. The witnesses present reported that they had never seen him in such a rage. He roared at both the men and the officers in the foulest language. He also gave a proper scolding to the captain of the *Orel,* Jung, for being too "liberal" with his men. In conclusion, Rozhestvensky informed the *Orel* officers that they were "shameful superiors of a shameful crew." Eight sailors were arrested and deported to one of the transports.

The incident on the *Orel* was not an isolated case. A new spirit of anger and despair had descended on the whole squadron. On the transport *Irtysh,* the captain, mate, and officers were constantly drunk and loud, causing indignation among the crew. The *Suvorov*'s captain, the painter Ignatsius, started appearing on the bridge barefooted and without his jacket. Many officers discovered opium cigarettes.

People were tired of everything. Officers were complaining that in St. Petersburg they would make a special trip to the Vasilievsky Island Spit just to watch the spectacular sunset, but here they had stopped feeling the amazing beauty of the nightly performance. For uncaring eyes, the descending sun gilded blue mountaintops, and the red ball of the moon rolled down from the hills to light up the majestic squadron in the bay.

A rumor spread that they would be returning to the foggy Baltic Sea. Amazingly enough, this piece of news invoked protest in many: "Did we suffer these millions of deprivations, storms, starvation, northern cold and tropical heat, spend eight months without news from home, cut off from the whole world, surrounded by constant anxieties, waiting for the attack of torpedo boats or submarines—to end this all in a draw?"

In the absence of news and action, a lot of vain talk occurred. The favorite theme was which ship would perish first in the forthcoming battle with Togo. Of course, the *Suvorov* had the best chance of all.

This caused much anxiety among the crews. Rozhestvensky's death could mean catastrophe for survivors. In spite of constant complaint about the admiral's rudeness, the majority of officers and crewmen still held their leader in the highest esteem. Even those officers who disliked him intensely still expressed their confidence in him when they wrote home from Indochina: "We all place our hopes in the admiral and firmly believe in his experience and knowledge, in spite of all his shortcomings." At about this time, French observers reported from Indochina that "high above the officers and men, there stood a lofty and noble figure—Admiral Rozhestvensky. Always calm and collected, keeping the secrets of his loneliness and gnawing anxieties locked up in his own bosom, he was the very incarnation of courage, energy, and determination."

Virtually nobody in the squadron, with the possible exception of Sivers, knew that the admiral was at the end of his tether. In letters to his wife, he explicitly said that "the continuation of war will result in more and more shameful catastrophes." He suspected that his squadron would perish. With some remorse, he admitted his own increasingly bad temper. He was ashamed of the fact that his chief of staff, Captain Kolong, wept after their meetings. Many people were sick, he reported. He himself had "fallen to pieces, having spent seven months in the tropics."

Good health was a particularly rare commodity in the squadron. Every prolonged stay on a tropical coast brought more diseases. Stomach problems were the most common. To make things worse, the men did not trust doctors. Like their rural ancestors in times past, who killed the doctors at every outbreak of cholera, suspecting that these mysterious men "poisoned" the water and food, the sailors would insist that the doctors had put some medicine into the water whenever it became foul.

In general, the men were bearing their illnesses quite patiently. The only thing that really scared them was vomiting; as soon as a man started throwing up, he would pronounce himself "dying" and the doctor would be informed that "so-and-so is passing away."

Such attacks would often occur after the local Vietnamese had visited a ship; the crew would buy tropical fruit from them and, hungry for nutritious food, eat it all immediately. Of course, both crewmen and officers needed things like fruit badly. The squadron was eating fresh meat every day, but the supply of fresh fruit and vegetables was scarce. Doctors were afraid that scurvy would soon break out.

All in all, the toll of disease and accidents was heavy. According to very incomplete data, the squadron had lost five officers and twenty-five crewmen between Kronshtadt and Indochina. Ten officers and forty-two crewmen had been sent back to Russia (three insane, twenty-eight with tuberculosis). If the squadron had not had its hospital ship, the toll would have been much heavier, though. The ship doctors had the luxury of sending a person with appendicitis to the white *Orel,* where proper surgery could be performed.

But hospital ship or not, no force in the world would have been able to heal the widespread depression, as long as the armada kept purposelessly wandering along the coast of French Indochina.

5

By April, Rozhestvensky and his squadron had become a huge diplomatic embarrassment for St. Petersburg. Nobody knew what to do with them. In addition, people in the capital suspected that Rozhestvensky was capable of openly defying the French.

The tsar instructed his uncle, Grand Duke Alexei, to contact the ferocious admiral. Grand Duke Alexei cabled Rozhestvensky with a stern warning: "Following the Sovereign Emperor's will, you are once again ordered to coordinate your moves with the French colonial administration, demanding nothing from them that would contradict the rules of neutrality." The next paragraph of the cable was nothing but plain hypocrisy: "The French government does not mind at all if the squadron uses the bays for anchoring, but it does not permit operations that might turn these bays into bases for a fleet at war."

Rozhestvensky felt frustrated, abandoned, and angry. On April 26, after yet another expulsion, he cabled Avelan: "It is a real pity that our diplomacy did not support firmly our right to use the bays for anchoring, provided we do not get involved in operations against an adversary. Having wandered around for one month, we are left with engines in disorder and a lot of coal used up."

However, there was an even bigger issue than how to deal with the French. Vladivostok was now only 2,500 miles away. But did it make sense to go there?

Even before reaching Cam Ranh, Rozhestvensky had asked the tsar for instructions. "If it is necessary to proceed, we have to do this very quickly," he stated bluntly, stressing both the urgency of the issue and his personal unwillingness to go any further. He said it would make sense to move on to Vladivostok only if the city still needed the squadron, if it had food for thirty thousand more people and coal for the ships. It was obvious he himself was answering all these "if's" negatively.

He suggested that if it was "too late" to send the squadron to Vladivostok (which was his opinion), then the squadron should return to Russia, for it could not function without a permanent base.

Anticipating that the tsar would insist on moving on, the admiral said that in that case he had to leave Indochina "immediately, not waiting for Nebogatov. The loss of even one week would be difficult to make up."

The cable was sent by the hospital ship *Orel* from Saigon. However, no urgent reply awaited Rozhestvensky when he arrived in Cam Ranh.

As in Madagascar, logistics made communications very difficult. It had been decided in St. Petersburg not to use Cam Ranh as Rozhestvensky's telegraph address; it would greatly embarrass the French. Cables for the admiral were to be sent to Saigon first and then sent on to Cam Ranh via local telegraph.

However, the Russian Foreign Ministry had no representative in Saigon—an incredible situation at such a critical time. As a result of this stupid bureaucratic blunder, the squadron felt "absolutely cut off." "This is outrageous," Rozhestvensky snarled in a cable to the naval minister.

Fortunately for the squadron, the Russian cruiser *Diana,* having escaped from Port Arthur to Saigon several months earlier, had to stay there until the end of the war, as international law demanded. Now her captain, Prince Liven, was to serve as an intermediary. However, he was not to decipher confidential cables to Rozhestvensky. To prevent confusion, such cables were to contain three Latin letters—ZIN, short for Zinovy Petrovich.

Having reached Cam Ranh and still hoping for a quick departure, Rozhestvensky ordered Liven to forward all mail to him immediately. He also demanded daily briefings from the Russian consuls in Singapore, Batavia, Hong Kong, and Shanghai. At first he even suggested that the French embassy in Tokyo might keep him informed as well, but this was nothing but wishful thinking.

The reports that Rozhestvensky started getting were, as usual, alarmist and contradictory. During the months of his forced stay in Indochina, Prince Liven had developed something of a spy network. Now he informed Rozhestvensky that Togo's main force was in Formosa, while other ships were spying on the squadron in Indochina's waters. The Russian Admiralty insisted that on March 23 Togo had left Sasebo with four battleships and the best cruisers for an unknown destination. Later, the Admiralty said that according to its British informants, Togo's main force was at Kure, a naval base in southwestern Honshu.

In April 1905, Admiral Togo still flew his flag on the legendary *Mikasa.* As a British observer remarked from Tokyo, now, after several months of "a life of ease" (since the fall of Port Arthur in December), his fleet had to "re-awake to the graver aspects of war."

British observers thought that Rozhestvensky would be a strong adversary. Togo could place four battleships "in line against a similar number of the best Russian ships," so the combatants were "well matched." Yet, the report continued, "heterogeneity will bring to the

Russians a reduction of speed," whereas Togo was perfectly capable of maintaining a battle speed of fifteen knots.

"The Baltic Fleet has been systematically cried down," the report said. "It may be beaten, but there seems no other reason for its being so than that the Japanese have won other victories."

Most likely, experts thought, during the forthcoming battle Togo would be using his favorite "T" maneuver: placing his line so as to cross ahead or astern the enemy, thus concentrating the fire of several ships upon head or tail of the Russian squadron. There was little doubt that Togo would make good use of such a maneuver; the Japanese fleet had given great attention to target practice recently, to say nothing of its impressive battle experience.

"It must be presumed," the report from Tokyo continued, "that Vladivostok rather than the Yellow Sea is the destination of the Baltic Fleet." It was indeed. But there were several routes leading to Vladivostok. Which one would Rozhestvensky choose? And where would Togo be waiting for him? The report was categorical about this:

> In their approach the Russians could be compelled to fight either in the neighborhood of Tsushima or, with somewhat less certainty, in the north. Should the Japanese go in search of their enemy, the seas are large, and they might miss him. On the other hand, should they await him in the best position they can find on or near their coasts, they must be prepared for the improbable event of their own coast towns being bombarded.
>
> The map shows that if Japan is willing to run this slight risk, she has it in her power to give her fleet a central watching-position, offering many advantages. Such a position may be found in one of the numerous bays in south-western Japan, or in south-eastern Korea. . . . From there, she could bar the Korea Strait.

At about the same time, Rozhestvensky's mind was turning over the same set of names mentioned in the British report: Togo,

Tsushima, the Korea Strait, Vladivostok. However, Rozhestvensky still hoped that the tsar would come to his senses and order the squadron back to Kronshtadt. But as soon as the first cables from St. Petersburg started arriving, Rozhestvensky learned to his immense disappointment that the stubborn monarch still wanted him to continue to Vladivostok.

Rozhestvensky did not know that on March 22, Grand Duke Alexei had chaired a special meeting on the future of the Russian navy. The grand duke himself expressed his trust in "Admiral Rozhestvensky's valor and courage." Yet, he continued, the squadron could not win the war and "master the sea." Russia could lose most of its fleet before his nephew, the tsar, would be ready to sign peace. Minister of Finance Kokovtsev suspected that Russia could lose not only its fleet but even Vladivostok, as it had already lost Port Arthur. Other participants in the conference, such as Foreign Minister Lamsdorf, Minister of War Sakharov, and Naval Minister Avelan, preferred not to make any explicit statement. Their silence spoke for itself.

Lamsdorf was also working on the tsar privately. Every week or so, Nicholas received him at Tsarskoe Selo and each time Lamsdorf tried to persuade him that peace with Japan was necessary.

In April 1905, virtually all St. Petersburg dignitaries thought the war had to be brought to an end and Rozhestvensky recalled. Only the soft-spoken tsar remained bellicose. He sought fame and recognition, and he also sought vengeance. That spring, keeping his yearly routine, Nicholas wrote in his diary on April 29: "The memorable day of Otsu."

But should the war continue, Vladivostok was not the only strategic choice. Another possibility for Rozhestvensky was to find a base somewhere on China's coast and wage war from there, avoiding exposing his squadron to attack on the perilous route to Vladivostok.

At the fateful conference in Peterhof the previous August, Rozhestvensky had mentioned that option. A likely candidate was the Chou-shan archipelago, a group of four hundred islands off Shanghai. The islands, with their steep peaks, covered with cave temples and monasteries, provided excellent harbors, and their location was strategically important for cutting supplies between Japan and its continental army.

But Rozhestvensky now knew that it was not a realistic option. He admitted that Britain would never allow this to happen. Other neutral powers like France would also be hostile to such a move, he thought. In addition, Japan had many excellent cruisers, which could easily blockade any island, thus depriving his squadron of all basic supplies. He also believed that with Port Arthur lost long ago, it made no sense to continue naval operations along China's coast. In other words, he did not like the Vladivostok option and thought all others were impossible. In his cables, he implicitly begged the tsar to prevent the slaughter and recall his fleet.

But the tsar would hear nothing of this defeatist talk. He instructed naval authorities to prepare Vladivostok for Rozhestvensky's arrival. On April 2, Virenius reported to the admiral that Vladivostok was not blockaded by the Japanese from land. Its seven submarines would soon be functional. Five older torpedo boats were ready, and three more would be fixed in a week's time. Three others had arrived and were being assembled. In three weeks, a powerful radio station would become operational as well. All available vessels were ready to depart at short notice to meet Rozhestvensky's squadron in the Sea of Japan.

The Admiralty knew that the squadron would not be able to reach Vladivostok without a major battle with Togo. Virenius sent a special cable to Rozhestvensky concerning Togo's tactics. Togo, Virenius said, preferred to stay at a long distance from his adversary—around 40 cables (8,000 yards). The Japanese admiral always stubbornly stuck to his original plan and therefore could be "easily" fooled by "a sudden, unexpected, perhaps even risky maneuver." Such a maneuver could actually deliver victory to "a weaker side," that is, to Rozhestvensky's squadron.

The instructions were not very helpful. What mattered most was the tsar's strategic decision. And Nicholas had made up his mind: Rozhestvensky was ordered to wait in Indochina for Nebogatov and then proceed to Vladivostok. In the admiral's eyes, this was asking for disaster, but he understood the futility of further arguing with the tsar.

6

If there was a helpless, frustrated diplomat in Southeast Asia in the first week of April 1904, it was Consul Rudanovsky. First he had spent weeks watching out for Rozhestvensky. The thunderous admiral had finally emerged from the waves of the Indian Ocean like angry Neptune and proceeded to his destination without so much as saying hello. For the consul, that humiliating episode had also become highly embarrassing. While talking to the *Suvorov* from his cutter and insisting on being received by the admiral, Rudanovsky had thought he was talking not to Rozhestvensky but to Enkvist.

In his triumphant cables to the Admiralty, the wretched man reported that on March 26 he had met "Admiral Enkvist's squadron" and that Rozhestvensky had taken his battleships by Singapore at nighttime, "positively unnoticed by anybody."

The Admiralty personnel had derived malicious joy from seeing an agent of the rival Foreign Ministry blunder. But now they had another top-secret errand to run, and Rudanovsky was the only person they could use in Southeast Asia. This time he had to find Admiral Nebogatov.

Admiral Nikolai Ivanovich Nebogatov might have been a mediocrity, but he was a very practical man. He knew he had to join Rozhestvensky at all costs. Otherwise his whole journey was meaningless. But when Nebogatov was in Djibouti, Rozhestvensky was quietly plowing the Indian Ocean, hoping to skip the unwelcome rendezvous. Nobody knew where he was.

On March 25, Nebogatov cabled Avelan: "Am leaving Djibouti to search for Rozhestvensky via the Strait of Malacca." He set three rendezvous points in the ocean. Russian agents were to contact him and brief him on Rozhestvensky's whereabouts.

Starting April 7, his transport, the *Kuronia*, would wait for two days at sea not far from Colombo. Then on April 12, his squadron would reach the Nicobar Islands and spend five days there, waiting for messengers. Finally, on April 22, he would be waiting for Commander

Polis, the Russian agent in Batavia, at 1°N and 105°23'E—in the South China Sea, roughly one hundred miles east of Singapore.

In the cable sent to Rudanovsky by the naval minister himself, the consul was instructed to select a "trusted person," put him on a steamer, and send him to the Nicobar Islands. There the messenger was to wait for Nebogatov and deliver to him Avelan's cable. After that the messenger was to take his steamer not to Singapore but to Bombay, thus preventing the crew from talking too much about Nebogatov in spy-infested Singapore.

In addition, Rudanovsky himself was to requisition a ship or cutter and intercept Nebogatov on April 21–22 in the South China Sea. He was to personally convey to the admiral more instructions from St. Petersburg and also the most recent news about Rozhestvensky.

The Russian consul in Colombo also received an enigmatic cable: "Top Secret. Immediately freight a steamer for one month for a secret mission and keep her ready. . . . You will have to take our cables to a certain place. . . . Report on the readiness of a steamer. Price does not matter."

The consul in Colombo started looking for a steamer, but very soon he found that no matter how much money he suggested, skippers just shook their heads. He panicked. The British secret service was clearly orchestrating the conspiracy. He reported the failure to St. Petersburg.

Naval Minister Avelan responded impatiently: "Try somehow, be it on a yacht, or a sailboat, or a cutter, or a fishing boat to reach the Russian transport *Kuronia* . . . ."

Finally, a boat was found and dispatched to the meeting place. On April 11, the consul sent a triumphal cable to Avelan: "Just received my messenger's ciphered telegram saying your instructions have been delivered promptly." The Admiralty could relax; Nebogatov had been briefed.

However, in several hours another cable from Colombo arrived: "Very urgent. My messenger is back. Spent three days at sea. Did not see our transport. Did not deliver the cable. I was misinformed."

Meanwhile, the *Kuronia* was there and could not locate the messenger. Apparently, the person dispatched by the consul was a bad navigator—or on the British payroll.

All that the Russian Admiralty could do now was curse diplomats and amateur secret agents in general. Disappointed, Nebogatov headed eastward, to celebrate Easter in an ocean so full of sharks that his crews christened the area Sharktown. Of course, Nebogatov did not suspect that had he received the message, he would have been even more frustrated.

The undelivered cable read: "To Rear Admiral Nebogatov. Admiral Rozhestvensky's squadron safely passed the Strait of Malacca. On April 4, he was in Cam Ranh Bay to the north of Saigon. His further route is unknown. Cannot wait for you. At the Nicobar Islands you will get further instructions."

Now Rudanovsky was again the Admiralty's only hope. However, he faced the same problem that his colleague in Colombo had had a couple of weeks earlier: There were no ships available for freighting. The Admiralty urgently instructed Prince Liven in Saigon to find one and send it to Rudanovsky immediately—but even in Saigon skippers kept saying no.

Finally, Rudanovsky did dispatch a boat to the Nicobar Islands. His messenger waited there for three days but did not see anybody and on April 21 returned to Penang.

The Admiralty was in despair. It had lost Nebogatov just as it had lost Rozhestvensky a month earlier!

The cables Nebogatov failed to receive at the Nicobar Islands contained a different message: Rozhestvensky was waiting for him in Van Fong.

While Nebogatov traveled between Ceylon and the Nicobars, the Admiralty suggested various options to the tsar. Nebogatov could disarm in a neutral port. He could return to Russia. He could cruise the Sunda Strait for a while, intercepting war contraband and then disarm in Saigon. He could try to reach Vladivostok on his own via the remote and foggy La Perouse Strait. But the tsar firmly insisted that Rozhestvensky wait for Nebogatov.

The Admiralty had only one more chance to find Nebogatov. Rudanovsky was to send a boat to the last rendezvous place—off Singapore.

This time the French allies did help their frustrated Russian colleagues: The French consul arranged for a merchant boat. The person who was to carry the vital mail was a Russian sailor, Vasily Baboushkin. He had been captured in Port Arthur on the cruiser *Bayan*, but his wounds were so bad that the Japanese let him go to Russia via Singapore. In Singapore the man heard that Nebogatov was expected to pass by soon (so much for Russian secrecy). Baboushkin jumped ship and reported to Rudanovsky. The consul, apparently now apprehensive of his own ability to distinguish one warship from another, was glad to make use of the brave man as a messenger.

The messenger boat, with Baboushkin onboard, left Singapore on April 20. They reached the designated area and waited. Two days passed, but there was no sign of Nebogatov. Two other men onboard were on the verge of mutiny. Baboushkin, a giant with muscles of steel, promised to "crack their heads like nuts." Grudgingly, they agreed to wait several hours more. Suddenly, scanning the horizon through his binoculars, Baboushkin muttered in a throbbing voice: "Ours are coming."

The boat steered to the battleship *Nicholas I.*

Having delivered the mail to an overjoyed Nebogatov, Baboushkin asked, "Your Excellency, may I stay on your battleship? I want to give the Japanese another thrashing." It goes without saying that Nebogatov enthusiastically agreed.

He unsealed the envelope. Rozhestvensky was waiting for him in Van Fong. Another cable bore alarming news: Russian agents in London reported that Togo planned to move south of Formosa to attack the Russians in Indochina. The third cable was a pleasant one: Nebogatov had been awarded the St. Anna's Cross.

Two days before, on April 20, Nebogatov had had his fifty-sixth birthday. Now, at least for a while, he could believe that a lucky star guided him.

7

On the night of April 25, having received a report from Singapore that Nebogatov had passed the Strait of Malacca, Rozhestvensky dispatched four cruisers to look for the 3rd Pacific Squadron.

He was angry and nervous. One of the ships reported that her radio operators had heard something that might have been Nebogatov's wireless. Rozhestvensky snarled, "If you motherfuckers want to gain favor, then raise a signal saying 'I want to gain favor,' and if I respond 'All right,' then go for it."

He was right; it was a false alarm. It was not until eleven o'clock in the morning on April 26 that the *Suvorov*'s radio was able to establish contact with Nebogatov's flagship. Rozhestvensky transmitted his curt instructions. At 2:25 P.M., officers on duty saw smoke to the west-northwest. It was Nebogatov.

At three o'clock, the two squadrons exchanged greeting salvos. At four, Nebogatov was on the *Suvorov*. He and Rozhestvensky embraced. The staff was invited to drink champagne to the "happy reunion."

Rozhestvensky kept them for exactly thirty minutes. Nebogatov boasted a safe and successful journey. The ships had behaved "ideally," he said. He also started briefing Rozhestvensky on his ideas about traveling to Vladivostok around Japan, via the La Perouse Strait. To save coal on this long journey, he said, battleships could be tugged by transports.

Apparently, Rozhestvensky was not sufficiently impressed by the image of his battleships being tugged by transports in hostile waters. He interrupted Nebogatov and began instructing him on taking on coal and making all necessary repairs in the next four days.

He did not discuss his strategy for the forthcoming battle. He did not even tell Nebogatov which route he planned to take. Then he indicated that it was time for Nikolai Ivanovich to leave.

In spite of generous congratulations and praise from Rozhestvensky, Nebogatov felt totally confused and slightly hurt. He supposed that they would have a proper conference later. Rozhestvensky already knew they would not.

By seven o'clock at night, both squadrons entered long and dark Kua Bay, just two miles north of Van Fong. They sneaked in like smugglers, anticipating trouble, but the French knew they would be leaving soon and did not bother to protest.

The ships stayed in Kua Bay for four days. As usual, they took on coal—this time for the final leg of their journey. Nebogatov's ships also had some minor repairs to do.

Rozhestvensky's and Nebogatov's officers exchanged visits. They spent hours retelling ordeals from their respective journeys. The Nebogatov squadron's stories, though, were blissfully void of drama.

The tsar sent a cable to Nebogatov, congratulating him on the "excellent" performance of a "difficult task." But Nebogatov's independent command was over. Rozhestvensky was in charge. He curtly informed the monarch: "On April 26, was joined by Nebogatov's detachment. . . . After inspection and repair of engines the squadron will go on." Nebogatov's battleships were now called the 3rd Armored Unit, and he was the commander. In the early morning of May 1, the reorganized and hopefully reinforced fleet weighed anchor.

10

"Be Prepared for Full Steam Ahead,"

MAY 1–13, 1905, PACIFIC OCEAN

1

IT WAS ELEVEN O'CLOCK IN THE MORNING ON MAY 1, AND THE shores of Indochina were melting into the distance. The squadron increased its speed to nine knots. The commander defined the course as NO 40—to Formosa Island. In the *Suvorov*'s wardroom, the officers were drinking Mumm champagne.

The admiral was taking his squadron into waters that had only recently seen Togo's ships. The battle could begin at any moment.

Rozhestvensky was leading the armada of fifty ships. He himself presided over the 1st Armored Unit—the *Suvorov, Alexander III, Borodino,* and *Orel*. The 2nd Armored Unit—the battleships *Oslyabya, Sisoi, Navarin,* and the armored cruiser *Nakhimov*—flew the flag of Admiral Felkersam. Nebogatov led the 3rd Armored Unit: four older battleships, the clunkers, *Nicholas I, Apraxin, Senyavin,* and *Ushakov*.

The cruisers were organized in two detachments: the 1st Unit led by Admiral Enkvist on the *Oleg*—the *Aurora, Donskoi, Vladimir*

Monomakh, Rion, and *Dnieper;* the 2nd Unit led by Captain Shein on the *Svetlana*—the *Kuban, Terek,* and *Ural.*

The torpedo boats were split into two units, the first one joined by the reconnaissance cruisers *Zhemchug* and *Izumrud.* Captain Radlov led the transports. Two hospital ships, the *Orel* and *Kostroma,* the latter brought to Van Fong by Nebogatov, were proceeding on their own.

Rozhestvensky's armada was one of the biggest fleets that had ever been amassed on the high seas, but that did not mean it surpassed Togo's. The Russians had more battleships, but Togo was much stronger in torpedo boats and cruisers. Rozhestvensky's ships had more heavy artillery guns; the Japanese prevailed in lighter weaponry.

Togo's hugest asset was speed. An admiral who commanded faster ships was normally a winner. The Russian heavy artillery guns were untested, the gunners unpracticed, and their shells scarce. Of Rozhestvensky's men, 99 percent had never heard a cannonade and never seen a person blown to pieces by a gun shell, to say nothing of a ship taking her final dive. Togo's fleet had spent the previous year in battle, he had as much ammunition as he could possibly wish for, and his artillery shells stuffed with *shimosa* were more powerful than any other gun shell in the world.

Rozhestvensky's crews had had a most demoralizing journey; many had spent the last nine months with scarcely a glimpse of shore, with the daily vodka ration as life's only pleasure. Just recently, they had spent a most frustrating month in an oppressive climate in their ally's colony, secretly crawling from one secluded bay to another like thieves, abandoned by their own government. As for Togo, in the Sea of Japan he would be at home.

For the next few days, the sea remained absolutely calm. Two battleships—the *Sisoi* and *Orel*—developed mechanical problems, but they were quickly fixed. All looked well.

However, officers had lost their peace of mind. Everybody was arguing about what the admiral planned to do and where he was taking the squadron. Only one person knew for sure: the admiral himself.

There were three possible routes to Vladivostok: through the Korea Strait, the Tsugaru Strait, or the La Perouse Strait.

The La Perouse Strait promised the longest journey—about 3,700 miles. It separated Russian Sakhalin Island from Japanese Hokkaido. The strait was only twenty-seven miles wide at its narrowest point and notorious for extremely strong currents. To reach it, ships had to first pass through the rough necklace of the Kuril Islands. The area promised a lot of fog, and the ships were likely to hit each other or the rocky coast while they forced their way through the misty and foamy chain of the Kurils. A slight mistake in navigation and several ships could perish in a matter of seconds. And Rozhestvensky did not have a high opinion of his navigators; in the Atlantic, in fine weather, they had already missed Gabon.

Even more important, he was sure his ships would not survive such a long journey without major breakdowns. A squadron could not abandon a peer immobilized by a mechanical problem in hostile waters. That meant that each time one ship slowed down or stopped, the whole squadron would be disabled, too. There had been dozens of such occasions throughout the journey. And what if a major mechanical failure occurred? The ship would have to be scuttled. How many ships would eventually be able to reach Vladivostok? And out of this number, how many would be fit for action? Of course, Togo would aspire to attack Vladivostok immediately after Rozhestvensky reached it. What a perilous trap it would be for his disabled ships—all of the labors of the immense journey would be in vain.

Then there was the problem of coal. To solve it, Nebogatov suggested towing battleships, as if they were cruising the roadstead of Kronshtadt and not Japan's backyard. Tow warships just one hundred miles away from the enemy's shores! What a battle-ready fleet that would be!

Also, who said Togo's ships would not be waiting at the La Perouse Strait? If Rozhestvensky's squadron disappeared for weeks after leaving Indochina, its route would become obvious. And it would be totally unrealistic to try to break through the narrow strait if it was guarded by Togo.

The admiral also discarded the second possible route—through the Tsugaru Strait. The Tsugaru separated two Japanese islands, Honshu and Hokkaido. It was merely fifteen to twenty-five miles wide and could be easily blockaded by a handful of torpedo boats. Also, its shores were populated not only by fishermen and woodcutters but also by Japanese troops who watched the coast zealously day and night. The city of Hakodate had all of the modern means of communication, a garrison, and naval facilities, and would be an excellent base for Togo. The squadron had no hope in the Tsugaru.

The final option was the Korea Strait. The Korea Strait separated Japan from continental Asia. It had a very comfortable depth of three hundred feet and was divided into two channels—western and eastern—by the Tsushima Islands. The eastern channel was often referred to as the Tsushima Strait. Its narrowest part was only twenty-five miles wide, but this bottleneck was very short. There were no rocks there, so misty weather would be the Russians' ally and not their enemy. It was also by far the fastest way to reach Vladivostok. After the squadron passed through the strait, the safe haven would be only six hundred miles away.

Yet, this option looked pretty bad, too. The strait was too close to central Japan to be left unprotected by Togo. It was very likely that his main force would be there. Nevertheless, in Rozhestvensky's eyes, the route through the Tsushima Strait was the "easiest," or in other words, the lesser evil.

The admiral knew the deficiencies of his fleet. Before leaving Van Fong he wrote to his wife: "Well, whatever the developments of the next few days might be, nothing will result from them but more shame for Russia." Yet, even given all the weaknesses of his squadron and all his pessimism, he did not mind a battle. The correlation of forces was far from being hopeless, he thought, and his duty was "to seek a battle in order to break through to Vladivostok, having caused all possible damage to the adversary."

Though choosing the Korea Strait, the admiral was sure that he would meet Togo's main force there and maybe even the whole fleet. Just before Rozhestvensky left Van Fong, he had received a cable from Virenius informing him that four Japanese cruisers and seven torpedo boats were on duty in the Tsushima Strait. Intelligence had deceived him many times in the past but he did not need it now. He knew that Togo would never leave the place unprotected.

However, why not play cat and mouse for awhile? Perhaps it made sense to slow down a bit. Let Togo get nervous. Let Togo, waiting at the Korea Strait, lose his sleep; let him send a few ships to look for the Russian armada in the misty waters of the Tsugaru or La Perouse.

Rozhestvensky also decided that he would dispatch four auxiliary cruisers in different directions to hunt for war contraband and thus stir trouble elsewhere, distracting Togo's attention from the Tsushima area.

But what kind of tactics would Togo apply? Crossing the "T"? What else? The Russian naval attaché in London reported that the four newest Russian battleships looked particularly awesome, especially if they stuck together. Apparently, Togo would attempt to disunite them. Allegedly, the Japanese Nelson planned to attack transports first, then lone cruisers, and finally deal with battleships. So what was Rozhestvensky to do? Send transports away? Protect his cruisers with the battleships' powerful guns?

He had to do all the planning alone. Togo had trusted subordinates. Rozhestvensky had none. He could not rely on any of his junior flag officers. Admiral Enkvist was a joke. He could lose his ships in daytime as easily as a toddler loses his toys in a sunlit garden. Admiral Nebogatov was too soft, too unmanly, too shy. Rozhestvensky trusted Admiral Felkersam, but in May 1905 Felkersam was dying.

That was a matter of special concern for Rozhestvensky; he was losing a friend and, even more importantly, a pillar. "Even on his deathbed he did not cease being a sensible associate, just like he has been a good servant of the throne for forty years," Rozhestvensky wrote to the Admiralty. Now he was asking the tsar to give Felkersam's widow "a guaranteed pension," for she had to take care of "many miserable relatives." He considered these personal matters urgent enough to report them to the capital before the battle.

With Felkersam waning quickly, he was losing the only junior flag officer he trusted. He did not think highly of most of his captains, either. Of course, there were several people whom he respected. One of them, Captain Dobrotvorsky, who had taken the detachment of cruisers from the Baltic Sea to Madagascar, even dared to make a bet with the thunderous admiral. Dobrotvorsky insisted that there would be no battle before Vladivostok. But even if he liked younger people like Dobrotvorsky, could he entrust them with independent command, passing over the two worthless but nevertheless senior admirals, Enkvist and Nebogatov? He could not.

Rozhestvensky felt he could endure no more of this job. He would take the squadron to Vladivostok, but then he would step down. On the eve of the departure from Indochina, he sent Grand Duke Alexei a very personal cable: "I beg you to send to Vladivostok a healthy and capable commander of the fleet or of the squadron. I can hardly walk and cannot move around the deck of my own ship. Therefore the situation of the squadron is very bad. If I am still alive, I can continue to command the squadron under the leadership of the commander of the fleet. . . ." He had asked for the same thing two months earlier, from Madagascar. The tsar had denied him his wish then. What would he say now?

Meanwhile, he had to decide who would lead the squadron if he were killed. There he made a smart move. He could not possibly disinherit Nebogatov and Enkvist officially. But they could lose leadership by default.

On May 10, Rozhestvensky issued a special order. Everybody knew that according to rules of subordination, the next in command was dying Felkersam, then Nebogatov, then Enkvist. But Rozhestvensky introduced a quiet revolution to the rules of succession. If his battleship, the *Suvorov,* was damaged or sunk, he said, then the next battleship in line—*Alexander III*—had to lead the squadron to Vladivostok; if the *Alexander* was damaged, then the *Borodino,* then the *Orel.* Basically, that meant that the commanders of the three newest battleships were given superiority over the two admirals.

No rendezvous in case the squadron became dispersed was indicated in the order. It was unnecessary. If they were to meet anywhere, it was in Vladivostok.

2

Late at night on May 5, the squadron caught its first prey. She was the British steamer *Oldhamia,* carelessly heading north without any papers.

The search took several hours. The squadron waited, not moving any further; Rozhestvensky was taking his time. The ship was sitting too deep in the water for the merchandise her captain had declared. Rozhestvensky decided to capture her. He was proven right, for underneath her trade goods, the ship was carrying artillery guns.

The admiral put a Russian crew on the smuggling vessel, provided her with coal, and sent her to Vladivostok via the La Perouse Strait. Before the Russian crew came aboard, the *Oldhamia*'s officers attempted to sink her. They were arrested and sent to the hospital ship *Orel,* while the rest of the crew went to the cruiser *Dnieper.*

The *Orel* was surprised. She signaled the *Suvorov,* "We have got five perfectly healthy Englishmen. What should we do with them?" Rozhestvensky replied, "Make sure they stay in good health until Vladivostok."

His subordinates, drunk on their first action, suggested the *Oldhamia* officers should be shot. Rozhestvensky was thoroughly surprised: "To shoot neutrals? Just because they are involved in war contraband?"

Meanwhile, the cruiser *Zhemchug,* her appetite whet, stopped a Norwegian steamer shortly before noon on May 6. The ship was inspected and then allowed to go, and the squadron continued on.

May 6 was the tsar's birthday. A whining mystic and reluctant fatalist, Tsar Nicholas II was very much upset by the patron saint he received at birth—Saint Job, the one who was tortured by God without any apparent reason. The tsar used this as an explanation for the numerous misfortunes of his reign.

To celebrate the tsar's birthday was a must. At 11:06 in the morning, Rozhestvensky signaled, "The admiral congratulates you all with the birthday of His Imperial Majesty, Sovereign Emperor." In nine minutes, another, more practical, signal was raised: "An extra glass of vodka to the crews."

The next day, they left the boundaries of the South China Sea. Wind brought waves. Shaky torpedo boats were now towed by transports. Despite the weather, Rozhestvensky started fulfilling his plan. He sent auxiliary cruisers to various parts of the Pacific to confuse Togo and make him withdraw at least some of his forces from the Korea Strait. Also, he was getting rid of transports. Between May 8 and 12, he sent away ten ships.

The cruisers *Kuban* and *Terek* went to the eastern coast of Japan— to make Togo believe Rozhestvensky was heading for either the La Perouse Strait or the Tsugaru Strait. Six transports, commanded by Captain Radlov, and accompanied by two cruisers, the *Dnieper* and the *Rion,* were sent to Shanghai—just ninety miles away from where the squadron was on May 12. The cruisers were to escort the transports to land and then head for the Port Arthur area. The *Dnieper* still carried the *Oldhamia* crew. Rozhestvensky's instructions were to set them free in the first foreign port.

The cruisers were ordered to inspect and, if necessary, to destroy all suspicious foreign merchant vessels. If they were chased, or when their supplies were used up, they were to go to Saigon and disarm there.

The three transports that the squadron kept—the *Kamchatka, Irtysh* and *Anadyr*—were military ships. Three others were indispensable. The *Korea* carried ammunition. The *Svir* and the *Rus* were tugboats.

There was one more unneeded light cruiser—the *Ural.* But Rozhestvensky decided to keep her. Reportedly, her captain intended to get to the nearest port and disarm there. Everybody on the *Suvorov* was saying that he could not be trusted.

On May 10 the squadron stopped and took on coal. Radios were receiving indecipherable signals. Rozhestvensky sent cruisers to probe for Togo's ships, but they did not find anything. It seemed they were in a void.

The world was of the same opinion. Even the British lost the squadron. On May 1 the Russians were spotted leaving Indochina. On May 2 they were seen 140 miles east, steering north. On May 12 their transports safely arrived at Shanghai. Otherwise Rozhestvensky's whereabouts were unknown.

The admiral ordered his ships "to be ready for battle at any time." After May 10, the ships shut down most of their lights every night. However, the two hospital ships, the *Orel* and *Kostroma,* were still easily detectable, lit as brightly as usual. Unfortunately, that was the only way to make them immune to a potential Japanese attack.

Rozhestvensky pretended he was not particularly alarmed or excited, yet it was obvious that the admiral was very unsettled. Sometimes he would send as many as fifty signals to various ships in an hour and a half.

Everybody was nervously preparing for the battle, each person in his own way. Uncertain what to do with their personal belongings, sailors were putting in bags all their portable treasures—icons, letters, family photographs. Some wrote letters back home and sent them with the transports going to Shanghai. Others were bravely saying that they would send their letters "from Vladivostok." Quite a few were carelessly laughing; they would be in Russia in a few days—and just imagine, they would get letters, newspapers, and news in Vladivostok! Many had friends or family there and were already inviting people to parties.

There were also some inspiring and reassuring examples. Several people had joined the squadron on their own initiative at the later, gloomier stage. One was Vasily Baboushkin, the one who had delivered mail to Nebogatov off Singapore and was now sailing on the *Nicholas I.* Another was Commander Polis—the Russian agent in Batavia. His sensitive mission over, he had boarded the *Alexander III* at Van Fong.

Crews still stuck to their rather relaxed routine: waking at 5:20, vodka and lunch around 10:40, then a long nap until 2:00, then tea, then drills for a couple of hours, then another shot of vodka and dinner at 5:40, and then to bed after prayers at 8:00.

On May 11, Admiral Felkersam died. Rozhestvensky was prepared for this blow; the doctors had warned him that Felkersam would probably not live beyond May 12. By Rozhestvensky's order, his death was concealed from the rest of the squadron, and his flag remained on the *Oslyabya*'s mast. Heading for battle was bad enough. Sailors were superstitious. The last thing Rozhestvensky wanted to hear was vain talk about "a bad omen." Captain Ber of the *Oslyabya* was now commanding the 2nd Armored Unit, though its crews believed they were following the orders of the bedridden Felkersam.

However, a potential disaster lay in wait. Treating Nebogatov with cold contempt, Rozhestvensky did not bother to inform him that now he, and not Felkersam, was to command the squadron if Rozhestvensky was killed or disabled. He probably thought that he had ensured proper succession already by entrusting command to the next battleship in line.

On May 12, at nine o'clock in the morning, in wind, rain, cold, and fog, the squadron turned to NO 73—to the Korea Strait. Some were hoping that if the fog continued, they would be able to sneak into the Sea of Japan unnoticed.

On that night, the ships' radios started getting Japanese signals. The closer they got to the Korea Strait, the clearer they could hear Togo's ships. The cruiser *Ural* had a strong wireless; her captain asked the admiral's permission to jam the air to cut the enemy's communications. Rozhestvensky answered in the negative. If the *Ural* had interfered, Togo would have immediately realized that the Russians were approaching.

For the same reason, he did not send out reconnaissance cruisers; Togo's scouts could spot them. The admiral was absolutely sure Togo was close.

At dawn, May 13, the Russians started hearing the Japanese quite clearly. The horizon was foggy. No ships could be seen. At night, all the wireless broadcasts abruptly stopped. Apparently, Togo had smelled the Russian steel.

That day the squadron moved very slowly. The Japanese fleet was so close that many were shocked. A popular explanation was that Rozhestvensky, fairly superstitious as an old school sailor, would never agree to seek a battle on Friday the 13th.

Unfriendly voices were saying that he wanted to kowtow to the tsar by scheduling the battle precisely for May 14—the anniversary of Nicholas's coronation. Others said he was waiting for cruisers from Vladivostok.

In all likelihood, the delay could be explained differently. The admiral had sent out the *Kuban, Terek, Dnieper,* and *Rion* just a few days ago. He wanted to allow them more time to attract Togo's attention.

At noon the Russians saw a white steamer—presumably a spy. Yet, the admiral did not order to pursue her. Instead, Rozhestvensky commanded time-consuming maneuvers from nine to eleven and then from two to four. Soon after, at 4:30 P.M., he raised a signal: "Get ready for battle."

Many were excited and even joyful; tomorrow the Japanese would have to pay for "Port Arthur, for our dear sunken ships, for our constant misfortunes in Manchuria—for everything." The *Aurora's* wardroom served champagne.

At six o'clock Rozhestvensky announced, "By tomorrow's dawn be prepared for full steam ahead." Both tea and dinner at his quarters passed in tense silence. Some officers were impressed by reports of their orderlies: Rats were crawling out of their holes and assembling on decks.

At dark, the ships turned on very few lights. "Unusual solemn silence descended."

At eight o'clock the silence ended. Drums roared their throbbing rhythm; crews were summoned for evening prayer. That night the priests' words seemed especially distinct and meaningful. For the first time during the voyage, crews did not go to their bunks that night.

In the "black velvet" of the night, the ships could not see each other. Only the hospital ships were bobbing on the waves like two "Christmas trees."

At ten o'clock they noticed brief light from a searchlight to the left. They were approaching the Tsushima Strait.

Suddenly, Japanese radio communications resumed. The Russians were able to make out several words: "Ten lights . . . They are like bright stars . . ."

The squadron had been detected.

PART THREE

BATTLE

11

"They Are All There!"

6:30 A.M.—5:30 P.M., MAY 14, 1905

1

DAWN DID NOT BRING MUCH LIGHT THAT CHILLY MORNING. The sun had climbed the sky, but the horizon remained shrouded in hazy gloom. It was impossible to see farther than three miles. The *Suvorov* raised a signal: "Keep the speed of nine knots."

Rozhestvensky had spent the whole night on the bridge. Now he stood there next to the *Suvorov*'s captain, Ignatsius.

The armada was entering Japanese waters in meticulous order. Three light cruisers, the *Svetlana, Ural* and *Almaz,* made a broad triangle in the vanguard. Two awesome columns followed them. Rozhestvensky on the *Suvorov* led the right one: the five best battleships (the *Suvorov, Alexander III, Borodino, Orel,* and *Oslyabya*) and three older battleships, the *Sisoi, Navarin,* and *Nakhimov.* Nebogatov led a symmetrical column to the left: four older battleships (the *Nicholas I, Apraxin, Senyavin, Ushakov*) and four armored cruisers—the *Oleg, Aurora, Donskoi,* and *Vladimir Monomakh.* The cruiser *Zhemchug* and two torpedo boats, the *Bedovy* and *Bystry,* escorted Rozhestvensky's column; the cruiser *Izumrud* and two other torpedo boats, the *Buiny* and

Bravy, accompanied Nebogatov. All of the transports and the remaining five torpedo boats kept in the middle, the hospital ships in the rear.

At 6:30 A.M., forty miles from Tsushima Island, they saw a warship six miles to the right. She had two masts and two funnels. Trained to make out enemy ships, the Russians immediately recognized the cruiser *Izumi*. In several minutes, when the gloom darkening the horizon started to shrink, they saw three more Japanese scouts.

Rozhestvensky ordered three light cruisers to move to the rear to guard the transports. He also commanded his battleships to aim at the *Izumi*.

Minutes passed, but nothing happened. The Japanese maintained their six-mile distance. Rozhestvensky waited. Meanwhile, many sailors were hastily putting on clean underwear; this was the customary Russian way of preparing for death.

At eight o'clock, the squadron raised flags to celebrate the tsar's coronation day, but there was no time for celebration. The hospital ship *Kostroma* informed Rozhestvensky that from her position in the rear, she could see four more Japanese ships—apparently Vice Admiral Dewa's unit.

2

In the early hours of May 14, Togo's main force was still on the southern coast of Korea. Vice Admiral Kataoka waited at Tsushima Island, and four cruisers were at Goto Island further south. Six more were shuttling back and forth between the islands, looking for Rozhestvensky.

At 2:45 A.M., the light cruiser *Shinano Maru* discovered bright lights piercing the velvet darkness. It was one of the two "Christmas trees," a Russian hospital ship. The *Shinano Maru* crawled forward cautiously. Her captain wanted to make sure that he had spotted the right prey. At four o'clock in the morning, he distinguished numerous dim silhouettes steering for the Tsushima Strait. It was the 2nd Pacific Squadron. The *Shinano Maru* withdrew quietly and sent a warning to Togo.

The news reached the *Mikasa* at 5:05 in the morning. Togo's adjutant rushed into the admiral's quarters to break the news. Togo did not conceal his joy. He commanded immediate departure.

By 6:45, Togo's main force had weighed anchor. But the Japanese commander-in-chief did not rush to the Tsushima Strait. First he wanted Rozhestvensky to get into its bottleneck. The Russians were not to see the whole Japanese fleet yet.

A British naval observer was present on one of the Japanese ships and described the scene:

> A very stiff breeze was blowing from the south and west, and though no heavy sea was able to rise, great inconvenience was suffered throughout the day from the water dashed through casemate and turret gun-ports, and from the constant wetting of the object glasses of the sighting telescopes. . . . Besides this wind, a rather thick haze hanging over the sea made ships indistinct outside ranges of 5,000 meters. The bright sun was quite unable to clear the air, and thus, though everyone was in high spirits at the prospect of the long-deferred meeting, the weather caused some anxiety.

The annoying thing was that the smaller torpedo-craft were unable to keep up with the fleet and were therefore ordered closer to the coast for shelter.

The first ship to detect Rozhestvensky in the daylight was the *Izumi*. She reported to Togo that she could distinguish the Russian fleet and that it was led by a vessel of the *Zhemchug* type. (It was indeed the *Zhemchug*.)

Togo decided to stay at a distance of thirty to forty miles. Light cruisers, dipping into the gloom, kept informing him of the Russian progress. He took his time. At eleven o'clock, he sent men to lunch.

"The haze continued, and ships in the rear of the line could hardly be distinguished."

Togo had been waiting for Rozhestvensky for nearly a year. Of course, until the fall of Port Arthur, he had been very much preoccupied with the diminishing, but still impressive 1st Pacific Squadron, but after its fall, Rozhestvensky was his only adversary.

Togo had made good use of Rozhestvensky's prolonged lingering at Madagascar. Just as Rozhestvensky had warned, Togo had utilized that time to get all of his ships repaired and ready for battle. The Japanese dockyards had worked around the clock, but still the work had been finished only in late February. If Rozhestvensky had left Madagascar on January 6, as he had hoped to do, he would have reached the Sea of Japan before Togo's ships had finished repairs. Now he faced the whole Japanese fleet.

Togo had had plenty of time to prepare. Reconnaissance ships were dispatched in all directions. All straits leading into the Sea of Japan were heavily patrolled. The Sea of Japan itself was divided into numbered squares—ten minutes of latitude and longitude each—to ease the planning.

Two cruisers, the *Hongkong Maru* and the *Nihon Maru*, were sent far south. On the morning of December 9, they arrived in Singapore and then headed to the Sunda Strait, Sumatra, Java, and Borneo. In February, Admiral Dewa, with four ships, explored southern waters again. On February 23 they visited Van Fong and Cam Ranh, then Singapore and Borneo.

While scouts were cruising remote waters, Togo was training his men, paying special attention to gunnery. By that time, many of his gunners had had plenty of battle practice, hitting Russian hulls at Port Arthur and in the Yellow Sea.

Spies kept Togo informed of the Russians' whereabouts. Still, no matter how hard they worked, there were long periods of uncertainty—when Rozhestvensky, Felkersam, Dobrotvorsky, or Nebogatov had plowed the ocean far from ports and popular trade routes. On such occasions, only a happy accident could help Togo—as happened on March 17, when Togo was informed by spies that eleven days earlier Rozhestvensky had been spotted in the Indian Ocean at 9°S and 53°E heading north. This was an invaluable piece of intelligence; having departed from Madagascar three days earlier, the squadron was heading not for the Australian coast and not for the Sunda Strait but for Singapore.

However, after Rozhestvensky made his spectacular appearance at Singapore, the Japanese admiral could only guess what the Russians would do next.

Togo thought Vladivostok was the most natural destination for the armada, yet he also suspected that the Russians might seize some island on China's coast and operate from there. Even if his guess about Vladivostok was right, he did not know which route the Mad Dog would choose.

Togo sent Admiral Kamimura to the Vladivostok area to lay mines and prevent the Vladivostok cruisers from assisting Rozhestvensky. From his base in Korea, he could easily watch and quickly reach all three straits—and the Chinese coast, should Rozhestvensky prefer after all to occupy some island there.

Nevertheless, mid-May was a difficult time for Togo. Rozhestvensky had left Indochina—but where was he going? Togo was waiting for him at the Korea Strait, but the Mad Dog was late for the fateful rendezvous. Had he indeed chosen some wild route around Japan?

On May 11, Togo cabled Tokyo that if Rozhestvensky did not appear in the next few days, then Togo would take his fleet to the Tsugaru Strait up north. But on May 13, he learned that the Russian ships had been spotted near Shanghai—a natural transit point for the Korea Strait. Togo was relieved and lay in wait for just one more day.

Now the Japanese admiral was standing on the forward bridge of his talisman ship the *Mikasa,* scanning the mist through binoculars. At 1:20 they met Admiral Dewa's squadron. Dewa was advancing ahead of the Russians.

Togo turned to the south-southwest, "but had not gone far on this course when the Russians suddenly hove into sight a little on his starboard bow. The moment was one calling for prompt and decided action," a British observer thought.

"It was now possible to see down the Russian lines. At the head of the right column the four big battleships loomed enormous, dwarfing all others to insignificance." The first one was the *Suvorov* with Rozhestvensky on the bridge.

3

Rozhestvensky seemingly paid no attention to Dewa's ships, which had accompanied the squadron since eight o'clock in the morning. At nine, he ordered regrouping. His column sped up to eleven knots to move ahead and to form a single formation with all the battleships and heavy cruisers. Now the squadron was moving in a straight thread four miles long.

He raised a signal: "At noon head for NO 23." Everybody knew this meant Vladivostok. Was it possible that Togo would allow the Russians to pass through the Tsushima Strait undisturbed?

At 10:20, four more enemy cruisers appeared to the west, but they made no attempt to attack. The *Zhemchug*, proceeding in the vanguard, noticed a Japanese steamer intending to cross the squadron's path—perhaps to check Russian alertness or launch a torpedo attack. The *Zhemchug* fired several shots at her. The intruder turned back. Rozhestvensky curtly commanded the *Zhemchug* not to pursue.

At 11:20 people on the *Suvorov* bridge heard another shot. It was the battleship *Orel*. She semaphored apologetically to the admiral that it had been an accidental discharge. But some other ships, uncertain who had fired, opened fire, too. Nebogatov's ships were especially active.

The Japanese cruisers spat several return shots and turned west into the fog. Rozhestvensky signaled, "Do not waste your ammunition."

Almost immediately he allowed crews to have lunch. While his men were having their meal, more Japanese ships emerged from the fog and then dived into it again. Drinking their daily rum, people held heated debates. What did such a limp start of the long-awaited battle promise? Quite a few were sure that the battle was practically over and that they could calmly proceed to Vladivostok. Officers went to wardrooms where a proper lunch was served and they drank champagne to the tsar's health.

At 12:05 the squadron changed its course to NO 23: to Vladivostok. They were in the middle of the Tsushima Strait. Haze on the horizon started to swell.

About this time, Rozhestvensky saw enemy ships again. This time Japanese light cruisers were accompanied by torpedo boats. It looked like they intended to cross the course of the Russian squadron. If this was their intention, the armada was in danger; the torpedo boats could lay drift mines on its way. Rozhestvensky decided to act.

The admiral ordered a new regrouping. He thought he needed a more awesome formation to drive the torpedo boats away and also to meet Togo's main force. He decided that he wanted all twelve of his battleships line-abreast.

Changing from line-ahead to line-abreast formation demanded quick and prompt maneuvering. The first four battleships were the first to perform it. The *Suvorov, Borodino,* and *Orel* executed it satisfactorily, but the *Alexander* misinterpreted the admiral's command and turned in the wrong direction. What resulted was the "ugly mob" predicted by Rozhestvensky three months earlier.

Rozhestvensky canceled the maneuver. As a result of the abortive regrouping, his ships were going in two parallel columns: he with the *Suvorov, Alexander III, Borodino,* and *Orel* in the right column, slightly ahead of the rest of the ships in the left. That was precarious. If the Japanese attacked from the left now, the four newest battleships would be unable to fire at them, for the other Russian ships were blocking the way.

But the Japanese did not want to attack yet. Their cruisers and torpedo boats turned back.

Having failed with the line-abreast formation, Rozhestvensky had
no better option but to bring all the ships back into the line-ahead,
single thread order. For that, he needed at least half an hour. But he
was not allowed that.

The *Suvorov* officers were eating their lunch in the wardroom
when they were suddenly summoned to combat position. At 1:20,
seven miles northeast of the Russian squadron, four battleships and
eight armored cruisers had appeared. One of the battleships was the
Mikasa, Togo's flagship.

4

As soon as Togo's main force was spotted in the distance, the *Suvorov*'s
commanding officers went to the conning tower. Rozhestvensky remained on the forward bridge, watching the new regrouping with a
full view of the sea. Yet he already knew that his brisk maneuvering
had got him into trouble. Now there was no chance that the Russians
could meet Togo in good battle formation.

In several minutes, the admiral would have to leave the bridge.
The battle could start any moment now.

One of the officers, a veteran of Port Arthur, having noticed familiar Japanese ships, said, "There they are, Your Excellency! All six of
them, like on July 28."

Rozhestvensky shook his head.

"No, more," he said. "They are all there!"

In the conning tower, everybody stood in complete silence. Officers expected the admiral to command fire, but he quietly monitored
Togo's moves instead. The Japanese main force was moving from right
to left, crossing the Russian squadron's "T".

Crossing the "T" was a winning weapon. The horizontal, advancing line of this "T" could shower the vertical with gun shells using all

its artillery might. The vertical line would be significantly disabled, for only its vanguard ships could use their guns properly—others could not, for their own peers were shielding the enemy. Crossing the "T" enabled the horizontal line to seriously damage, if not destroy, the vertical line in a matter of several minutes.

However, crossing the "T" was a risky tactic for the attacker. At a certain point during the maneuver, each ship had to turn around, which required staying in the same place and therefore becoming an excellent target for the enemy. Until all ships involved in the maneuver regrouped, the attacker could not open fire.

Russians on the *Suvorov* were excited: "In another minute we shall be hammering their flagship!" A British observer aboard one of Togo's vessels was equally astonished: "The Japanese approach could hardly have been worse. . . . In the few minutes the approach lasted, the fate of Japan depended upon what happened to her leading ships."

Rozhestvensky knew this as well and ordered to open fire immediately. The *Suvorov* shot the first shell at the *Mikasa.* The duel of the two admirals began. The clocks stood at 1:49 P.M.

However, due to the previous unfortunate maneuvering, the Russians were unable to use their advantage fully. Only three battleships—the *Suvorov, Alexander,* and *Borodino*—could participate in the battle; the others were still taking their place in line.

Despite this, the first shell dropped only twenty yards astern of Togo's flagship. Others, equally close, succeeded it. The Japanese position became critical. For those onboard the *Mikasa,* "minutes were like hours." The Japanese flagship had come under fire that grew hotter and hotter as she passed into the fire range of each successive Russian ship. The sole object of the Russian fire, the *Mikasa* did not return a single shot. Togo wanted to accomplish the regrouping of his formation first.

Rozhestvensky had less than five minutes to hammer Togo. Timing was perfect, but marksmanship was not. The sea around the *Mikasa* churned with Russian shells, but only nineteen hit the Japanese flagman in the first fifteen minutes. Inexperienced and nervous Russian gunners did better than they might have but much worse than they should have.

At 1:52, the *Mikasa* replied. Minutes earlier she had raised a signal: "The empire's fate depends upon the outcome of this battle. Let everyone do his best."

The first shots of the Japanese were chaotic, but in five minutes Togo's gunners started hitting the Russian ships, using the advantage of the "T" maneuver to its fullest. The *Mikasa* and other battleships concentrated on the *Suvorov*. Cruisers fired on the *Oslyabya*. Felkersam's flag was still flying on her mast, and Togo had no way of knowing that the Russian second-in-command was lying dead in a zinc coffin in the ship's chapel.

The Russians were immediately overwhelmed by Togo's fire. His guns spat steel incessantly, and his gunners targeted well. The shelling was so heavy that the sea around the *Suvorov* "seemed to be boiling." The Russians still had not straightened out their battle line, and ships in the rear could not yet respond.

The first staff officer to be wounded was Midshipman Prince Tsereteli, a young aristocrat from Georgia who had charmed the French ladies in Nosy Be with his dazzling looks and great tennis game. He had chosen to stay on the *Suvorov*'s forward bridge and now was carried away on a blood-stained stretcher.

At 2:15 the *Suvorov* experienced its first fire when one of the shells hit the captain's quarters. The *Suvorov* was now feeling the terrible destructive power of the *shimosa*. The Japanese shells were not just tearing her into pieces, they were also burning her.

Shimosa was a picric acid explosive that the Japanese had developed a new type of shell for. The shell was thin-skinned, allowing more space for the explosive itself—10 percent of the total weight of the shell instead of the normal 2–3 percent. These shells bore the name of *furoshiki*, after the thin Japanese kerchief. Also, a research group headed by Admiral Ijuin Goro had developed the Ijuin fuse. It caused the shell to explode upon impact, instead of just piercing the armor like the Russian shells did.

The Russian sailors were terrified by what looked like "liquid flame" leaping on the sides of the ship as if the steel itself was on fire. But it was just *shimosa* feeding on paint.

Binoculars became useless. The air over the decks got so hot that officers could only see fluid streams of heat, blurring everything from sight. Sailors were stumbling over numerous dead bodies; a single shell could easily kill as many as a dozen. Blood covered the decks.

Several splinters hit the inside of the armored conning tower. Two sailors and Colonel Bersenev were killed on the spot. When another officer grabbed the helm he discovered that its handles were covered with blood. His own uniform was spotted with pieces of the dead men's brains. "It stunk terribly."

Rozhestvensky was not hurt. He was standing next to Captain Ignatsius. Both were looking through the embrasures. It quickly become impossible to watch the battle from this allegedly safe place; more and more splinters were penetrating the tower. Smoke, chips of wood, and splashes of water reached the admiral. All he could see outside was fire and smoke.

The *Suvorov*'s captain kept begging him to change the course, saying that Togo's gunners had adapted to the existing distance. Contrary to his normally short temper, the admiral patiently repeated, "Vasily Vasilievich, calm down. We have adapted to it too." Only when it was reported that the battleship had an underwater hole did the admiral command to turn to starboard.

Then a number of splinters pierced the embrasures again. One of them hit the admiral, but the wound was not serious. Rozhestvensky sat down in a chair and continued his watch. Six dead people were lying around him. When an officer reached the tower to report that there was a severe fire in one of the turrets, the admiral shrugged his shoulders: "Try to extinguish it. There is nothing I can do from here."

Five minutes later, more splinters hit him. This time the wounds were quite serious, both in the head and legs, but he did not leave the tower. He kept sitting there, his head bandaged with a towel. Almost immediately another splinter hit the *Suvorov*'s captain. The skin of his skull opened "like an envelope," and blood poured from the wound. He was taken below to the doctors. He never returned.

5

At 2:25 the *Suvorov's* situation became precarious. An officer in the conning tower next to Rozhestvensky thought, "Hell has started." Fires erupted at the stern and on the bridge. Because of the underwater hole, the ship was now helplessly listing left. Her masts were gone, and worse, her steering gear was damaged. Half an hour after the battle started, the Russian flagship was already destroyed.

Range finders and other artillery devices were heavily damaged or totally smashed, but the battleship kept stubbornly shelling the Japanese ships. The Japanese thought it was "surprising" that the Russian gunners were able to continue targeting and firing at all.

Staying in the conning tower no longer made sense. There were only four survivors there: the admiral, his flag-captain, the flag-navigator, and one sailor. They could not see anything outside because of the flames and smoke. Fire had made the air unbearably hot. They decided to move to the lower fighting position through a special armored shaft. In order to open the hatch leading to the shaft, they had to push dead bodies aside.

Rozhestvensky did not spend much time at the lower fighting position either. He instructed his officers to try to keep the battleship on the original course. He was leaving, he said, to find a place from which he could observe the battle.

He must have seen a hellish spectacle. One of the Japanese shells had exploded over the upper deck, and "forty men instantly fell there without a single groan." Burnt corpses were spread all over the ship. Many people were trapped by fire below decks. If they were lucky, they rushed topside through flame; if not, they died screaming in the steel grill.

The ship herself was mortally wounded. She left the column, moving slowly and unsteadily. When the *Suvorov* turned aside, the *Alexander*, *Borodino,* and *Orel* followed her sheepishly. They did not realize that with the masts gone, Rozhestvensky simply could not send them any signal. In a few minutes, the captain of the *Alexander III*, Rozhestvensky's favorite, Bukhvostov, realized what had happened. Following Rozhestvensky's instructions issued before the battle, the *Alexander* steered north, bravely leading the squadron. By that time, the Russian formation had straightened up, but it was too late to make a difference now.

It was half past two, and for the flag ship the battle was already over. The *Suvorov* could not move any farther. She stayed in one place—a stationary target. Captain Bukhvostov took the squadron away from her.

Rozhestvensky wandered slowly through the burning ruin that had been his ship. All around lay dead sailors, some totally disfigured, some pinned by handrails, some still handsome, some burnt beyond recognition. Finally, he made it to a place from which he could watch the sea.

The new leader of the squadron, the *Alexander III,* was steaming away. She was under the heaviest shelling. Togo knew that for a real massacre, he had to keep decapitating the Russian line. The *Alexander* was already struggling with several fires.

Another gigantic ironclad, the *Oslyabya,* was sinking. The battleship was listing to port more and more. Several hundred sailors crowded on her starboard side, hesitating between diving or staying for a few more minutes. Some of them were already completely naked.

Suddenly, the *Oslyabya* started capsizing. Her glossy bottom emerged from the sea like the skin "of an enormous sea monster." Knowing that if they waited longer, the terrifying maelstrom would suck them under, the *Oslyabya* crew were ready to jump into the sea. But they could not dive, for the keel was barring the way. So they slid downward, some on their stomachs, others balancing on their feet, others head over heels. Many of them were hitting the keel and breaking their bones.

Those who were already in the water were crushed by frantic, yelling peers. The Japanese kept firing on the drowning mob. Togo's men "watched the tragic spectacle intently; this was something they had never seen—a mighty warship, sunk by their gunfire, going to the bottom."

In a matter of a few moments, the *Oslyabya* disappeared under the gray surface of the sea. Four hundred survivors remained in the icy water. Russian torpedo boats, the *Izumrud* cruiser, and the *Svir* tugboat rushed under fire to rescue them. Somewhere inside the huge hull, quickly sinking to the sea bottom, rolled Admiral Felkersam's zinc coffin.

The *Oslyabya* was the only ship that Rozhestvensky saw sink. After that he wandered around the *Suvorov* without any evident purpose. After a while, nobody knew where he was or whether he was still alive.

6

At 3:20, the *Alexander III,* ablaze with fire, left her place in the column. The suicidal position of the leader was assumed by the *Borodino.*

Battleships were Togo's prey. He left the Russian cruisers and transports to other predators, but he would not let the battleships go. From two o'clock until four, the Russian column made two full circles, trying to shake off the pursuers like a hunted bear shakes off hounds, but the Japanese were following them closely and watchfully. Suddenly, at 4:10 P.M., the fog intensified. The Russians and Togo could not see each other. The battle between the two main forces stopped, but in the rear, Japanese cruisers and torpedo boats continued massacring disabled Russian ships. One of these ships, left far behind, was Rozhestvensky's *Suvorov.*

At 4:45 four Japanese torpedo boats rushed to the Russian flagship to finish her off. One of their torpedoes hit the *Suvorov*'s stern, but the disabled ship kept responding. The Japanese sailors watched her in awe: "It was hard to imagine how any living creature could still find a foothold on that mass of twisted, fire-blasted iron." The torpedo boats retreated. There was no rush. They would get the *Suvorov* after dusk if she did not sink by herself.

It was clear that the ship was doomed. Should it be abandoned? But where were the torpedo boats that were supposed to evacuate the admiral in case his ship was badly damaged? And where was Rozhestvensky?

The flag-captain started rushing about the hull, asking everybody, "Where is the admiral?" Nobody seemed to know. He had been seen at various places. Reportedly, he had been wounded one more time.

Finally, he was spotted in the right six-inch turret. He was sitting by himself on a box amid steel debris and torn human flesh. He had been badly wounded indeed. A splinter had hit his left ankle, and apparently a nerve was damaged, for his foot was paralyzed. When staff officers reached him around four o'clock, he told them to find new gunners. But the turret had been totally disabled, and no gunner would be of any use.

Having been told that, the admiral just sat there immobile on his box, sometimes asking what was happening outside. An hour later he fell unconscious.

In despair, his officers went to the deck. Suddenly they spotted a Russian torpedo boat. She came very close. They could even recognize the face of her captain—Kolomeitsev. That meant she was the *Buiny*.

They started semaphoring him with their hands, asking her to take the admiral on board. Kolomeitsev told them to send a boat. The flag-captain yelled, "Move closer—there are no boats left." Indeed, all of them had already burned.

Kolomeitsev said he would give it a try. He started cautiously approaching the ship's starboard side. He had seen a lot of destruction during the day, but still could not believe his eyes: "Yes, it was the *Suvorov*, but how terrible she looked. Masts gone, funnels gone, the board beaten and holed, paint burnt, tongues of fire leaping from inside the ship. . . . It looked like a roaster full of charcoal."

Finally, the torpedo boat came close enough. It was now or never. They ran into the tower, lifted the admiral, and brought him to the deck. Rozhestvensky was very pale, his features totally changed. If not for his uniform and his staff members around him, he would have been unrecognizable.

He had lost a lot of blood but was conscious again. He did not groan and said nothing, even when the people carrying him made an awkward move, causing him pain. Then he ordered all the staff officers to be assembled to accompany him.

The ladders were long gone. Fortunately, the sea was swelling and the torpedo boat could rock up to meet the deck of the *Suvorov*. The men carrying the admiral stopped in hesitation. Suddenly he said in a quiet but firm voice: "Listen, folks, do not cast me."

Having chosen the right moment, they transported the admiral to the *Buiny*—actually, almost cast him there. The *Buiny*'s crew yelled, "Hurrah!"

There was not a moment to spare. Those who wanted to leave the *Suvorov* had to do so immediately. Rozhestvensky's staff officers jumped on the torpedo boat. So did some other officers and men who happened to be around. As for the rest, the *Buiny* could not wait for them any longer; a Japanese shell could hit her any moment.

Leaving the sinking ship, Rozhestvensky's staff officers looked at her in anguish: no masts, no funnels, all electric lights out, decks on fire, most of the guns destroyed. They noticed that Rozhestvensky's quarters had been annihilated. On the deck stood two officers who had refused to leave the ship—Lieutenant Vyrubov and Ensign Von Kursel. A third, Lieutenant Bogdanov, had already vanished in the viscera of the burning hulk.

It was 5:30. The evacuation was complete. The admiral was on the *Buiny*, unconscious again.

12

"Follow the Admiral,"

5:30 P.M., MAY 14–1 P.M., MAY 15, 1905

1

IN LATE AFTERNOON, MAY 14, ADMIRAL NEBOGATOV FELT LOST. So far, his ships had been doing not badly at all, but everything else he saw from the bridge of his flagship, the battleship *Nicholas I,* was awful; the Russians were losing the battle.

Nebogatov's ships, now called the 3rd Armored Unit, were the ones that had started shelling Admiral Dewa's cruisers in the morning. They had fired barely thirty-five shots when Rozhestvensky curtly commanded them to stop. They had not hit a ship.

When the real battle finally commenced, Nebogatov's ships were at the end of the Russian formation. They could not fire at Togo's force because their peers were blocking the way. When their chance eventually came, Nebogatov, pacing the bridge impatiently, commanded to "hit the crowd." He did not single out a major target. As a result, the ships of the 3rd Armored Unit were firing at random, mostly at Japanese armored cruisers. At 2:09 a shell from the *Nicholas* hit the *Asama.* But the cruiser stayed disabled for only forty minutes. Nebogatov's ships also started hitting two other cruisers—the *Nissin* and the *Kassuga*—but these immediately moved away at the enviable speed of fifteen knots.

Unable to damage the adversary seriously, Nebogatov concentrated on the survival of his own ship. The *Nicholas* started zigzagging, and the Japanese could not keep her under constant fire. That paid off; only a few shells hit the battleship. Inspired by this relative safety, Nebogatov decided to remain on the unprotected front bridge.

Nebogatov's unit was following Rozhestvensky in a line-ahead column. Togo was not interested in reaching them yet. His fire was concentrated on the Russian leaders—first the *Suvorov*, then the *Alexander*, and then the *Borodino*. The *Suvorov* lasted thirty-five minutes, the *Alexander* forty-five. At 3:20 she too became disabled. Now the squadron was led by the *Borodino*. In spite of fierce fire, the gallant ship stayed at the head of the squadron for almost four hours, by the end of the day reduced to just a burning shell.

Enveloped in flames, the *Borodino* was heeling heavily, her aftermast already gone. Still, she "continued to work her foremost guns vigorously." Meanwhile, she herself was receiving the fire of the whole Japanese battle line. A British observer watching her agony from one of Togo's ships described the scene:

> The unexampled lengths to which human bravery and fortitude were carried in defence of this ship were such as reflect undying glory not only on her gallant crew, but on their navy, their country, on humanity. . . . Flames had crept to the stern, and the dense smoke emitted was being rolled horizontally away by the wind. Less than half the ship could have been habitable; yet she fought on.

Although he was next in command, Nebogatov did not attempt to replace the floundering *Borodino* at her suicidal place at the head of the column. He was disheartened and confused. He had seen the *Suvorov* leave the column barely half an hour after the battle started. He had watched her plight with utter terror. In his own words, the *Suvorov* looked like "a peasant hut on fire." But where was Rozhestvensky?

Lying dead under a pile of bodies on his flagship? Still sheltered somewhere inside the dying ironclad? Or had he moved to another ship?

By evening, Nebogatov could not distinguish the *Suvorov* at all. She was left far behind. The admiral finally decided to act on his own. He thought it was time "to at least go somewhere"; "it made no sense to stick around." Uncertain whether Rozhestvensky was still trying to command the squadron from some other ship, Nebogatov nevertheless raised a signal: "Course NO 23"—to Vladivostok. Only the ships of his unit acknowledged it.

By that time, the commander of the *Nicholas,* Captain Smirnov, had been wounded and had left the bridge. Nebogatov assumed command of the battleship himself.

At around six o'clock the admiral saw a torpedo boat cruising the column. Apparently, she was a messenger. When the torpedo boat finally reached the *Nicholas,* with voice and semaphore she announced that Admiral Rozhestvensky had been wounded, was now on the torpedo boat *Buiny,* and was surrendering command to Nebogatov, ordering him to proceed to Vladivostok.

In the heat and chaos of battle, Nebogatov and his staff misinterpreted the message. They failed to apprehend that Rozhestvensky was surrendering actual command. All they understood was the instruction to proceed to Vladivostok. "Thank God," Nebogatov announced with relief, "this means I have given the right order."

2

At 6:20 Nebogatov raised a signal: "Follow the admiral. Course NO 23."

The very first instants of his independent command coincided with two disasters. In ten minutes, at around 6:30, the *Alexander,* on fire, suddenly capsized and sank almost instantly. Forty minutes later, at 7:12, the *Borodino* also capsized.

In the blood-red rays of the setting sun, the overturned hull of the *Borodino* looked like a bleeding whale. Several sailors were still standing on it, scared to dive. Many more were already in the water. The overturn had been sudden, and dozens remained trapped inside the ship to die in anguish, darkness, and pain. Witnesses on the other Russian ships shuddered in terror. The next battleship in line, the *Orel,* to the consternation of her crew, inadvertently passed over the fresh grave of her mate.

At the sight of the *Borodino* sinking, Nebogatov was "shaken." The overturned battleship reminded him of a great fish. On the spine of that fish "stood about eight men, screaming something to us, but we did not hear what." He did not stop. Battleships were not supposed to get involved in rescue missions. He had one particularly terrifying thought—perhaps the wake created by his ship had swept those miserable people off and sent them into the drink.

He was glad that the dusk was bringing the massacre to an end. He thought that his own ship, the *Nicholas,* would have been sunk in two to three minutes, totally destroyed, "as a pile of wood," if she had found herself under direct fire. But the dusk did not promise calm. Enemy torpedo boats were spotted on the horizon—harbingers of a night of fear.

Only after the *Alexander* and the *Borodino* sank and the badly damaged *Orel* slowed down, did Admiral Nebogatov dare to lead the force. His timing was superb; at 7:40 P.M., in the advancing twilight, Togo stopped action and withdrew into the night.

Nebogatov's situation was not bad at all. His ships were hardly damaged. Rozhestvensky's four battleships had been hit by no less than 250 shells, Nebogatov's by just 12. Only eleven of his sailors had been killed. The *Senyavin* had not experienced a single hit at all. Nebogatov's *Nicholas* had lost just one gun. The only ship that was considerably damaged was the *Ushakov* whose bow was smashed.

Now Nebogatov's major concern was how to escape from enemy torpedo boats, the hounds of the dark. With several already sniffing the terrain nearby to the northeast, he turned southwest, away from Vladivostok.

At eight o'clock, already in total darkness, Nebogatov dared to turn back northeast. He was followed by his unit and by five other ships that happened to be around. The squadron as a whole had collapsed. Instead of the armada, the Sea of Japan carried dispersed ships independently struggling for survival.

By nine o'clock, Nebogatov started losing followers. The *Ushakov* was one. She was too badly damaged to keep the required speed. Captains of three other ships did not trust Nebogatov and decided to act on their own. As a result, by midnight the only ships left with the *Nicholas* were the *Apraxin*, *Senyavin*, the cruiser *Izumrud*, and the badly damaged battleship *Orel*.

Nebogatov had no idea how many ships were following him. He did not dare to check by sending light signals. He still was not entirely sure he was commanding the squadron. He thought that if Rozhestvensky had survived, he would perhaps join him during the night. Some ship was probably carrying him, say, the *Izumrud*.

Between dusk and dawn, torpedo boats attacked several times. Luckily, Nebogatov's ships escaped. The admiral spent the whole night on the bridge in fear and doubt.

At dawn, Nebogatov discovered that just four ships followed him. He did not know where the others were. For all he knew, they all might have perished.

3

The morning of May 15 brought bad news: bright sun and no fog. It was the worst possible weather for any ship wanting to sneak away from her enemies unnoticed.

Soon after dawn, at 5:15, Nebogatov saw several plumes of smoke on the horizon. The next forty-five minutes passed in agitation and uncertainty. The ships were too far away and nobody could make them out. All binoculars targeted them, but to no avail. They were warships, not steamers; that was clear. Some argued that they could distinguish the *Nakhimov* and the *Sisoi.* Nebogatov dispatched his fastest ship, the *Izumrud,* to take a closer look. She quickly returned reporting that it was the enemy.

The ships belonged to Admiral Kataoka's 5th Unit; they were older and inferior to Togo's main force. Nebogatov cheered up. At 7:15 he asked his ships, "Are your guns all right?" The captains responded affirmatively. Nebogatov commanded, "Get ready for battle." He started taking his ships toward the enemy; Kataoka retreated.

Nebogatov's ships were poor pursuers; their speed could not match Kataoka's. So Nebogatov gave up and ordered a course to Vladivostok instead. He started praying to St. Nicholas for divine help. But St. Nicholas turned a deaf ear to Russian prayers that morning: more smoke was spotted on the horizon. It was Togo.

Nebogatov made inquiries about the prospects of an artillery duel. He was told that the Japanese were too far away and that the Russian guns had no chance of reaching them. He felt "crushed" by that response.

Meanwhile, the captain of the *Nicholas,* Smirnov, had no intention of dying a hero. Having received a light wound the day before, he never returned to the bridge again. Around nine o'clock he sent a messenger to carry his advice to Nebogatov: Surrender! "Well, we will see," Nebogatov replied to the officer who whispered Smirnov's words into his ear.

The picture the admiral observed from the bridge was disheartening. Five Russian ships found themselves surrounded by twenty-seven Japanese vessels, led by Admiral Togo himself. However, the enemy's ring was imperfect; there was a considerable gap in it to the east.

Nebogatov lingered. Finally, he summoned the defeatist captain to the conning tower. This time crafty Smirnov felt strong enough to climb the ladders. He was persuasive. After a conference with him, Nebogatov told staff officers that resistance would be impossible and ordered them to raise the capitulation signal. But unexpectedly he faced something very close to mutiny.

The senior officer of the *Nicholas,* Commander Vedernikov, insisted on an urgent war council. Nebogatov agreed. Meanwhile, his ship raised a signal indicating surrender.

As the custom demanded, junior officers were the first to speak. They vigorously advocated opening fire or sinking the battleship. Nebogatov repeated that resistance was useless. "Look," said the admiral pointing at younger sailors outside, "some of them haven't even started living yet, and we are going to drown them." Captain Smirnov openly advocated surrender. The flagship's artillery officer, Commander Kurosh, expressed his readiness "to fight until the last drop of blood"—but his voice did not carry much weight. Kurosh was drunk. The conference was only about five minutes long; the Japanese started shelling the ship, and the officers had to go to their battle stations.

Nebogatov made up his mind. "God help me," the admiral said. "I do not want to drown my people."

He ordered not to respond. He did not understand Togo. Had not he already raised the capitulation signal? Meanwhile, the Japanese fire continued. In a matter of ten minutes, the *Nicholas,* her guns muted by Nebogatov's order, had six ruptures. Finally, exasperated Nebogatov ordered the Japanese flag raised.

Nebogatov's crews were shocked. Some people stood frozen in disbelief, some wept, and others rushed to commanders and pressed for the immediate sinking of their ships.

But the captains were adamant; they had to obey the admiral's order. The acting commander of the *Orel* (her captain had been mortally wounded the day before) thought resistance was utterly impossible. There was no time for real decision-making. No lifeboats were left; even the crewmen's floating bunks had been destroyed by fire. They had already been defeated yesterday, and battle today would be just a "senseless massacre." Almost no ammunition was left. Out of nineteen officers only three were not injured; he himself had been hit twice. All rangers had been destroyed—and so on and so forth.

The *Orel, Apraxin,* and *Senyavin* started preparing for surrender. Not so the *Izumrud.* She had repeated the capitulation signal, XGH, like everybody else, but then hastily pulled it down. Instead, Captain Ferzen commanded full steam ahead to the east. As she was boldly breaking through Togo's blockade, thousands of envious and admiring eyes followed her. Togo ordered his torpedo boats to pursue.

Meanwhile, the three other ships were swiftly raising Japanese flags.

4

Nebogatov summoned the *Nicholas*'s crew. He told his men that he did not want two thousand people to die purposelessly. Few cheered, many wept. A junior officer exclaimed in anguish, "But I have given my oath!" Nebogatov responded, "They will get to it in time." Meanwhile, Captain Smirnov was feverishly distributing the ship's purse among officers, as custom suggested.

At 10:53 A.M. Togo dispatched two officers to the Russian flagship. They were taken straight to Nebogatov's cabin. The Russian admiral looked friendly and invited them to sit down. The senior messenger announced: "Admiral Togo is glad that the ferocious battle is approaching its end. He wants your squadron to have an honorable surrender and thus will allow you to keep your personal weapons." The messenger informed Nebogatov that Togo was expecting him to visit the *Mikasa* immediately. The admiral was also to instruct his subordinates to keep all machinery and guns intact.

Nebogatov and his staff departed for the *Mikasa* on a Japanese torpedo boat. As they passed by Togo's ironclads, the Russians could not believe their eyes; no matter how closely they looked, they could not find a single mark of a Russian shell. It looked like Togo's main force had passed through yesterday's battle unharmed.

Approaching the charmed *Mikasa,* Nebogatov could see only a couple of minor holes. The Russians did not know that the *Mikasa* had actually been hit thirty times, that eight people had been killed, and that her bridges had been seriously damaged. Apparently, they were blinded by the striking contrast between the *Mikasa* and their own ships.

Togo's chief of staff met the Russians. The Japanese Nelson was waiting for them in his cabin.

"What are your conditions?" Togo asked.

"I cannot insist on any conditions," Nebogatov replied.

"But still."

" First, I want you to let me immediately report my misfortune to my emperor. Second, the personal belongings of officers and crews should be left to them. Then, if the emperor allows us to return to Russia, the Japanese should not try to prevent this."

Togo responded that only the Mikado could sanction the last request. But he would ask him. As for the two other requests, he was happy to grant them.

They also discussed the practicalities—where to take Russian crews and when. Nebogatov begged the Japanese to treat his men "well." He was assured that such was the custom of his hosts. In return, Togo demanded that the Russians should not attempt to damage their ships. He advised Nebogatov to give stern instructions to all captains to this effect. Finally, Togo served champagne and congratulated Nebogatov on the termination of the cruel battle.

Simple-hearted Nebogatov asked: "How did you conclude that our squadron would pass through the Korea Strait instead of the La Perouse or the Tsugaru and that we should advance on the east side of Tsushima? It appears to me almost supernatural."

Togo answered modestly, "I only thought so." Then he changed the conversation, congratulating Nebogatov on bringing his fleet without harm from the Baltic Sea to the Pacific Ocean.

Meanwhile, Togo was watching attentively to see whether Russians would show "any sign of resentment" while drinking to his health. "As, however, they raised their glasses quietly," he concluded, "I felt assured that there would be no danger in sending only a few of our men to the surrendered vessels to take them with all their crews on board to our country."

Soon, the Japanese started arriving on the Russian ships. Nebogatov summoned all captains and briefed them on his meeting with Togo. He met no resistance or strong comments.

The crews became totally demoralized. On the flagship, men sacked the wine cellar and got drunk. Many officers involuntarily contributed to the spirit of chaos. On the *Orel*, Colonel Parfenov was running around, urging the crew to leave all machinery and guns in fine order; otherwise the Japanese would get angry, he said. Another officer was almost in tears: "We will be stripped of our nobility!" The bursar, having had a quiet exchange with the senior officer in French, started distributing the ship's purse among officers. Later he claimed he had thrown part of the money overboard.

People kept saying that Rozhestvensky would have never allowed such a thing to happen. But they did not know where he was or whether he was still alive.

13

"Slutty Old Geezer,"

MAY 14–21, 1905

1

IN THE NAVY, ADMIRAL OSKAR ADOLFOVICH ENKVIST HAD A reputation as a dummy. His powerful, if somewhat short, figure and magnificent white beard gave him an imposing and sometimes majestic look—as long as he kept his mouth shut.

Enkvist had had a very undistinguished career and was appointed to Rozhestvensky's squadron only because his relative, Avelan, was naval minister. Enkvist was kind-hearted and soft-spoken; unlike Rozhestvensky, he always treated his men well. He also knew that he was not fit for the job and relied on the advice and guidance of others. His favorite expression was, "If we do this, is it going to be all right?" The officer who answered yes or no would thus make the decision for him.

Rozhestvensky disliked Enkvist intensely. He hated nepotism, a traditional Russian malady, and he despised weak and shy males. On the bridge of the *Suvorov*, Rozhestvensky contemptuously referred to his junior flag officer as "the Slutty Old Geezer." As early as in Tangier, he had deprived him of independent command, choosing Felkersam instead of Enkvist to lead the separate unit through the Suez Canal.

On the eve of the battle, Rozhestvensky virtually stripped Enkvist of any significant leadership. On May 14, out of the squadron of thirty-eight vessels, Enkvist commanded just two cruisers—the *Oleg* and the *Aurora*.

The crewmen of every ship that Enkvist had ever commanded sneered at the admiral. He knew that he was unpopular, and during the voyage he kept moving from one ship to another: from the *Almaz* to the *Nakhimov* and then, in Van Fong, to the *Oleg*. The *Oleg* officers started grumbling even before he came aboard. Their own captain, Dobrotvorsky, was a capable and strong-willed officer who had brought a whole detachment intact from the Baltic Sea to Madagascar. Enkvist immediately found himself under Dobrotvorsky's influence. The latter treated his superior with cold disdain and complained that no captain could "grow into a Nelson" as long as he had to share a ship with an admiral like Enkvist.

On May 14, Enkvist's ships fired their first shots at 11:13 A.M., aiming at Admiral Dewa's cruisers. Both his captains hoped for an active role that day. Between 11:13 and 11:19, the *Oleg* fired twenty-two shells, until Rozhestvensky's curt order advised "not to waste ammunition."

Dobrotvorsky was ambitious. He had taken the trouble of preparing detailed instructions for the upcoming battle. Gloomily, but realistically, he started with an order to figure out a way of either sinking or exploding the *Oleg* in case she was overwhelmed by the enemy (points one and two of the instruction). Other entries discussed how to straighten the cruiser if she started listing, what wooden parts of the ship had to be dismantled before the battle—and so on, forty-five entries in all.

The commander of the *Aurora*, Captain Evgeny Yegoriev, was also well known to the squadron. He had the reputation of a fearless sailor, a model commander, and a father figure for both officers and crew. Unlike on many other ships, the *Aurora* crewmen were always well fed and wore clean clothes. Never harassed, they gave the impression of a "merry and energetic" bunch of people, "not walking, but flying over the deck, to fulfill orders." In striking contrast with the *Suvorov*, they were not afraid to look an officer in the eye. The *Aurora* officers were mostly young and exceptionally friendly to each other and all visitors. They took pride in their ship and boasted that Rozhestvensky had called the *Aurora* a model vessel. He had indeed. The *Aurora* was one of his favorites. Probably, he also felt a bit guilty about the cruiser; at Dogger Bank, several shells had hit the *Aurora,* one of them killing her chaplain.

Both officers and crew loved the *Aurora's* band. Its merry "Yankee Doodle" accompanied the most loathsome work, like taking on coal. They even had their own the *Aurora* march. It was decided that musical instruments would not be put away for the battle. Perhaps they would be needed, for even a sinking ship could go down "with her flag on and her march playing."

When the battle started in earnest, Dobrotvorsky and Yegoriev realized that they could not participate in it as actively as they would have liked; both the *Oleg* and the *Aurora* were at the end of the battle line. They had to helplessly watch the swift destruction of the four Russian leaders. Only at 3:12, when the *Suvorov* had already been disabled and the *Alexander* was leading the squadron, did the *Oleg* and *Aurora* find themselves under Japanese crossfire. The *Oleg* experienced a fire on board. But the *Aurora* suffered more; a Japanese shell exploded in the conning tower lightly wounding three officers and killing Captain Yegoriev.

Admiral Enkvist was just a passive observer that day. In dismay, he watched the *Suvorov,* engulfed by flame, leave the column—obviously to fall prey to the enemy's torpedo boats. "We did not recognize the *Suvorov,*" one of his officers admitted. "It was not a ship, but some burnt black chunk with tongues of fire." Yet this paralyzed heap of iron, "which used to be the battleship *Prince Suvorov,* was still shooting at the *Nishin* and the *Kasuga.*"

Soon after they passed by the dying flagship, the helmsman of the *Oleg* spotted a torpedo. It was a short torpedo, cutting the surface of the water and approaching the *Oleg.* The cruiser zigzagged and miraculously survived. Soon after, they saw a second torpedo heading for the *Aurora.*

Fortunately, the *Aurora* was warned. Those two torpedoes led Captain Dobrotvorsky to believe that Japanese submarines were around.

At 6:05 the squadron's ships repeated an important signal: "The admiral transfers command to Admiral Nebogatov." It was unclear what had happened to Rozhestvensky and what Nebogatov could do now, for to the people on the *Oleg* and *Aurora,* it seemed that Togo's battleships were intensifying their fire. Did the Japanese want to finish the Russians off before dusk? The day of May 14 was ending in an obvious defeat. The best Russian ships had been lost, and the commander-in-chief was apparently handicapped.

At sunset, Enkvist saw several lines of Japanese torpedo boats. They menacingly loomed in the north, not moving forward, but effectively sealing the way to Vladivostok. The *Oleg* fired a shot at them, but to no avail; they were too distant. Shortly afterward, they witnessed the terrible death of the *Borodino.*

Only a minute before, the battleship had been stubbornly shooting at the enemy, and now she was lying on the sea bottom; the *Borodino* sank in barely thirty seconds. A whiff of white steam flew to the sky, "as if it were the soul" of the sunken ship. The survivors on Enkvist's ships could not help imagining the agony of the *Borodino* crew, especially those staying with the engines. Now they were dying slowly, tortured by boiling water and hot steam, perhaps even chewed alive by the machinery.

Dobrotvorsky again emphatically maintained that Japanese submarines were cruising beneath the surface. He argued that it was too difficult to sink a battleship with only artillery shells. Not a single ship throughout that war had been sunk by artillery fire, he said. Ships had been sent to the bottom of the sea by either torpedoes or mines.

Torpedoes or not, they had to think about their own survival. Although Enkvist's ships were not as severely damaged as the battleships, they still had their share of destruction. No matter how few people had been killed or wounded, the effect was nevertheless terrifying. Wounds made by the shells' splinters were horrible, incomparable to those inflicted by bullets; flesh was torn and burnt, threads of cloth mixed with blood and broken bones. The wounded had to suffer without any anesthetic. Morphine was being saved exclusively for people dying in fierce agony; chloroform was not applied, as there were too many wounded and doctors had little time. On the *Aurora,* a sailor entered the sick bay. He looked lost and was holding a dirty bloody lump in his hand. "What do I do with this, Your Honor?" he asked the doctor. The doctor looked and shuddered. The man was holding the scalped face of his mate.

In the dusk, the battle started receding. Cannonade was heard here and there, but the terrifying unceasing roar stopped. Willing to break away from the enemy, they turned south. This did not help. At around eight o'clock came the first attack of torpedo boats. It was pitch-dark, and it was impossible to tell the enemy from the Russian ships. But they knew a torpedo boat was close when they heard a characteristic dry coughing sound: The hostile ship was discharging deadly tubes.

Luckily, the two cruisers remained unhurt. At 8:30 P.M. they turned north. Then northwest. Then northeast. But no matter where they tried, the terrifying coughing sound kept reaching them from the gloom. Togo's torpedo boats were guarding the road to Vladivostok.

At ten o'clock at night, having lost all hope of continuing north-ward, the *Oleg* and *Aurora* turned southwest.

2

In the night, on rough seas, Enkvist's ships started patching their wounds. The *Oleg* had twelve holes. Several areas had been flooded. Two officers had been lightly wounded, twelve crewmen were killed, and fifty-six wounded. By the standards of May 14, that was moderate damage. The *Aurora* was even better off. The bad news was that she had used up a lot of ammunition. But, of course, the greatest loss was the death of her commander, Captain Yegoriev.

Meanwhile, Admiral Enkvist had to make a decision. In a matter of several hours, the sun would rise. Where would he head then? He had no idea how many ships were following the *Oleg*. Perhaps quite a few? After all, he was an admiral.

He decided the Korea Strait was out of the question; Togo was there. Should he proceed to Russia via the La Perouse Strait or the Tsugaru Strait? He thought his ships would not make it. The *Oleg*'s engines were damaged. She could not move very fast. Also, they might run out of coal.

Enkvist decided to turn south. Away from the battle, away from the squadron, away from Russian shores.

By dawn the sea calmed down. The faces of people assembled for morning prayer were pale and expressionless. Many heads were bandaged. Though all pools of blood and pieces of flesh had been swept overboard, a terrible smell of rotting flesh pervaded the deck.

By that time, Enkvist had discovered that only the *Aurora* and *Zhemchug* followed him. He also learned that Captain Yegoriev had been killed. The admiral immediately announced that he would move to the *Aurora*.

His decision seemed strange. The *Aurora*'s senior officer, Arkady Nebolsin, had proved in the last twelve hours that he was perfectly capable of commanding the cruiser. He had suffered several wounds, but that had not prevented him from visiting every corner of the ship during the battle the day before. The truth was that Enkvist was tired of Dobrotvorsky. The admiral liked advice but not the disdain it came with. He decided to flee with his staff, who were also annoyed with Dobrotvorsky. They started packing enthusiastically. But very soon they were interrupted.

The senior officer of the *Oleg* came to the bridge and reported that the *Oleg* officers had taken a vote on whether to continue to the south or to turn back north. Going north, they could either reach Vladivostok or seek battle, inflict as much damage on the enemy as possible, and then die. They chose north.

Enkvist instantly knew that it was not a mutiny. His authority was not challenged. He did not have to worry. With tears in his eyes, he thanked the patriotic officers:

I understand you only too well! As an officer I share your feelings completely, but as an admiral I cannot agree. We kept trying throughout the whole night, but we could not go north. First the enemy's squadron, then his torpedo boats blocked the way. We had changed our course many times before we turned south. Now it is too late. To go north means to doom your cruiser and also the *Aurora* and the *Zhemchug*. I am an old man already, I don't have much longer to live, but besides me there are 1,200 younger lives, which will be able to serve the fatherland. No, dear, tell the officers that though I wholeheartedly share and appreciate their choice, I cannot agree. The whole responsibility will be mine.

When briefed on the admiral's stance, the officers became indignant. To start with, Enkvist had not been trying to break through to Vladivostok "throughout the whole night"; he had turned south at ten o'clock. One of the officers tried to persuade the senior officer to give him a boat—to summon volunteers and try to reach Vladivostok under sail. But that was a totally unrealistic plan.

Enkvist started hesitating. He asked the *Aurora*'s acting commander, Nebolsin, what he thought. Nebolsin interviewed his officers and then replied that during the next night the unit should try to break through the Korea Strait once again.

Enkvist was not convinced. He decided he would take his ships to either Shanghai or Saigon. But that was not the end of his tribulations that day. Everybody seemed to be willing to interfere with his decision-making. At lunch, Captain Dobrotvorsky, seeing that his customary prey was hastily leaving the ship, decided to try his way one more time. He suggested Manila as their destination. At the American-owned Philippines, he argued, they were less likely to be disarmed. Also, it was unlikely that they would meet the Japanese on their way there.

Enkvist quickly agreed with Dobrotvorsky, as he always did. His chief concern was to leave the ship and her domineering captain as soon as possible.

Admiral Enkvist arrived on the *Aurora* at 1:30 P.M., accompanied by his whole staff. The crew was not there to greet him; the men were allowed their daily nap. But the kind-hearted admiral did not mind.

Those who still happened to be on deck at the time of Enkvist's arrival saw an "imposing old man with a long gray beard, who was, apparently, shaken by the outcome of the battle." They started guessing what he planned to do.

Rumors were abundant. The *Aurora*'s officers believed that they were going to Shanghai to get more coal and then to Vladivostok via the La Perouse Strait, or perhaps they would even return to the Baltic Sea.

As soon as they learned their actual destination, Manila, officers and crewmen became equally angry; they were leaving the battle area, basically deserting. Many agreed that last night the *Aurora* should have "lost" the *Oleg* with the wretched admiral on board. But there was nothing they could do about it.

Now, in the postbellum calm, Enkvist could afford to complain. He said no meeting place had been designated for dispersed ships. That was a lie. Rozhestvensky had made it clear that if the ships were to meet at all, it was to be in Vladivostok.

Enkvist still hoped to come across other ships of the squadron. Apparently, he was uncomfortable with his new safety and wanted others to share it. For a while, no ship crossed their path. But suddenly a steamer was noticed to the northeast.

At first, the Russians thought it was the *Irtysh*. But no, she was British. She could be Togo's spy, but that was not sufficient reason for an attack. Instead of being sent to their battle stations, the men were sent to do repairs.

At 3:55 the *Aurora* slowed down and lowered the flag at her stern. The men killed the day before were buried at sea. Enkvist attended. The dead were sewn into canvas and covered by the St. Andrew's flag. Numerous splinters had pierced the flag itself. From the strain of the previous day, the priest had lost his voice, and words of prayers were now inaudible. It was decided that the captain's body, placed in a hastily made zinc and wooden coffin, should be buried later, in firmer soil.

3

The way to Manila was long—around 1,500 miles. Meanwhile, the condition of several of the wounded started worsening. The ship's drummer kept groaning: "What for? What for? What have I done to the Japanese? I was not shooting at all. . . ." Soon he developed acute psychosis and started hallucinating. Day and night, the unfortunate man was saying that he kept seeing the overturning battleships and the two awesome admirals, Makarov and Rozhestvensky, the first one dead for more than a year, the second one probably buried at sea just several days earlier.

On May 16, they saw smoke again. The unit stopped. It was finally a Russian ship—the tugboat *Svir.* She carried the officers and crew of the sunken cruiser *Ural.*

Enkvist took a megaphone: "Where is our squadron? How is it doing?" A lieutenant, saved by the *Svir* from the *Ural,* responded loudly and clearly: "You, Your Excellency, are in a better position to know where our squadron is."

Enkvist reddened and put the megaphone down. Then he advised the *Svir* to go to Shanghai.

He started hesitating again. Should he perhaps take his unit to Shanghai after all, leave the two damaged ships—the *Oleg* and the *Zhemchug*—there, take on more coal, and bring the *Aurora* to Vladivostok via the La Perouse Strait? But he was advised that this was impossible. In order to enter the harbor of Shanghai, the ships would have to wait for a tide, and only then would they be able to move in and start coaling. That meant that the *Aurora* would spend more than twenty-four hours in Shanghai, and according to the rules of neutrality, a ship of a belligerent who did that was supposed to disarm immediately.

Enkvist let himself be persuaded by the argument, though in reality it did not make any sense. The *Aurora* could wait for a tide outside China's territorial waters, then go to Shanghai and accomplish the coaling speedily within twenty-four hours.

The admiral decided that the *Svir* would go to Shanghai all by herself. From there, she was to send a cable to Saigon asking for two transports with coal to be sent to Manila.

They continued. Soon people started feeling that their existence had become meaningless. "Life seems so boring," one of the officers complained. The stench of rotting flesh kept torturing sailors. They discovered that blood had got under the linoleum. They took it off and threw it overboard.

The ship's doctor, Kravchenko, finally assembled the X-ray apparatus, borrowed from Nikolaevsky hospital in Kronshtadt. In spite of the recent trials, the fragile device was working, and he was able to locate many hidden splinters in his patients' bodies. It was the first time that an X-ray apparatus had been used on a Russian warship after a battle. To many men, it looked supernatural. One sailor, who had been patiently enduring ten painful wounds, fainted when he saw his own skeleton on the screen.

It became hot; they were back in the tropics. On May 19, at 11:35 A.M., they finally saw land—an island to the north of Luzon. At 6:20 P.M., a German steamer passed by. She raised a friendly signal saying she had met the cruiser *Dnieper* to the northeast. Rozhestvensky had selected the *Dnieper* for independent cruising; she was still hunting.

By the end of the day, they stopped in Sual Bay in Luzon. An officer was dispatched ashore to get news, send urgent cables, and if possible, negotiate some coal.

But they got neither news about Rozhestvensky nor coal. The place was abandoned. There were no coal supplies and no telegraph. The captains of the *Oleg* and *Zhemchug,* Dobrotvorsky and Levitsky, met with Enkvist for a conference. Both looked exhausted by the long and frustrating journey. There was not much to discuss. Now they had no other option but to proceed to Manila.

That night, a thunderstorm swept over the harbor. The sky above the bay pulsated with lightning, and the echo of thunder roared in the mountains. In the morning, they left the harbor, heading south.

On May 21, at noon, the *Aurora* stopped her engines so that Captain Yegoriev could be given a funeral before they reached land. It was becoming hotter and hotter, and his body had started to decompose in spite of all precautions.

The *Aurora* crew mourned their commander, a soft-spoken man with an iron will, a perfect "gentleman." When they had been approaching the Korea Strait, he was anticipating seeing his son soon; the boy was a lieutenant on one of the cruisers in Vladivostok.

Having fired a salute of seven salvos, the cruiser resumed her journey. Ten minutes later, they saw five plumes of smoke to the right. They were moving in a column. Perhaps Togo, or one of his admirals, Dewa or Uriu, had reached them after all.

Manila was one hundred miles away—roughly seven or eight hours. There was no chance that the Japanese would allow them to pass by unharmed. At 12:30 P.M., Admiral Enkvist commanded alarm.

He stood on the bridge, gleaming with satisfaction and pride. His whole appearance had changed. Instead of a tired old man, people saw an inspired military leader. He thought that he would now be able to redeem himself. Men were sent to their battle stations. Suddenly the signalman yelled, "These are not Japanese!"

Instead of Togo they met Americans: two battleships and three cruisers, the *Oregon, Wisconsin, Cincinnati, Raleigh,* and *Ohio.*

Enkvist was obviously crestfallen. He frowned and slumped. All he could do was order a salute to the American admiral's flag. He did that and went downstairs to shut himself in his cabin.

At 7:45 that night, they reached Manila. The American squadron, closely following them, anchored nearby. In several minutes, they would learn what had happened to Admiral Rozhestvensky and their squadron.

14

"Throw Me Overboard,"

5:30 P.M., MAY 14—6 A.M., MAY 16, 1905

1

IT WAS HALF PAST FIVE IN THE EVENING OF MAY 14. THE *Buiny* was moving away from the *Suvorov* amid dark fountains raised by Japanese shells. One of them fell so close that water splashed all over the *Buiny's* bow.

The torpedo boat was overcrowded that night. Earlier she had rescued two hundred survivors from the *Oslyabya*. Her officers' quarters were full of naked men. Rozhestvensky's staff—six officers in all—dispersed. Some stayed with the admiral, some went on deck.

Rozhestvensky's condition looked critical. To make things worse, there was no doctor on board, only a medical assistant, Kudinov, who was summoned immediately to deal with the admiral's wounds. The man was terrified by what he saw. He thought the admiral would soon die.

Rozhestvensky had a large bleeding wound in the forehead and a bleeding wound under his right shoulder blade; a piece of flesh had been torn from his right thigh; and an artery on his left heel was damaged, and blood was streaming from it.

"How do you feel, Your Excellency?"

Instead of replying, the admiral asked, "How is the *Suvorov*?" and added, "For Christ's sake, tell them not to lower the flag." That could sound delirious, but it was not. When Kudinov informed the admiral that the *Suvorov*'s masts were gone, and that there was no place for the flag, Rozhestvensky angrily retorted: "Let them somehow find a way. It could be put up on an oar or on some hook."

Kudinov started dressing the admiral's wounds. During the extremely painful process, Rozhestvensky kept talking to his staff and the torpedo boat's commander, Kolomeitsev. He ordered the squadron to head for Vladivostok. He also commanded the raising of a signal: "The admiral transfers command to Admiral Nebogatov." Later everybody agreed that the signal was raised almost immediately after the *Buiny* departed from the *Suvorov*—around 5:35 P.M.

The signal was kept on the mast for at least half an hour, until several ships of the squadron repeated it. Then another signal was raised: "The admiral is on the torpedo boat."

To prevent possible confusion, another torpedo boat, the *Bezuprechny*, was ordered to go straight to Nebogatov's flagship and orally inform somebody there that Rozhestvensky was transferring command to Nebogatov and was ordering Nebogatov to take the squadron to Vladivostok. The *Bezuprechny* departed but didn't come back to report on the reply.

Until nightfall, the *Buiny* traveled with four cruisers—the *Oleg, Aurora, Monomakh,* and *Donskoi*. For the admiral's safety, the signal indicating his presence on board had been quickly taken off, and now the *Buiny* looked like an ordinary torpedo boat carefully staying away from the epicenter of the battle. Meanwhile, Togo was finishing off the Russian battleships. From the *Buiny*'s bridge, the panic-stricken members of Rozhestvensky's staff gawked at the sinking of the *Borodino*. When darkness fell, the *Buiny* moved closer to the *Donskoi*. Together, they headed south.

Shortly before eight o'clock, Rozhestvensky opened his eyes. He asked for an officer of the staff. The person who arrived first was the veteran of Port Arthur, Semenov. He briefed the admiral on what he had seen from the bridge. His report did not last longer than a few minutes, but it was too long for Rozhestvensky. Semenov believed that during that time the admiral became delirious twice.

At 9:30, the admiral regained consciousness again. He was told that together with the *Donskoi* they were heading south. The admiral ordered both ships to proceed to Vladivostok. If he had any plan for the squadron now, it was for all ships to go to Vladivostok independently.

However, his order was not transmitted to the *Donskoi*. It was too dangerous to use lights, for other Russian ships could take the *Buiny* for a Japanese torpedo boat and shell her. In darkness, no other means of communication were available. While staff members discussed what to do, the *Donskoi* started moving northward on her own initiative. The torpedo boat followed the cruiser.

At night the *Buiny* developed a mechanical problem. They slowed down to nine knots and as a result lost the *Donskoi*. They were moving toward Vladivostok by themselves. Late at night, the wounded officers from the *Oslyabya* heard Rozhestvensky issuing delirious incoherent orders.

2

Meanwhile, the senior members of the staff assembled in the wardroom. All bunks there were occupied by the wounded, so they settled on the floor.

At around 3 A.M., Captain Kolomeitsev entered the wardroom. He woke up the flag-captain, Constantine de Kolong. In the darkness, they started conferring. Kolomeitsev informed Rozhestvensky's chief of staff that the torpedo boat could not continue for much longer. Her engine was damaged, and she did not have enough coal. He recommended that they go to the Japanese coast, land all people ashore, and explode the ship.

De Kolong approved. The flag navigator Colonel Vladimir Filippovsky, who was lying next to him, also woke up. He said that in order to save the admiral's life, they should not become engaged in battle even if they met enemy ships.

De Kolong lingered. At least two other officers—Commander Vladimir Semenov and Lieutenant Evgeny Leontiev—also woke up and agreed that they would have to surrender in order to save the admiral. Kolomeitsev refused to consider surrendering his ship. He suggested asking the admiral himself.

Rozhestvensky was lying in a separate cabin. Kolomeitsev and Filippovsky went in and de Kolong stayed at the door, the cabin being too tiny for the three of them.

The admiral was dozing. Kolomeitsev took his hand. Rozhestvensky opened his eyes.

Filippovsky started arguing that they would have to surrender if they met with the enemy. He bluntly informed the admiral that his life was more important than a torpedo boat. Rozhestvensky gave a reply that was later misinterpreted. Feebly he answered that they should not feel bound by his presence. They should act as if he were not on the torpedo boat at all.

At that point, the officers had no doubt about what the admiral meant: His life was not worth any special consideration. In other words, if they met the enemy, they should fight.

Yet when they left the cabin, Filippovsky repeated his point: Rozhestvensky's life was too important to risk a fight with the Japanese. Kolomeitsev, to the contrary, thought the admiral's reply had summed it all up: No surrender was possible.

He demanded from de Kolong a written protocol of this debate about surrender and returned to the bridge. In darkness, Kolomeitsev waited in vain; the protocol was never delivered to him. Finally, he sent a messenger downstairs. When the man returned, he reported that the staff officers were fast asleep.

Kolomeitsev shrugged his shoulders. He had more than enough to worry about that night.

The officers were not asleep at all. They were quietly continuing their conference. After a while, they reached a consensus. If they met a Japanese ship, they would raise a white flag and also a Red Cross flag, to indicate that the torpedo boat was carrying many wounded.

De Kolong ordered Lieutenant Vourm to find a bed sheet and give it to the commander to use as a white flag at the time of surrender. Vourm took the sheet upstairs. Kolomeitsev, outraged at the staff's duplicity, angrily threw it away: "What a tragicomic thing! I, a commander of a naval ship, should take my admiral to captivity! This will never be."

In the morning, the debate resumed. Kolomeitsev confirmed that the torpedo boat had coal for just twelve hours more and that her engines were damaged.

Soon after seven o'clock, they spotted the cruiser *Donskoi* and two torpedo boats—the *Bedovy* and the *Grozny*.

Kolomeitsev went downstairs to talk to the admiral. He told Rozhestvensky that he was running out of coal and that the engine was seriously damaged. The suggestion was explicit: move to another torpedo boat. In all likelihood, Kolomeitsev wanted to get rid of de Kolong and Filippovsky. But the only way to get rid of them was to send the admiral away.

Rozhestvensky agreed to go to the *Bedovy*. The admiral liked the clean and tidy torpedo boat and her handsome and imposing captain, Commander Nikolai Baranov. Generally, Baranov was not liked in the squadron; he was rightfully accused of careerism, stinginess, and pompousness. He probably appealed to Rozhestvensky because they were both disciplinarians and the *Bedovy* was always as spotless and orderly as a royal yacht.

On the previous day, May 14, Baranov had steered his torpedo boat away from the heat of the battle. He failed to assist the drowning crews of two ships—the first victim of the day, the *Oslyabya,* and the *Suvorov*. He deliberately passed by both. However, he had vested interests in the fate of another ship, the *Alexander;* his young son was a midshipman there.

When the *Alexander* left the battle line, quickly turning into a hellish bonfire, Baranov took his torpedo boat to the side of the dying ironclad. He yelled and semaphored, trying to make somebody on the *Alexander* respond and go find the boy, but his efforts were in vain. Those on the *Alexander* who had not been killed or wounded were busy extinguishing fires. Baranov wept and steered away.

The *Donskoi* sent a cutter to transport Rozhestvensky and his staff to the *Bedovy.* The admiral was carried on a stretcher. His first words on the *Bedovy* were "Throw me overboard." Yet he greeted the crew. He also shook Baranov's hand and said, "They've smashed us."

The *Bedovy* steamed north. She carried a doctor, borrowed from the *Donskoi,* who inspected Rozhestvensky's wounds. The admiral's condition was very bad. From time to time, he lost consciousness and when he was awake, the doctor suspected that often his mind was just not there.

Meanwhile, the torpedo boat was to go to Vladivostok together with the *Grozny.* Only four hundred miles separated them from Russian shores.

3

They were moving at twelve knots. But soon two of the *Bedovy*'s four boilers were shut down. It was explained to the crew that they were short of coal.

Men started getting angry. In the heat of their flight, Rozhestvensky's officers forgot about decorum and dignity and were openly discussing surrender. Colonel Filippovsky said that they had to have the two flags ready. "We are a hospital ship now!" he explained. Baranov was overheard saying that if he encountered enemy ships, he would not fight. Rozhestvensky himself was lying in the captain's cabin, from time to time shouting unintelligible words and orders.

At around ten o'clock, Midshipman O'Brien de Lassi ordered signalman Sibirev to make a white flag from the wardroom's tablecloth. "Are we really going to surrender?" the man asked. "The admiral has ordered us to prepare it just in case," the midshipman replied.

Three hours later, at one o'clock, they noticed smoke. Baranov and Rozhestvensky's officers assembled on the bridge. The officers asked each other whether the ships were Russian or Japanese. Should the torpedo boat increase its speed?

By three o'clock, it became clear that the ships belonged to the enemy. The two Japanese torpedo boats were the *Sazanami* and the *Kagero*.

The *Bedovy* crew, having received no orders from the captain, went to their battle stations. They watched the officers, conferring on the bridge with anxiety; unlike them, the crewmen wanted to fight.

The *Grozny*'s captain was confused. He brought his ship closer to the *Bedovy* and raised a signal: "The Japanese torpedo boats are approaching. What shall we do?"

The *Bedovy* asked, "How fast can you go?"

"Twenty-two knots," the *Grozny* answered.

"Go to Vladivostok," the *Bedovy* advised.

Even more confused, the *Grozny*'s captain, Commander Andrzhievsky, asked, "Why flee and not fight?"

He did not receive a reply. The officers on the *Bedovy* were too busy. Midshipman O'Brien de Lassi was now firmly commanding signalman Sibirev to prepare the white flag. Baranov and de Kolong were driving the crew away from the guns.

De Kolong ordered Leontiev to go downstairs and inform Rozhestvensky that the ship was raising a white flag and a Red Cross flag because two Japanese torpedo boats were approaching.

Leontiev went downstairs, accompanied by a *Bedovy* officer, and reported as he had been ordered. But Rozhestvensky was almost unconscious. Leontiev did not get anything from him but a few incoherent words: "What? How?"

Leontiev returned to de Kolong and briefed him that there had been no response.

The enemy was already very close. All the officers went on deck. Even the *Donskoi* doctor left the cabin where he had been staying with the admiral. Rozhestvensky was left alone.

At 3:25 P.M. the Japanese opened fire. The *Grozny* responded. The *Bedovy* stopped and raised a signal: "Am carrying heavily wounded."

Baranov ordered the Russian flag down and the two others raised. Seeing that the *Bedovy* was surrendering, the *Grozny* sped up in disgust.

Sailors downstairs heard the admiral's shouts: "Steam ahead, they will sink us!" At about the same time, Semenov heard the admiral cursing. The officer peeped into the cabin. Rozhestvensky was lying with his eyes wide open.

"What is going on, who is shooting?" he thundered.

"Probably, the Japanese," Semenov replied.

"Why aren't we answering? Find out, God damn it, find out!"

When Semenov returned to report that it was already too late, Rozhestvensky did not recognize him. He was delirious again.

The *Bedovy* crew was on the verge of mutiny. Men demanded a fight, saying that it was one torpedo boat against another. But de Kolong, Filippovsky, and Leontiev kept telling them that the admiral's life was more important.

The *Grozny* was disappearing in the distance, chased by the *Kagero*. It was 4:30 P.M., May 15.

The *Sazanami* paid no attention to the flags raised and fired again.

4

The *Sazanami*'s shells did not hit the *Bedovy*. The fire ceased. The Japanese launched a boat to inspect their trophy.

The *Sazanami* commander badly wanted distinction, for the previous day his ship had developed a condenser problem and had been forced to withdraw to port for urgent repairs. At 9:30 in the morning, she was back to the hunt together with the *Kagero*.

The Japanese were surprised when one torpedo boat started slowing down, while the second one sped up, angrily firing at them. Then they saw the two flags.

The *Sazanami* sent a party of several armed men and one officer to the Russian torpedo boat. Unexpectedly, de Kolong informed them that the awesome commander, the thunderous Mad Dog, Admiral Rozhestvensky, was lying downstairs, barely conscious.

The captain of the *Sazanami,* Commander Aiba, became deliriously happy. He wanted to bring the precious captive to his own ship, but the Russian doctor begged him not to risk the admiral's life. Aiba agreed.

He ordered the *Bedovy*'s guns and torpedoes disabled. Four officers from the *Bedovy* and several crew members were transferred to the *Sazanami.* Rozhestvensky, his six staff officers, the *Bedovy*'s captain, and seventy-seven crewmen stayed on board. Commander Aiba took the two ships toward Urusan.

At 7:20 P.M., already close to Urusan, they heard a cannonade and then saw several plumes of smoke. Both the Russians and the Japanese were anxious, but they encountered no ships, Russian or otherwise.

The next morning, at around six o'clock, the *Sazanami* met the Japanese cruiser *Akasi.* The cruiser was entrusted with the task of towing the *Bedovy.* The victorious *Sazanami* proudly escorted them, taking her prized trophy to the main Japanese base, triumphant Sasebo.

15

"Return Soon,"
MAY—NOVEMBER 1905

1

NEWS ABOUT THE TSUSHIMA DISASTER STARTED REACHING ST. Petersburg on May 16. Until then, the Admiralty kept working on the Vladivostok end of Rozhestvensky's journey. Vice Admiral Birilev departed for Vladivostok as a new naval commander-in-chief; Rozhestvensky had informed the tsar that he would be unable to command anything bigger than a squadron. The local commander, Admiral Greve, was sent a cable headed "Extremely urgent. Extremely secret. For your eyes only": "According to our information, General Adjutant Rozhestvensky's squadron departed the shores of Annam around May 1, heading north." But every effort was in vain.

The initial unconfirmed reports quoted enormous Russian casualties. Japanese losses were not mentioned at all. The only thing St. Petersburg knew for sure at first was that there had been a battle and that strikingly few ships were reaching Vladivostok.

The first ship to reach Russian shores was the cruiser *Almaz.* On May 16, her commander cabled that the *Suvorov,* the *Oslyabya,* and the cruiser *Ural* had sunk, the *Alexander* had been badly damaged, and Rozhestvensky had been wounded and taken to the destroyer *Buiny.*

The *Almaz* had left when the squadron was still whole, and now her captain's cable asked incredulously: "Could it be that none of the squadron's ships has reached Vladivostok?"

The next day, on May 17 at ten o'clock in the morning, the torpedo boat *Grozny* arrived, the same one that had left the *Bedovy* shortly before her fateful surrender. Her captain, though he might have had his own ideas about what had happened on the *Bedovy,* dryly reported: "Fate of the admiral unknown." If the *Bedovy* had sped up, Rozhestvensky would have been in Vladivostok, too.

The third warship to come to Vladivostok was the torpedo boat *Bravy.* She had reached Russian shores with much difficulty; in order to hide from enemy torpedo boats, she had cut down her mast and hastily painted her funnel white to become inconspicuous on the misty silvery sea.

For a while, reports from these three ships were the only solid material in a liquid world of hearsay and gossip. In 1905, there were few less reliable networks than the news agencies. When the squadron had been staying at Indochina, they had reported ferocious battles in the Strait of Malacca; now they were trumpeting that Rozhestvensky had made it to Vladivostok on the *Suvorov.* The tsar called the incomplete and contradictory information "terribly depressing."

Hour by hour, however, reports were becoming clearer—and gloomier. By May 19 it was confirmed that almost all the Russian ships had sunk and that Rozhestvensky was in captivity. No other ship reached Vladivostok out of the squadron of thirty-eight. The cruiser *Izumrud* came very close, but became shipwrecked. Yet she still deserved all the praise in the world. Surrounded by twenty-seven Japanese ships together with Admiral Nebogatov's battleships, the *Izumrud* had decided to break through. The tsar included the *Izumrud* on the list of survivors and thanked all four ships for "a self-sacrificial heroic deed in the battle, which happened to be ill-fated for us."

St. Petersburg society was terrified. The country was already seized by revolution, with peasants setting landlords' estates on fire and workers marching the streets with red banners, and a defeat like Tsushima promised more revolt. "There is no person who would not say that the result of this battle will be a constitution," a society lady wrote down in her journal.

Seasoned admirals like Skrydlov were wrestling with the surrender of Nebogatov's ships. They knew their captains personally and insisted that they would have been incapable of such cowardice. They suspected that the crews had mutinied and made the captains surrender. Of course, they could not have been farther from the truth.

Eleven days later, the tsar's uncle, Grand Duke Alexei, the august chef of the navy, resigned on his own initiative; the public was violently accusing him of ineffectual and corrupt leadership. He wrote to his nephew that he had to step down because he was too tired and also because now he "did not believe in human beings." The tsar agreed, but felt badly about it. "Poor soul!" he wrote in his diary.

Vice Admiral Birilev, dispatched to Vladivostok, received the news about the disaster while still traveling on the Trans-Siberian Railroad. From Kliukvennaya Station, he cabled the emperor: "With a feeling of mortal anguish learnt about the annihilation of the fleet which I was to command. Unfortunately, the naval war in this campaign is finished." He begged the tsar to let him return to the capital, as he no longer had a mission in Vladivostok. Nicholas satisfied his wish.

Now peace was the tsar's only option. He agreed to let President Theodore Roosevelt mediate and sent Sergei Witte, a notorious opponent of the war, to the United States, to negotiate a treaty with Tokyo.

Nicholas received the reports of all three of the admirals who had survived the battle. Of course, Rozhestvensky's was by far the most important. It was sent from Tokyo on May 24 and was fairly brief and formal. Rozhestvensky started by saying that on May 14 his squadron had been confronted by twenty-four Japanese ships, including Togo's main force. After the *Suvorov* had been disabled, he continued, he himself, "losing consciousness," and several staff officers were put on the *Buiny,* and he had "transferred command to Nebogatov." The next day he had been "carried" to the *Bedovy.* "On the evening of the 15th learnt that the *Bedovy* had surrendered to two Japanese torpedo boats.

The *Bedovy* was brought to Sasebo on the 18th. Was informed that Nebogatov was in Sasebo."

The latter phrase, of course, was a euphemism for Nebogatov's surrender. Also from Tokyo on May 24, but five hours later, came Nebogatov's cable to the tsar. Unlike Rozhestvensky's, it was in French. The admiral reported to the sovereign that on May 15, while heading for Vladivostok, his ships had been surrounded by twenty-seven enemy warships, not counting torpedo boats. With resistance impossible, he had decided to capitulate, unwilling to sacrifice his men. He admitted that the cruiser *Izumrud* had escaped.

No matter how contemptuous Rozhestvensky could be toward Nebogatov, he thought that it was his duty to protect his subordinates from the wrath of the tsar. He wanted no scapegoats.

He cabled the tsar, asking for "grace" for those who had found themselves in such a "cruel position." In yet another cable, he insisted that Nebogatov's surrender was exclusively his—Rozhestvensky's—"sin." He explicitly asked the emperor to forgive Nebogatov and his officers.

The third admiral, Enkvist, cabled not from Japanese captivity, but from Manila, on May 21: "With the cruisers *Oleg, Aurora,* and *Zhemchug,* arrived at Manila where I hope to make repairs, take on coal, and proceed according to the expected instructions."

Nicholas responded with a gracious cable. They could relax; he did not consider them deserters. Instead, he called their performance "exceptional and honest."

But for quite a while, the sovereign, typically indecisive, had no idea what to do with those who were in captivity. Together with the endless lists of Russian officers killed at Tsushima or missing in action, he was now getting long rolls of those on Japanese terrain. Naturally, the first person on the register was General Adjutant Rozhestvensky.

2

For Nicholas, Rozhestvensky's case was the most difficult one. He forgave Enkvist; after all, the admiral had not surrendered. His three

cruisers would eventually return to Russia and be used in future battles. Nebogatov's case was also a relatively simple one. The surrender of
four battleships by a perfectly healthy admiral, unscathed by a single
splinter, could not go unpunished. But what to do with Rozhestvensky? He was in captivity—but hadn't he been seriously wounded, unconscious, and therefore blameless? His fleet had been destroyed, but
who was responsible for that, Rozhestvensky or Providence?

Finally, the tsar sent a gracious cable to Sasebo. He thanked Rozhestvensky and the squadron for having "honestly fulfilled their duty."
"The Almighty chose not to crown your feat with success," the fatalis-
tic monarch wrote, "but the fatherland will be always proud of your
exceptional courage. I wish you a fast recovery and let the Lord console
you all."

It was practically an absolution. But Rozhestvensky still thought
he could not keep the material privileges he was entitled to as head of
Naval General Staff. He cabled the Admiralty to give up his spacious
subsidized apartment. Their response was amazingly friendly: His initiative had been reported to the tsar, who was "very much surprised
and ordered to cancel your instruction. Your family is fine, they are at
the dacha. . . . Return soon."

It looked like the tsar did not want to hold him responsible for the
catastrophe. Nevertheless, the admiral now had to master the role of
perpetual culprit. The destruction had been too ugly and too complete
for the public to exempt him. He was gradually accumulating the details of what had happened to his ships and his men. It was a terrifying
picture.

His own ship, the *Suvorov,* had sunk on the evening of May 14, finished off by Togo's torpedo boats. Nobody lived to tell the tale of her
final hours.

The heroic *Borodino* had just one survivor, Semen Yushchenko, a
peasant from Tambov province. During the battle, he was in the stern
turret with a 75-millimeter gun and never left his post. Finally, after
two shells hit the area almost simultaneously, a fire started. Commanded by the only surviving mate to seek help, Yushchenko rushed
outside.

He did not meet a living soul. He saw just destruction, corpses, and flames. He panicked, forgot about his mate, and headed for the upper deck to jump into the water. Racing along the abandoned corridors, he thought he was "the only living person on the ship."

The *Navarin* also had just one survivor. The *Alexander,* with a crew of nine hundred, had none.

The old battleship *Admiral Ushakov* had no chance when surrounded by enemy ships on May 15. Admiral Shimamura raised a signal: "Advising surrender. Your admiral has already capitulated." When a sailor started reading the message to the *Ushakov* commander, Captain Miklukha, the latter interrupted: "I do not need to hear the end— we are starting a fight." In forty minutes, the crippled *Ushakov*, sunk by her crew, went to the bottom of the sea, "teasing the Japanese with her Russian flag." Captain Miklukha did not outlive his ship. After the battleship sank, the Japanese kept the Russian survivors in the water under fire for several minutes. When a shell hit a group of twenty, witnesses saw a red fountain rise to the sky. Later, the Japanese told their Russian captives that they had not expected resistance from "such an insignificant enemy."

The light cruiser *Svetlana* was a royal yacht, yet on May 15 she died a warship. Surrounded by Japanese cruisers, she was massacred by their fire. Captain Shein, wounded, having sent off his officers and crew, refused to leave his ship. The cruiser sank proudly, still carrying the St. Andrew's flag. The Japanese did not stop the shelling until the ship was already half-submerged.

The odyssey of one particular ship looked almost ludicrous. On June 17, more than a month after the battle had ended, the tsar got a cable from the transport *Anadyr* from Madagascar. Her captain informed the sovereign that on May 14, he had not been able to get to Vladivostok on his own and had decided to head south instead. He had been too afraid to call on any port and, using up coal reserved by Rozhestvensky for several warships, had finally reached the tropical island.

Rozhestvensky surely recalled that it was the same clownish *Anadyr* whose anchor had caught a telegraph cable in Tangier. But that story belonged to another age.

3

On May 21, Admiral Rozhestvensky, staying in the Sasebo Naval Hospital, had an unexpected visitor. His archenemy, Admiral Togo, came to the ward where Rozhestvensky, bandaged and still weak, was lying and shook his hand. "Defeat," he said magnanimously, "is an accident common to the lot of fighting men, and there is no occasion to be cast down by it if we have done our duty. I can only express my admiration for the courage with which your sailors fought during the recent battle, and my personal admiration for yourself, who carried out your heavy task until you were seriously wounded."

Rozhestvensky kept Togo's hand in his own for a few moments and then said quietly, "Thank you for having come to see me. With you, I am not ashamed to come off a loser."

In the summer of 1905, Admiral Togo was, arguably, the most popular man in the world. He knew this. When immediately after the battle a British naval officer, Jackson, called on Togo in Sasebo, he thought that he had "never seen anyone so thoroughly happy. He sat and chuckled delightedly and asked many questions: 'Did you think they would sink so fast?' 'Did you expect me to steer north during the night and fight again the next day?' 'What did you think of the surrender?' and many others." During the battle, Togo had had "a close shave with a shell fragment. A matter of inches only, and very few of them." Admiral Shimamura had had his cabin wrecked. Admiral Misu, the only one using a conning tower, had been wounded in the head, but not seriously. So much for the losses of the Japanese admirals.

Togo suggested that Jackson visit some of the "prizes." The British officer chose the *Apraxin*. The Russian crew had been brought ashore, and the ship was manned by Japanese. Nebogatov's people had left the ship hastily; Jackson even found a chart "that was in use which gave us information as to the Russian movements for twenty four hours or so before the battle."

No matter how willingly Rozhestvensky would have sent Togo to the bottom of the sea, he had a lot of personal respect for him. In September, Togo's *Mikasa* blew up in the Sasebo harbor. The official explanation was that her powder magazine had exploded. However, it was suspected that this had been a terrorist act—a protest against the soft peace treaty negotiated with Russia. This was quite possible; at that point Japan was experiencing riots in the streets and even mob violence against officials. In any case, Rozhestvensky found it proper to send Togo his condolences. Togo replied with a laconic thank-you note.

But correspondence with Togo or, for that matter, with the tsar was a burden to the unhappy admiral. Luckily, he was getting other messages. Since the beginning of June, he had been in touch with the four women who were central in his life. The first to contact him were his wife and daughter: "Take good care of yourself. Waiting. Missing you." Admiral Makarov's widow, beautiful Capitolina, cabled: "My heart is always with you. Makarova." His love of the last troubled year, Nataliya Sivers, also wrote to him. The first message from her was from Nagasaki. The white *Orel* had also been captured by the Japanese. This was partially his fault; he had ordered the hospital ship to take the smuggling *Oldhamia*'s British crew, which gave the Japanese sufficient reason to arrest the ship. But Sivers was soon released and went to Europe. She next cabled him from the Hotel Orleans Richelieu in Paris.

4

Russian prisoners of war were held at Sasebo, Osaka, and Maizuru. Never before had Russian soldiers or sailors been held in captivity in such numbers or under such strict confinement.

By the beginning of August, most Russians were taken to Kyoto and put in Buddhist monasteries. Guarded by high walls, these spaces of refinement and learning became prisons. The Japanese allowed officers to take walks in the city; a foreigner did not have much chance of getting lost in Japan. They were also allowed to write three letters a month and could subscribe to Russian and Western newspapers. The Japanese government paid each officer six rubles a month, and fifty rubles were paid by St. Petersburg through the French consulate. Meals were on the hosts.

Rozhestvensky and his staff occupied a separate wing of a monastery, facing a narrow pond. Otherwise, they did not have any special privileges. Even the admiral had to attend a lecture given by the local garrison commander on how to behave in captivity. Rozhestvensky did not say anything during the talk, but the muscles on his cheekbones kept twitching. When addressed by Japanese officials, he was curtly polite. Normally his responses went no further than "Thank you" or "All right." When he was offered permission to leave the monastery between eight in the morning and six o'clock in the evening, he said he wasn't interested. In any case, as one of his officers remarked, the monastery was "much bigger than a battleship."

No matter how much the Russians admired the amazing bonsai trees and elaborate bridges and ponds, they felt awful. In order to cheer up, younger officers studied languages and staged tactical games. They often replayed Tsushima. Games and classes did not help much; people complained that the "nightmares" of the battle—particularly the sinking of the *Oslyabya, Borodino,* and *Alexander*—were still "torturing and haunting" them.

Another thing that made officers unhappy was the collapse of discipline among the sailors. Their respect toward officers after the catastrophic battle had naturally diminished, and news about revolution in Russia aggravated the situation. On the way to Sasebo, the *Nicholas's* crew had looted the officers' food supplies. To their enormous indignation, the officers were left with only tea and dried black bread for two days. Sailors also used the officers' toilets, taking delight in making the places as foul as possible. Officers called them "rude swine"; sailors started talking exploitation and class struggle.

In the monastery, Rozhestvensky lived with the *Suvorov*'s crew and Nebogatov lived with the crew of the *Nicholas*. Nebogatov was friendly to practically everybody. After a young officer from the *Orel*, Kostenko, gave a shocking talk on the Russian performance in the battle, Nebogatov invited him to his room, summoned all his staff, and asked Kostenko to repeat the lecture. The admiral was probably motivated by more than just curiosity; Kostenko's talk was a ferocious critique of Rozhestvensky.

Rozhestvensky was not interested in the strategic analysis of midshipmen and lieutenants. He was preparing for something different. Peace was in hand. Soon he would be able to go to St. Petersburg and, hopefully, launch a reform of the navy.

He did not in the least like the new liberalism in the prisoners' camps. Discussing Tsushima and even blaming him for everything was one thing. Sympathizing with revolution was another. When the same troublemaker Kostenko started receiving revolutionary pamphlets by mail, Rozhestvensky summoned him to his study. The admiral looked as fearsome as he had on the *Suvorov*'s bridge. Scars on his head did not lend him any joviality. He curtly advised Kostenko not to go back to Russia, but rather to move to Hawaii "to plant bananas." He reminded him that distributing antigovernment pamphlets was a crime, but still dutifully returned the officer's mail, which had been intercepted by his associates.

Nebogatov visited the Mad Dog several times. Their talks were long. Nebogatov insisted that he had done the right thing. If he had not surrendered, his ships would have been massacred. He knew that in Russia he would be prosecuted, and he repeated that he was ready to face all the consequences. If Rozhestvensky did not approve, he did not say so.

In September Nebogatov left for Russia. He and his officers had been discharged by the angry tsar. As they automatically ceased being soldiers, the Japanese government decided to let them go. Before leaving

Kyoto, Nebogatov visited Rozhestvensky for the last time. The subject of their talk remains unknown, but in all likelihood nothing new was said.

Very soon after Nebogatov left, Rozhestvensky needed all his willpower to stay calm. The emperor of Japan conferred decorations on British allies—Admiral Sir Gerard Noel of His Majesty's Navy China Station and his senior officers. In October, Noel brought twelve ships to Japan. Some of them had been involved in shadowing Rozhestvensky in Indochina.

The British officers were received by the emperor himself and then entertained by him at a luncheon for eighty guests. Junior officers and crewmen spent their time in the parks with excellent meals for all, fencing, jiujitsu, wrestling, fireworks, and band music. "Nothing could exceed the heartiness of their welcome," Noel noted with satisfaction in his report to London.

A group of British sailors toured Kyoto. The Japanese hosts advised Rozhestvensky's officers to stay indoors that day "to prevent possible trouble."

Several weeks earlier, Russia and Japan had signed a peace treaty. Russian diplomacy had done surprisingly well. Kaiser Wilhelm sent the tsar his insincere "most heartfelt compliments"; he had hoped the war would last longer, keeping Nicky's attention distracted from Europe. King Edward VII, to the contrary, spoke his mind when he called this peace "a universal blessing." Russia lost the southern half of Sakhalin Island and Manchuria—but it was a small cost of defeat. In mid-October, people of the squadron were allowed to go back to Russia.

Rozhestvensky refused to travel to St. Petersburg on a foreign steamer via the Suez Canal. He asked for permission to board a Russian ship bound from Japan straight for Vladivostok. A week later, the Russian military responsible for the repatriation finally agreed.

On the eve of his departure from Kyoto, he received many visitors. Several crews sent official delegations to wish him well. On October 31, he went to Kobe and boarded the steamer *Voronezh*. Like half a year before, Vladivostok was just a few hundred miles away.

16

"The Insulted Russian People,"

NOVEMBER 3, 1905–JANUARY 1, 1909

1

On the night of November 3, the *Voronezh* left Kobe. She was bringing twenty-five hundred soldiers and sailors, angry and in poor health, home to Russia. They were agitated, singing revolutionary songs, swearing by the red banner hidden in a dark corner of the hold, and drinking vodka by the mugful.

The very first day ended in a riot over the disgusting meal served to the men. After that, sailors and soldiers started holding rallies almost around the clock. Many of them stared at officers with unreserved hatred. An anonymous letter was found in the wardroom: "Wait until we get to the sea—you will all go overboard."

These twenty-five hundred were confronted by fifty-six officers, one general, two admirals, and five revolvers. The second admiral was the Port Arthur commander, Admiral Viren. The two admirals had been in touch during their captivity, and Rozhestvensky had invited Viren to join him on the *Voronezh*.

They started their travel in relative comfort. The captain gave Rozhestvensky his cabin. Although this concession may have been granted because of his high rank, the admiral did need privacy because of his ailments. The Tsushima wounds had not healed in six months. He had become much thinner and still walked with a cane. His head, pierced by a fragment of a Japanese shell half a year earlier, still had to be rebandaged daily. But if anybody thought the admiral was now a crippled old man, he was mistaken.

Soon after departure, Rozhestvensky went on deck to take a stroll. There he stumbled upon a group of men leisurely lying on the deck and paying no attention to him. For the first time since May, Rozhestvensky exploded in public: "Take these dirty scum away! *Now!*"

Not waiting for officers to carry out his order, he limped into the group himself, and with few energetic kicks made them jump and hastily retreat in amazement and fear. Soon the whole steamer knew: The Mad Dog had recuperated and was out for drills.

Only in the night did they dare to take revenge. Several sailors crept to the admiral's cabin. They were drunk, yet only a single person was bold enough to peep in.

Rozhestvensky was lying on his bunk reading a book. He looked up.

"What do you want?"

"I want to talk to you."

"About what?"

"About your behavior."

Then the sailor started yelling. He called Rozhestvensky a coward; beating Russian sailors was much easier than beating Togo! Rozhestvensky should leave the ship! They should be given as much vodka as they wanted! They had sacrificed their blood and now deserved respect!

The noise attracted attention, and the sailor fled. After that incident, officers were posted outside the admiral's cabin at night.

In the morning, the captain was informed that they could not go to Russia; Vladivostok was experiencing political unrest and rioting. They anchored in Nagasaki.

Every day at lunchtime the ship's band played merry marches and waltzes under the windows of the admiral's cabin. Rozhestvensky thanked the musicians and dutifully paid for their drinks. For several days everything was fine. He liked the music, and the musicians appreciated free liquor. But eventually their peers started rebuking them: They were betraying "the free proletariat." The band hastily learned to play the *Marseillaise*. Rozhestvensky was highly displeased, and the musicians had to pay for their own drinks.

Meanwhile, revolutionary chieftains demanded that they sail for red Vladivostok immediately. Otherwise, they were saying, they would throw Rozhestvensky and Viren overboard. Now the *Marseillaise,* which played all the time, sounded threatening.

The situation began looking very dangerous. The officers decided to appeal to their former enemies. The Nagasaki police promised to help. Indeed, seventy policemen immediately boarded the steamer. That night, five Russian officers bribed local boatmen and quietly escaped from the mutinous vessel. Rozhestvensky stayed on board.

By the next morning, November 6, four Japanese torpedo boats had arrived from Sasebo. With their torpedoes demonstratively ready for launching, they menacingly cruised the waters around the *Voronezh.*

General Danilov, responsible for the repatriation of Russian prisoners of war from Japan, arrived on board. There was no love lost between him and Rozhestvensky. When Danilov had been in Kyoto, he had chosen not to visit the admiral. Now he was very glad that Rozhestvensky was in trouble.

Danilov met with the revolutionary leaders. He talked to them for quite a while and then informed the officers that he had been reassured that there would be no violence on board. They could depart for Vladivostok, where the rioting had stopped.

This time the captain of the *Voronezh* lost his patience. He announced that he and his crew refused to risk their lives by taking a mutinous vessel to the sea.

Danilov took this opportunity to inflict his revenge. He rightfully noted that the revolutionaries were upset by Rozhestvensky's presence on board and, even more importantly, by his challenging behavior. With obvious pleasure, he suggested that Rozhestvensky and Viren move to another ship.

They did not argue. On November 10, they sailed from Nagasaki on the *Yakut* transport. In three days they saw Russian shores.

2

The first thing they encountered in the Vladivostok harbor was a number of small warships—all that was left of the Russian fleet in the Pacific. The next thing they noticed was even more disturbing: Several buildings on the waterfront had been destroyed by fire. The Japanese had not reached Vladivostok; these were the signs of the recent rioting, when drunken mobs had looted the city. The commander of the port, Admiral Greve, took Rozhestvensky and Viren ashore.

Rozhestvensky received two greetings by cable—one from the local garrison commander and another from the city mayor. Both were rather ambivalent. The garrison commander welcomed him "as an honest Russian officer" but reserved the right of history "to judge" him; the mayor stressed the admiral's role in "taking the squadron through the great space full of dangers," no matter what the ultimate result of "his mission" had been. Nevertheless, for Russians to hail a defeated military leader returning home from captivity was highly unusual; Russia had never been known for empathy toward failed generals. It was obvious that at least some people hoped that the admiral, a man of steel will and impeccable honesty, would be able to bring about change in the capital.

This was becoming clearer with every day. Rozhestvensky received an invitation from the commander-in-chief, General Linevich: "If your health allows, I am begging Your Excellency to visit me at the army." Rozhestvensky cabled an immediate response, apologizing that he had to spend several days in Vladivostok to have a new uniform made. (Naturally, all his clothes had sunk with the *Suvorov*.) Another prominent commander, Kuropatkin, also was eager to see him.

He spent just four days in the city. On November 17, Rozhestvensky and his staff officers left Vladivostok. The Trans-Siberian Railroad was to take them straight to the capital.

On his way westward, Rozhestvensky stopped to meet with both Linevich and Kuropatkin. The generals were hopeful; they thought that Rozhestvensky was now in a position to turn St. Petersburg upside down and root out corruption and incompetence in the military establishment. As Rozhestvensky left, Kuropatkin said, "You are our only hope. Tell them the truth, the whole truth . . . if they are willing to listen."

As they rode through Siberia, it was roaring with revolution. Trains were delayed; railway stations were crowded with yelling mobs parading red flags; many buildings carried the signs of recent fires. On November 21, snow reached them. So, it seemed, did the epicenter of the revolution.

They were detained at a small station. Rozhestvensky's car was blocked. The crowd assembled around it was immense. The staff panicked; they thought the admiral would be lynched.

But the revolutionary masses were not detaining Rozhestvensky's train to kill him. They wanted to ask how his health was. They were soldiers discharged from hospitals. Their wounds had healed, but their frustrations had not. Having gone through the first, senseless stage of revolt with its frenzied drinking and destruction, they were now looking for icons. Rozhestvensky was one.

Having been told by his staff that he was all right, the soldiers asked to see him. Neglecting to put on his coat in spite of bitter cold and snow, Rozhestvensky opened the door of the car.

"An old man," he heard, "and still chose to spill his blood . . . may God bless you."

The crowd cried, "Hurrah!"

"Thank you!" the admiral said. "Is this your delegate?" he asked, as he embraced a soldier and kissed him. The crowd roared, the man cried. The train jerked and moved on.

On that day, the admiral must have conceived some new ideas about his future.

The cities they passed through—Chita, Irkutsk, and others—were chaotic and deafeningly loud. Local authorities were powerless. Many officers, fed up with Nicholas II, participated in revolutionary rallies. All cables were censured not by police but by local strike committees.

Barely two weeks after the near mutiny on the *Voronezh*, Rozhestvensky was inspiring adoration among the lower classes. Often soldiers would run to the railway station to cheer the admiral from a revolutionary rally at which they had been discussing the prospects of building an independent republic in the area. If he had been interested, he would have stood a good chance of becoming the new ruler of Siberia, if not Russia.

Revolutionary committees, having learned that the train carried Rozhestvensky, were giving it the green light, while detaining all other trains indefinitely. In Samara on the Volga River, the admiral was summoned to the platform three times to answer the cheering crowd. Later in the day, two thousand soldiers blocked the railway to stop his train. They were yelling and throwing their fur hats in the air, welcoming the martyr of Tsushima.

However, when Rozhestvensky finally reached St. Petersburg on December 6, after nineteen days of travel, no official was waiting on the platform to meet him.

3

While Rozhestvensky was slowly crossing Siberia, numerous sources reported that the tsar was going to promote him and perhaps even entrust him with naval reform. But only the tsar himself knew whether this was true.

They met two days after Rozhestvensky's arrival. It is not known what they talked about, but eleven days later it was announced that the Admiralty was starting an investigation of the Tsushima debacle. Not a single member of the authoritative commission had participated in the recent war.

Instead of launching naval reform, Rozhestvensky had to protect his honor. In a matter of days, he became the chief target of the mass media, the public whipping boy for the colossal defeat. The sly, weak, and ineffective tsar and the lazy and corrupt leaders of the Admiralty wanted Rozhestvensky persecuted and preferably punished. Their own opinions on responsibility were irrelevant. They needed a scapegoat.

Nebogatov was too insignificant to be a viable target for popular outcry. Enkvist was a mock admiral from a farcical charade (his ships were currently bound for Russia, having spent five months in Manila). Rozhestvensky's stature was towering. It was worth trying to blame him.

For a while, he went through the piles of accusations calmly, then with more and more fury. Finally, he wrote a letter to a leading daily, *Novoye vremya* in St. Petersburg, responding to the most frequent criticisms.

He never addressed all the accusations filed against him. Some sounded like total rubbish to him; some he could not respond to because they involved his loyalty to the tsar; some were too true to dispute.

The chief, and perhaps the only, reason for Togo's victory had been the outstanding Japanese artillery, including its explosive power and its rate and volume. Of course, reports by Russian sailors about every Japanese shell hitting the target were an overstatement. "The actual ratio of hits to shots fired by Togo's force was low," a modern historian asserts, "probably well below 10 percent. . . . Japanese preponderance, then," he continues, "was not so much due to the number of hits as to the relative damage per hit." The Japanese shells were "sturdy"; the Russians' "often were duds." Also, the Japanese shells were endowed with a "dreadful force"; their explosive charge was roughly four times greater than that of Russian shells. They could not penetrate Russian armor, but *shimosa* caused numerous fires, which destroyed everything within a ship's armored shell. It also exploded into abundant shrapnel, massacring Russian crews.

Togo also had an advantage in speed. He was not burdened with slower and older ships. His fleet was much better trained, and his ships could perform all required maneuvers with precision.

In his public response, Rozhestvensky could not state any of these reasons for defeat. The tsar was in some way responsible for all of them. From the very start, Rozhestvensky had expressed skepticism about the success of the mission and had not wanted to sail for the Far East. He had not had nearly enough time to train his men, nor enough ammunition for artillery practice. Inadequate gunnery and poor maneuvering had been his constant concern throughout the voyage. From the start, he had also opposed sending older and slower ships. He had been made to linger for more than two months in Madagascar and for yet another month in Indochina, allowing Togo to repair all his ships.

But Rozhestvensky would not discuss this. He was not a revolutionary. He had given his oath of loyalty to the tsar and would keep it.

Instead, he addressed a number of relatively minor subjects. His squadron, he said in the letter, was accused of being "an unmanageable and slow bunch" at Tsushima. This was not true. The Russian squadron had entered the battle not as an unmanageable and slow bunch but in several well-organized detachments.

Another accusation was that the squadron had been caught unaware. Untrue also, he continued. He had anticipated the battle exactly on that day. Two days prior to the battle, he had known about the presence of Japanese scouts. True, he had not let the *Ural* cruiser use her powerful radio station to suppress the Japanese transmissions and had not sent his cruisers for reconnaissance. But that had been unnecessary. He insisted that many hours before the battle he had guessed where the Japanese would wait. In addition, he asserted that he had also succeeded in deceiving Togo. The Japanese had planned to attack the weakest Russian ships first, but as a result of proper maneuvering, they had faced the best battleships instead.

Always good at dramatic effect, Rozhestvensky reserved his major bombshell until the very end. He said that during the Tsushima battle, the British fleet had been at the Weihaiwei base "anticipating an order to annihilate the Russian fleet," if Togo had failed to do so himself.

London howled in rage. The Mad Dog, having miraculously survived the battle, was snapping at His Majesty's Government again!

Russian Anglophiles were equally enraged. Foreign Minister Lamsdorf had hated Rozhestvensky wholeheartedly since the Dogger Bank incident. Now, beside himself with fury, he demanded an explanation.

Rozhestvensky was glad that he had hurt the Foreign Ministry. He held Russian diplomacy, and Lamsdorf personally, responsible for the gross mistreatment of his squadron by neutral powers. He willingly wrote the demanded explanation. Knowing that it would be circulated in the corridors of power, he made it sarcastic and pungent.

One of his major critics was the Russian ambassador to London. The ambassador maintained that Rozhestvensky had published his letter only to deny his responsibility for Tsushima. "I am sure," the admiral responded with venom, "that the Russian ambassador to London knew to what degree the Russian enterprise in the Far East was incompatible with the interests of the English state and nation." British diplomats, he continued, had "acted skillfully, forcing the governments of Europe and of the United States to close all oceanic highways to the Russian reinforcements proceeding to the Pacific."

"Perhaps, the Russian ambassador to London is unaware of all the ordeals that the Russian squadron went through during its 35,000 *versts* journey thanks to the role of England." Rozhestvensky was reminding the ambassador that the British government had forced foreign coal and food merchants to limit supplies to his squadron. "But surely," he continued, "the Russian ambassador could not be unaware of the joint plan for a naval campaign prepared for the English squadrons in China, Australia, and East India, reinforced by the Mediterranean squadron."

The ambassador knew that after the Russian squadron had passed Singapore, the English government forbade selling it coal in all its eastern colonies other than by the special permission of local high authority.

The ambassador also had to know about the friendly pressure of England on France, 'allied' to us . . . due to which the Russian squadron, tired to death, could not show up in a single wild bay of Annam without causing immediate protest and threats from the French government. . . . While the Russian squadron was wandering at Annam (though far beyond the territorial waters), it was prohibited not only from seizing contraband, but even from inspecting English merchant vessels, which were appearing in abundance for reconnaissance purposes.

Britain was resented in St. Petersburg that winter. Naval Minister Avelan supported Rozhestvensky. In an angry letter to Lamsdorf, he wrote, "I cannot understand why Mr. Z. Rozhestvensky cannot express his opinion, even if it is very much to the dislike of England and the English, our traditional foes."

"I think," the minister concluded, "the English are too spoiled by our slavish attitude toward them and are therefore more demanding and haughty than they should be."

Lamsdorf got so angry that he could hardly contain himself. On New Year's Eve, 1905, he sent his colleague a challenging letter. His ministry, he informed Avelan icily, "has never and nowhere demonstrated a 'slavish attitude' toward foreign powers or ignored Russia's basic interests." As for Rozhestvensky's allegations about the planned British military action against his squadron, the British base at Weihaiwei had been hosting just one light cruiser and one auxiliary ship at the time of the Tsushima battle.

Sergei Witte, who after the signing of the peace treaty was made Count Witte and a full-time prime minister again, wrote a letter to the tsar explaining that he could not possibly appoint Rozhestvensky as deputy naval minister, given the way he was insulting London.

If Tsar Nicholas II still had any intentions of promoting Rozhestvensky, he abandoned them after the scandal. By the end of 1905, it was becoming increasingly clear that another and greater conflict awaited Russia in the future—with the tsar's cousin, Kaiser Wilhelm, and his German empire. At such a time, it was unwise to risk London's goodwill. The Mad Dog had to pay for his audacity.

Meanwhile, Rozhestvensky was not going to keep a low profile. On January 31, 1906, he attended a conference of the Imperial Technological Society. The issue discussed was a highly relevant one—the future of the fleet. In the revolutionary atmosphere of the day, the speakers venomously attacked corruption in the navy. Nobody could say that Rozhestvensky liked corrupt officials, but generalizations always drove him mad. He stood and gave a spontaneous talk, finishing it in an emphatic way: "It is quite possible I made many mistakes in my preparations and also during the battle itself; it is possible I have been ignorant and lazy; it is possible my associates were not too good. But I would ask you to believe me that the people now buried in the Korea Strait did not steal." He was met with thunderous applause.

His new popularity was too much for the tsar. The sovereign had probably also been briefed on Rozhestvensky's success with war veterans on his way from Vladivostok to St. Petersburg. Nicholas decided that the admiral should be put on trial to prove that he had not ordered the surrender of the *Bedovy* torpedo boat the previous May.

Rozhestvensky made up his mind instantly. He would not beg the tsar for mercy. He wrote a letter of resignation.

The tsar did not protest. On May 8, 1906, Rozhestvensky retired "due to health problems."

4

The trial started on June 21, 1906, in Kronshtadt. The accused were divided into several groups. Two of Rozhestvensky's staff officers—Captain Constantine de Kolong and Colonel Vladimir Filippovsky—were accused of having initiated the surrender. Commander Nikolai Baranov, the captain of the *Bedovy*, was accused of having violated his duty by lowering the Russian flag. One staff officer—Lieutenant Evgeny Leontiev—and three of the *Bedovy* officers—Lieutenant Nikolai Vecheslov and midshipmen Terenty O'Brien de Lassi and Alexander Tsvet-Kolyadinsky—were accused of compliance to surrender. Commander Vladimir Semenov, Lieutenant Nikolai Krzhizhanovsky, Midshipman Vladimir Demchinsky—all of Rozhestvensky's staff officers—and the *Bedovy* mechanic Alexander Iliutovich were accused of not having prevented the surrender. Vice Admiral Zinovy Petrovich Rozhestvensky was charged with failure to prevent the capitulation.

Rozhestvensky refused to engage a lawyer. He pleaded guilty and then continued to maintain that he was the only person responsible for the *Bedovy's* surrender. However, Rozhestvensky did want to make a statement.

Having briefly summarized the course of the battle prior to his arrival on the first torpedo boat to host him, the *Buiny*, Rozhestvensky proceeded to explain his staff's obsession with saving his life. He blamed this on himself: "If my order had stated bluntly that a disabled admiral shared the fate of the crew of his ship, the Tsushima chronicle would have had no such sad page." But that had been only one of his grave faults, he continued.

In spite of considerable evidence presented at the hearing showing otherwise, the admiral maintained that he had never been unconscious. "Witnesses saying that I was delirious are mistaken. I was weak, often dozing . . . but I saw everything, heard everything, recognized everybody, and was in sound mind." When Kolomeitsev had asked him what to do with the torpedo boat if they met the adversary, he, Rozhestvensky, had responded that he should not be taken into account. "Instead of energetically reminding the people who had come to me to seek moral support about their duty, I responded with a trite remark."

The only accusations that Rozhestvensky rejected belonged to the two sailors from the *Bedovy*. They testified that he had directly ordered the surrender.

Then the other accused spoke. None of them pleaded guilty. When cross-examined, each said that he had been seriously wounded and did not realize what was going on, or was fast asleep, or unaware of the consequences of his ambiguous and quite innocent statements.

The prosecution played with these people like gleeful cats play with mice; their responsibility for the surrender was obvious. But at the end of the hearings, the admiral expressed his desire to make yet another statement. That smelled of sensation.

However, Rozhestvensky's speech had little to do with the *Bedovy*'s surrender. He simply felt outraged by the prosecutor saying that the objection of a single junior officer would have been enough to raise the *Bedovy*'s crew against the treacherous commanders. Furthermore, Rozhestvensky caustically continued, the prosecutor was advocating that a junior officer should have provoked the crew's mutiny and thrown all his superiors overboard. "In our times," Rozhestvensky ominously stressed, meaning the current revolutionary fervor, this was a dangerous idea. Did it mean that any midshipman who had joined the service only yesterday could stage a revolt against his commander's order if he found it criminal?

He concluded by saying that he did not mean that what had happened on the *Bedovy* was not criminal. It was. But "the guilty party should be the senior commander solely. And I was such on the *Bedovy*. Your Honors, the navy and the insulted Russian people trust you and are longing for my punishment."

The trial lasted for six days. The final conference of the judges on June 26 took almost ten hours. Finally, the verdict was voiced.

De Kolong, Filippovsky, Baranov, and Leontiev were sentenced to death. However, the verdict asked the emperor to change this to a ten-year imprisonment. Moreover, the judges begged the emperor to take into consideration the ordeal that the accused had been through, their fatigue, and also their noble desire to save the admiral. The bottom line was that they deserved to be just discharged.

Admiral Rozhestvensky and the rest of the accused were acquitted.

5

The day after his acquittal, June 27, Rozhestvensky wrote to Makarova: "I feel humiliated by the sentence and would be happier if I had been found guilty. I would be better able to deal with a shameful label." Yet, he still had to go through Nebogatov's trial, this time as a witness.

It was a long trial. It took the judges fifteen days to hear the case. But unlike Rozhestvensky's, this case was clear-cut. In the case of the *Bedovy,* the judges were dealing with a tiny ship, hardly larger than the courtroom, carrying the semi-conscious, badly wounded commander of the squadron and his panicking officers, some of whom were wounded as well. In Nebogatov's case, they were dealing with four functioning battleships under the command of a person in perfect health, single-handedly making consistent and consequential decisions.

Before Nebogatov and his officers could return home from captivity, the tsar had stripped the admiral and the three captains (of the *Nicholas, Apraxin,* and *Senyavin*) of their military ranks. The tsar could hardly be blamed for this; in August 1905, when he announced the punishment, three of the four surrendered battleships were already serving in the Japanese navy.

Nebogatov's statement was undignified. Retreating from his original argument, that he had acted out of humanitarian concern for his men, he now claimed that he had been responsible solely for his own battleship, the *Nicholas,* and that all other commanders could have disobeyed if they had wished to do so. He also falsely testified that none of his officers had opposed his decision at the improvised war council that fateful morning. His memory had started failing him, he admitted, and he could not recall some important details of the day. He also maintained that on the evening of May 14, he had had no idea that Rozhestvensky was surrendering command to him, though officers of several ships confirmed that signals and messages sent from the *Buiny* had been clear.

On November 29, the defense summoned Admiral Rozhestvensky as a witness. He answered all questions curtly and angrily.

Yes, his message to Nebogatov about surrendering command had been repeated by several other ships. Yes, Nebogatov's ships had had guns good for further fighting. Yes, the squadron had failed to significantly damage the Japanese ships.

DEFENSE: If you had found yourself in Admiral Nebogatov's shoes and had been surrounded by twenty-seven Japanese

ships, absolutely fresh, without a single scratch, would
you have been surprised?

ROZHESTVENSKY: I had seen those ships in such condition
on the 14th, so they would not have overwhelmed me.

Just as at his own trial, he was particularly annoyed by the notion
that junior officers on Nebogatov's ships should have disobeyed and
raised a rebellion: "Apparently, this is the recent doctrine," he commented acidly. The defense, unabashed, continued:

DEFENSE: So you believe that an officer, having opposed the
surrender at a war council, had already fulfilled his duty,
for he had no other means of resistance?

ROZHESTVENSKY: First of all, I must say that junior officers should not be held responsible at all, because the law
holds a commander responsible. In this sense I regard the
commanders of the squadron as the first and the sole culprits. The trial should deal with me and Admiral Nebogatov; all others are not guilty and are sitting on the dock by
mistake.

But the defense kept returning to the question of whether junior
officers should have disobeyed Nebogatov, thus driving Rozhestvensky
mad with fury.

DEFENSE: If you had ordered a retreat or surrender and one
bold officer had started stirring the crew to disobey your
order, what would have you done?

ROZHESTVENSKY: I would have shot him.

CHAIRMAN: No other questions to the witness?

RANDOM VOICES: No.

Two weeks before Christmas, the verdict was announced. Nebogatov and the captains of the *Nicholas, Apraxin,* and *Senyavin* were

sentenced to death. However, the court, like its predecessor in June, appealed to the tsar to change that sentence to a ten-year confinement. Four officers were sentenced to four months of confinement. Others were acquitted, the acting commander of the battleship *Orel*, Shvede, among them; his ship had been severely damaged on the previous day, May 14.

6

Tsar Nicholas II was not a vengeful man. The officers who had surrendered the *Bedovy* were only discharged. Admiral Nebogatov was released early from his ten-year prison sentence. When on May 15, 1905, the day of the surrender, the admiral declared his readiness to take the consequences, he did not know that he would live for twenty-nine more years and die in 1934 in Communist Russia, some of whose leaders had been sailors in the Imperial Navy. He kept a low profile, largely forgotten by his contemporaries. In 1920, during the ferocious civil war, he lived in territory occupied by the Whites, in the village of Mikhailovka in northern Tavria. Unlike most other former admirals, he preferred not to leave Russia.

Russian spymaster, Arkady Garting, returned to his duties as chief of police in the Berlin bureau. He had saved 22,000 rubles out of the 150,000 assigned by the government to protect Rozhestvensky's squadron in the Baltic Sea; the tsar graciously allowed him to keep 10,000 as his cut. At Garting's request, several Swedes, Norwegians, and Germans were awarded the Cross of St. Anna or were sent personal precious gifts from the tsar—watches, cigarette cases, rings, and earrings—the last suggesting that some of Garting's agents were female.

The tsar's uncle, Grand Duke Alexei, died three years after his forced retirement. His bastard brother, Admiral Alexeev, lost his job as Viceroy of the Far East. There was not much left of his empire, in any case. Caustic Count Witte, also sent into retirement by the tsar who disliked clever ministers, was saying that it was good that Alexeev kept his beard long; it was covering the Cross of St. George. Otherwise, the unforgiving Witte continued, this ultimate military distinction on Alexeev's chest would have led people to think "sad thoughts about the ways some people in our country get to such high positions."

To commemorate the Russian sailors who had died at Port Arthur, Tsushima, and Vladivostok, 12,000 people in all, a church was built in St. Petersburg. It had no decorations other than bronze plates with the names of the fallen. A special monument made of red granite—the stone of martyrs—was also put in St. Petersburg to honor the nine hundred men from the *Alexander III* battleship, which had sunk leaving no survivors.

Admiral Togo lived the rest of his life as a national hero. He became Count Togo and Chief of Imperial General Staff. In 1911 he visited Britain to participate in the coronation of King George V. He went to his old training ship, the *Worcester,* and was received aboard with great honors. From Britain he sailed to America as a guest of President William Howard Taft. The Secretary of State, Philander C. Knox, gave a dinner in his honor. On the table was a model of Togo's talisman ship, the *Mikasa,* made of flowers.

In 1915 Togo went to an artillery training exercise. The ship to be shelled and ultimately destroyed was the *Iki*—the former *Nicholas I,* Nebogatov's flagship. His officers wondered whether that day the admiral was troubled by memories of the past.

Soon thereafter he withdrew from public life. He died in May 1934, the same year as Nebogatov, at the age of eighty-six.

If for Togo longevity was a blessing, for the admirals he had defeated it must have become a curse. Such was the case with Nebogatov. Zinovy Petrovich Rozhestvensky, however, was spared that.

After he retired from the navy, foreign newspapers offered him huge sums of money for a memoir about Tsushima, but he was not interested. He became a private person. He spent the last years of his life with his family at 8 Ertelev Lane in St. Petersburg, a prestigious and wealthy neighborhood. He celebrated New Year's Eve, 1908, at home with his wife, daughter, son-in-law, and four-year-old grandson, Nikolai, the one who had been born while his squadron was heading for Madagascar. On that night, he impressed everybody as being very fit; he told many jokes and made many toasts for "the bright future." At around two o'clock in the morning, he left the festive table. Suddenly the family, continuing the party, heard a crash. They rushed to his room to find the admiral lying dead on the floor.

Notes

Several abbreviations are used in the endnotes:

ADM   Admiralty
BA   Bakhmetieff Archive at Columbia University, New York
CAB   Cabinet
CO   Colonial Office
FO   Foreign Office
GARF   Gosudarstvenny Arkhiv Rossiiskoi Federatsii (State Archives of
            the Russian Federation), Moscow
PRO   Public Record Office, London, U.K.
RGAVMF   Rossiisky Gosudarstvenny Arkhiv Voenno-Morskogo Flota
            (Russian State Naval Archives), St. Peterburg
RGVIA   Rossiisky Gosudarstvenny Voenno-Istorichecsky Arkhiv (Russ-
            ian State Military History Archives), Moscow
f.   "fond" (collection)
op.   "opis" (file)
d.   "delo" (folder)
ed. khr.   "edinitsa khraneniya" (folder)
l.   "list" (page)

See Select Bibliography for full citations of references.

CHAPTER 1

3   Alexeev's telegram: RGAVMF, f. 469, op. 1, d. 64, 1a, Alexeev to
Nicholas II, January 27, 1904.

3   That night: Rossiiskaya diplomatiya, 299; *Dnevniki imperatora Nikolaya II*, 193.

4   "War—so be it": Rossiiskaya diplomatiya, 318.

4   After the opera: ibid., 299.

4   Throughout the whole day: *Dnevniki imperatora Nikolaya II*, 193.

5   "God will help us!": ibid.

5   Before going to bed: Rossiiskaya diplomatiya, 300.

5   Count Lamsdorf: ibid.

5   General Kuropatkin: Kuropatkin, *Dnevnik A. N. Kuropatkina*, 132.

5   The next morning brought more news: *Dnevniki imperatora Nikolaya II*, 193.

5   The tsar issued a war manifesto: GARF, f. 601, op. 1, ed. khr. 524, Manifest Nikolaya II ob obyavlenii voiny.

5   At 3:30 P.M.: GARF, f. 650, op. 1, d. 3, Grand Duke Andrew's diary, January 27, 1904; *Dnevniki imperatora Nikolaya II*, 193.

6   Even students: *Dnevniki imperatora Nikolaya II*, 193.

6   Passing in a carriage: Vitte, vol. 2, 291.

7   Przhevalsky: Rayfield, 151.

8   He also was quite familiar with teenagers: Rayfield, 21.

11   In his letters home: GARF, f. 677, op. 1, d. 919, Nicholas to Alexander III, January 20, 1891.

11   "Shot out like a fountain": GARF, f. 677, op. 1, d. 919, Nicholas to Alexander III, May 7, 1891.

12   Nicholas in Vladivostok: GARF, f. 677, op. 1, d. 919, Nicholas to Alexander III, June 11, 1891.

12   Chekhov's journey: Pritchett, 85–94.

14   "Looked like a crocodile": Bakhrakh, 166.

14–15   Nicholas II and the Far East: Kontsesiya na Yalu, 89–107; Rossiiskaya diplomatiya, 301–318; Kuropatkin, *Dnevnik A. N. Kuropatkina*, 108–128; Nish, 238–253; White, 1–49; Okamoto, 96–102.

17   Description of Nicholas: Gurko, 8–11, 33; Vitte, vol. 2, 5–6.

17–18   Description of the kaiser: Rohl, 38–50; Palmer, 104.

18   "Filthy": GARF, f. 676, op. 1, ed. khr. 109, l, 30, Telegram of Grand Duke Alexander Mikhailovich to Grand Duke George Mikhailovich.

18   Wilhelm was fascinated: My Early Life, 220–228; Palmer, 13–15.

19   Badmaev: Semennikov, 57.

20   Grand Duke Alexander's memorandum: GARF, f. 645, op. 1, ed. khr. 729, Zapiska velikogo kniazya Alexandra Mikhailovicha o neobhodimosti sozdaniya silnogo flota na Dalnem Vostoke.

21   "His handsome face": My Early Life, 244.

21   He had nearly drowned: BA, Meshcherskii, Grand Duke Alexander Alexandrovich to Meshcherskii, October 2, 1868.

21   "Seven puds": Novikov-Priboy, vol. 1, 95.

22   "In order to prevent revolution": Vitte, vol. 2, 291.

22   "A walking archive": Vitte, vol. 2, 177.

22   He sent a Cossack officer: *Dnevniki imperatora Nikolaya II*, 191; Kuropatkin, *Dnevnik A. N. Kuropatkina*, 121–122.

22–23   Badmaev: Semennikov, 110.

23   The *Nishin* and the *Kasuga*: Gribovsky and Poznakhirev, 138–146.

23   Sinister speed: PRO, ADM 1/7726, Captain of HMS *Diana* to Admiral Domvile, January 20, 1904.

23   Willy's cable: GARF, f. 601, op. 1, ed. khr. 1428, Wilhelm II to Nicholas II, January 6 and January 19, 1904.

CHAPTER 2

25   "A terrible event": *Dnevniki imperatora Nikolaya II*, 193.

25   On January 31: *Dnevniki imperatora Nikolaya II*, 193.

26   Cooler heads like Witte: GARF, f. 645, op. 1, d. 19, Witte to Grand Duke Alexander Mikhailovich, July 1, 1896.

27   The *Majestic*: Evans, 55–56.

28   Bureaucracy and corruption: RGAVMF, f. 763, op. 1, d. 29, Admiral N. K. Reitzenshtein's memoir.

28   In 1904: Semenov, *Flot*, 4–24.

29–30   The Japanese navy: Evans, 57–81.

30   Port Arthur: RGAVMF, f. 763, op. 1, d. 32; *Port-Artur*, 13.

30–32   Togo Heihachiro: Lloyd, 42–49; Ogasawara, 9–33, 150–162.

32–33   Togo at Port Arthur: Lloyd, 98–103; Evans, 61, 98–100.

33   Russian losses: Kuropatkin, *Dnevnik A. N. Kuropatkina*, 129–133.

34   Expert in oceanography: RGAVMF, f. 17, op. 1, d. 281, S. O. Makarov's diary.

34   "Excellent machine of slaughter": Tolstoy, 35.

34   February 4: Dnevniki imperatora *Nikolaya II*, 194.

34   "Thank God": *Dnevniki imperatora Nikolaya II*, 201.

34   March 17: RGAVMF, f. 763, op. 1, d. 180, Yu. V. Vasiliev's diary, 73.

34   On March 31: BA, Vereshchagin, Box 1.

34   Decapitated: RGAVMF, f. 763, op. 1, d. 180. Yu. V. Vasiliev's diary, 123.

34–35   The *Petropavlovsk* was cloaked: RGAVMF, f. 763, op. 1, d. 171, Cherakosov's diary, 21–22.

34   Masses: RGAVMF, f. 763, op. 1, d. 173, V. E. Egorov to his father, April 3 and April 16, 1904, 12.

35   "Sad": *Dnevniki imperatora Nikolaya II*, 202.

35   The kaiser cabled: GARF, f. 601, op. 1, ed. khr. 1428, Wilhelm II to Nicholas II, March 31 and April 13, 1904.

36   Nicholas decided: RGAVMF, f. 417, op. 1, d. 2925, l.1, Grand Duke Alexei's order #81, April 17, 1904.

37   All of the short lists: GARF, f. 543, op. 1, ed. khr. 77; Kuropatkin, *Dnevnik Kuropatkina*, 129; Semenov, *"Flot,"* 35.

37   On April 19: RGAVMF, f. 417, op. 1, d. 2925, l, 2, Nicholas II's order, April 19, 1904.

37–38   Rozhestvensky: Shtenger, 29–31.

39–43   Rozhestvensky's career: RGAVMF, f. 1233, op. 1, d. 5, l.9–13, Polnyi posluzhnoi spisok Rozhestvenskogo; Gribovsky and Poznakhirev, 9–35, 40–46, 52–119; Khoudyakov, 143; Novikov-Priboy, vol. 1, 353–355.

44   Rozhestvensky's memo: RGAVMF, f. 1233, op. 1, d. 5, l.16–21, Rozhestvensky to War Minister.

44   Rozhestvensky' s special report: RGAVMF, f. 1233, op. 1, d. 5, l.26, Rozhestvensky to War Minister.

44   Prince Alexander's decree: RGAVMF, f. 1233, op. 1, d. 5, l.4, decree of Prince Alexander, September 29, 1883.

45   The tsar ordered: RGAVMF, f. 1233, op. 1, d. 5, l.61, Cable from Russian Foreign Ministry to Russian diplomatic mission in Bulgaria, September 13 and September 25, 1885.

55   He was very critical of using Port Arthur: RGAVMF, f. 763, op. 1, d. 381, Rozhestvensky to the Head of Naval General Staff, February 8, 1906.

56   "Hostilities": Semenov, 37.

56   Thunderous fits: Novikov-Priboy, vol. 1, 355.

56   Rozhestvensky volunteered: Gribovsky and Poznakhirev, 118–157.

56   "Had decided to get rid": Shtenger, 31–32.

57   Courtiers: GARF, f. 543, op. 1, ed. khr. 77, Count Geiden to Nicholas II, March 21, 1904.

57   Rozhestvensky was busier than ever: Shtenger, 29–31.

57   It was June 16: RGAVMF, f. 417, op. 1, d. 2925, l.17, Felkersam to Rozhestvensky, June 16, 1904.

57   On July 1: RGAVMF, f. 417, op. 1, d. 2925, l.22, Virenius to Birilev, June 30, 1904.

57   August 1: RGAVMF, f. 417, op. 1, d. 2925, l.27.

58–59   Preparing the squadron: Shtenger, 32–38.

60   Ginsburg: A.D., Tsushima, 100–106.

60   On June 15: Suvorin, 460–463.

60   The next day: ibid.

61   After Makarov's death: Evans, 101.

61–62   July 28: ibid., 102–107.

62   After dusk: Nojine, 8–9.

62   The Japanese kept shelling: RGAVMF, f. 763, op. 1, d. 108, Istoricheskii zhurnal shtaba komanduyushchego eskadroi kontr-admirala Virena, September 17, 1904.

62–64   August 11: RGAVMF, f. 1233, op. 1, d. 4, l.29–30, photos of two Chilean cruisers; *Russko-yaponskaya voina. Rabota istoricheskoi komissii,* vol. 7, 4–8, 14–15; Vitte, vol. 2, 385–386; Iz dnevnika Konstantina Romanova, 94–95; Zolotarev, 152–153; *Dnevniki imperatora Nikolaya II,* 226.

66   White Eagle: Taube, 11.

67   "Refrigerator!": GARF, f. 601, op. 1, ed. khr. 513, Na kreisere *Dmitry Donskoi,* 17.

67   Lebedev: GARF, f. 601, op. 1, ed. khr. 513, Na kreisere *Dmitry Donskoi,* 19–21.

67–68   The tsar in Kronshtadt: *Dnevniki imperatora Nikolaya II,* 225–226.

68   "Horrifying to think": GARF, f. 662, op. 1, ed. khr. 22, Grand Duchess Xenia Alexandrovna's diary, August 23, 1904.

68   "You wish us victory": Ugriumov, 92–93.

CHAPTER 3

70   The Russians snorted: GARF, f. 568, op. 1, ed. khr. 82, Letter to Lamsdorf, November 23, 1898, 10.

70   "Hurt": GARF, f. 645, op. 1, ed. khr. 729, Zapiska velikogo knyazya Alexandra Mikhailovicha, 50.

70   King Edward VII's manifesto: PRO, FO 211/249, Proclamation of Edward VII, February 11, 1904.

70   The Russians suspected: GARF, f. 601, op. 1, ed. khr. 513, Na kreisere *Dmitry Donskoi,* 14.

70   Britain was preventing Russian cruisers: RGAVMF, f. 763, op. 1, d. 381, Rozhestvensky to the Head of Naval General Staff, February 8, 1906.

71   "Any inconvenience": PRO, FO 46 589, F. H. Villiers's letter to Colonial Office, July 16, 1904.

71   "Greatly disappointed": PRO, FO 46 589, MacDonald to Lansdowne, July 18, 1904.

71   The Japanese ambassador: PRO, FO 46 589, Lansdowne to MacDonald, July 27, 1904.

71   Lansdowne yielded to pressure: PRO, FO 46 589, Lansdowne to MacDonald, July 28, 1904.

71–72   British moves in Tibet: PRO, FO 181/823, Lansdowne to Hardinge, September 27, 1904.

72   Word spread: "Pisma V. V. Vereshchagina Nikolayu Romanovu v 1904 g.," 167–168.

72   "Would come shortly": PRO, FO 181/823, Extract from the diary of the political residency in the Persian Gulf for the week ending June 25, 1904.

72   The Admiralty advised: PRO, ADM 1/7729, Government of India to John Brodrick, March 24, 1904.

72   Commander of Aden Division: PRO, ADM 1/7729, Commander of Aden Division to Commander-in-Chief, East Indies, August 4, 1904.

72   A warm cable: GARF, f. 601, op. 1, ed. khr. 1428, Prince of Wales to Nicholas II, April 1 and April 14, 1904.

73   The kaiser reported: GARF, f. 601, op. 1, ed. khr. 1428, Wilhelm II to Nicholas II, April 6 and April 19, 1904.

74   The *Petersburg* and *Smolensk*: PRO, ADM 1/7726, Captain R. Tupper to the Commander-in-Chief in Mediterranean, July 24, 1904; Captain R. Tupper to Commander-in-Chief in Mediterranean, July 25, 1904; R. Tupper to Commander-in-Chief in Mediterranean, July 26, 1904; V. J. Hughes Laferla to R. Tupper, July 26, 1904.

75   The British ambassador: GARF, f. 568, op. 1, ed. khr. 65, Lamsdorf's notes for meetings with Nicholas II.

76   In Manchuria: Tainy, 159–160, 180–181, 239–240; RGVIA, f. 165, op. 1, d. 1123, Svodki svedenii razvedyvatelnogo otdeleniya shtaba glavnokomanduyushchego o protivnike; Alexeev, 190–191.

77   Routine reconnaissance: RGVIA, f. 165, op. 1, d. 1123, Svodki svedenii.

77   Piles of telegrams: GARF, f. 568, op. 1, ed. khr. 197, Doneseniya o peredvizhenii inostrannyh sudov.

78   Pavlov: RGVIA, f.165, op.1, d.1077, l.1–2, Pavlov's reports from Shanghai; GARF, f. 568, op. 1, ed. khr. 199, 1–15.

78   War Ministry: Kuropatkin, *Zapiski,* 193.

78   They did not speak the language: Alexeev, 204.

78   Rozhestvensky had been supervising: RGAVMF, f. 417, op. 1, d. 3149.

78   Lowdill: RGAVMF, f. 417, op. 1, d. 3018, Letter to Rozhestvensky, January 27, 1904.

79   Vinecken: RGAVMF, f. 417, op. 1, d. 3018, Letter from the naval attaché in the U.S., August 20, 1904.

79   Avelan: RGAVMF, f. 417, op. 1, d. 3018, Avelan to Lamsdorf, January 31, 1904.

79   His typical response: RGAVMF, f. 417, op. 1, d. 3018, 13.

79   Grand Duke Alexander: RGAVMF, f. 417, op. 1, d. 3018, 1.66, Grand Duke Alexander Mikhailovich to Grand Duke Sergei Mikhailovich, November 13, 1904.

79   To penetrate the Middle East: RGAVMF, f. 417, op. 1, d. 3149, l.4.

79   Bekker: RGAVMF, f. 417, op. 1, d. 3018.

80   Japanese agents: Kuropatkin, *Zapiski,* 193.

80   The French cruiser: RGVIA, f. 165, op. 1, d. 1077, l.1, Pavlov's report from Shanghai, February 5, 1904.

80   The Japanese were preparing an ambush: RGAVMF, f. 417, op. 1, d. 3144, Biuzov to Lamsdorf, July 7 and July 20, 1904; d. 3126, Report of Major-General Desino, April 9, 1904; Bostrem to Rozhestvensky, March 22, 1904; GARF, f. 568, op. 1, ed. khr. 197, Izvolsky to Lamsdorf, February 1 and February 14, 1904; RGAVMF, f. 417, op. 1, d. 3126, 49–50 and d.3018, 19.

81   Avelan immediately ordered vigilance: RGAVMF, f. 417, op. 1, d. 3018, l.19.

81   Garting: RGAVMF, f. 417, op. 1, d. 3144, Garting's letter, August 18 and August 31, 1904.

81   Alarming reports: RGAVMF, f. 417, op. 1, d. 3144, Garting's reports, September 6 and 19 and September 11 and 24, 1904.

82   Garting divided: RGAVMF, f. 417, op. 1, d. 3144, Garting's report, September 6 and September 19, 1904.

82   Danish minister of foreign affairs: RGAVMF, f. 417, op. 1, d. 3144, Letter from Izvolsky, July 2 and July 15, 1904.

82   Danish government: RGAVMF, f. 417, op. 1, d. 3144, 52–53.

82–83   His activities were reported: RGAVMF, f. 417, op. 1, d. 3144, Garting's letter, August 14 and August 27, 1904, 80–89; letter to Virenius, September 1, 1904; Garting's letter August 7 and August 20, 1904; Russian Consul General's Instruction, 21–23; f. 417, op. 1, d. 3018, Rozhestvensky's letter, July 5, 1904, 35–36; Virenius to Avelan, June 14, 1904; A. Gamm to Genrikhovich, October 9 and October 22, 1904, 67–69.

83   "It would be hardly pleasing": RGAVMF, f. 417, op. 1, d. 3144, Biutzov to Lamsdorf, July 7 and July 20, 1904.

83   August 30: GARF, f. 601, op. 1, ed. khr. 1428, Rozhestvensky to Nicholas II, August 29, 1904; August 30, 1904.

83   "We have stationed": RGAVMF, f. 417, op. 1, d. 3144, Director of Police Department to Virenius, September 19, 1904, 120.

84   Reval: Thiess, 126–129.

84   Hopeful and ready for the journey: Vyroubov, 107.

84   To drown their sorrows: Paleologue, 118.

84   Rozhestvensky in Reval: GARF, f. 601, op. 1, ed. khr. 1428, Rozhestvensky to Nicholas II, September 9, 1904.

85   The tsar arrived: *Dnevniki imperatora Nikolaya II*, 231.

85   September 27: GARF, f. 601, op. 1, ed. khr. 513, Na kreisere *Dmitry Donskoi*, 22.

85   He repeated: GARF, f. 681, op. 1, d. 46, Nicholas II to Grand Duke Alexei Alexandrovich, December 4, 1904, 3.

85   In good spirits: *Dnevniki imperatora Nikolaya II*, 231.

85   The squadron's departure: GARF, f. 601, op. 1, ed. khr. 513, Na kreisere *Dmitry Donskoi*, 22–23.

85   September 28: GARF, f. 601, op. 1, ed. khr. 1428, Rozhestvensky to Nicholas II, September 28, 1904.

86   "Foreign war vessels": PRO, FO 211/249, Half-yearly List of Foreign War Vessels of which Photographs are Required, January 1904.

86   The British monitored: PRO, ADM 1/7726, Captain of HMS *Diana* to Admiral Domvile, January 20, 1904.

86   "Rumors from the bazaar": PRO, ADM 1/7726, Captain of HMS *Venus* to Commander-in-Chief, Mediterranean, July 26, 1904.

87   The London *Times*: PRO, FO 46/589, Lamsdorf's cable, April 1 and 14, 1904, Admiralty's letter, April 22, 1904.

87   "Considerable assistance": PRO, FO 46/589, Report from Weihaiwei, March 5, 1904; Captain of HMS *Thetis* letter, March 4, 1904.

87   "If Great Britain": PRO, FO 46/589, Admiralty's letter, April, 22, 1904.

87   "Would become inviolable": PRO, FO 211/249, Admiralty to Foreign Office, March 5, 1904.

87–88   "You are to have": PRO, FO 46/589, Vice Admiral Noel to the secretary of the Admiralty, March 15, 1904.

88   By May: PRO, FO 46/589, Commissioner J. H. Stewart to Colonial Office, May 8, 1904.

88   At Russian naval bases: PRO, FO 211/249, Report, November 27, 1904.

88   British ambassadors: PRO, FO 211/249, Report from Copenhagen to Lansdowne, August 1, 1904.

88   Consular officers: PRO, FO 211/249, Foreign Office, April 2, 1904.

88   "Purpose of": PRO, FO 46/579, MacDonald to Lansdowne, October 21, 1904; John Hutchison to secretary of the Admiralty, October 20, 1904.

88   On October 1: PRO, FO 211/249, Report from Copenhagen to Lansdowne, October 14, 1904.

89   The day scheduled for departure: Semenov, 270.

89   "I cannot think": Gribovsky-Poznakhirev, 180.

89   October 2: Semenov, 271–275.

89   The armada departed: Gribovsky-Poznakhirev, 184–185.

89   "With ships": GARF, f. 601, op. 1, ed. khr. 1428, Rozhestvensky to Nicholas II, October 2, 1904.

89   "Bless its path": *Dnevniki imperatora Nikolaya II*, 232.

CHAPTER 4

91   "This morning": GARF, f. 601, op. 1, ed. khr. 1428, Empress Maria Fedorovna to Nicholas II, October 7 and October 20, 1904.

91   "29 ships": GARF, f. 601, op. 1, ed. khr. 516, Report from Garting, October 7 and October 20, 1904.

91   Three days earlier: RGAVMF, f. 531, op. 1, d. 15, Dnevnik plavaniya 2-i eskadry Tikhogo okeana s 28 sentiabria po 14 oktiabria.

91   The ships were unreliable: Thiess, 134–137.

92   "Russian fleet": PRO, FO 211/249, Cable to Lansdowne, October 17, 1904.

92   A celebratory telegram: GARF, f. 601, op. 1, ed. khr. 1428, Rozhestvensky to Nicholas II, October 5 and October 18, 1904.

93   The pleas of Paris: Paleologue, 118.

93   The first warnings: Vyroubov, 112.

93   The Russian freighter *Bakan*: RGAVMF, f. 531, op. 1, d. 15, Dnevnik plavaniya.

93   King Christian IX: GARF, f. 601, op. 1, ed. khr. 513, Na kreisere *Dmitry Donskoi*, 24.

94   Captains were informed: RGAVMF, f. 531, op. 1, d. 15. Dnevnik plavaniya.

94   The night of October 7: Novikov-Priboy, vol. 1, 84.

95   A shortcut: Semenov, 293.

95   "As if to announce": ibid., 86.

95–97   At 8:45 P.M. on October 8: RGAVMF, f. 531, op. 1, d. 15, Dnevnik plavaniya; RGAVMF, f. 763, op. 1, d. 303, Pisma michmana D. S. Golovnina, l.9; Novikov-Priboy, vol. 1, 28–31; Semenov, 293–297.

97   "Was lucky to have disappeared": RGAVMF, f. 531, op. 1, d. 15, Dnevnik plavaniya.

97   "Since the fishing trawlers' behavior": ibid.

98   Throughout all four nights: RGAVMF, f. 763, op. 1, d. 303, l.2, Pisma michmana D. S. Golovnina.

98   Take the wounded: GARF, f. 601, op. 1, ed. khr. 513, Na kreisere *Dmitry Donskoi*; Yegoriev, 5.

98   "Arrived with": GARF, f. 601, op. 1, ed. khr. 1428, Rozhestvensky to Nicholas II, October 13 and October 26, 1904.

98   "English Fishing Fleet": Thiess, 143.

98   "Our filthy enemies": *Dnevniki imperatora Nikolaya II*, 234.

99   The Russian ambassador: Paleologue, 120.

99   The British press: ibid., 119–121.

99   "A most dastardly outrage": Howarth, 84.

99   "Squadron of mad dogs": Thiess, 143.

99   The Home Fleet: Paleologue, 121.

99–100   British preparations for war: PRO, ADM 1/7729, Order to Captain C. H. Mayhew, October 31, 1904; PRO, ADM 1/7729, Summary of Vice-Admiral's intended procedure on being ordered to act against the Russian Fleet; PRO, ADM 1/7729, Beresford's report to the Admiralty, December 2,

1904; Beresford to his captains, October 27, 1904; Beresford' memorandum to the Senior Officer, 27 October 1904; Beresford's memorandum to Captain Arthur W. Ewart, October 27, 1904; Beresford's memorandum to Captain Alban G. Tate, October 28, 1904.

100   The *Lancaster*: PRO, ADM 1/7729, Captain of the *Lancaster* to Vice-Admiral Beresford, October 30, 1904.

102   "I have steam": PRO, FO 181/823, Beresford to Admiralty, No. 232, November 1, 1904.

102   "I have no words": Willy-Nicky, 74.

102   "How very unpleasant": GARF, f. 601, op. 1, ed. khr. 1428, Maria Fedorovna to Nicholas II, October 16 and 29, 1904.

102   The Dowager Empress had decided: PRO, FO 211/249, Cable to Lansdowne, October 21, 1904.

102   "I am sorry": Willy-Nicky, 70.

103   "The press": ibid., 70.

103   "Would have to be faced": ibid., 68–69.

103   "To get the Tsar": Paleologue, 124.

103   "I can see": ibid., 121.

103   "And, a few hours later": ibid., 122.

104   Conversation with Nelidov: ibid., 120.

104   "Russia has been": GARF, f. 892, op. 1, ed. khr. 201, Nelidov to A. A. Girs, October 2 and October 15, 1904.

104   "The Russian government": PRO, FO 181/823, Lansdowne to Hardinge, October 24, 1904.

104   "That security": PRO, FO 181/823, Lansdowne to Hardinge, October 25, 1904.

105   Rozhestvensky's telegram: PRO, FO 181/823, Lansdowne to Hardinge, October 27, 1904.

106   An unsuccessful search: PRO, FO 211/249, Lansdowne's letter to the embassy in Copenhagen, October 27, 1904.

106   Negotiations: PRO, FO 181/823, Lansdowne to Hardinge, October 28, 1904; Lansdowne to Hardinge, October 31, 1904.

106   King Alfonso XIII: Aronson, 163–164.

107   "Everyone": Novikov-Priboy, vol. 1, 104.

107   "We will be able": Semenov, 311.

107   "The enemy of our enemy": ibid.

107   "All my thoughts": ibid.

107   "The entire squadron": ibid., 312.

107   On October 16: Willy-Nicky, 74.

108   "Have already acknowledged": ibid., 76.

108   London accepted: Paleologue, 124–125.

108   "You can imagine": GARF, f. 892, op. 1, ed. khr. 107, A. A. Girs to P. S. Girs, October 10, 1904.

108   "We have become": RGAVMF, f. 763, op. 1, d. 17, Rozhestvensky to his wife, October 19, 1904.

108   Rozhestvensky recognized: Vyroubov, 115.

108   "We could not get": RGAVMF, f. 763, op. 1, d. 303, l.2, Pisma michmana D. S. Golovnina.

108   "What a squadron": Semenov, 314.

108–109   The Admiralty informed: PRO, FO 181/823, Admiralty to Beresford, No. 90, November 1, 1904.

109   In another cable: PRO, FO 181/823, Admiralty to Beresford, No. 89, November 1, 1904.

109   Beresford responded: PRO, FO 181/823, Beresford to Admiralty, No. 237, November 2, 1904.

109   The Dowager Empress: PRO, FO 211/249, Embassy in Copenhagen to Lansdowne, November 1, 1904.

109   "Only a few": Von Tirpitz, 168.

109   Rozhestvensky's explanation: Paleologue, 125.

110   The infuriated French: ibid., 126.

110   His itinerary: ibid.

110   "Making all the arrangements": ibid.

111   Rozhestvensky immediately ordered: Gribovsky and Poznakhirev, 198.

111   The *Diana*: PRO, ADM 6/104–92, Remarks on Russian Fleet, which arrived at Tangier on 28th and 29th October 1904.

111   The *Aurora*: PRO, ADM 6/104–92, the *Diana*'s captain's report, November 5, 1904.

112   "Very powerful": PRO, ADM 6/104–92, the *Diana*'s captain's report, November 5, 1904.

112   "Also continued": PRO, ADM 6/104–92, the *Diana*'s captain's report, November 5, 1904.

112   The *Ariel*: PRO, ADM 1/7729, Beresford's report, December 2, 1904.

112   The *Anadyr*: RGAVMF, f. 763, op. 1, d. 303, l.3, Pisma michmana D. S. Golovnina.

113   "May God": GARF, f. 601, op. 1, ed. khr. 1428, Rozhestvensky to Nicholas II, October 22 and November 3, 1904.

113   "One has to": RGAVMF, f. 763, op. 1, d. 17, Rozhestvensky to his wife, October 22, 1904.

CHAPTER 5

115   Seasoned sailors: Politovsky,30.

115   Three columns: ibid., 29.

116   An immediate cable to the tsar: RGAVMF, f. 763, op. 1, d. 292, l.6, Captain of the *Rion* cruiser to Nicholas II, November 27 and December 10, 1904.

116   Known to foreign royals: GARF, f. 601, op. 1, ed. khr. 1219, George Prince of Wales to Nicholas II, January 3, 1902, l.13.

116   "Iron monsters": Novikov-Priboy, vol. 1, 35.

117   "Dog": Vyroubov, 114.

117   Each warship: Novikov-Priboy, vol. 1, 34–35.

118   Otto Richter: ibid., 418–419.

118   A good orderly: Politovsky, 30.

118   *Vashe blagorodie*: Semenov, 128.

119   Church attendance mandatory: Novikov-Priboy, vol. 1, 132.

119   Meals: ibid., 145.

120–121   A day on a warship: ibid., 62–66; 82.

121   Short of supplies: Politovsky, 29–30.

121   Officers complained: ibid., 30.

121   The heat: ibid., 30–31.

122   They were thirsty: Semenov, 316.

122   The *Malaya*: Politovsky, 28.

122   "I never thought": Gribovsky and Poznakhirev, 202.

123   "The people who were left": ibid., 166.

123   "Tell the den": Thiess, 201–202.

123   Nicknames: RGAVMF, f. 763, op. 1, d. 303, Pisma michmana D. S. Golovnina, l.15; Novikov-Priboy, vol. 1, 363–364.

123–124   Black balls: Gribovsky and Poznakhirev, 205.

124   A signal sent to the *Orel*: ibid.

124   Marconi: PRO, ADM 1/7809, Information Supplied by Marconi, March 7, 1905.

124   Scrupulously recorded: PRO, ADM 1/7727, Record of wireless telegraphy received onboard H.M.S. *Duncan* from Poldhu between May 7 and May 14, 1904.

125   Telegraph terminals: Gribovsky and Poznakhirev, 128.

125   The Russian consulate in Chefoo: PRO, FO 46/579, MacDonald to Lansdowne, December 22, 1904.

125   Precautions: *Port-Artur*, 61–81.

126   Officers' letters: Vyroubov, 107; Politovsky, 27–28.

126   Totally isolated: Vyroubov, 116.

126   October 30: Politovsky, 31.

126   Sivers: ibid., 32.

126   Ten German steamers: Thiess, 161.

126   He hoped to start loading: Politovsky, 32.

127   Western reporters: Thiess, 161.

127   The governor's visit: ibid., 162.

127   The work was frantic: Novikov-Priboy, vol. 1, 135.

128   "In the mixed juice": Vyroubov, 116.

128   All drinks: Politovsky, 32–34.

128   Ivan Nelidov: RGAVMF, f. 417, op. 1, d. 3147, l.195, Rozhestvensky to Nicholas II, November 2, 1904, Dakar.

128   Nelidov's body: GARF, f. 601, op. 1, ed. khr. 513, Na kreisere *Dmitry Donskoi*, 29–30; Politovsky, 35.

128–129   Dakar: Vyroubov, 116; Politovsky, 32–37.

129   Two Japanese: Politovsky, 35.

129   "It is believed": RGAVMF, f. 417, op. 1, d. 3147, l.177, Virenius to Rozhestvensky.

129   Cape Lopez: Paleologue, 145.

129–130   King Edward VII: ibid., 148–149.

130   "Influx of troops": PRO, FO 181/823, Viceroy to the Foreign Office, October 5, 1904.

130   "Persian ambassador": PRO, FO 181/823, Cable from Teheran, November 8, 1904.

130   Prime Minister Balfour: PRO, CAB 41/29/38, Balfour to the King, November 19, 1904.

130–131   Three top naval commanders: PRO, ADM 1/7728, Report of a conference in Singapore, November 7, 1904.

131   Prime Minister Arthur Balfour informed: PRO, CAB 41/29/38, Balfour to the King, November 19, 1904.

131   The letter: PRO, FO 46/660, Letter sent to certain Chambers of Commerce, associations, etc., and communicated to press.

131   Lists of all ships: PRO, FO 46/660, List of Cargoes of coal.

131   Destinations of colliers: PRO, FO 46/660, Particulars of coal cargoes suspected as being intended for Russian Fleet, October 24, 1904; Coal cargoes suspected of being intended for the Russian Fleet, October 24, 1904.

131   British consuls: PRO, FO 46/660, Telegram from Commander-in-Chief, Cape Station.

131   When a British collier: PRO, FO 46/660, British Consulate in Cadiz to Board of Trade, November 7, 1904.

131–132   The Japanese also had the names: PRO, FO 46/660, Lansdowne to MacDonald, November 16, 1904.

132   The Japanese were prodding: PRO, FO 46/579, MacDonald to Cambell, November 11, 1904.

132   Tokyo never tired of thanking: PRO, FO 46/579, McDonald to Lansdowne, December 22, 1904.

132   Ito Hirobumi: PRO, FO 46/579, Memorandum by Mr. Hohler, November 13, 1904.

132   Komura Jutaro: PRO, FO 46/579, McDonald to Lansdowne, November 23, 1904.

132   "Gabulen": RGAVMF, f. 417, op. 1, d. 3147, l.208, Rozhestvensky to Nicholas II, November 3 and November 16, 1904.

132   A detailed report: PRO, FO 46/660, Report to Lansdowne, November 17, 1904.

133   The rains: GARF, f. 601, op. 1, ed. khr. 513, Na kreisere *Dmitry Donskoi,* 27–29; Politovsky, 37–38, 43.

134   The *Suvorov* nearly rammed: Politovsky, 37.

134   The *Borodino* and *Malaya*: Semenov, 324.

134   The *Donskoi*: Politovsky, 38.

134   His navigators: RGAVMF, f. 763, op. 1, d. 303, l.6, Pisma michmana D. S. Golovnina.

135   Their first coaling in the open sea: Vyroubov, 117–118.

135   The local French governor: ibid., 118.

135   The French officers: ibid., 118.

135   Rozhestvensky ignored the order: Politovsky, 44.

135   News from the front: RGAVMF, f. 417, op. 1, d. 3147, l.257, Virenius to Rozhestvensky, November 17, 1904.

136   The British government: RGAVMF, f. 417, op. 1, d. 3147, l.251, Avelan to Rozhestvensky, November 16, 1904.

136   "I beg you to": RGAVMF, f. 417, op. 1, d. 3147, l.263, Rozhestvensky to Virenius, November 17, 1904.

136   Uncoded: Semenov, 332.

136   Lamsdorf: RGAVMF, f. 417, op. 1, d. 3147, l.268–269, Lamsdorf to Avelan, November 20, 1904.

137   Libreville: Vyroubov, 118; Politovsky, 43–50.

137–139   The *Donskoi* and *Orel*: RGAVMF, f. 763, op. 1, d. 303, l.7, Pisma michmana D. S. Golovnina; Thiess, 202–204; GARF, f. 601, op. 1, ed. khr. 513, Na kreisere *Dmitry Donskoi,* 30–32; RGAVMF, f. 417, op. 1, d. 3147, l.264, Rozhestvensky to Virenius, November 17, 1904.

139   The feast: Politovsky, 51–52.

139   The Christmas fast: ibid., 52–53.

140   After the ships crossed the equator: ibid., 54.

140   The *Limpopo*: PRO, FO 181/854, 204–205, Extract; Thiess, 170–171.

141   Great Fish Bay: Politovsky, 54–5.

141   The *Barrosa*: PRO, ADM 1/7728, Captain of the Barrosa to Commander-in-Chief, Cape Station.

141   Monotonous: Politovsky, 56; Vyroubov, 121.

142   A storm: Vyroubov, 121.

142   Pets: ibid., 121; Politovsky, 66.

142   "Disgusting dump": Vyroubov, 119.

142   Its harbor: ibid., 119–120; Politovsky, 58.

142   The first friendly port: Thiess, 181.

143   Coaling: Vyroubov, 121; Politovsky, 60–61.

143   On December 1: Semenov, 331.

143   A suspicious steamer: Politovsky, 59.

143   A flotilla of schooners: Thiess, 182.

143   Weather: Politovsky, 59–63.

143   A British newspaper: ibid., 60–61.

143   Another newspaper: ibid., 64.

144   He summoned: Semenov, 331.

144   Rozhestvensky dispatched: Vyroubov, 121.

144   Ominous signs: Politovsky, 67–68.

145   December 6: ibid., 68.

145   Tempest came: GARF, f. 601, op. 1, ed. khr. 513, Na kreisere *Dmitry Donskoi,* 34; Politovsky, 68.

145   The shores of South Africa: Politovsky, 70.

145   Rozhestvensky was waiting: ibid.

145   No schooner: ibid., 71–72.

145   On December 9: ibid., 72–75.

146   "Tell them": Semenov, 335.

146   On the night of December 12: Politovsky, 75–76.

147   After the storm: Semenov, 337.

CHAPTER 6

151   On November 1: Bogdanovich, 304.

151–152   Felkersam's career: Gribovsky and Poznakhirev, 13, 84, 173.

152   Felkersam's appearance: Novikov-Priboy, vol. 1, 53.

152   The *Navarin*: Bogdanov, "Navarin," 50–63.

152   Felkersam's ships: Gribovsky and Poznakhirev, 161.

152   Felkersam's character: Thiess, 198–200.

153   Kaiser Wilhelm: Palmer, 160–161.

153   Crete: Kravchenko, 35–36.

153–154   Felkersam's men: RGAVMF, f. 417, op. 1, d. 3129, l.28, Bronevsky's report, November 18, 1904.

154   As early as April 1904: RGAVMF, f. 417, op. 1, d. 3018, l.17, Director of the Police Department to Rozhestvensky, April 24, 1904.

154   Foreign Minister Lamsdorf discussed the situation with the tsar: RGAVMF, f. 417, op. 1, d. 3018, l.21–22, Virenius to Avelan, June 14, 1904; RGAVMF, f. 417, op. 1, d. 3150, l.19, Organizatsiya okhrany Suetskogo kanala.

154   Loir: RGAVMF, f. 417, op. 1, d. 3150, l.19, Organizatsiya okhrany Suetskogo kanala; RGAVMF, f. 417, op. 1, d. 3018, l.21–22, Virenius to Avelan, June 14, 1904.

154   Maximov: RGAVMF, f. 417, op. 1, d. 3125, l.25, 27, 65, Virenius to Rozhestvensky, October 1, 1904.

155   On October 28: RGAVMF, f. 417, op. 1, d. 3125, Lamsdorf to Avelan, October 28, 1904.

155   Japanese spies were monitoring: *Opisanie deistvii na more*, 2.

155   Loir was an easy target: PRO, ADM 1/7727, Captain of HMS *Hermione* to Commander-in-Chief, Mediterranean.

156   Felkersam in Port Said: RGAVMF, f. 417, op. 1, d. 3129, l.179, Maximov to Lamsdorf, November 20 and December 3, 1904.

156   One warned: RGAVMF, f. 417, op. 1, d. 3129, l.127, Virenius to Felkersam, November 9, 1904.

156   Another informed: RGAVMF, f. 417, op. 1, d. 3129, l.130, Virenius to Felkersam, November 10, 1904.

157   Their watchdog: PRO, ADM6/104–92, Captain of HMS *Hermione* to Commander-in-Chief, Mediterranean, December 7, 1904; PRO, ADM6/104–92, Copies of telegrams, November 20, 1904.

157   Many perceived: Clado, 36.

157   The Admiralty cabled: RGAVMF, f. 417, op. 1, d. 3129, l.153, Virenius to Felkersam, November 16, 1904.

157   Felkersam curtly replied: RGAVMF, f. 417, op. 1, d. 3129, l.175, Felkersam to Virenius, November 20, 1904.

158   On November 21: RGAVMF, f. 417, op. 1, d. 3129, l.191, Virenius to Felkersam, November 21, 1904.

158   Felkersam protested: RGAVMF, f. 417, op. 1, d. 3129, l.222, Felkersam to Virenius, November 22, 1904.

158   Felkersam exploded with indignation: RGAVMF, f. 417, op. 1, d. 3129, l.241, Felkersam to Virenius.

158   Avelan cabled: RGAVMF, f. 417, op. 1, d. 3129, l.233, Avelan to Felkersam, November 25, 1904.

159   Cable number 5305: RGAVMF, f. 417, op. 1, d. 3129, l.256, Avelan to Felkersam, November 27, 1904.

159   Felkersam responded: RGAVMF, f. 417, op. 1, d. 3129, l.256, Felkersam to Avelan, November 29, 1904.

159   Spies reported: RGAVMF, f. 417, op. 1, d. 3129, l.282, Virenius to Felkersam, December 11, 1904.

159–160   Dobrotvorsky's career: RGAVMF, f. 406, op. 7, d. 419, l.110–122.

160–163   Dobrotvorsky's journey from Libava to Crete: Kravchenko, 21–35.

163   The *Merlin*: PRO, ADM 1/7800, captain of HMS *Merlin* to Commander-in-Chief, Mediterranean.

163–164   The stay on Crete: Kravchenko, 36–38.

164   The British watched: PRO, FO 211/249, Cable to Lansdowne from Copenhagen, November 21, 1904.

164–166   The Red Sea: Kravchenko, 37–48.

166–168   The journey from Djibouti to Madagascar: ibid., 49–52.

CHAPTER 7

169   "Arrived Sainte-Marie": RGAVMF, f. 763, op. 1, d. 291, l.12, Rozhestvensky to Nicholas II.

169   A Japanese squadron: Vyroubov, 122–123.

170   According to rumors: GARF, f. 601, op. 1, ed. khr. 513, Na kreisere, 34.

170   Its garrison: GARF, f. 601, op. 1, ed. khr. 516, l.131, Stessel to Nicholas II, November 15, 1904.

170   On November 30: GARF, f. 601, op. 1, ed. khr. 516, l.135, Stessel to Nicholas II, November 30, 1904.

170   The tsar wrote: GARF, f. 681, op. 1, d. 46, l.3, Nicholas II to Grand Duke Alexei, December 4, 1904.

170   Communications with the besieged fortress: GARF, f. 601, op. 1, ed. khr. 516, l.137, Tideman to Nicholas II, December 3 and December 16, 1904.

170   On December 16: GARF, f. 601, op. 1, ed. khr. 516, l.142, Stessel to Nicholas II, December 16, 1904.

170   "The torpedo boats": GARF, f. 601, op. 1, ed. khr. 516, Tideman to Nicholas II, December 20, 1904.

170   Stessel cabled: GARF, f. 601, op. 1, ed. khr. 516, Stessel to Nicholas II, December 20, 1904.

170   "Shocking": *Dnevniki imperatora Nikolaya II*, 243.

171   "Indifference": Bogdanovich, 326.

171   Delcasse: Paleologue, 171.

171   Kaiser Wilhelm: GARF, f. 601, op. 1, ed. khr. 1428, l.254, Wilhelm II to Nicholas II.

171   "The order to Felkersam": RGAVMF, f. 417, op. 1, d. 3147, l.372, Rozhestvensky to Avelan.

171   The Admiralty had repeatedly tried: RGAVMF, f. 417, op. 1, d. 3129, l.191, Virenius to Felkersam, November 21, 1904; RGAVMF, f. 417, op. 1, d. 3147, l.276, 328, 329, Avelan to Rozhestvensky, November 27, 1904, November 30, 1904, December 7, 1904.

172   "The 3rd Squadron": RGAVMF, f. 417, op. 1, d. 3147, Bezobrazov to Rozhestvensky, December 18, 1904.

172   Grand Duke Alexei, disliked: GARF, f. 601, op. 1, ed. khr. 1152, l.26–27. Grand Duke Alexei to Nicholas II, December 3, 1904.

172   High society salons: Bogdanovich, 310.

172   Unknown avengers: ibid., 319.

172   On December 4: GARF, f. 681, op. 1, d. 46, l.3–4, Nicholas II to Grand Duke Alexei, December 4, 1904.

173   Said Grand Duke Alexei: GARF, f. 601, op. 1, ed. khr. 1152, l.27, Grand Duke Alexei to Nicholas II, December 3, 1904.

173   Rozhestvensky loathed: "Do Tsushimy," 197; RGAVMF, f. 417, op. 1, d. 3147, l.398, Avelan to Rozhestvensky, December 3, 1904.

173   "Sunda Strait": RGAVMF, f. 417, op. 1, d. 3147, l.398, Rozhestvensky to Avelan, December 23, 1904.

173   He intended: RGAVMF, f. 763, op. 1, d. 303, k.12, Pisma Golovnina.

173   Joyful news: RGAVMF, f. 417, op. 1, d. 3147, l.348, Cable to Rozhestvensky, December 18, 1904.

174   Sainte-Marie: Politovsky, 83–84; Vyroubov, 123.

174–175   The journey to Nosy Be: Vyroubov, 123–124; Politovsky, 86.

174   "My own fuckers": RGAVMF, f. 763, op. 1, d. 303, l.16, Pisma michmana Golovnina.

175   December 25: Semenov, 346–347.

175   Charts: ibid., 348.

175   "It is all right": ibid.

175   They safely reached: Politovsky, 88–89.

175   Rozhestvensky met Felkersam: ibid., 89.

175   A report from the Russian spymaster: RGAVMF, f. 417, op. 1, d. 3129, l.186, Virenius to Felkersam, November 21, 1904.

176   In a more recent cable: RGAVMF, f. 417, op. 1, d. 3147, l.522, Bezobrazov to Rozhestvensky, January 1, 1905.

176   Both the Sunda Strait: RGAVMF, f. 417, op. 1, d. 3147, l.418a, Virenius to Kolong, December 25, 1904.

176   Ceylon: RGAVMF, f. 417, op. 1, d. 3129, l.130, Virenius to Felkersam, November 10, 1904.

176   Durban: RGAVMF, f. 417, op. 1, d. 3129, l.184, Virenius to Felkersam, November 21, 1904.

176   Even its consul: RGAVMF, f. 417, op. 1, d. 3147, l.448, Russian consul in Kaapstad to the Foreign Ministry, December 14, 1904.

176   Count Katsura: PRO, FO 46/579, MacDonald to Lansdowne, December 22, 1904.

176   The Russian naval attaché: RGAVMF, f. 417, op. 1, d. 3147, l.441, Bezobrazov to Rozhestvensky, December 29, 1904.

176   Insiders: PRO, ADM 1/7840, S.S.O. Japan, report No. 1/05, January 2, 1905, from Tokyo.

176   "I ask you": RGAVMF, f. 417, op. 1, d. 3147, l.421, Rozhestvensky to Naval General Staff, December 28, 1904.

177   The Portuguese government: RGAVMF, f. 417, op. 1, d. 3129, l.194, Virenius to Felkersam, November 21, 1904.

177   To exchange stories: Politovsky, 89–90.

177–178   Nosy Be: ibid., 93–94, 96, 100; Kravchenko, 59–61; Semenov, 349; "Do Tsusimy," 197.

179   In the *Suvorov*'s wardroom: Vyroubov, 125.

179   Two cables: GARF, f. 601, op. 1, ed. khr. 1428, l.255, Rozhestvensky to Nicholas II, December 31, 1904; f. 645, op. 1, d. 254, Rozhestvensky to Grand Duke Alexander, December 31, 1904.

179   "I am not": Gribovsky and Poznakhirev, 209.

179–180   January 4–7: Vyroubov, 125; Politovsky, 95; GARF, Na kreisere, 37.

180   The Black Sea Fleet: Vitte, vol. 2, 386–387.

180   On December 26: RGAVMF, f. 417, op. 1, d. 3147, l.426, Avelan to Rozhestvensky, December 26, 1904.

180   "Being unable": RGAVMF, f. 417, op. 1, d. 3147, l.434, Rozhestvensky to Avelan, December 30, 1904; RGAVMF, f. 417, op. 1, d. 3147, l.467, Rozhestvensky to Grand Duke Alexei.

180   Virenius reported: RGAVMF, f. 417, op. 1, d. 3147, l.332, Virenius to Rozhestvensky, December 11, 1904.

180   They would not allow him: RGAVMF, f. 417, op. 1, d. 3147, l.353, Vice-Admiral Bezobrazov to Rozhestvensky, December 19, 1904.

180   Grand Duke Alexei: GARF, f. 568, op. 1, ed. khr. 294, l.2, Grand Duke Alexei to Lamsdorf, December 13, 1904.

181   "As long as it needs": RGAVMF, f. 417, op. 1, d. 3147, l.407, Avelan to Rozhestvensky, December 29, 1904.

181   He just curtly advised: RGAVMF, f. 417, op. 1, d. 3147, l.533a, Rozhestvensky to Avelan, received January 9, 1905.

181   On January 3: RGAVMF, f. 417, op. 1, d. 3147, l.472, Avelan to Rozhestvensky, January 3, 1905.

181   The German colliers: RGAVMF, f. 417, op. 1, d. 3147, l.526, Rozhestvensky to Avelan, received January 9, 1905; Semenov, 351.

181   "Having prepared": RGAVMF, f. 417, op. 1, d. 3147, l.499, Rozhestvensky to Nicholas II, January 6, 1905.

181   "We should not": RGAVMF, f. 417, op. 1, d. 3147, l.500, Rozhestvensky to Nicholas II, received January 9, 1905.

181   In a cable to Avelan: RGAVMF, f. 417, op. 1, d. 3148, l.8, Rozhestvensky to Avelan, received January 9, 1905.

182   He also appealed: RGAVMF, f. 417, op. 1, d. 3147, l.508, Rozhestvensky to Avelan, received January 9, 1905.

182   The kaiser's birthday: Politovsky, 117.

182   To send a cable: Thiess, 210.

182   "Cables sent": RGAVMF, f. 417, op. 1, d. 3147, l.484, Rozhestvensky to Avelan.

182   It also distorted: RGAVMF, f. 417, op. 1, d. 3110, l.6, Sventorzhetsky to Golovkin.

182   "I am deprived": RGAVMF, f. 417, op. 1, d. 3148, l.14, Rozhestvensky to Avelan, received January 14, 1905.

183   On January 12: RGAVMF, f. 417, op. 1, d. 3147, l.543, Avelan to Rozhestvensky, January 12, 1905.

183   January 11: *Dnevniki imperatora Nikolaya II*, 246.

183   "Your mission": RGAVMF, f. 417, op. 1, d. 3148, l.64–65, Nicholas II to Rozhestvensky, January 12, 1905.

183   January 6: Bogdanovich, 330.

184   "By staying here": RGAVMF, f. 417, op. 1, d. 3148, l.54, Rozhestvensky to Nicholas II, received January 22, 1905.

184   Japanese minister of foreign affairs: PRO, FO 46/579, MacDonald to Lansdowne, November 23, 1904.

184   A British observer: PRO, ADM 1/7840, S.S.O. Japan, report No. 1/05, January 2, 1905.

184   "Nebogatov will reach": RGAVMF, f. 417, op. 1, d. 3148, l.112, Rozhestvensky to Avelan, received January 26, 1905.

185   "English cruisers": RGAVMF, f. 417, op. 1, d. 3147, l.362, Rozhestvensky to Avelan, December 18, 1904.

185   He was informed: PRO, FO 181/854, Foreign Office to Hardinge, January 11, 1905.

185   "After the departure": PRO, FO 181/854, Foreign Office to Hardinge, January 11, 1905, second letter.

185   When his aide: Semenov, 343.

186   Rozhestvensky knew: Gribovsky and Poznakhirev, 75, 79, 105.

186   Rozhestvensky knew him, too: ibid., 57, 88.

186   "Rot": ibid., 209.

186   "Pikes": ibid., 210.

187   Chukhnin: ibid.

187–191   The stay at Nosy Be: Vyroubov, 125, 130; Politovsky, 100–104, 106–108, 117–118, 132–133, 137, 144, 153, 156; Kravchenko, 61, 66–68; Novikov-Priboy, vol. 1, 238–239; GARF, Na kreisere, 41; Semenov, 382–385.

189–192   Discipline started collapsing: Politovsky, 105.

192   The *Nakhimov*: ibid., 109; Novikov-Priboy, vol. 1, 215.

192   Demoralization: Politovsky, 131, 140, 143, 144, 147; Novikov-Priboy, vol. 1, 233.

193   On torpedo boats: Politovsky, 138.

193   Rozhestvensky reported: RGAVMF, f. 417, op. 1, d. 3148, l.94, Rozhestvensky to Virenius, received January 29, 1905.

193   "If the squadron": RGAVMF, f. 417, op. 1, d. 3148, l.111, Rozhestvensky to Avelan, received January 26, 1905.

193   "I am not": Semenov, 376.

193   Funerals: Politovsky, 127; Kravchenko, 62.

193   Diseases: ibid., 63–64.

194   Many sailors: ibid., 53.

194   Now the Russian officers regretted: Politovsky, 134–135.

194   Mail: ibid., 121–123, 125, 128, 139.

195   Rozhestvensky allowed: RGAVMF, f. 417, op. 1, d. 3148, l.19, Virenius to Kolong, January 15, 1905.

195   He never hesitated: RGAVMF, f. 417, op. 1, d. 3148.

195   He and other top officers: RGAVMF, f. 417, op. 1, d. 3147, l.455, Virenius to Kolong.

195   His share of family problems: RGAVMF, f. 417, op. 1, d. 3148, l.136, Rozhestvensky to Ziloti, l.144, Ziloti to Rozhestvensky, l.70, Rozhestvenskaya to Rozhestvensky.

195   Rozhestvensky's illness: Politovsky, 132–133, 140.

195   Twenty years older: Kravchenko, 53.

195–196   Affair with Sivers: Novikov-Priboy, vol. 1, 289; RGAVMF, f. 763, op. 1, d. 303, l.12–15, Pisma Golovnina; Yegoriev, 39.

196   The hospital ship: RGAVMF, f. 417, op. 1, d. 2943, l.3, Vice-Admiral Zeleny to Naval General Staff, December 31, 1904.

196   Seeing apathy all around: RGAVMF, f. 763, op. 1, d. 303, l.12–13, Pisma Golovnina.

196   Torpedo boats: Vyroubov, 132.

197   Artillery practice: ibid., 126.

197   Rozhestvensky said: Semenov, 356.

197   "Ugly mob": Semenov, 357.

197   On February 8: RGAVMF, f. 763, op. 1, d. 303, l.11, Pisma Golovnina; Semenov, 366.

197   The stock of artillery shells: Semenov, 356.

197   The *Aurora*: Kravchenko, 64–65.

198   He finally briefed: Gribovsky and Poznakhirev, 216.

198   "Your Imperial Majesty": RGAVMF, f. 417, op. 1, d. 3110, l.5, Rozhestvensky to Nicholas II, received February 3, 1905.

198   "On February the second": RGAVMF, f. 417, op. 1, d. 3148, l.166, Avelan to Rozhestvensky.

198   A cable of condolence: RGAVMF, f. 417, op. 1, d. 3184, l.190, Rozhestvensky to Nicholas II, received February 15, 1905.

199   "I let you": RGAVMF, f. 417, op. 1, d. 3184, l.170, Nicholas II to Rozhestvensky, February 8, 1905.

199   "The 1st Squadron": RGAVMF, f. 763, op. 1, d. 291, l.18, Rozhestvensky to Nicholas II, February 17, 1905.

200   The Admiralty reported: RGAVMF, f. 417, op. 1, d. 3148, l.298, Virenius to Rozhestvensky.

200   "We are very sorry": RGAVMF, f. 417, op. 1, d. 3148, l.298, Rozhestvensky to Virenius, received February 24, 1905.

200   "In their final statement": RGAVMF, f. 417, op. 1, d. 3148, l.238, Avelan to Rozhestvensky, February 17, 1905.

200   Grand Duke Alexei: GARF, f. 568, op. 1, ed. khr. 294, l.4, Grand Duke Alexei to Lamsdorf, February 20, 1905.

200   "It is not known": PRO, ADM 1/7840, S.S.O. report No. 4/05.

201   On the morning of March 2: Semenov, 389–391.

201   He assembled: Yegoriev, 41; Gribovsky and Poznakhirev, 216.

201   Coal: Vyroubov, 132.

202   "On March third": RGAVMF, f. 417, op. 1, d. 3110, l.7–9, Rozhestvensky to Nicholas II, Grand Duke Alexei, Avelan, received March 5, 1905.

202   Twenty hours: Paleologue, 207.

202   "The route": RGAVMF, f. 417, op. 1, d. 3140, l.217, Avelan to Nebogatov, March 21, 1905.

202   A final cable: RGAVMF, f. 417, op. 1, d. 3110, l.12, Rozhestvensky to Avelan, received March 5, 1905.

CHAPTER 8

203   They thought: Kravchenko, 82.

205   The consul's informants: RGAVMF, f. 763, op. 1, d. 25, Vypiska iz otcheta byvshego rossiiskogo konsula v Singapure nad. sov. Rudanovskogo, l.3–4.

205   "I have to warn you": RGAVMF, f. 417, op. 1, d. 3144, l.161, Cable from Rudanovsky, November 3 and November 16, 1904.

206   "The alleged movements": PRO, CO 1273/308, Governor of Singapore to Lyttelton, January 27, 1905.

206   "A close watch": PRO, FO 181/854, 66, Anderson to Lyttelton, received December 27, 1904.

206   "I don't believe": PRO, CO 1273/308, Memorandum by the chief police officer, Singapore, on the subject of stories circulated by Russians as to intended attacks on the Baltic Fleet, January 25, 1905.

206   He thought the prolonged stay: RGAVMF, f. 763, op. 1, d. 25, Vypiska . . . , l.3–4.

207   Noel: PRO, ADM 1/7804, Noel to the Secretary of the Admiralty, May 2, 1905.

207 On March 20: RGAVMF, f. 763, op. 1, d. 25. Vypiska . . . , l.4.

208 "In three days": RGAVMF, f. 417, op. 1, d. 3140, l.232, Nebogatov to Avelan, March 20, 1905.

208–213 Nebogatov's journey: Gribovsky, "Krestny put' otryada Nebogatova," 16–22.

209 In 1904: Dubrovsky (Nebogatov), 421–422.

209 On January 11: *Dnevniki imperatora Nikolaya II*, 246.

209 On February 2: Gribovsky, 22.

209 Nebogatov insisted: *Pamyati kreisera "Vladimir Monomakh,"* 3; *Bronenosets "Admiral Ushakov,"* 11.

209 Alarming news: RGAVMF, f. 417, op. 1, d. 3140, l.26, Virenius to Nebogatov, February 6, 1905.

210 On Crete: RGAVMF, f. 417, op. 1, d. 3140, ll.142, 144, 153, Lamsdorf to Avelan, March 5, 1905, Bezobrazov to Nebogatov, Nebogatov to Bezobrazov, March 6, 1905.

211 The British squadron at Corfu: PRO, ADM 1/7800, Commander-in-Chief, Mediterranean, to the Secretary of the Admiralty, April 15, 1905.

211 Essen: RGAVMF, f. 417, op. 1, d. 3140, l.112, Virenius to the commander of the canon boat *Khrabry* at Soudha, February 28, 1905.

211 Alarmed, Nebogatov: RGAVMF, f. 417, op. 1, d. 3140, ll.251–253, Stroevoi raport Nebogatova v. k. Alexeyu; *Pamyati kreisera "Vladimir Monomakh,"* 3–4; Gribovsky, *Krestny,* 22–23.

211 The secret network: RGAVMF, f. 417, op. 1, d. 3150, l.89, Maximov to Lamsdorf, February 9 and February 22, 1905.

212 Commander Shvank: RGAVMF, f. 417, op. 1, d. 3150, l.94, Avelan to Lamsdorf, February 14, 1905.

212 Local French bureaucrats: RGAVMF, f. 417, op. 1, d. 3140, l.264, Shvank's report, March 20, 1905.

212 Djibouti: *Bronenosets "Admiral Ushakov,"* 11.

212 "His destination": RGAVMF, f. 417, op. 1, d. 3140, l.163, Virenius to Nebogatov, March 6, 1905.

212 "Try to": RGAVMF, f. 417, op. 1, d. 3140, l.217, Avelan to Nebogatov, March 21, 1905.

212 On March 25: RGAVMF, f. 417, op. 1, d. 3140, l.241, Nebogatov to Avelan, March 25, 1905.

212 In Tangier: RGAVMF, f. 417, op. 1, d. 3140, l.251, Stroevoi raport Nebogatova v. k. Alexeyu Alexandrovichu, March 7, 1905.

213 "An experienced": RGAVMF, f. 417, op. 1, d. 3140, l.112, Nebogatov to Bezobrazov, March 1, 1905.

213–215 Rudanovsky meets the squadron: RGAVMF, f. 763, op. 1, d. 25, Vypiska, ll.4–5; *Russko-yaponskaya voina. Materialy dlia opisaniya,* 143; Kravchenko, 82–83.

214   "They were steaming": PRO, ADM 1/7804, Captain of HMS *Sutlej* to the Senior Naval Officer, Singapore, April 12, 1905.

CHAPTER 9

217   March 26: *Russko-yaponskaya voina. Materialy dlia opisania,* 143.

217–218   Rozhestvensky's choices: Semenov, 402.

218   "Nobody thought": *Dnevniki imperatora Nikolaya II,* 255.

218–221   Crossing the Indian Ocean: Politovsky, 206, 208; Semenov, 399–401.

221–222   The Strait of Malacca: Kravchenko, 73–83; *Russko-yaponskaya voina. Materialy . . . ,* 142; Politovsky, 161–185, 196–201; Vyroubov, 133.

221   The British commander-in-chief: PRO, ADM 1/7804, Noel to the Secretary of the Admiralty, May 2, 1905; PRO, ADM 1/7804, Captain of HMS *Sutlej* to Senior Naval Officer, Singapore, April 12, 1905.

222   "In several minutes": Semenov, 402.

222   Cotton: Politovsky, 202.

222   Rozhestvensky himself thought: *Russko-yaponskaya voina. Materialy . . . ,* 144.

223   On March 28: *Russko-yaponskaya voina. Materialy . . . ,* 144.

223   They met the British: Semenov, 407; PRO, ADM 1/7804, Noel to the Secretary of the Admiralty, May 2, 1905; PRO, ADM 1/7804, Captain of HMS *Sutlej* to Senior Naval Officer, Singapore, April 12, 1905.

223   The *Orel*: Politovsky, 207.

223   The cables sent: RGAVMF, f. 417, op. 1, d. 3110, ll.71–73, Rozhestvensky to Grand Duke Alexei, Avelan, Nicholas II, all received April 1, 1905.

223–224   On March 30: Semenov, 412.

224   On March 31: *Russko-yaponskaya voina. Materialy . . . ,* 144–146.

225   Delcasse: Paleologue, 219–220.

225   The shores: Politovsky, 212–213.

225   Rozhestvensky sent: Vyroubov, 134–135.

225   The *Aurora*: Kravchenko, 92–93.

226   March 31 and April 1: Politovsky, 213; *Russko-yaponskaya, Materialy . . . ,* 147.

226   Felkersam: Politovsky, 216, 231.

226–227   Cam Ranh: Kravchenko, 89, 95.

227   On April 2: Semenov, 416–417, 419.

228   A poem: Politovsky, 247.

228   Delcasse: Paleologue, 224–225.

228   "Insolent summons": PRO, FO 46/592, S.S.O. Report, Japan, No. 51, April, 26, 1905.

229   Rozhestvensky decided: Semenov, 425.

229–230   The second conference: ibid., 422–425.

230   "A hole coated in iron": ibid., 421.

230   A new anchorage: ibid., 422–428.

230   Van Fong: Vyroubov, 135; Politovsky, 214–216, 231, 233, 237; Kravchenko, 94–101.

231   Easter: Vyroubov, 136; Politovsky, 220; Kravchenko, 107–108.

231   The *Orel*: Novikov-Priboy, vol. 1, 293–311.

232   Spirit of anger and despair: Kravchenko, 97.

233   "We all place": RGAVMF, f. 763, op. 1, d. 303, l.20, Pisma michmana Golovnina.

233   "High above": Paleologue, 223.

233   In letters: Gribovsky and Poznakhirev, 229.

233–234   Health: Kravchenko, 101–103; 105; 112.

234   "Following the Sovereign Emperor's will": RGAVMF, f. 417, op. 1, d.
3110, l.109, Grand Duke Alexei to Nicholas II.

235   Rozhestvensky felt frustrated: RGAVMF, f. 417, op. 1, d. 3110, l.142,
Rozhestvensky to Virenius, received April 25, 1905.

235   "It is a real pity": RGAVMF, f. 417, op. 1, d. 3110, l.149, Rozhestvensky to Avelan, received April 26, 1905.

235   "If it is": RGAVMF, f. 417, op. 1, d. 3110, l.71, Rozhestvensky to
Grand Duke Alexis.

235   "Too late": RGAVMF, f. 417, op. 1, d. 3110, l.73, Rozhestvensky to
Nicholas II, received on April 1, 1905.

236   "Absolutely cut off": RGAVMF, f. 417, op. 1, d. 3110, l.114, Rozhestvensky to Avelan, received April 4, 1905.

236   ZIN: RGAVMF, f. 417, op. 1, d. 3110, l.29, Virenius to Liven, March
29, 1905.

236   Rozhestvensky ordered Liven: RGAVMF, f. 417, op. 1, d. 3110, l.77,
Liven to Virenius, April 2, 1905.

236   He also demanded: RGAVMF, f. 417, op. l, d. 3110, l.91, Avelan to
Lamsdorf.

236   Prince Liven had developed: RGAVMF, f. 417, op. 1, d. 3110, l.34,
Liven to Virenius, March 27, 1895.

236   The Russian Admiralty insisted: RGAVMF, f. 417, op. 1, d. 3110,
l.47, Virenius to Liven, March 29, 1905.

236   At Kure: RGAVMF, f. 417, op. 1, d. 3110, l.168, Virenius to Rozhestvensky, April 22, 1905.

236   British observers: PRO, ADM 1/7840, Report, Tokyo, April 17, 1905.

238   On March 22: GARF, f. 601, op. 1, ed. khr. 528, l.4–19, Zhurnal
soveshchaniya 22 marta 1905 goda.

238   Lamsdorf was also: GARF, f. 568, op. 1, ed. khr. 66, Konspekty vse-
poddaneishih dokladov Lamsdorfa za 1905 g., l.5, January 25, 1905, l.6, February 1, 1905.

238   "The memorable day": *Dnevnik imperatora Nikolaya II*, 259.

238   Conference in Peterhof: GARF, f. 543, op. 1, ed. khr. 84.

239   But Rozhestvensky now knew: RGAVMF, f. 763, op. 1, d. 290, l.2, Raport Rozhestvenskogo morskomu ministru.

239   On April 2: RGAVMF, f. 417, op. 1, d. 3110, l.84, Virenius to Rozhestvensky, April 2, 1905.

239   All available vessels: RGAVMF, f. 417, op. 1, d. 3110, l.53, 58, Virenius to Vladivostok's port commander, March 28, 1905, Avelan to Linevich, March 29, 1905.

239   Togo's tactics: RGAVMF, f. 417, op. 1, d. 3110, l.19, Virenius to Rozhestvensky, March 21, 1905.

239   The tsar's strategic decision: RGAVMF, f. 417, op. 1, d. 3110, l.142, Rozhestvensky to Nicholas II, received April 15, 1905.

240   On March 26: RGAVMF, f. 417, op. 1, d. 3110, ll.24–25, Rudanovsky to Virenius, March 27, 1905 (two cables).

240   "Am leaving Djibouti": RGAVMF, f. 417, op. 1, d. 3140, l.241, Nebogatov to Avelan, March 25, 1905.

241   The consul was instructed: RGAVMF, f. 417, op. 1, d. 3140, l.313, Avelan to Rudanovsky, April 9, 1905.

241   "Top Secret": RGAVMF, f. 417, op. 1, d. 3140, l.248, Virenius to consul in Colombo.

241   "Try somehow": RGAVMF, f. 417, op. 1, d. 3140, l.280, Avelan to Burnashev.

241   On April 11: RGAVMF, f. 417, op. 1, d. 3140, l.328, Burnashev to Avelan, April 11, 1905.

241   "Very urgent": RGAVMF, f. 417, op. 1, d. 3140, l.330, Burnshev to Avelan, April 11, 1905.

242   Sharktown: *S eskadroi admirala Rozhestvenskogo*, 89.

242   The undelivered cable read: RGAVMF, f. 417, op. 1, d. 3140, l.281, Avelan to Nebogatov.

242   Prince Liven: RGAVMF, f. 417, op. 1, d. 3140, ll.305, 307, Virenius to Liven, April 4, 1905, Liven to Virenius.

242   His messenger: RGAVMF, f. 417, op. 1, d. 3140, l.362, Rudanovsky to Virenius, April 21, 1905.

242   The Admiralty suggested: RGAVMF, f. 417, op. 1, d. 3140, l.278–279, 298.

243   French allies: RGAVMF, f. 417, op. 1, d. 3140, l.380, Rudanovsky to Virenius, May 9, 1905.

243   Baboushkin: Novikov-Priboy, vol. 1, 325–330.

243   Rozhestvensky was waiting: RGAVMF, f. 417, op. 1, d. 3140, l.283, Avelan to Nebogatov.

243   Togo planned: RGAVMF, f. 417, op. 1, d. 3140, l.317, Virenius to Nebogatov, April 9, 1905.

243   St. Anna's Cross: RGAVMF, f. 417, op. 1, d. 3140, l.312, Bezobrazov to Nebogatov.

244   "If you": Khoudyakov, 140.

244   Able to establish contact: *Russko-yaponskaya, Materialy . . . ,* 157.

244–245   The reunion: Politovsky, 251–252.

245   Kua Bay: Kravchenko, 114–124.

245   The tsar sent: RGAVMF, f. 417, op. 1, d. 3140, l.374, Nicholas II to Nebogatov.

245   "On April 26": RGAVMF, f. 417, op. 1, d. 3110, l.201, Rozhestvensky to Nicholas II.

CHAPTER 10

247   May 1: Semenov, 460.

247   The armada of fifty ships: Gribovsky and Poznakhirev, 221–224.

248   For the next few days: *Russko-yaponskaya, Materialy . . . ,* 180–183.

250   The admiral knew the deficiencies: RGAVMF, f. 763, op. 1, d. 290, l.2–6, Rozhestvensky's report to the naval minister, July 1905; d. 17, Rozhestvensky to his wife, April 16, 1905; f. 417, op. 1, d. 3110, l.186, Virenius to Rozhestvensky, April 27, 1905; Kravchenko, 116–117.

251   The Japanese Nelson planned: RGAVMF, f. 417, op. 1, d. 3147, l.441, Bezobrazov to Rozhestvensky, December 29, 1904.

251   "Even on his deathbed": RGAVMF, f. 417, op. 1, d. 3110, l.206, Rozhestvensky to Grand Duke Alexei, received May 2, 1905; l.242, Rozhestvensky to Avelan, received May 14, 1905.

252   Dobrotvorsky insisted: RGAVMF, f. 763, op. 1, d. 304, l.11, Zapisnaya knizhka leitenanta A. A. Paskina.

252   "I beg you": RGAVMF, f. 417, op. 1, d. 3110, l.206, Rozhestvensky to Grand Duke Alexei, received May 2, 1905.

252   On May 10: Gribovsky, "Krestny," 26.

253   The *Oldhamia*: Semenov, 461–464.

253   The *Zhemchug*: *Russko-yaponskaya, Materialy . . . ,* 183–185.

253   May 6: RGAVMF, f. 763, op. 1, d. 309, Dnevnik ofitsera s otryada vspomogatelnyh kreiserov.

254   Rozhestvensky started fulfilling his plan: *Russko-yaponskaya, Materialy,* 185–189; Politovsky, 258–260.

255   Even the British: PRO, ADM 1/7804, Noel to the Secretary of the Admiralty, June 13, 1905.

255   After May 10: Kravchenko, 104–113.

256   Crews still stuck: RGAVMF, f. 870, op. 1, d. 33717, l.23–25, Vakhtenny zhurnal kreisera "Avrora", May 6 and May 19, 1905.

256   On May 11: *Russko-yaponskaya, Materialy,* 188; Gribovsky, *Kresnty,* 26.

256   On May 12: ibid., 188–189; Kravchenko, 125.

256   The cruiser *Ural*: *Russko-yaponskaya voina, Materialy,* 190.

257   May 13: Kolong, 49.

257   At dark: *Russko-yaponskaya voina, Materialy,* 190–191; Kravchenko, 124–129; *Pamyati kreisera "Vladimir Monomakh,"* 4; Taube, 37; RGAVMF, f. 763, op. 1, d. 290, Rozhestvensky's report, 8.

CHAPTER 11

261–262   The dawn of May 14: RGAVMF, f. 763, op. 1, d. 312, l.25, Donesenie Krzhizhanovskogo; *Russko-yaponskaya, Materialy,* 194–196; Kolong, 51.

262–264   Togo on morning May 14: RGAVMF, f. 763, op. 1, d. 517, Togo's report; *Russko-yaponskaya, Materialy,* 194; Ogasawara, 335; PRO, FO 46/592, Tokyo, N. A. Report 12/05, 193–195.

264   Togo had been waiting: Evans, 110–118; Ogasawara, 324–333; *Opisaniye voennyh deistvii na more,* 4–44, 76–80.

265   Now the Japanese admiral: PRO, FO 46/592, Tokyo, N. A. Report 12/05, 195–196.

266–268   9:00 A.M. to 1:20 P.M.: RGAVMF, f. 763, op. 1, d. 327, l.2–3, Dnevnik pisarya Nikolaya Stepanova; *Russko-yaponskaya, Materialy,* 196–199.

268–272   1:20 P.M. to 2:25 P.M.: Semenov, 493–507; PRO, FO 46/592, Tokyo, N. A. Report, 12/05, 196–197, 222.

272–274   2:25 P.M. to 3:20 P.M.: RGAVMF, f. 763, op. 1, d. 335, l.6–14, Zapiski leitenanta Kryzhanovskogo; d. 312, Doneseniye Krzhizhanovskogo; d. 325, Report of Commander Chagin; *Russko-yaponskaya, Materialy,* 199–202; Ogasawara, 337; Evans, 63, 119–120; Chistyakov, 188–206; Blond, 221–225; Kolong, 53–54; *Russko-yaponskaya voina, Deistviya flota,* 2–5, 9, 33–41, 51; Nebogatov's trial, 277.

274–276   3:20 P.M. to 5:30 P.M.: *Russko-yaponskaya, Materialy,* 202–206; Ogasawara, 340; Taube, 55–69; Blond, 227–228; RGAVMF, f. 763, op. 1, d. 335, l.20, Raport Kolomeitseva; d. 327, l.7, Dnevnik pisarya Stepanova; Kolong, 54–55, *Russko-yaponskaya voina, Deistviya flota,* 5–6, 10, 23–24 41–44.

CHAPTER 12

277–279   May 14 until 6:20 P.M.: PRO, FO 46/592, Tokyo, N. A. report 12/05, 202–205; *Otchet po delu o sdache Nebogatova,* 54–55; *Russko-yaponskaya voina, Deistviya,* 207; Gribovsky, "Krestny," 26–30.

279–181   The night of May 14–15: *Otchet po delu o sdache Nebogatova,* 4, 55–57,189; RGAVMF, f. 763, op. 1, d. 330, l.5, Lieutenant I. G. Time's letter; *Russko-yaponskaya, Deistviya,* 207–213; Gribovsky, "Krestny," 32.

281–284   The morning of May 15: RGAVMF, f. 763, op. 1, d. 330, Lieutenant I. G. Time's letter; *Otchet po delu o sdache Nebogatova,* 4–7, 14–19, 59–61; GARF, f. 543, op. 1, ed. khr. 111, the Orel's senior officer's report;

Taube, 84–93; *Russko-yaponskaya, Deistviya,* 213–214; Gribovsky, *Krestny,* 32–34.

284–286   The surrender: *Otchet po delu o sdache Nebogatova,* 7, 125–126, 191–192; Taube, 93–94; *Opisaniye voennyh deistvii na more,* 93, 150–151; Ogasawara, 361.

CHAPTER 13

288–291   May 14: Novikov-Priboy, vol. 2, 390–392; Politovsky, 219; Kravchenko, 57–59, 143–144, 158, 189, 192–196, 204, 218; RGAVMF, f. 870, op. 1, d. 33717, l.45, 47–50, Vakhtenny zhurnal kreisera "Avrora"; Posokhov, 76–77; *Russko-yaponskaya, Deistviya,* 175–178; 283–291; Dobrotvorsky, 6.

291–295   May 15: RGAVMF, f. 870, op. 1, d. 33717, l.50–58, 61; Posokhov, 77–78; Kravchenko, 207–213, 217.

295–297   The way to Manila: Novikov-Priboy, vol. 2, 398–401; Kravchenko, 153, 213–225; *Russko-yaponskaya, Materialy,* 211; RGAVMF, f. 870, op. 1, d. 33717, l.69–80; Posokhov, 79.

CHAPTER 14

299–300   The evening of May 14: *Russko-yaponskaya, Deistviya,* 7–8, 17–18, 24–25, 44, 53; Kolong, 55–56; *Russko-yaponskaya, Materialy,* 206–207; Dubrovsky, *Delo o sdache minonostsa "Bedovy,"* 7–8, 15.

300–303   On the *Buiny:* Novikov-Priboy, vol. 2, 221–226; *Russko-yaponskaya, Deistviya,* 18–19; Kolong, 57; *Russko-yaponskaya, Materialy,* 214; *Otchet po delu o sdache Nebogatova,* Bedovy, 2–5, 10, 15, 22, 25, 28, 37.

304–306   On the *Bedovy: Russko-yaponskaya, Deistviya,* 19; *Russko-yaponskaya, Materialy,* 216; *Otchet po delu o sdache Nebogatova,* Bedovy, 4–8, 31–32, 14–23, 26, 29.

306–307   The surrender: *Opisaniye voennyh deistvii na more,* 162–163; *Otchet po delu o sdache Nebogatova,* Bedovy, 8, 22, 27.

CHAPTER 15

309   "Extremely urgent": RGAVMF, f. 417, op. 1, d. 3148, l.341, Virenius to Greve, May 13, 1905.

309   The *Almaz:* RGAVMF, f. 763, op. 1, d. 291, Linevich to Nicholas II, May 16, 1905, 13:10.

310   The *Grozny:* RGAVMF, f. 763, op. 1, d. 292, Linevich to Nicholas II, May 17, 1905, 13:45.

310   The *Bravy:* RGAVMF, f. 763, op. 1, d. 325, Durnovo's report.

310   On the *Suvorov:* Bogdanovich, 349.

310   "Terribly depressing"; *Dnevniki imperatora Nikolaya II,* 261.

310   By May 19: *ibid.,* 262.

310   The *Izumrud*: RGAVMF, f. 417, op. 1, d. 3325, l.1, Fersen's cable from Olga, May 18, 1905.

310   The tsar thanked: RGAVMF, f. 470, op. 1, d. 30, Nicholas II to Chagin, May 28, 1905.

311   "There is no person": Bogdanovich, 350.

311   Seasoned admirals: ibid., 349.

311   Grand Duke Alexei: GARF, f. 601, op. 1, ed. khr. 1152, Grand Duke Alexei to Nicholas II, May 29, 1905, l.6.

311   "Poor soul!": *Dnevnik imperatora Nikolaya II*, 263.

311   Birilev: RGAVMF, f. 763, op. 1, d. 291, l.5, Birilev to Nicholas II, May 19, 1905.

311   Rozhestvensky's cable: GARF, f. 601, op. 1, ed. khr. 2426, l.9, Rozhestvensky to Nicholas II.

312   Nebogatov's cable: GARF, f. 601, op. 1, ed. khr. 2426, l.10, Nebogatov to Nicholas II.

312   He cabled the tsar: GARF, f. 601, op. 1, ed. khr. 2426, l.11, Rozhestvensky to Nicholas II.

312   In yet another cable: RGAVMF, f. 1233, op.1, d.30, l.73, Rozhestvensky to Nicholas II.

312   Enkvist's cable: RGAVMF, f. 763, op. 1, d. 292, l.22, Enkvist to Nicholas II, May 21 and June 3, 1905.

312   A gracious cable: Kravchenko, 232.

312   The first person: RGAVMF, f. 470, op. 1, d. 30, cable, May 31, 1905.

313   Cable to Sasebo: RGAVMF, f. 1233, op. 1, d. 30, l.20–21, included in Harmand's cable to Rozhestvensky, June 8, 1905.

313   Their response: RGAVMF, f. 1233, op. 1, d. 30, l.27, Ziloti to Rozhestvensky, June 14, 1905.

313   The *Borodino*: RGAVMF, f. 763, op. 1, d. 335, l.114, Zapiski, dnevniki i pisma ofitserov i matrosov korablei 2-i tikhookeanskoi eskadry.

314   The *Admiral Ushakov*: RGAVMF, f. 763, op. 1, d. 309, the *Ushakov*'s officer's letter, October 19, 1905; *Bronenosets "Admiral Ushakov,"* 523.

314   The *Svetlana*: GARF, f. 543, op. 1, ed. khr. 112, Boevaya sluzhba kreisera "Svetlana" v Tsusimskom boiu.

314   The *Anadyr*: RGAVMF, f. 763, op. 1, d. 292, l.41–42, the *Anadyr*'s captain Commander Ponomarev to Nicholas II.

315   On May 21: Blond, 237.

315–316   Jackson's visit: PRO, FO 46/592, V. Jackson to MacDonald, June 2, 1905.

316   Togo replied: RGAVMF, f. 1233, op. 1, d. 30, l.57, Togo to Rozhestvensky, September 22, 1905.

316   The four women: RGAVMF, f. 1233, op. 1, d. 30, l.8, cable from the family, June 1, 1905; l.32, Makarova to Rozhestvensky, June 27, 1905; l.41, Sivers to Rozhestvensky, June 10, 1905; l.54, Sivers to Rozhestvensky, September 8, 1905.

317–319   Captivity in Kyoto: Semenov, 630–639; Kostenko, 469–483; RGAVMF, f. 763, op. 1, d. 297, l.4, Lieutenant L. Larionov's letter to his mother, August 6, 1905; d. 309, Pismo ofitsera s *Ushakova,* October 19, 1905; d. 330, l.9, Lieutenant I. G. Time's letter to his parents.

319   Noel in Japan: PRO, ADM 1/7804, Noel to the Secretary of the Admiralty, November 11, 1905.

319   "To prevent": Semenov, 643.

319   Kaiser Wilhelm: Willy-Nicky, 128.

319   King Edward VII: Lee, 307.

319   The departure: Semenov, 640–655.

CHAPTER 16

321–324   On the *Voronezh:* Semenov, 657–659; RGAVMF, f. 1233, op. 1, d. 30, l.2, Viren to Rozhestvensky, June 2, 1905; Novikov-Priboy, vol. 2, 486–488; Semenov, 659–665.

324   In Vladivostok: Semenov, 666–668.

324   Two greetings by cable: RGAVMF, f. 1233, op. 1, d. 14, l. 20, Komendant kreposti Vladivostok Rozhestvenskomu, November 14, 1905; l.21, i. o. gorodskogo golovy Vladivostoka Rozhestvenskomu, November 15, 1905.

324   Linevich: RGAVMF, f. 470, op. 1, d. 30, Linevich-Rozhestvenskomu, November 14, 1905, Rozhestvensky to Linevich, November 14, 1905.

324–326   On the Trans-Siberian Railroad: Semenov, 669–679; Thiess, 387.

326   Meeting with the tsar: Gribovsky and Poznakhirev, 267–268.

327   "The actual ratio": Evans, 124–125.

327–328   Rozhestvensky's letter: GARF, f. 543, op. 1, ed. khr. 86, Rozhestvensky, Pismo v redaktsiyu.

329–330   Rozhestvensky's explanation: GARF, f. 568, op. 1, ed. khr. 210, Raport Rozhestvenskogo, December 25, 1905.

330   Avelan: GARF, f. 568, op. 1, ed. khr. 210. Naval minister to foreign minister, December 26, 1905.

330   Lamsdorf: GARF, f. 568, op. 1, ed. khr. 210, Lamsdorf to Naval Minister, December 31, 1905.

330   Witte: GARF, f. 543, op. 1, ed. khr. 86, Witte, Vsepoddaneishy doklad, December 21, 1905.

330   On January 31: Khoudyakov, 145.

331–333   Rozhestvensky's trial: Dubrovsky, *Delo o sdache minonostsa "Bedovy,"* 1–93.

333   "I feel humiliated": Gribovsky and Poznakhirev, 270.

334–336   Nebogatov's trial: *Otchet po delu o sdache 15 maya 1905 g. nepriyateliu sudov otryada byvshego admirala Nebogatova*, 1–654; Gribovsky, "Krestny," 34.

336   Nebogatov: Gribovsky, "Krestny," 34, Alexander, Grand Duke of Russia, 205–207.

336   Garting's cut: RGAVMF, f. 417, op. 1, d. 3144, l.176, 187.

336   Awards: RGAVMF, f. 417, op. 1, d. 3144, l.204.

336   Alexeev: Vitte, vol. 2, 389.

337   The *Alexander III*: Kann, 389.

337   Togo: Blond, 245–251.

337–338   Rozhestvensky in retirement: GARF, f. 543, op. 1, ed. khr. 81, Vedomosti uvolennyh iz morskogo vedomstva v 1905–1906 gg.; Thiess, 389.

338   The admiral's death: RGAVMF, f. 417, op. 2, d. 1163, O pokhoronakh vitse-admirala Z. P. Rozhestvenskogo.

Selected Bibliography

PRIMARY SOURCES

Unpublished

Bakhmetieff Archive (BA), Columbia University, New York.
   Meshcherskii
   Vereshchagin
Gosudarstvenny Arkhiv Rossiiskoi Federatsii (GARF)(State Archives of the Russ-
   ian Federation, Moscow).
   Emperor Alexander III. Fond 677.
   Grand Duke Alexander Mikhailovich. Fond 645.
   Grand Duke Alexei Alexandrovich. Fond 681.
   Grand Duke Andrei Vladimirovich. Fond 650.
   Grand Duke Georgy Mikhailovich. Fond 676.
   Girs. Fond 892.
   Lamsdorf. Fond 568.
   Emperor Nicholas II. Fond 601.
   Tsarskoselsky Palace Collection. Fond 543.
   Grand Duchess Xenia Alexandrovna. Fond 662.
Public Record Office (PRO), London, United Kingdom.
   ADM 1/7726
   ADM 1/7727
   ADM 1/7728
   ADM 1/7729
   ADM 1/7800
   ADM 1/7804
   ADM 1/7809
   ADM 1/7840

ADM 6/104–92
CAB 41/29/38
CO 1273/308
FO 46/579
FO 46/589
FO 46/592
FO 46/660
FO 181/823
FO 181/854
FO 211/249

Rossiisky Gosudarstvenny Arkhiv Voenno-Morskogo Flota (RGAVMF) (Russian State Naval Archives), St. Petersburg.

Fond 17.
Fond 406.
Fond 417.
Fond 469.
Fond 470.
Fond 531.
Fond 763.
Fond 870.
Fond 1233.

Rossiiskii Gosudarstvenny Voenno-Istoricheskii Arkhiv (Russian State Military History Archives) (RGVIA), Moscow.

Fond 165.

Published

Alexander, Grand Duke of Russia. *Once a Grand Duke.* Garden City: Garden City Publishing, 1932.

"Bezobrazovskii kruzhok letom 1904 g." *Krasny arkhiv* 4 (1926): 17.

Bogdanovich, Alexandra. *Tri poslednikh samoderzhtsa.* Moscow: Novosti, 1990.

Bronenosets "Admiral Ushakov," ego put' i gibel. Petersburg, 1906.

Chegodaev-Sakonsky, A. *Na "Almaze" ot Libavy cherez Tsusimu vo Vladivostok.* Moscow, 1910.

Dnevnik Alexeya Sergeevicha Suvorina. Moscow: Nezavisimaya gazeta, 1999.

Dnevniki imperatora Nikolaya II. Moscow: Orbita, 1991.

"Do Tsuhimy," *Krasnyi arkhiv* 6 (1934):67.

Dubrovsky, Evgeny. *Dela o sdache yapontsam (1) minonostsa "Bedovy" i (2) eskadry Nebogatova.* Petersburg, 1907.

Egoriev, E. *Vokrug Starogo Sveta v 1904–1905 godu.* Petersburg, 1915.

Hare, James, H., ed., *A Photographic Record of the Russo-Japanese War.* New York: P. F. Collier & Son, 1905.

Kostenko, Vladimir. *Na "Orle" v Tsusime*. Leningrad: Sudostroyeniye, 1968.

Kuropatkin, Alexei N. *Dnevnik A. N. Kuropatkina*. Nizhpoligraf, 1923.

_____. *Zapiski generala Kuropatkina o russko-yaponskoi voine. Itogi voiny*. Berlin: J. Ladyschnikov, 1909.

Magdalinsky, Alexander. *Na morskom rasputye. Zapiski uchastnika Tsusimskogo boya*. Yaroslavl: Knizhnoye izdatelstvo, 1954.

Morskiye srazheniya russkogo flota. Moscow: Voenizdat, 1994.

Nakamura, Koya. *Admiral Togo: A Memoir*. Tokyo: Togo Gensui Hensankai, 1934.

"N. N. Romanov i amerikanskaya kontsessiya na zheleznuyu dorogu Sibir— Alaska v 1905 g.," *Krasny arkhiv* 6 (1930):43.

Opisaniye voennyh deistvii na more v 37–38 gg. Meiji, vol. 1–4. Petersburg, 1909–1910.

Otchet po delu o sdache 15 maya 1905 g. nepriyateliu sudov otryada byvshego admirala Nebogatova. Petersburg: Tip. Morskogo Ministerstva, 1907.

Paleologue, Maurice. *The Turning Point: Three Critical Years, 1904–1906*. London: Hutchinson, 1935.

Pamyati kreisera "Vladimir Monomakh." Odessa, 1906.

"Pisma V. V. Vereshchagina Nikolayu Romanovu v 1904 g.," *Krasnyi arkhiv* 2 (1931): 45.

Politovsky, Evgeny. *Ot Libavy do Tsusimy*. Petersburg, 1906.

Port-Artur: sbornik vospominanii uchastnikov. New York: Izdatelstvo imeni Chekhova, 1955.

Russko-yaponskaya voina, 1904–1905. Deistviya flota. Dokumenty, vol. 1–4. Petersburg, 1913.

Russko-yaponskaya voina, 1904–1905 gg. Materialy dlya opisaniya deistvii flota. Khronologicheskii perechen' voennyh deistvii flota v 1904–1905 gg., vol.1–2. Petersburg, 1910–1912.

S eskadroi admirala Rozhestvenskogo. Petersburg: Oblik, 1994.

Sbornik donesenii o Tsusimskom boye 14 maya 1905 g., Petersburg: Voenno-morskoi uchenyi otdel Glavnogo Morskogo Shtaba, 1907.

Sbornik Pnrikazov i tsirkulyarov po II eskadre flota Tihogo okeana za 1904 i 1905 goda. Vladivostok, 1905.

Semennikov, V.P., ed., *Za kulisami tsarizma. Arkhiv tibetskogo vracha Badmaeva*. Leningrad: Gosudarstvennoye izdatelstvo, 1925.

Semenov, V. *"Flot" i "morskoye vedomstvo" do Tsusimy i posle*, Petersburg: M. O. Wolf, 1911.

_____. *Rasplata*. Petersburg: Gangut, 1994.

Taube, G. N. *Posledniye dni vtoroi Tihookeanskoi eskadry*. Petersburg, 1907.

Tolstoy, Leo. *"Bethink Yourselves." Tolstoy's letter on the Russo-Japanese War*. Boston: American Peace Society, 1904.

Vitte, S. Yu. *Vospominaniya*, vol. 1–3. Moscow: Sotzekgiz, 1960.

Voronovich, N. *Russko-yaponskaya voina: vospominaniya*. New York: n.p., 1952.

Vyroubov, P. A. *Desyat' let iz zhizni russkogo moryaka, pogibshego v Tsusimskom boyu*. Kiev, 1910.

Westwood, J. N. *Witnesses of Tsushima*. Tokyo: Sophia University, 1970.

Wilhelm II. *The Kaiser's Memoirs, 1878–1918*. New York: Harper, 1922.

SECONDARY SOURCES

Alexandrovsky, Grigory. *Tsusimsky boi*. New York, 1956.

Andrew, Christopher M. *Her Majesty's Secret Service: The Making of the British Intelligence Community*. New York: Viking, 1986.

Aronson, Theo. *A Family of Kings: The Descendants of Christian IX of Denmark*. London: Cassell, 1976.

_____. *Grandmama of Europe: The Crowned Descendants of Queen Victoria*. Indianapolis and New York: Bobbs-Merrill, 1973.

Balfour, Michael L. *The Kaiser and His Times*. Boston: Houghton, 1964.

Beskrovny, L. G. *Armiya i flot Rossii v nachale XX veka. Ocherki voenno-ekonomicheskogo potentsiala*. Moscow: Nauka, 1986.

Blond, Georges. *Admiral Togo*. New York: Macmillan, 1960.

Bodley, R. V. C. *Admiral Togo*. London: Jarrolds, 1935.

Bogdanov, M. A. "Navarin." *Gangut* 4 (19): 50–63.

_____. "Sisoi Velikii." *Gangut* 3 (19): 46–60.

Busch, N. F. *The Emperor's Sword: Japan vs. Russia in the Battle of Tsushima*. New York: Funk & Wagnalls, 1969.

Bykov, P. D. *Russko-yaponskaya voina, 1904–1905 gg. Deistviya na more*. Moscow: Voenmorizdat, 1942.

Cecil, Lamar. *Wilhelm II, Prince and Emperor, 1859–1900*. Chapel Hill: University of North Carolina Press, 1989.

Chudakov, A. "'Neprilichnye" slova i obraz klassika. O kupiurah v izdaniyah pisem Chekhova." *Literaturnoye obozreniye* 1991, 11.

Connaughton, R. M. *The War of the Rising Sun and Tumbling Bear: A Military History of the Russo-Japanese War, 1904–5*. London: Routledge, 1988.

Dennett, Tyler. *Roosevelt and the Russo-Japanese War*. New York: Doubleday, 1925.

Dobrotvorsky, Leonid. *Uroki morskoi voiny*. Kronstadt: Kotlin, 1907.

Doing Naval History: Essays Towards Improvement. Newport, R.I.: Naval War College Press, 1995.

Dotsenko, V. D. *Rossiiskii bronenosny flot, 1863–1917*. Petersburg: Sudostroeniye, 1994.

Egoriev, V. E. *Operatsii vladivostokskih kreiserov v russko-yaponskuyu voinu 1904–1905 gg*. Moscow, Leningrad, 1939.

Eremeev, L. *Admiral Makarov. Biografichesky ocherk.* Moscow, Leningrad: Voenmorizdat, 1939.

Evans, David C., *Kaigun: Strategy, Tactics, and Technology in the Imperial Japanese Navy, 1887–1941.* Annapolis, Md.: Naval Institute Press, 1997.

Ginzburg, B. *K razyasneniyu zagadok v Tsusimskom boyu,* Petersburg, 1907.

Gribovsky, V. Yu. Eskadrennye bronenostsy tipa "Borodino" v Tsusimskom srazhenii. *Gangut* 2 (19): 25–43.

_____. "Katastrofa 31 marta 1904 goda (gibel bronenostsa 'Petropavlovsk.'" *Gangut* 4 (19): 30–49.

_____. "Krestny put' otryada Nebogatova." *Gangut* 3 (19): 16–34.

Gribovsky, V. Yu., and V. P. Poznakhirev. *Vitse-admiral Z. P. Rozhestvensky.* St. Petersburg: Tsitadel, 1999.

Hough, Richard. *The Fleet That Had to Die.* London: Severn House, 1958.

Howarth, Stephen, *The Fighting Ships of the Rising Sun: The Drama of the Imperial Japanese Navy, 1895–1945.* New York: Atheneum, 1983.

Hull, Isabel V., *The Entourage of Kaiser Wilhelm II, 1888–1918.* Cambridge: Cambridge University Press, 1982.

Ignatiev, E. P. "K ziuidu ot ostrova Russkii." *Gangut* 2 (19): 53–56.

Khoudyakov, Petr. *Put' k Tsusime.* Moscow, 1907.

Klado, N. *Posle uhoda vtoroi eskadry Tihogo okeana.* Petersburg, 1905.

_____. *Sovremennaya morskaya voina.* Petersburg, 1905.

Lee, Sidney. *King Edward VII,* vol. 2. New York: Macmillan, 1927.

Lloyd, Arthur. *Admiral Togo.* n.p. 1905.

Lloyd, Christopher, *Atlas of Maritime History.* New York: Arco, 1975.

Lourie, Abram. *S. O. Makarov.* Moscow: Voenizdat, 1949.

Ludwig, Emil. *Wilhelm Hohenzollern: The Last of the Kaisers.* New York: Putnam, 1927.

Mahan, A. T. *The Influence of Sea Power upon History, 1660–1805.* Englewood Cliffs, N.J.: Prentice-Hall, 1980.

McCully, Newton A. *The McCully Report: The Russo-Japanese War, 1904–1905,* ed. R. A. von Doenhoff. Annapolis: Naval Institute Press, 1977.

McLachlan, Donald. *Room 39: A Study in Naval Intelligence.* New York: Atheneum, 1968.

Miller, J. Martin. *Thrilling Stories of the Russian-Japanese War.* Chicago: n.p., 1904.

Nemitz, A. *Russko-yaponskaya voina 1904–1905 gg. (strategicheskii obzor).* Petersburg, 1909.

Nish, Ian Hill. *The Origins of the Russo-Japanese War.* London: Longman, 1985.

Novikov-Priboy, A. S. *Tsusima,* vol. 1–2. Moscow: Pravda, 1984.

Ogasawara, Nagayo. *Life of Admiral Togo*. n.p. 1934.

Okamoto, Shumpei. *The Japanese Oligarchy and the Russo-Japanese War*. New York: Columbia University Press, 1970.

Palmer, Alan W., *The Kaiser: Warlord of the Second Reich*. New York: Scribner, 1978.

Polenov, L. L. "Kreiser 'Avrora' v Velikom srazhenii Yaponskogo morya," *Gangut* 2 (19): 43–52.

Rayfield, Donald. *The Dream of Lhasa: The Life of Nikolai Przevalsky, Explorer of Central Asia*. Columbus: Ohio Unversity Press, 1977.

Russkii morskoi mundir, 1696–1917. Petersburg: Logos, 1994.

Smirnov, S. N., ed. *Khram-pamyatnik moryakam*. Petersburg: Logos, 1995.

Tainy russko-yaponskoi voiny. Moscow: Progress, 1993.

Thiess, Frank. *The Voyage of Forgotten Men (Tsushima)*. Indianapolis: Bobbs-Merrill, 1937.

Tomich, V. M., *Warships of the Imperial Russian Navy*. San Francisco: B. T. Publishers, 1968.

Ugriumov, A. I. "Mekhanik s 'Suvorova.'" *Gangut* 2: 86–93.

United States War Department, General Staff. *Epitome of the Russo-Japanese War*. Washington, D.C.: GPO, 1907.

White, John Albert. *The Diplomacy of the Russo-Japanese War*. Princeton, New Jersey: Princeton University Press, 1964.

Zolotarev, V. A., and I. A. Kozlov. *Russko-yaponskaya voina, 1904–1905 gg. Borba na more*. Moscow: Nauka, 1990.

Index

Aden, 154, 157
Admiral Nakhimov (cruiser), 57
Admiral Seniavin (cruiser), 186
Admiral Ushakov (cruiser), 186, 314
Afghanistan, 70, 72
Africa, 63, 69, 72, 80, 131. *See also*
    specific countries
Agriculture, impossibility of, where
    permafrost was present, 8
Aiba, Commander, 307
Alexander, Grand Duke, 20–21, 26, 51,
    55, 60
    and the attack on Port Arthur, 62–63
    and the Black Sea Fleet, 180
    and Britain, 70
    and espionage, 79
    as a naval leader, 28
    official communications with, 179
    in Reval, 85
Alexander Nevsky (frigate), 21
Alexander III (battleship), 64–65, 68,
    94, 95, 115, 123, 146, 224,
    247, 251, 255, 267, 269,
    273–274, 278–280, 304, 309,
    314, 317, 337
Alexander III (tsar), 5, 7, 11–12, 45
    death of, 14, 49
    and Witte, 13, 14
Alexander III Technological College, 194
Alexander II (tsar), 7, 11, 39, 53, 59,
    66–67
Alexandra (queen of Britain), 72, 73,
    102

Alexandra (wife of Tsar Nicholas II), 6,
    58, 64
Alexandria, 154
Alexeandrovich, Sergei, 198
Alexeev, Evgeny, Admiral, 3, 21, 33, 50,
    55–56
    cruisers which belonged to, 64
    and Kriger, 66
    and the Military High Command, 76
    retirement of, 336
    and Rozhestvensky's dissatisfaction
        with his men, 122–123
    and the use of radio communications,
        86
Alexei, Grand Duke, 6, 21–22, 28, 54–55,
    58, 172–173, 180, 200, 202, 209
    and the attack on Port Arthur, 62–63,
        170
    and the battle at Tsushima, 251, 311
    cruisers which belonged to, 64
    death of, 336
    and the Dutch, 180
    and French Indonesia, 234, 238
    meetings with, 98
    and Skrydlov, 173
    and the *Svetlana*, 152
Alexei (son of Nicholas II), 64, 92
Alfonso XIII (king), 106
Algeria, 77
Algiers, 48
Almaz (cruiser), 57, 64, 152, 223, 261,
    288, 310
Amphitrite (battleship), 221

Anadyr (transport), 95, 112, 115, 254, 314
Andrzhievsky, Commander, 305
Anglophobia, 185
Angola, 140
Angra Pequena, 142–144. 171
Annam, 309
Antarctica, 145
Antipova, Olga, 41
Apraxin (battleship), 66, 208, 247, 281, 283, 315–316, 335
Arabia, 157
Arctic Ocean, 8–9, 29, 159
Argentina, 23, 63, 136, 173, 180
Artillery Committee, 40, 43
Artillery Practice Unit, 50, 52, 186
Asama (cruiser), 277
Athens, 77
Aurora (cruiser), 23, 64–65, 97, 98, 111–112, 116, 123, 174, 197–198, 219, 222–223, 225, 227, 247, 258, 261, 288–297, 300, 312
Australia, 13, 130, 218, 265
Austria, 156
Autocracy, xvi
Avelan, Fedor, 54–56, 58, 81, 158
  and the attack on Port Arthur, 62–63
  and Enkvist, 111, 287
  and espionage, 79
  and French Indonesia, 235, 238, 240, 241
  and Ginsburg, 60
  and Klado, 172
  meetings with, 98
  and Nebogatov, 180, 198
  and the Nosy Be option, 180–184, 198, 200, 202
  and Rozhestvensky's passage to Vladivostok, 208, 210, 212
  and Rozhestvensky's return to Russia, 330
  and Skrydlov, 173
  wounding of, 183

Bab El Mandeb, 72
Baboushkin, Vasily, 243, 255
Badmaev, Peter, 19, 22–23
Bakan (freighter), 93
Balfour, Prime Minister, 130–131

Bali-Lombok, 180
Baltic Sea, 8, 29, 36, 45–46, 50–51, 63, 285, 288, 294
  and Denmark, 82, 86
  and espionage, 88
  and French Indonesia, 232
  Japanese ambush in, 75
  shortest route from, to the Yellow Sea, 69
  and Skagerrak, 94. *See also* Baltic Sea Fleet
Baltic Sea Fleet, 36, 40, 136, 176, 208, 237. *See also* Baltic Sea
Bangkok, 77
Baranov, Nikolai, 41, 43
  and the battle at Tsushima, 303, 304, 305, 331–333
  trial of, 331–333
Barrosa (cruiser), 140
Batavia, 181, 204, 207, 215, 236, 241, 255
Battenberg, Alexander (prince), 43, 44
Battleships: *Alexander III,* 64–65, 68, 94, 95, 115, 123, 146, 224, 247, 251, 255, 267, 269, 273–274, 278–280, 304, 309, 314, 317, 337
  Amphitrite, 221
  Apraxin, 66, 208, 247, 281, 283, 315–316, 335
  Borodino, 64–65, 94–95, 134, 177, 247, 251, 267, 269, 273–274, 278–280, 290, 300, 313, 317
  Cincinnati, 297
  Emperor Nicholas I, 172, 186
  Iki, 337
  Iphigenia, 221, 223
  Kiev, 219
  Korea, 115
  Lancaster, 100–101, 108
  Majestic, 27
  Malaya, 115, 122, 134, 141–142, 146, 192, 193
  Meteor, 115
  Mikasa, xvii, 33, 61, 86, 236, 263, 265, 268–270, 284, 316, 337
  Nakhimov, 116, 174, 192, 247, 261, 282
  Navarin, 64, 65, 152, 247, 261, 314
  Nicholas I, 208, 209, 247, 255, 277–281, 283, 317–318, 334, 337

Ohio, 297

Oregon, 297

Oslyabya, 23, 64, 65, 92, 115, 192, 247, 257, 270, 273–274, 299, 301, 303, 309, 317

Pervenetz, 40, 50, 186

Petropavlovsk, 34–36, 56, 60, 72

Prince Suvorov, 57, 64, 65, 67

Raleigh, 297

Senyavin, 172, 208, 247, 280, 281, 283, 335

Sevastopol, 211

Sisoi, 64, 89, 92, 152–153, 156, 157, 175, 247, 248, 261, 282

Suvorov, 86, 89, 94–97, 115–118, 120, 122–124, 126–129, 134–143, 146–147, 174, 177, 179, 193–197, 214, 218–232, 240, 244, 251, 253–254, 261, 266–279, 287–289, 299–300, 303, 309–313, 318

Thetis, 221

Tsesarevic, 3

Ushakov, 172, 208, 247, 280, 281

Wisconsin, 297

Worcester, 337

Yashima, 61

Bay of Biscay, 98, 210. *See also* Ships

Bayan (cruiser), 243

Bedovy (torpedo boat), 174, 214, 261, 303–307, 310–312, 331–334, 336

Beijing, 15–16, 77

Benkendorf, Count, 99, 105

Ber, Captain, 257

Beresford, Charles, 100–102, 108–109

Bersenev, Colonel, 271

Bezobrazov, Alexander, 20

Bezuprechny (torpedo boat), 226–227, 300

Bible, 32

Birilev, Alexei, 37, 56, 58, 309, 311

Bitter Lakes, 157

Black Sea, xvii, 29, 41, 43, 199, 209. *See also* Black Sea Fleet

Black Sea (cruiser), 179

Black Sea Fleet, 39, 41, 180, 187, 199. *See also* Black Sea

Bloody Sunday, 184, 209

Boats. *See* Ships

Bo Hai Gulf, 15

Boers, 145

Bogdanov, Lieutenant, 276

Bolshevik Revolution (1917), xviii–xvi, 183–184, 325–326

Bombay, 241

Borneo, 176, 214, 215, 226, 264

Borodino (battleship), 64–65, 94–95, 134, 177, 247, 251, 267, 269, 273–274, 278–280, 290, 300, 313, 317

Bosphorus, 10

Bostrom, Captain, 104–105

Bourgeois class, 17

Boyarin (cruiser), 25

Bravy (torpedo boat), 262, 310

Britain, 7, 31–32, 46–48, 69

and China, 15

and the Crimean War, 10

and the Dogger Bank incident, 96–112, 116, 123, 136

and the Entente Cordiale, 103

and espionage, 47, 80–81, 86, 201

and French Indonesia, 217–218, 229

and the Great Game in Central Asia, 10, 69–70

merchants from, 9

new military technology used by, 27

the North Sea as a domain of, 93

number of admirals in, 28

and Portugal, 140

purchase of ships from, 23, 29

and the Romanov family, 11, 72–73

and the Satsuma clan, 30

and shipbuilding, 23, 29, 46–47

and Tibet, 71–72

and war contraband, 75

and the "Yacht Squadron," 157, 164. *See also* English Channel

British East India Company, 204

Brussels, 77

Buddhism, 22. *See also* Buddhist monasteries

Buddhist monasteries, 317, 318

Buiny (torpedo boat), 261, 275–276, 279, 299–301, 309, 311, 332, 334

Bukara, 70

Bukhvostov, Captain, 68, 123

Bulgaria, 43–45, 48, 65, 67

Bureaucracy, 28–29, 75

Butakov, Vice Admiral, 42

Bystry (torpedo boat), 92, 118, 261
Byzantine Empire, 10, 75

Cairo, 77, 154, 156, 211. *See also* Egypt
Calendars, use of different, xviii
Cam Ranh Bay, 217, 223–230, 235–236, 242, 264
Cape Guardafui, 166
Cape Horn, 93, 109–110
Cape Horn-Polynesian Archipelago route, 109–110
Cape Lopez, 129
Cape of Good Hope, 93, 111, 145, 177
Cape of Storms, 145
Cape Town, 143, 144, 145
Cartography, 9
Catholicism, 32, 118–119. *See also* Christianity
Celebes, 215, 218
Celebes Sea, 218
Ceylon, 13, 156, 169, 176, 204, 242
Chagos Island, 164
Channel Fleet, 100–101
Chefoo, 125, 170
Chekhov, Anton, 12–13, 17, 33
Cherbourg, 45
Chile, 23, 63, 136, 173, 180
Chimosa explosive, 29
China, 238, 239, 265
    and Alexeev, 76
    and Badmaev, 19
    Beijing, 15–16, 77
    and espionage, 76–80, 175
    exploration of, 7
    and Hirobumi, 132
    and Makarov, 49
    merchants from, 9
    neutrality of, 64, 125
    and settlement patterns, 9
    and the "Yacht Squadron," 156
China Station, 71
Chloroform, use of, 291
Chou-shan archipelago, 238
Christianity, 32, 85, 118–119
    Christmas celebrations, 139–140, 164
    and hatred of the Japanese, 19
Christian IX (king), 93
Chukhnin, Grigory, 37, 187, 199, 202
Cincinnati (battleship), 297

Class: bourgeois, 17
    tensions, 119
Cocos Islands, 176
Colombo, 45, 77, 240, 241
Colonialism, 128
Concentration camps, xv
Confucius, 30
Constantine, Grand Duke, 39, 42, 48
Constantinople, 10
Contraband, 70, 74–75
Copenhagen, 27, 45, 82–83, 91–92, 102, 109
Coral Sea, 218
Corfu, 153, 211
Corporeal punishment, 120
Corruption, xvi, 7, 28–29
Court of Saint James, 129–130
Crete, 151, 153–154, 162–164, 177, 201, 210–211
Crimean War, 10, 29, 39, 66
Cross of St. Anna, 336
Cross of St. George, 337
Cruisers: *Admiral Nakhimov*, 57
    Admiral Seniavin, 186
    Admiral Ushakov, 186, 314
    Almaz, 57, 64, 152, 223, 261, 288, 310
    Asama, 277
    Aurora, 23, 64–65, 97, 98, 111–112, 116, 123, 174, 197–198, 219, 222–223, 225, 227, 247, 258, 261, 288–297, 300, 312
    Barrosa, 140
    Bayan, 243
    Black Sea, 179
    Boyarin, 25
    Descartes, 230
    Dmitri Donskoi, xvi, 23, 58, 64, 65, 97, 98, 116, 123, 134, 137–139, 159, 189, 214, 223, 247, 261, 300–301, 303, 305–306
    Dnieper, 65, 159, 223, 248, 253–254, 258, 296
    Drake, 108
    Guichen, 230
    Hermes, 108
    HMS Barrosa, 141
    HMS Glory, 130–131
    Hong Kong, 176

Hongkong Maru, 264
Izumi, 262
Izumrud, 64–65, 159–163, 221, 223, 248, 261–263, 274, 281–282, 310, 312
Kuban, 65, 179, 248, 254, 258
Nihon Maru, 264
Niiataka, 176
Nippon Maru, 176
Nishin, 23, 278
Oleg, 64, 65, 159, 162–163, 184, 198, 214, 223, 261, 288–296, 300, 312
Pascal, 80
Petersburg, 74
Rion, 65, 159, 223, 248, 254, 258
Shinano Maru, 262–263
Svetlana, 64, 152, 174, 248, 261, 314
Terek, 65, 179, 248, 254, 258
Ural, 65, 179, 193, 248, 254, 257, 261, 328, 295, 309
Vladimir Monomakh, 48, 50, 65–66, 208, 247–248, 261
Yoshino, 61
Zhemchug, 64, 65, 92, 152, 219, 223, 253, 261, 263, 266, 312, 292–296. *See also* Vessels

Dachnik (steamer), 67
Daimo of Satsuma, 30
Dakar, 110, 115–148, 187
Danilov, General, 323
Danube, 42
Dar es Salaam, 167–168
Dates, disparity in, xviii
De Jonquieres, Admiral, 227–228, 230
De Kolong, Constantine, 233, 301–303, 305–307, 333
De Lassi, O'Brien, 305, 331
Delcasse, Theophile, 103–104, 225, 228
Demchinsky, V., 331
Denmark, 80–82, 86, 88, 91, 93. 160, 164
Depression, among crew members, 116–117
Descartes (cruiser), 230
Devil's Island, 13
Dewa, Admiral, 264, 266, 288, 297
Diana (warship), 111–112, 236
Dias, Bartolomeu, 142

Djibouti, 56, 135, 226, 172, 180, 240
  and Rozhestvensky's passage to Vladivostok, 208, 212–214
  and the "Yacht Squadron," 154, 157, 159, 164–166
Dmitri Donskoi (cruiser), xvi, 23, 58, 64, 65
Dnieper (cruiser), 65, 159, 223, 248, 253–254, 258, 296
Dobrotvorsky, Captain, 135, 147, 180, 184, 211
  and the battle at Tsushima, 251, 264, 288–290, 292–293, 296
  and the "Yacht Squadron," 159, 160–166
Dogger Bank incident, 116, 123, 136, 177, 200, 221, 328
  and Edward VII, 98–99, 102, 106, 109
  overview of, 96–112
  and Rozhestvensky's passage to Vladivostok, 209, 210
  and the "Yacht Squadron," 154, 155, 160
Donskoi (cruiser), 97, 98, 116, 123, 134, 137–139, 159, 189, 214, 223, 247, 261, 300–301, 303, 305–306
Donskoi, Dmitri (prince), 64, 65, 67
Dowager Empress. *See* Federovna, Maria (Dowager Empress)
Draft, of men from prisons, 59
Drake (cruiser), 108
Drake, Sir Francis, 106
Drug use, introduction of, by Badmaev, 19
Dubasov, Fedor, 37
Durban, 136, 143, 176
Dutch East India, 182
Dutch Indonesia, 180

Edward VII (king), 17, 70, 72–73, 319
  and the Dogger Bank incident, 98–99, 102, 106, 109
  and the French ambassador to the Court of Saint James, 129–130
Egypt, 77, 154–156, 164, 211
Elizabeth (queen), 75
Emperor Nicholas I (battleship), 172, 186
England, 7, 31–32, 46–48, 69
  and China, 15

England (continued)
  and the Crimean War, 10
  and the Dogger Bank incident,
    96–112, 116, 123, 136
  and the Entente Cordiale, 103
  and espionage, 47, 80–81, 86, 201
  and French Indonesia, 217–218, 229
  and the Great Game in Central Asia,
    10, 69–70
  merchants from, 9
  new military technology used by, 27
  the North Sea as a domain of, 93
  number of admirals in, 28
  and Portugal, 140
  purchase of ships from, 23, 29
  and the Romanov family, 11, 72–73
  and the Satsuma clan, 30
  and shipbuilding, 23, 29, 46–47
  and Tibet, 71–72
  and war contraband, 75
  and the "Yacht Squadron," 157, 164.
    See also English Channel
English Channel, 95, 98–100, 162, 210
Enkvist, Oskar, 57, 65, 84, 89, 111, 116,
    123, 152
  appointment of, to Rozhestvensky's
    squadron, 287
  and the battle at Tsushima, 247, 251,
    287–297, 312, 327
  and battle simulations, 197
  and French Indonesia, 221, 240
  and the Nosy Be option, 174–175,
    186, 197
  and Rozhestvensky's return to Russia,
    327
  and Sventorzhetsky, 186
Entente Cordiale, 103
Ermak (icebreaker), 51
Esperance (refrigerator boat), 116, 194
Espionage, 74–83, 110
  and the battle at Tsushima, 264–265
  and Britain, 47, 80–81, 86, 201
  and China, 76–80, 175
  and Denmark, 82
  and Garting, 81–83, 91, 204, 336
  and Germany, 77, 79–80, 143
  and Nosy Be, 178, 182–183
  and the Sea of Japan, 201
  and Singapore, 204, 205
  and telegraph lines, 124–126

  and the use of radio communications,
    86
  and the "Yacht Squadron," 154–156,
    159
Essen, Nikolai, 211
Eulenburg, Philipp, 18
Eurasia, 8–9, 12, 14, 70
Eurasian forest, 8–9

Far Eastern Committee, 22
Federovna, Maria (Dowager Empress), 7,
    91, 102, 109
Felkersam, Dmitry Gustavovich, 57, 65,
    84, 89, 115–116, 147
  and the battle at Tsushima, 251–252,
    264
  and battle simulations, 197
  death of, 256
  departure of, for Djibouti, 135
  and French Indonesia, 226
  illness of, 226, 251–252
  movement of, through the Suez, 111
  and Nosy Be, 171–177, 197
  and Rozhestvensky's passage to
    Vladivostok, 210, 211
  and Sventorzhetsky, 185–186
  and the "Yacht Squadron," 151–159,
    164
Ferdinand of Bulgaria (king), 18
Fersen, Baron, 221
Ferzen, Captain, 284
Filippovsky, Vladimir, 302, 304, 306,
    331–333
Firearms, advent of, 9
First Pacific Squadron, 36, 169, 170, 199,
    264
Fitingof, Bruno, 65
Foreign Enlistment Act, 131
Foreign Ministry, 21, 22, 76
Forestry, 21
Formosa, 32, 236, 243, 247
Formosa Channel, 32
France, 16, 182, 316
  and the Crimean War, 10
  and the Entente Cordiale, 103
  and espionage, 80–81
  and the Golden Horn, 10
  and Kaiser Wilhelm, 73
  neutrality of, 127
  new military technology used by, 27

and the "Yacht Squadron," 156–158, 161. *See also* French Indochina
French Indochina, 181, 217–245
Furoshiki shells, 270

Gabon, 129, 133–137, 141, 249
Garting, Arkady M. (Abram Gekkelman), 81–83, 91, 204, 336
Gatchina Palace, 7
Gekkelman, Abraham. *See* Garting, Arkady M. (Abram Gekkelman)
George (prince), 211
George V (king), 337
Germany, 15–18, 43, 52, 167, 182–183
    colliers from, in Dakar, 126–127
    and the Dogger Bank incident, 102–103
    and espionage, 77, 79–80, 143
    merchants from, 9
    new military technology used by, 27
    number of admirals in, 28
    settlements of, in Southwest Africa, 142
Gerta (ship), 167
Gibraltar, 99–102, 108–109, 115, 153, 162. *See also* Gibraltar Strait
Gibraltar Strait, 162, 210, 111. *See also* Gibraltar
Gilyak (gunboat), 159
Ginsburg, Moisei, 60, 126
Glasgow, 47
Glastnost, 39
Glory, pursuit of, 17, 19
God, 17, 253
Gogland Island, 50–51
Golden Hall, of the Winter Palace, 5–6
Golden Horn harbor, 10
Goro, Ijuin, 270
Goto Island, 262
Grad (gunboat), 208
Great Belt Straits, 80, 91
Great Fish Bay, 140, 141
Great Game, in Central Asia, 7, 10, 69–70
Great Trans-Siberian Railroad, xvi, 311, 324
    launch of, 10, 12
    Makarov's travels via, 34
    Witte and, 14
Greece, 48–49, 163
Greve, Admiral, 309, 323

Grozny (torpeodo boat), 167, 303–306, 310
Guichen (cruiser), 230

Hague Conference protocol, 107
Hague Tribunal, 108
Haimun (vessel), 86
Hakodate, 250
Hamburg, 59–60, 77, 183
Hamburg-American Line, 59–60, 183
Hamilton, George, 46
Harbin, 16
Hardinge, Charles, 75, 155
Hatred, of the Japanese, 11, 18–19
Hatsuse (battleship), 61
Havas telegraph agency, 201
Hegemony, xvi
Heihachiro, Togo, xvii, 23, 30–33, 39, 202
    and the attack of Port Arthur, 32–33, 70, 132
    and the battle at Tsushima, 248, 250–251, 257–258, 261–273, 277–278, 282–285, 292, 294, 297, 313, 315–316, 327
    and Britain, 31–32, 101
    control of the Sea of Japan by, 173
    death of, 337
    difficulties encountered by, after Makarov's death, 61
    and the Dogger Bank incident, 107
    and French Indonesia, 218, 220, 222, 226, 232, 236–239, 243
    meetings with, 285–286, 315–316
    as a national hero, 337
    omnipotent appearance of, 117
    and Rozhestvensky's passage to Vladivostok, 205–207, 214
    and the Sunda archipelago, 180
    and Weihaiwei, 70–71
    and Witgeft, 61-62
Hermes (cruiser), 108
Hermione (battleship), 157
Hirobumi, Ito, 132
Historical sources, contradictions among, xvii–xviii
HMS Barrosa (cruiser), 141
HMS Glory (cruiser), 130–131
Hohenzollern (yacht), 211
Hokkaido, 250, 249

Holland, 25, 180–181
Home Fleet, 99
Homosexuality, 18, 22
Hong Kong, 13, 45, 156, 176, 221,
    223–224, 236
Hong Kong (cruiser), 176
Hongkong Maru (cruiser), 264
Honshu, 236, 250
Hotel Orleans Richelieu, 316
Hutchison, Captain, 88

Ignatsius, Captain, 96, 261, 271
Iki (battleship), 337
Iliutovich, Alexander, 331
Imperial Marinsky Theater, 4
Imperial Navy, 6, 45, 119, 336
Imperial Technological Society, 330–331
India, 9, 72, 130
Indian Ocean, 136, 143, 176, 202, 240,
    254
    and Rozhestvensky's passage to
        Vladivostok, 205–208
    and the "Yacht Squadron," 156, 164,
        166
Indochina, 181, 217–245, 251, 265
Industrialists, 16
Intelligence gathering, 74–83, 110
    and the battle at Tsushima,
        264–265
    and Britain, 47, 80–81, 86, 201
    and China, 76–80, 175
    and Denmark, 82
    and Garting, 81–83, 91, 204, 336
    and Germany, 77, 79–80, 143
    and Nosy Be, 178, 182–183
    and the Sea of Japan, 201
    and Singapore, 204, 205
    and telegraph lines, 124–126
    and the use of radio communications,
        86
    and the "Yacht Squadron," 154–156,
        159
Iphigenia (battleship), 221, 223
Iran, 70, 130
Irkutsk, 325
Irtysh (transport), 232, 254, 294
Island of Sakhalin, The (Chekhov), 13
Italy, 18, 23, 75, 156
Izumi (cruiser), 262

Izumrud (cruiser), 64–65, 159–163, 221,
    223, 248, 261–263, 274, 281–282,
    310, 312

Jackson, Commander, 88, 315
Japan: absolutist monarchy of, 16
    and Badmaev, 23
    British support for, 70–71, 132, 143
    and China, 15, 16
    and espionage, 62, 76–78, 80
    ground troops of, 61
    and hatred of the Japanese, 11, 18–19
    and Korea, 21
    national ego of, xvi
    naval strength of, 29, 30
    new military technology used by, 27
    purchase of ships by, 23, 29
    severing of diplomatic relations with,
        23
    Tsar Nicholas II's travels to, 11
    treaty negotiations with, 311, 319,
        330. *See also* Heihachiro, Togo
Java, 176, 215, 218, 264
Jews, 60, 81, 178
John II (king), 145
Johor Strait, 205
Journalists, 78
Jung, Captain, 123, 232
Jutaro, Komura, 132
Jutland, battle of, xvii

Kaapstad, 143, 144, 145, 176, 196
Kagero (torpedo boat), 305, 306
Kagoshima Bay, 30
Kaiser Wilhelm II, 15, 52, 73–74, 73, 211
    and the battle at Tsushima, 319, 330
    and the Dogger Bank incident,
        102–103, 106–108
    and the fall of Port Arthur, 171
    incendiary letters personality of, 17–19
    sent by, to the tsar, 130
    and the peace treaty, 319
    residence of, 153
Kajiya, 30
Kamchatka (repair ship), 95–96, 105,
    115, 123, 146–147, 192, 254
Kamimura, Admiral, 265
Kataoka, Admiral, 262, 282
Katsura, Count, 176

Kedah, 176
Kerch, 41
Khrabry (gunboat), 153
Kiev (battleship), 219
King James Bible, 32
Klado, Nikolai, 135–136, 157, 172–173, 186
Klemm, Miss, 138
Kliukvennaya Station, 311
Knox, Philander C., 337
Kobe, 319, 321
Kolomeitsev, Commander, 275, 300–303, 332
Komura, Foreign Minister, 22, 83
Koran, 166
Korea, 16, 32, 262, 265
    and Alexeev, 76
    and Bezobrazov, 20–21
    and espionage, 80
    and negotiations with Japan, 22. *See also* Korea Strait
Korea (battleship), 115
Korea Strait, xvi, 61, 238, 249, 250–251, 254, 257, 265, 285, 292–293, 297. *See also* Korea
Kostenko, 318
Kostroma (hospital boat), 248, 255, 262
Kotlin Island, 66
Krakatau, 218
Kravchenko, Doctor, 296
Kronshtadt, 45, 48, 56, 63, 238
    assembly of ships in, 66
    debauchery of officers at, 84
    departure of Nebogatov from, 208, 209
    founding of, 66–67
    and Makarov, 52
    prisons in, men drafted from, 59
    return of the Apraxin to, 51
    Rozhestvensky's departure from, 68, 69, 83
Krzhizhanovksy, Nikolai, 331
Kua Bay, 245
Kuban (cruiser), 65, 179, 248, 254, 258
Kudinov, 299, 300
Kure, 236
Kuril Islands, 249
Kurnoia (transport), 240–242
Kuropatkin, Alexei, 5, 135, 214, 325

Kurosh, Commander, 283
Kyoto, 317, 319, 323
Kyril, Grand Duke, 34–35, 72

Lancaster (battleship), 100–101, 108
Landsdowne, Lord Henry, 71, 88, 92, 133
Langeland Belt, 92
La Perouse Strait, 244, 249, 251, 253–254, 285, 292, 294–295
Lamsdorf, Count, 5, 22, 98, 210, 238, 328
    and the attack on Port Arthur, 62–64
    and the Black Sea Fleet, 180
    and the Dutch, 180
    and espionage, 77, 79
    and Nosy Be, 180, 200
    as Rozhestvensky's enemy, 136
    and Rozhestvensky's return to Russia, 328–330
    and the "Yacht Squadron," 154, 155
Law of Nations, 131
Lawrence of Arabia, 7
Le Perouse Strait, 243
Lebedev, Ivan, 138, 139
Lenin, V. I., xv
Leontiev, Evgeny, 302, 305–306, 331–333
Lepanto, battle of, xvii
Levedev, Ivan, 65, 67
Liaodong Peninsula, 15–16, 30, 125
Libava, 69, 83, 86, 89, 91–94, 159, 160, 200, 208–209
Libel, 43
Libreville, 110, 129, 135, 137, 139, 187
Limpopo (gunboat), 140, 141
Linevich, General, 214, 323, 325
Lisbon, 48, 177
Liven, Prince, 236, 242
Loir, Maurice, 154, 155
London, 46–48. *See also* Britain
Lowdill, Edward, 78–79
Luderitz, Franz Adolf, 142
Luzon, 296

Macao, 177
MacDonald, Claude, 71, 88
Madagascar, 63–64, 110–111, 136, 144, 146–147, 159, 206, 264, 338. *See also* Nosy Be; Sainte-Marie
Mahajanga, 159, 182

Mahan, Alfred Thayer, 28
Maizuru, 316–317
Majestic (battleship), 27
Makarov, Capitolina, 51–52, 179, 316
Makarov, Stepan Osipovich, 33–37, 43,
    49–52
    and the battle at Tsushima, 295, 316,
        333
    death of, 56, 72
    and Ginsburg, 60
    and Rozhestvensky's dissatisfaction
        with his men, 122–123
    and the *Yermak,* 92
Makassar, 215
Malacca, 164, 176, 213, 222
Malaga, 162, 163
Malagasy, 187, 189
Malaya (battleship), 115, 122, 134,
    141–142, 146, 192, 193
Malaysia, 204, 205
Malta, 77, 99
Mammoths, 8
Manchuria, 3–5, 15–16, 49, 58, 72, 143,
    214
    and Grand Duke Alexander, 20
    and the Great Game, 70
    and intelligence operations, 76
    and Kuropatkin, 135
    and military communications,
        125–126
    Military High Command in, 76
    and negotiations with Japan, 22, 319
    restoration of, to China, 132
    and the use of radio communications,
        86
    and the "Yacht Squadron," 160
Manila, 293–297, 312
Marconi (company), 124
Maslyannaya carnival, 197
Masqat, 157
Maugham, Somerset, 75
Mediterranean Fleet, 99–100
Mediterranean Sea, 10, 48, 121
    and the Great Game, 70
    Kaiser Wilhelm's reports from, 73–74
    Tsar Nicholas's travel to, 11
    and the "Yacht Squadron," 163
Meiji, Emperor, 16, 29
Mekong River, 223, 226

Merbal Bay, 157
Merchant Marine Department, 20
Merlin (ship), 163
Messina Strait, 163
Meteor (battleship), 115
Middle Ages, 20
Middle class, 17
Middle East, 7, 14, 72, 79, 80, 154
Midway, battle of, xvii
Mikado, 285
Mikasa (battleship), xvii, 33, 61, 86,
    236, 263, 265, 268–270, 284,
    316, 337
Miklukha, Captain, 314
Military High Command, 76
Mines, use of, 25, 26–27
Ministry of War, 21
Misu, Admiral, 315
Modernity: and glastnost, 39
    sinister aspects of, xv
Monasteries, 317, 318
Mongolia, 7, 19
Morocco, 95, 110–111
Morphine, use of, 291
Motono, Japanese Minister, 228
Mozambique, 182

Nagasaki, 77, 316, 322, 323
Nakhimov (battleship), 116, 174, 192,
    247, 261, 282
Namib Desert, 142
Napoleon Bonaparte, 39
Narcotics, xv
National ego, of Japan, xvi
Naval Academy, 37, 39, 40, 66, 152
Naval General Staff, 76, 78, 195
Navarin (battleship), 64, 65, 152, 247,
    261, 314
Nebogatov, Nikolai Ivanovich, 318, 327,
    333–336
    and the battle of Tsushima, 248–249,
        251, 255, 257, 262, 264, 266,
        277–286, 290, 300, 310–313,
        316–319
    death of, 337
    early release of, from prison, 336
    and French Indonesia, 224, 226,
        229–230, 239–245
    meeting with Togo, 285–286

and the Nosy Be option, 172, 180,
    183–186, 198, 199–202
return of, to Russia, 318–319
and Rozhestvensky's passage to
    Vladivostok, 208–213
transfer of command to, 300
Nebolsin, Arkady, 292
Nelidov, Alexander, 104
Nelidov, Ivan, 128
Nepotism, 28
Neutrality, 36, 64, 70, 125, 127
Neva River, 4–5, 183
Nevsky Prospect, 4–5, 219
Nevsky shipyard, 60, 166
Nicholas I (battleship), 208, 209, 247,
    255, 277–281, 283, 317–318,
    334, 337
Nicholas I (tsar), 34, 39
Nicholas II (tsar), 4–25, 113, 313–314
    and the battle at Tsushima, 311, 319
    birthday of, celebration of, 253–254
    childhood of, 6–7
    decision of, to put Rozhestvensky on
        trial, 331
    and the Dogger Bank incident,
        102–103
    and Emperor Alexander II, 66–67
    and French Indonesia, 218, 239–240
    journal entries written by, 89
    and the king of Denmark, 82
    and the naval buildup, 26
    and Nebogatov, 183–184
    and the peace treaty, 319
    and revolutionary rallies, 325
    and Rozhestvensky's return to Russia,
        330
    and Saint Job, 253–254
    sentencing by, 336
    son of, birth of, 58
    and Togo, 30
    visit of, to Rozhestvensky's unit, 52–54
    and Wilhelm, 73–74
    and Witte, 14–15
Nicobar Islands, 240–242
Nihon Maru (cruiser), 264
Niiataka (cruiser), 176
Nile River, 154
Nippon Maru (cruiscr), 176
Nishin (cruiser), 23, 278

Noel, Gerard, 207, 221, 319
Nogueria, Silva, 140
North Sea, 82, 93–94, 102, 161, 213
Norway, 82, 93
Nossibeisk, 169–202. *See also* Nosy Be
Nosy Be option, 158–159, 169–202, 207,
    219, 225
Novoye vremya (newspaper), 327
Nyborg, 80

Ocean (training ship), 159
Ochakov, 41
Odessa, 41, 126
Ohio (battleship), 297
Old Believers, 9
Oldhamia (steamer), 253, 254, 316
Oleg (cruiser), 64, 65, 159, 162–163,
    184, 198, 214, 223, 261, 288–296,
    300, 312
Olga (queen of Greece), 48–49, 85, 153,
    211
Oligarchs, 16, 22–23
Oranienbaum, 67
Order of St. George, 42
Order of St. Vladimir, 42
Oregon (battleship), 297
Orel (vessel), 65, 66, 92, 94, 95, 115–118,
    123–134, 137–138, 126, 128, 144,
    196, 223, 226, 231–232, 234–235,
    247–248, 252, 253, 255, 267, 273,
    280–281, 283, 286, 318, 336
Osaka, 316–317
Oslyabya (battleship), 23, 64, 65, 92, 115,
    192, 247, 257, 270, 273–274, 299,
    301, 303, 309, 317
Ottoman Empire, 10, 42–43

Pacific Ocean, 8, 10, 72
    and the battle at Tsushima, 247–258,
        285
    Tsar Nicholas's travel to, 11. *See also*
        Pacific Squadrons
Pacific Squadron(s)
    First, 36, 169, 170, 199, 264
    Second, 36, 64–65, 56, 163, 169–170,
        199, 263
    Third, 135–136, 172–173, 209, 210,
        244
Padang, 215

Pakenham, Captain, 88, 184
Pallada (cruiser), 3
Parfenov, Colonel, 286
Pascal (cruiser), 80
Patriotism, 6
Pavlov, Alexander, 78, 79, 80, 176, 204
Pavlovskaya, Miss, 196
Peace treaty, 311, 319, 330
Peasants, xvi
Penang, 213, 242
Permafrost, 8–9
Persian Gulf, 72
Pervenetz (battleship), 40, 186
Pescadore Islands, 32, 64
Peter the Great (Tsar), 6, 25–26, 66, 139
Peterhof, 62
Petersburg (cruiser), 74
Petropavlovsk (battleship), 34–36, 56, 60, 72
Petrovich, Zinovy, 50
Philippines, 293
Phoenix Hotel, 82
Photography, as a new technology, 86
Piraeus, 48–49, 211
Police Department, 76, 79–81, 83, 154
Polis, Commander, 204, 207, 240–241, 255
Politovsky, Evgeny, 65–66
Polynesian Archipelago, 109–110
Port Arthur, 3, 5, 16, 56, 60–61
    assignment of Makarov to, 33–34
    attack, 5–6, 23, 30, 61–64, 132, 135, 143–144
    fall of, 70–71, 130, 160, 169–171
    founding of, 15–16
    and military communications, 124–126
    reinforcements sent to, 23, 36–37
    suppliers for, 60
    Togo's closure of, 70
    use of, during the winter, 29
    Witgeft's attempts to break from, 71
Port Said, 45, 86, 206
    and the Nosy Be option, 178, 187, 201
    and the "Yacht Squadron," 154–156, 164
Portugal, 9, 110, 140, 145
Poseidon, 26
Prince George of Greece, 11

Prince of Wales, 72
Prince Suvorov (battleship), 57, 64, 65, 67
Prisoners of war, 316–317
Prisons, 9, 59, 317, 336
Propaganda, xvi
Protestants, 118. *See also* Christianity
Prozorlivy (torpedo boat), 92, 164
Przhevalsky, Nikolai, 7–8, 11–12, 19

Radio communications, 27, 36, 86–87, 88, 124
Radlov, Captain, 248
Raffles, Stamford, 204
Railroad(s): in Britain, 46–47
    in Manchuria, 132
    pivotal role of, 13–14
    stations, 14
    Trans-Siberian, xvi, 10, 12, 14, 34, 311, 324
Raleigh (battleship), 297
Ras Hafun Bay, 167
Red Sea, 23, 69, 72–75, 83, 121, 135, 143, 151–168, 184, 211
    Chekhov's travels to, 13
    and the "Yacht Squadron," 154, 157, 165
Renaissance, 75
Retvizan (battleship), 3
Reuters news agency, 153
Reval, 68–69, 83–85, 88, 153
Revolution(s): Bolshevik (1917), xviii–xvi, 183–184, 325–326
    committees for, 326
    rallies for, 325
Rhodes, Cecil, 7
Rhodesia, 7
Richelieu, Cardinal. 171
Richter, Otto, 118
Rion (cruiser), 65, 159, 223, 248, 254, 258
Riurikovichi dynasty, 9
River Thames, 47
Romanov dynasty, 4–6, 11
    members of, description of, 17–20
    naval leaders among, 28
    and the new technological age, 9
    strong ties of, with Britain, 72–73. *See also specific individuals*
Roosevelt, Theodore, 311

Rozhestvensky, Nikolai, 173, 195, 337–338
Rozhestvensky, Zinovy Petrovich, 37–69, 75
  acquital of, 333–334
  and the Anadyr, 112–113, 314–315
  in Angra Pequena, 142–144
  and the Aurora, 288
  and Balfour, 130
  and the battle at Tsushima, 248–273, 277–279, 281, 286–288, 290, 296–309
  and Bostrom, 104–105
  and the Cape Horn-Polynesian Archipelago route, 109–110
  in captivity, 310, 312–313, 315–319
  and corporeal punishment, 120
  in Dakar, 115–148
  death of, 338
  departure of, from Kronshtadt, 83
  detention of, at Vigo, 132
  and deserters, 177
  and the Dnieper, 296
  and the Dogger Bank affair, 96–99, 101–110, 123, 136
  and Enkvist, 111
  and espionage, 78–79, 82, 88
  explosive temper of, 122–123, 136
  and the fall of Port Arthur, 169–171
  in French Indochina, 217–245
  and Garting, 204
  illness of, 195–196
  and Klado, 135–136
  last years of, 337–338
  in Libava, 86–87, 89, 91–92, 94
  meeting with the Lancaster captain, 100–101
  and Nebogatov's trial, 333–336
  at Nosy Be, 169–202
  passage of, to Vladivostok, 203–215
  retirement of, 331, 337
  return of, to Russia, 319–327, 300–331
  in Reval, 83–86, 88
  and Sivers, 66, 126, 137–138, 195, 196, 316
  in Skagen, 92–97
  and Skrydlov, 173
  in Tangier, 110–112, 115
  trial of, 331–333
  at Vigo, 98–102, 104–109
  and the "Yacht Squadron," 151–168
  and the Yellow Sea, 80–81
Rudanovsky, Mr., 203–208, 213, 240
Rumelia, 45
Rus (tugboat), 115, 135, 146, 169, 172, 200, 208, 209, 254
Russia (merchantman), 32
Russo-Turkish War, 59

Sadebo, 175
Sahara Desert, 115
Saigon, 181, 204, 225–226, 228, 235, 236, 242, 296
Saint Job, 253–254
Saint Nicholas, 145, 173, 175, 282
St. Petersburg, 20, 22
  College of Transportation, 40
  Kronshtadt as the guardian of, 66
  patriotic demonstrations in, 6
  and the naval bureaucracy, 28
  prisons in, men drafted from, 59
  transport of gold from, xvi
  vulnerability of, to naval attacks, 27
Sainte-Marie, 144, 147, 169. See also Madagascar
Sakhalin Island, 12–13, 249, 319
Samara, 326
Sasebo, 29, 236, 307, 312–317
Sazanami (torpedo boat), 305, 306–307
Scandals, 43
Scotland, 99
Sea of Japan, xvi, xvii, 10, 64, 173, 176, 198, 199–201, 239
  and the battle at Tsushima, 248, 257, 264, 281
  and espionage, 201
  Golden Horn harbor, 10
  Togo's knowledge of, 248
Second Pacific Squadron, 36, 64–65, 56, 163, 169–170, 199, 263
Semenov, Vladimir, 144, 301, 302, 306, 331
Senegal, 115. See also Dakar
Senyavin (battleship), 172, 208, 247, 280, 281, 283, 335
Sevastopol, 29, 53
Sevastopol (battleship), 211
Sfakteria (warship), 211

Shandong, 15, 125
Shanghai, 77, 79, 156, 204, 236, 238
    and the battle at Tsushima, 295, 296
    safe arrival of transports in, 255
Shein, Captain, 223, 248, 314
Shimamura, Admiral, 314
Shinano Maru (cruiser), 262–263
Shipbuilding, 25–28, 46–47
Ships: *Admiral Nakhimov* (cruiser), 57
    Admiral Seniavin (cruiser), 186
    Admiral Ushakov (cruiser), 186, 314
    Alexander Nevsky (frigate), 21
    Alexander III (battleship), 64–65, 68,
        94, 95, 115, 123, 146, 224, 247,
        251, 255, 267, 269, 273–274,
        278–280, 304, 309, 314, 317, 337
    Almaz (cruiser), 57, 64, 152, 223,
        261, 288, 310
    Amphitrite (battleship), 221
    Anadyr (transport), 95, 112, 115, 254,
        314
    Apraxin (battleship), 66, 208, 247,
        281, 283, 315–316, 335
    Asama (cruiser), 277
    Aurora (cruiser), 23, 64–65, 97, 98,
        111–112, 116, 123, 174, 197–198,
        219, 222–223, 225, 227, 247, 258,
        261, 288–297, 300, 312
    Bakan (freighter), 93
    Barrosa (cruiser), 140
    Bayan (cruiser), 243
    Bedovy (torpedo boat), 174, 214, 261,
        303–307, 310–312, 331–334, 336
    Bezuprechny (torpedo boat), 226–227,
        300
    Black Sea (cruiser), 179
    Borodino (battleship), 64–65, 94–95,
        134, 177, 247, 251, 267, 269,
        273–274, 278–280, 290, 300, 313,
        317
    Boyarin (cruiser), 25
    Bravy (torpedo boat), 262, 310
    Buiny (torpedo boat), 261, 275–276,
        279, 299–301, 309, 311, 332,
        334
    Bystry (torpedo boat), 92, 118, 261
    Cincinnati (battleship), 297
    Dachnik (steamer), 67
    Descartes (cruiser), 230
    Diana (warship), 111–112, 236

Dmitri Donskoi (cruiser), xvi, 23, 58,
    64, 65
Dnieper (cruiser), 65, 159, 223, 248,
    253–254, 258, 296
Donskoi (cruiser), 97, 98, 116, 123,
    134, 137–139, 159, 189, 214, 223,
    247, 261, 300–301, 303, 305–306
Drake (cruiser), 108
Emperor Nicholas I (battleship), 172,
    186
Ermak (icebreaker), 51
Esperance (refrigerator boat), 116, 194
Gerta (ship), 167
Gilyak (gunboat), 159
Grad (gunboat), 208
Grozny (torpedo boat), 167, 303–306,
    310
Guichen (cruiser), 230
Haimun (vessel), 86
Hatsuse (battleship), 61
Hermes (cruiser), 108
Hermione (battleship), 157
HMS Barrosa (cruiser), 141
HMS Glory (cruiser), 130–131
Hohenzollern (yacht), 211
Hong Kong (cruiser), 176
Hongkong Maru (cruiser), 264
Iki (battleship), 337
Iphigenia (battleship), 221, 223
Irtysh (transport), 232, 254, 294
Izumi (cruiser), 262
Izumrud (cruiser), 64–65, 159–163,
    221, 223, 248, 261–263, 274,
    281–282, 310, 312
Kagero (torpedo boat), 305, 306
Kamchatka (repair ship), 95–96, 105,
    115, 123, 146–147, 192, 254
Khrabry (gunboat), 153
Kiev (battleship), 219
Korea (battleship), 115
Kostroma (hospital boat), 248, 255,
    262
Kuban (cruiser), 65, 179, 248, 254,
    258
Kurnoia (transport), 240–242
Lancaster (battleship), 100–101, 108
Limpopo (gunboat), 140, 141
Majestic (battleship), 27
Malaya (battleship), 115, 122, 134,
    141–142, 146, 192, 193

Merlin (ship), 163
Meteor (battleship), 115
Mikasa (battleship), xvii, 33, 61, 86, 236, 263, 265, 268–270, 284, 316, 337
Nakhimov (battleship), 116, 174, 192, 247, 261, 282
Navarin (battleship), 64, 65, 152, 247, 261, 314
Nicholas I (battleship), 208, 209, 247, 255, 277–281, 283, 317–318, 334, 337
Nihon Maru (cruiser), 264
Niiataka (cruiser), 176
Nippon Maru (cruiser), 176
Nishin (cruiser), 23, 278
Ocean (training ship), 159
Ohio (battleship), 297
Oldhamia (steamer), 253, 254, 316
Oleg (cruiser), 64, 65, 159, 162–163, 184, 198, 214, 223, 261, 288–296, 300, 312
Oregon (battleship), 297
Orel (vessel), 65, 66, 92, 94, 95, 115–118, 123–134, 137–138, 126, 128, 144, 196, 223, 226, 231–232, 234–235, 247–248, 252, 253, 255, 267, 273, 280–281, 283, 286, 318, 336
Oslyabya (battleship), 23, 64, 65, 92, 115, 192, 247, 257, 270, 273–274, 299, 301, 303, 309, 317
Pascal (cruiser), 80
Pervenetz (battleship), 40, 50, 186
Petersburg (cruiser), 74
Petropavlovsk (battleship), 34–36, 56, 60, 72
Prince Suvorov (battleship), 57, 64, 65, 67
Prozorlivy (torpedo boat), 92, 164
Raleigh (battleship), 297
Rion (cruiser), 65, 159, 223, 248, 254, 258
Rus (tugboat), 115, 135, 146, 169, 172, 200, 208, 209, 254
Russia (merchantman), 32
Sazanami (torpedo boat), 305, 306–307
Senyavin (battleship), 172, 208, 247, 280, 281, 283, 335

Sevastopol (battleship), 211
Sfakteria (warship), 211
Shinano Maru (cruiser), 262–263
Shtandart (yacht), 85
Sisoi (battleship), 64, 89, 92, 152–153, 156, 157, 175, 247, 248, 261, 282
Skory (torpedo boat), 170
Smolensk (cruiser), 74
Sutlej (warship), 221, 223
Suvorov (battleship), 86, 89, 94–97, 115–118, 120, 122–124, 126–129, 134–143, 146–147, 174, 177, 179, 193–197, 214, 218–232, 240, 244, 251, 253–254, 261, 266–279, 287–289, 299–300, 303, 309–313, 318
Svetlana (cruiser), 64, 152, 174, 248, 261, 314
Svir (tugboat), 254, 274, 295, 296
Terek (cruiser), 65, 179, 248, 254, 258
Thetis (battleship), 221
Tsarevna (yacht), 68
Tsesarevich (battleship), 3
Ural (cruiser), 65, 179, 193, 248, 254, 257, 261, 328, 295, 309
Ushakov (battleship), 172, 208, 247, 280, 281
Vesta (steamer), 41–43, 49, 55, 59
Viper (torpedo boat), 27
Vladimir Monomakh (cruiser), 48, 50, 65–66, 208, 247–248, 261
Vlastny (torpedo boat), 170
Voronezh (steamer), 319, 321–323, 326
Wisconsin (battleship), 297
Worcester (battleship), 337
Yakut (transport), 323
Yashima (battleship), 61
Yenisei (transport), 25
Yermak (icebreaker), 92
Yoshino (cruiser), 61
Zhemchug (cruiser), 64, 65, 92, 152, 219, 223, 253, 261, 263, 266, 312, 292–296
Vesta (steamer), 41–43, 49, 55, 59
Shtandart (yacht), 85
Shvank, Commander, 212
Siberia, 9, 326
Silk Road, 8

Singapore, 45, 77, 156, 264–265
  Chekhov's travels to, 13
  and French Indonesia, 217–218,
    221–222, 241, 243
  and Rozhestvensky's passage to
    Vladivostok, 203–207, 213, 214
Singapore Strait, 218. *See also* Singapore
Sisoi (battleship), 64, 89, 92, 152–153,
    156, 157, 175, 247, 248, 261,
    282
Sivers, Natalia, 66, 126, 137–138, 195,
    196, 316
Skagen, 81, 91–97, 160, 200, 209
Skagerrak, 93–94
Skory (torpedo boat), 170
Skrydlov, Nikolai, 37, 56, 79, 173, 311
Slander, accusations of, 43
Smirnov, Captain, 279, 282, 283, 284
Smolensk (cruiser), 74
Snowstorms, 9
Socotra Island, 166–167
Soudha, 153, 154, 162, 163, 210–213
South Africa, 7, 142–145
South China Sea, 217, 222, 224, 241,
    254
Southern Cross, 134
Spain, 9, 26, 98–99
Spanish Armada, 26
Spys, 74–83, 110
  and the battle at Tsushima, 264–265
  and Britain, 47, 80–81, 86, 201
  and China, 76–80, 175
  and Denmark, 82
  and Garting, 81–83, 91, 204, 336
  and Germany, 77, 79–80, 143
  and Nosy Be, 178, 182–183
  and the Sea of Japan, 201
  and Singapore, 204, 205
  and telegraph lines, 124–126
  and the use of radio communications,
    86
  and the "Yacht Squadron," 154–156,
    159
Steam engine, importance of, 13–14. *See
  also* Railroads
Stessel, General, 170
Strait of Gibraltar, 162, 210, 111. *See also*
  Gibraltar

Strait of Lombok, 218
Strait of Malacca, 176, 207, 212, 217–218,
    220–222, 240, 242, 244, 310
Suez Canal, 45, 69, 110–111, 206, 287
  Chekhov's travels to, 13
  contraband traveling via, 70
  and Felkersam, 111
  and the "Yacht Squadron," 153–155,
    164
Sumatra, 176, 215, 217, 218, 264
Sunda archipelago, 180
Sunda Strait, 173, 176, 177, 180–181,
    201, 202, 207, 218, 242, 264, 265
Sutlej (warship), 221, 223
Suvorov (battleship), 86, 89, 94–97,
    115–118, 120, 122–124, 126–129,
    134–143, 146–147, 174, 177, 179,
    193–197, 214, 218–232, 240, 244,
    251, 253–254, 261, 266–279,
    287–289, 299–300, 303, 309–313,
    318
Sventorzhetsky, Lieutenant, 185
Svetlana (cruiser), 64, 152, 174, 248,
    261, 314
Svir (tugboat), 254, 274, 295, 296
Sweden, 82, 83

Taft, William Howard, 337
Tambov province, 313
Tangier, 94, 100–102, 107, 110–112,
    115, 126, 135, 162, 178, 185, 210,
    287
Tavria, 336
Teheran, 130
Terek (cruiser), 65, 179, 248, 254, 258
Terrorism, 7
Thailand, 77, 204
Thetis (battleship), 221
Third Armored Unit, 277
Third Pacific Squadron, 135–136,
    172–173, 209, 210, 244
Tibet, 7, 19, 22–23, 71–72
Times Literary Supplement, xvi
Timor Sea, 218
Togo Heihachiro, xvii, 23, 30–33, 39,
    202
  and the attack of Port Arthur, 32–33,
    70, 132

and the battle at Tsushima, 248,
    250–251, 257–258, 261–273,
    277–278, 282–285, 292, 294, 297,
    313, 315–316, 327
and Britain, 31–32, 101
control of the Sea Japan by, 173
death of, 337
difficulties encountered by, after
    Makarov's death, 61
and the Dogger Bank incident, 107
and French Indonesia, 218, 220, 222,
    226, 232, 236–239, 243
meetings with, 285–286, 315–316
as a national hero, 337
omnipotent appearance of, 117
and Rozhestvensky's passage to
    Vladivostok, 205–207, 214
and the Sunda archipelago, 180
and Weihaiwei, 70–71
and Witgeft, 61–62
Tokyo, 22, 71, 215, 229, 236, 237, 311
Tolstoy, Leo, 34
Torpedo boats. *See* Boats
Torres Strait, 218
Totalitarianism, xv
Trafalgar, battle of, xvii, 26
Trans-Siberian Construction Committee,
    14
Trans-Siberian Railroad, xvi, 311, 324
    launch of, 10, 12
    Makarov's travels via, 34
    Witte and, 14. *See also* Railroads
Treaty negotiations, 311, 319, 330
Trieste, 77
Trinkomali, 156
Tropic of Capricorn, 142
Tsar Alexander III, 5, 7, 11–12, 45
    death of, 14, 49
    and Witte, 13, 14
Tsar Alexander II, 7, 11, 39, 53, 59,
    66–67
Tsar Nicholas I, 34, 39
Tsar Nicholas II, 4–25, 113, 313–314
    and the battle at Tsushima, 311, 319
    birthday of, celebration of, 253–254
    childhood of, 6–7
    decision of, to put Rozhestvensky on
        trial, 331

and the Dogger Bank incident,
    102–103
and Emperor Alexander II, 66–67
and French Indonesia, 218, 239–240
journal entries written by, 89
and the king of Denmark, 82
and the naval buildup, 26
and Nebogatov, 183–184
and the peace treaty, 319
and revolutionary rallies, 325
and Rozhestvensky's return to Russia,
    330
and Saint Job, 253–254
sentencing by, 336
son of, birth of, 58
and Togo, 30
visit of, to Rozhestvensky's unit,
    52–54
and Wilhelm, 73–74
and Witte, 14–15
Tsarevna (yacht), 68
Tsarskoe Selo, 238
Tsesarevich (battleship), 3
Tsugaru Strait, 249–251, 254, 265, 285,
    292
Tsushima, battle at, xvi–xvii, 33, 238,
    247–286
    books about, discovery of, xvii
    historical information about,
        contradictions among, xvii–xviii
    Rozhestvensky's descriptions of,
        327–328
Tsvet-Kolyadinsky, Alexander, 331
Turkey, 10, 41–43, 70

Ural (cruiser), 65, 179, 193, 248, 254,
    257, 261, 328, 295, 309
Ural Mountains, 9, 12
Urbanization, 12
Uriu, Admiral, 297
Urusan, 307
Urya, Rear Admiral, 32
Ushakov (battleship), 172, 208, 247, 280,
    281

Van Fong Bay, 230–231, 243, 248–251,
    255, 264, 288
Vasilievich, Vasily, 271

Vasilievsky Island, 232
Vedernikov, Commander, 283
Vereshchagin, Vasily, 34
Vessels:
  Admiral Nakhimov (cruiser), 57
  Admiral Seniavin (cruiser), 186
  Admiral Ushakov (cruiser), 186, 314
  Alexander Nevsky (frigate), 21
  Alexander III (battleship), 64–65, 68,
      94, 95, 115, 123, 146, 224, 247,
      251, 255, 267, 269, 273–274,
      278–280, 304, 309, 314, 317, 337
  Almaz (cruiser), 57, 64, 152, 223,
      261, 288, 310
  Amphitrite (battleship), 221
  Anadyr (transport), 95, 112, 115, 254,
      314
  Apraxin (battleship), 66, 208, 247,
      281, 283, 315–316, 335
  Asama (cruiser), 277
  Aurora (cruiser), 23, 64–65, 97, 98,
      111–112, 116, 123, 174, 197–198,
      219, 222–223, 225, 227, 247, 258,
      261, 288–297, 300, 312
  Bakan (freighter), 93
  Barrosa (cruiser), 140
  Bayan (cruiser), 243
  Bedovy (torpedo boat), 174, 214,
      261, 303–307, 310–312, 331–334,
      336
  Bezuprechny (torpedo boat), 226–227,
      300
  Black Sea (cruiser), 179
  Borodino (battleship), 64–65, 94–95,
      134, 177, 247, 251, 267, 269,
      273–274, 278–280, 290, 300, 313,
      317
  Boyarin (cruiser), 25
  Bravy (torpedo boat), 262, 310
  Buiny (torpedo boat), 261, 275–276,
      279, 299–301, 309, 311, 332,
      334
  Bystry (torpedo boat), 92, 118, 261
  Cincinnati (battleship), 297
  Dachnik (steamer), 67
  Descartes (cruiser), 230
  Diana (warship), 111–112, 236
  Dmitri Donskoi (cruiser), xvi, 23, 58,
      64, 65

  Dnieper (cruiser), 65, 159, 223, 248,
      253–254, 258, 296
  Donskoi (cruiser), 97, 98, 116, 123,
      134, 137–139, 159, 189, 214, 223,
      247, 261, 300–301, 303, 305–306
  Drake (cruiser), 108
  Emperor Nicholas I (battleship), 172,
      186
  Ermak (icebreaker), 51
  Esperance (refrigerator boat), 116, 194
  Gerta (ship), 167
  Gilyak (gunboat), 159
  Grad (gunboat), 208
  Grozny (torpedo boat), 167, 303–306,
      310
  Guichen (cruiser), 230
  Haimun (vessel), 86
  Hatsuse (battleship), 61
  Hermes (cruiser), 108
  Hermione (battleship), 157
  HMS Barrosa (cruiser), 141
  HMS Glory (cruiser), 130–131
  Hohenzollern (yacht), 211
  Hong Kong (cruiser), 176
  Hongkong Maru (cruiser), 264
  Iki (battleship), 337
  Iphigenia (battleship), 221, 223
  Irtysh (transport), 232, 254, 294
  Izumi (cruiser), 262
  Izumrud (cruiser), 64–65, 159–163,
      221, 223, 248, 261–263, 274,
      281–282, 310, 312
  Kagero (torpedo boat), 305, 306
  Kamchatka (repair ship), 95–96, 105,
      115, 123, 146–147, 192, 254
  Khrabry (gunboat), 153
  Kiev (battleship), 219
  Korea (battleship), 115
  Kostroma (hospital boat), 248, 255,
      262
  Kuban (cruiser), 65, 179, 248, 254,
      258
  Kurnoia (transport), 240–242
  Lancaster (battleship), 100–101, 108
  Limpopo (gunboat), 140, 141
  Majestic (battleship), 27
  Malaya (battleship), 115, 122, 134,
      141–142, 146, 192, 193
  Merlin (ship), 163

Meteor (battleship), 115
Mikasa (battleship), xvii, 33, 61, 86, 236, 263, 265, 268–270, 284, 316, 337
Nakhimov (battleship), 116, 174, 192, 247, 261, 282
Navarin (battleship), 64, 65, 152, 247, 261, 314
Nicholas I (battleship), 208, 209, 247, 255, 277–281, 283, 317–318, 334, 337
Nihon Maru (cruiser), 264
Niiataka (cruiser), 176
Nippon Maru (cruiser), 176
Nishin (cruiser), 23, 278
Ocean (training ship), 159
Ohio (battleship), 297
Oldhamia (steamer), 253, 254, 316
Oleg (cruiser), 64, 65, 159, 162–163, 184, 198, 214, 223, 261, 288–296, 300, 312
Oregon (battleship), 297
Orel (vessel), 65, 66, 92, 94, 95, 115–118, 123–134, 137–138, 126, 128, 144, 196, 223, 226, 231–232, 234–235, 247–248, 252, 253, 255, 267, 273, 280–281, 283, 286, 318, 336
Oslyabya (battleship), 23, 64, 65, 92, 115, 192, 247, 257, 270, 273–274, 299, 301, 303, 309, 317
Pascal (cruiser), 80
Pervenetz (battleship), 40, 50, 186
Petersburg (cruiser), 74
Petropavlovsk (battleship), 34–36, 56, 60, 72
Prince Suvorov (battleship), 57, 64, 65, 67
Prozorlivy (torpedo boat), 92, 164
Raleigh (battleship), 297
Rion (cruiser), 65, 159, 223, 248, 254, 258
Rus (tugboat), 115, 135, 146, 169, 172, 200, 208, 209, 254
Russia (merchantman), 32
Sazanami (torpedo boat), 305, 306–307
Senyavin (battleship), 172, 208, 247, 280, 281, 283, 335
Sevastopol (battleship), 211

Sfakteria (warship), 211
Shinano Maru (cruiser), 262–263
Shtandart (yacht), 85
Sisoi (battleship), 64, 89, 92, 152–153, 156, 157, 175, 247, 248, 261, 282
Skory (torpedo boat), 170
Smolensk (cruiser), 74
Sutlej (warship), 221, 223
Suvorov (battleship), 86, 89, 94–97, 115–118, 120, 122–124, 126–129, 134–143, 146–147, 174, 177, 179, 193–197, 214, 218–232, 240, 244, 251, 253–254, 261, 266–279, 287–289, 299–300, 303, 309–313, 318
Svetlana (cruiser), 64, 152, 174, 248, 261, 314
Svir (tugboat), 254, 274, 295, 296
Terek (cruiser), 65, 179, 248, 254, 258
Thetis (battleship), 221
Tsarevna (yacht), 68
Tsesarevich (battleship), 3
Ural (cruiser), 65, 179, 193, 248, 254, 257, 261, 328, 295, 309
Ushakov (battleship), 172, 208, 247, 280, 281
Vesta (steamer), 41–43, 49, 55, 59
Viper (torpedo boat), 27
Vladimir Monomakh (cruiser), 48, 50, 65–66, 208, 247–248, 261
Vlastny (torpedo boat), 170
Voronezh (steamer), 319, 321–323, 326
Wisconsin (battleship), 297
Worcester (battleship), 337
Yakut (transport), 323
Yashima (battleship), 61
Yenisei (transport), 25
Yermak (icebreaker), 92
Yoshino (cruiser), 61
Zhemchug (cruiser), 64, 65, 92, 152, 219, 223, 253, 261, 263, 266, 312, 292–296
Vesta (steamer), 41–43, 49, 55, 59
Victoria (queen), 17, 73
Vietnam, 227, 230–231, 234. *See also* Saigon
Vigo, 98–102, 104–109, 132

Vigo Fleet, 102

Viper (torpedo boat), 27

Viren, Admiral, 321, 323

Virenius, Admiral, 23, 56–57, 66, 129, 158, 180, 239

Vladimir, Grand Duke, 18

Vladimir Monomakh (cruiser), 48, 50, 65–66, 208, 247–248, 261

Vladivostok, 12, 173, 177, 203–215
   and the battle of Tsushima, 249–258, 265–267, 279–280, 282, 290, 292–297, 300–301, 309–312, 314, 319, 331
   Chekhov's travels to, 13
   closure of, during the winter, 29, 63
   and espionage, 79
   founding of, 10
   and French Indonesia, 224, 225, 229, 235, 238–239, 242–244
   the Korea Strait as a gateway to, 61
   return of the Kreiser to, 45
   Rozhestvensky's return to, 323
   and Singapore, 203
   transport of gold to, xvi
   and the Trans-Siberian Railroad, xvi, 14
   Witgeft's attempts to get to, 71

Vlastny (torpedo boat), 170

Volga River, 326

Von Kursel, Ensign, 276

Voronezh (steamer), 319, 321–323, 326

Vyrubov, Lieutenant, 276

Vysoka Hill, 143–144, 170

Walvis Bay, 141

War Ministry, 76, 78

Weihaiwei, 70–71, 87–88, 330

"White Tsar," legend of, 19

Wilhelm II, Kaiser, 15, 52, 73–74, 73, 211
   and the battle at Tsushima, 319, 330
   and the Dogger Bank incident, 102–103, 106–108
   and the fall of Port Arthur, 171
   incendiary letters sent by, to the tsar, 130

personality of, 17–19
   and the peace treaty, 319
   residence of, 153

Winter Palace, 4–6, 170, 184

Wisconsin (battleship), 297

Witgeft, Admiral, 61–62, 66, 71

Witte, Sergei, 6, 13–15, 19, 311, 330
   and Grand Duke Alexander, 20, 22
   and the naval buildup, 26
   retirement of, 336–337

Worcester (battleship), 337

World War I, 75

World War II, xv–xvi

World Wide Web, xv

Xenia, 20, 68, 85

Yachts. See Ships

Yakut (transport), 323

Yalta, xvii

Yangtze Valley, 23

Yashima (battleship), 61

Yegoriev, Evgency, 89, 219, 227, 288–289, 291, 292

Yellow Sea, 15, 29, 33, 63, 80, 237 264
   death of Witgeft in, 66
   and the Great Game, 70
   shortest route from the Baltic Sea to, 69
   use of radio communications in, 86

Yenisei (transport), 25

Yenisei River, 159

Yermak (icebreaker), 92

Yokohama, 30, 60

Yoshino (cruiser), 61

Younghusband, Colonel, 71

Yushchenko, Semen, 313

Yutland, 21

Zaionchakovsky, Sub-lieutenant, 193

Zanzibar, 182

Zeitgeit, 26

Zhemchug (cruiser), 64, 65, 92, 152, 219, 223, 253, 261, 263, 266, 312, 292–296